COMPLICITY IN INTERNATIONAL CRIMINAL LAW

This book tackles one of the most contentious aspects of international criminal law—the modes of liability. At the heart of the discussion is the quest for balance between the accused's individual contribution and the collective nature of mass offending. The principle of legality demands that there exists a well-defined link between the crime and the person charged with it. This is so even in the context of international offending, which often implies 'several degrees of separation' between the direct perpetrator and the person who authorises the atrocity. The challenge is to construct that link without jeopardising the interests of justice.

This monograph provides the first comprehensive treatment of complicity within the discipline and beyond. Extensive analysis of the pertinent statutes and jurisprudence reveals gaps in interpreting accessorial liability. Simultaneously, the study of complicity becomes a test for the general methods and purposes of international criminal law. The book exposes problems with the sources of law and demonstrates the absence of clearly defined sentencing and policy rationales, which are crucial tools in structuring judicial discretion.

Volume 63 in the Studies in International Law series

Studies in International Law
Recent titles in this series

Democratic Statehood in International Law: The Emergence of New States in Post-Cold War Practice
Jure Vidmar

International Law and the Construction of the Liberal Peace
Russell Buchan

The OIC, the UN, and Counter-Terrorism Law-Making: Conflicting or Cooperative Legal Orders?
Katja Samuel

Statelessness: The Enigma of the International Community
William E Conklin

The Reception of Asylum Seekers under International Law: Between Sovereignty and Equality
Lieneke Slingenberg

International Law and Child Soldiers
Gus Waschefort

The Contractual Nature of the Optional Clause
Gunnar Törber

Non-State Actors in International Law
Edited by Math Noortmann, August Reinisch and Cedric Ryngaert

The Rule of Law at the National and International Levels: Contestations and Deference
Edited by Machiko Kanetake and André Nollkaemper

Human Rights Obligations of Non-State Armed Groups
Daragh Murray

Security and International Law
Edited by Mary E Footer, Julia Schmidt and Nigel D White

Complicity and its Limits in the Law of International Responsibility
Vladyslav Lanovoy

For the complete list of titles in this series, see 'Studies in International Law' link at www.hartpub.co.uk/books/series.asp

Complicity in International Criminal Law

Marina Aksenova

·HART·
PUBLISHING
OXFORD AND PORTLAND, OREGON
2016

Hart Publishing
An imprint of Bloomsbury Publishing Plc

Hart Publishing Ltd
Kemp House
Chawley Park
Cumnor Hill
Oxford OX2 9PH
UK

Bloomsbury Publishing Plc
50 Bedford Square
London
WC1B 3DP
UK

www.hartpub.co.uk
www.bloomsbury.com

Published in North America (US and Canada) by
Hart Publishing
c/o International Specialized Book Services
920 NE 58th Avenue, Suite 300
Portland, OR 97213-3786
USA

www.isbs.com

HART PUBLISHING, the Hart/Stag logo, BLOOMSBURY and the Diana logo are trademarks of Bloomsbury Publishing Plc

First published 2016

British Library Cataloguing-in-Publication Data
A catalogue record for this book is available from the British Library.

ISBN: HB: 978-1-50990-008-4
ePDF: 978-1-50990-010-7
ePub: 978-1-50990-009-1

Library of Congress Cataloging-in-Publication Data

Names: Aksenova, Marina, author.

Title: Complicity in international criminal law / Marina Aksenova.

Description: Oxford ; Portland, Oregon : Hart Publishing, an imprint of Bloomsbury Publishing Plc, 2016. | Series: Studies in international law ; volume 63 | Based on author's thesis (doctoral - European University Institute, Florence, Italy, 2014). | Includes bibliographical references and index.

Identifiers: LCCN 2016034352 (print) | LCCN 2016036386 (ebook) | ISBN 9781509900084 (hardback : alk. paper) | ISBN 9781509900091 (Epub)

Subjects: LCSH: Accomplices (International law)

Classification: LCC KZ7094 .A47 2016 (print) | LCC KZ7094 (ebook) | DDC 345/.04—dc23

LC record available at https://lccn.loc.gov/2016034352

Series: Studies in International Law, volume 63

Typeset by Compuscript Ltd, Shannon
Printed and bound in Great Britain by Lightning Source UK Ltd

To all those suffering from violence.

Contents

Table of Cases

International Military Tribunals (Nuremberg and Tokyo)

Post-World War II Jurisprudence

International Court of Justice

International Criminal Court

International Tribunal for Rwanda

Special Court for Sierra Leone

Extraordinary Chambers in the Courts of Cambodia

International Tribunal for the Former Yugoslavia

European Court of Human Rights

Human Rights Committee

UK Courts

German Courts

French Courts

Italian Courts

Russian Courts

Indian Courts

Chinese Courts

US Courts

Canadian Supreme Court

1

Introduction

COMPLICITY IS A notoriously difficult legal notion to grasp. KJM Smith wrote: 'Surveying complicity's hazy theoretical landscape can, depending on the commentator's nerve, temperament, and resilience, induce feelings running from hand-rubbing relish to hand-on-the-brow'.[1]

Complicity is a doctrine that attributes criminal responsibility to those who do not physically perpetrate the crime.[2] Thus, its function is to construct a link between the accomplice and the criminal act of another person. This is not an easy task if one accepts the distinct moral importance of the perpetrator's role.[3] Criminal law is premised on the principle of individual autonomy that views individuals as rational persons responsible for their own acts.[4] If the perpetrator is the one ultimately responsible for the act, why do we need to punish those who *merely* influence or aid him?

Smith referred to the difficulties of researching complicity in domestic law. Undertaking the same journey in the context of international criminal law presents even more challenging obstacles. Consider the following cases:

— The commander of the Bosnian Serb troops, positioned around Sarajevo during the siege of the city, does nothing to prevent the forces under his command from targeting—by shelling and sniping—the civilians trapped in the city. This situation lasts for 23 months. In this period, the commander remains passive: sometimes he decreases the level of attacks, only to increase them later. The commander's complicity for ordering crimes perpetrated by the troops is established

[1] KJM Smith, *A Modern Treatise on the Law of Criminal Complicity* (Oxford, Clarendon, 1991) 4.

[2] Jackson provides a similar definition: complicity is 'a derivative form of responsibility for participation in wrongdoing committed by another actor'. See M Jackson, *Complicity in International Law* (Oxford, Oxford University Press, 2015) 11. Kutz defined complicity slightly differently as a concept that renders one person liable for the criminal act of another when the accomplice intentionally aids, encourages, or both intentionally aids and encourages, the direct perpetrator in the commission of act. See C Kutz, 'The Philosophical Foundations of Complicity Law' in J Deigh and D Dolinko (eds) *The Handbook of Philosophy of Criminal Law* (Oxford, Oxford University Press, 2011) 151.

[3] Smith (n 1) 81.

[4] A Ashworth, *Principles of Criminal Law*, 2nd edn (Oxford, Clarendon, 1995) 83.

based on his lack of reaction to these crimes. There is no direct evidence that he ordered the attacks. The commander is sentenced to life imprisonment.[5]

— The most senior officer in the Yugoslav Army knowingly provides logistical and personnel assistance to the Army of the Republika Srpska, which is committing crimes in Sarajevo and Srebrenica.[6] He is acquitted of aiding and abetting crimes against humanity, including murder, persecutions and attacks on civilians. The rationale for the acquittal is a failure to establish that the officer's assistance is specifically directed at supporting the criminal activities, and not just aimed at winning the war.[7]

— The acting President of Liberia supplies financial aid and other forms of practical assistance to warlords in the neighbouring Sierra Leone, where he knows crimes are being committed on a large scale.[8] He is convicted of aiding and abetting and planning murders, rapes and other acts of violence committed during the Sierra Leonean civil war. He is sentenced to 50 years' imprisonment.[9]

— A pharmacy owner in Rwanda participates in a meeting where the demolition of a local church is discussed. Approximately 2000 Tutsi men, women and children are known to have taken refuge in this church. After the meeting, the businessman gets a bulldozer that is subsequently brought to the parish and used to demolish the church, crushing those inside.[10] The businessman is sentenced to 30 years' imprisonment for planning genocide and extermination.[11]

These examples demonstrate the complexity of holding an individual complicit in crimes against humanity, war crimes and genocide. International criminality breeds an infinite number of factual scenarios; the accused range from local businessmen to the former (or acting) heads of state. Because international criminal law targets organized, large-scale offending, the distance between the accomplice and the harm is usually greater when compared to the regular domestic law situations. This peculiarity creates much room for inferential analysis as to the mental state of the

[5] *Prosecutor v Galić*, ICTY Case No IT-98-29-T, Trial Judgment, 5 December 2003 ('*Galić* Trial Judgment'), paras 741–49.

[6] *Prosecutor v Perišić*, ICTY Case No 04-81-A, Appeal Judgment, 28 February 2013 ('*Perišić* Appeal Judgment'), paras 2, 62 and 68.

[7] ibid, paras 62 and 68.

[8] *Prosecutor v Taylor*, SCSL-03-1-T, Trial Judgment, 11 May 2012 ('*Taylor* Trial Judgment'), paras 6920. 6952, 6956.

[9] *Prosecutor v Taylor*, SCSL-03-1-A, Appeal Judgment, 26 September 2013 ('*Taylor* Appeal Judgment').

[10] *Prosecutor v Kanyarukiga*, ICTR Case No 02-78-T, Trial Judgment, 1 November 2010 ('*Kanyarukiga* Trial Judgment'), paras 644-653.

[11] *Prosecutor v Kanyarukiga*, ICTR Case No 02-78-A, Appeal Judgment, 8 May 2012 ('*Kanyarukiga* Appeal Judgment'), para. 285.

accused and fosters creativity in the application of traditional legal doctrines. Different interpretations of the same doctrine lead to startlingly different results in each particular case—from life sentence to an acquittal.

The state of mind of an accomplice in mass atrocities presents another difficulty as it differs from the state of mind of a complicit individual in ordinary crimes. In the context of domestic law, criminality is a form of deviance from the norm. The principal perpetrator chooses to offend with the knowledge and understanding that he is defying the rules accepted in his society. The accomplice, for his part, takes a culpable decision to assist the principal. The responses of the domestic criminal justice system are consequently tuned towards ensuring conformity and preventing deviance.[12]

In contrast, participation in international crimes often stems from obedience rather than deviance. Political violence creates circumstances whereby authority is exercised to induce offending on the part of subordinates and creates a culture of impunity. Experiments aimed at testing human capacity to resist authority when put under pressure to perform acts going against human conscience show that on average, less than half of those tested were able to do so.[13] As a consequence, the will of the principal perpetrator in international criminal law is frequently compromised—he becomes part of the system that makes it easier for him to offend than to desist. In contrast, the accomplice who occupies a senior position in the state or army apparatus may have more leeway than the foot soldier to resist authority and make the right choices. Thus, international criminal law modifies the assumption that the act of the principal has distinct moral importance: the accomplice is often more culpable than the actual perpetrator.

The purpose of this work is to explain what complicity means within the international criminal law context and to define the legal requirements of its various forms, as well as to delimit complicity from neighbouring concepts such as co-perpetration and common design.[14] The book uses

[12] In the words of Hart, criminal law sets up, in its rules, standards of behaviour to encourage certain types of conduct and discourage others. See HLA Hart and J Gardner, *Punishment and Responsibility: Essays on Philosophy of Law* (Oxford, Oxford University Press, 2009) 6.

[13] S Milgram, *Obedience to Authority: An Experimental View* (Tavistock, Pinter & Martin, 1974).

[14] This book does not address in detail another neighbouring concept—command responsibility, also referred to as superior responsibility. This notion shares some common features with accomplice liability in that they are both accessory to principal crimes committed by primary perpetrators. The key difference that distinguishes command responsibility from complicity is the fact that the superior is liable not for his part in the commission of crimes by his subordinates, but for his own personal failure to adopt measures to prevent and punish those acts. The superior is sanctioned for a culpable omission. This divergence is so fundamental that it places command responsibility in a category separate from all other liability modes. See *Prosecutor v Orić*, ICTY Case No IT-03-68-T, Trial Judgment, 30 June 2006 ('*Orić* Trial Judgment'), para 292; G Mettraux, *The Law of Command Responsibility* (Oxford, Oxford University Press, 2009) 39.

legal tools to tackle complicity. It must be noted, however, that the concept lies at the intersection of law, philosophy, human psychology, sociology and criminology. Under what circumstances an individual is responsible for the act of another person is a serious dilemma that can be approached from different angles.

The task of defining complicity is not an easy one—it creates much uncertainty. What elements should be included in the various forms of complicity? Is it possible to come up with a single formula for complicity that would suit the plethora of factual scenarios in international criminal law or is this an unattainable goal? Do we need to distinguish between different forms of liability at all? And if so, why? The quest for complicity and its consequences also inevitably raises questions relating to the general nature of international criminal law, its sources and its punishment rationales. Thus, complicity serves an additional function in this book: it is used as a test to assess the method and purposes of international criminal law.

Four main points will take shape on the basis of the discussion in the subsequent chapters:

1. Crafting a blanket provision defining complicity does not appear feasible in international criminal law. A single formula that would magically assist in the attribution of individual criminal responsibility to those removed from the crime is akin to a Kafkian castle—an unachievable objective.
2. Having said this, it is essential to define most comprehensively the constituent elements of the various forms of complicity—the conduct requirement and the fault requirement. Thoroughly researched doctrine serves as a solid basis for the subsequent evaluation of facts.
3. Complicity in its various manifestations is a useful tool in describing the conduct of the accused in the most accurate terms. It has the advantage over its alternatives—extended co-perpetration and joint criminal enterprise—of being deeply rooted in domestic criminal law and thus enjoying more acceptance and legitimacy at the national and international levels. This is so because complicity as a 'general principle of law' has a solid foundation in the sources of international law, while its alternatives do not enjoy the same status.
4. The key to the successful application of various forms of complicity is a careful balancing of its different elements on the basis of the facts of the case: in instances when the accomplice is in the physical proximity to the unfolding atrocities, his culpability may be inferred from the surrounding circumstances, while his contribution to the crime needs to be spelled out in detail—mere presence at the scene is not sufficient to attract criminal responsibility. In cases where the accomplice is removed from the principal perpetrator—in time or in space—the emphasis should be on the accomplice's guilty state of mind. The

> more tenuous the connection between the accomplice and the crime, the less an inferential analysis of his mental state is to be allowed. In the end, it is the faulty choice to assist another in the commission of the crime that makes accessory participation punishable.

The following chapters explore complicity from various angles. Chapter two supports one of the main claims of this book, namely that *systematic* analysis of domestic law may enhance the coherence and legitimacy of international criminal law. There is a notable trend in international jurisprudence to disregard traditional forms of liability in favour of newly developed concepts that are not expressly provided by their respective statutes.[15] This paradox served as an inspiration for the comparative analysis of complicity in various domestic jurisdictions around the world in an attempt to find the roots of complicity and to legitimise this concept in an international arena.

Complicity in one form or another appears to be recognised by all legal systems under review. The comparative exercise is instructive for two reasons: first, it grounds complicity, in legal terms, as a 'general principle of law';[16] and, second, it helps to reach a deeper understanding of what distinguishes complicity from perpetration.[17] From the overview of domestic legal systems, it becomes clear that international courts at times 'cherry picked' particular features of the various modes of participation in different legal orders in an attempt to create a form of criminal responsibility best suited to international criminal law.[18] Whether such 'cherry picking' is appropriate in lieu of the comprehensive analysis of different approaches is a relevant question.

Chapter three turns to international criminal law proper. It discovers the historical origins of complicity in international criminal law—a field of law that, from its very inception, has struggled with the attribution of individual responsibility for collective wrongdoing. The discussion focuses on different mechanisms of addressing the collective dimension of international crimes, including complicity. A historical perspective also showcases the importance of domestic criminal law in shaping modern international criminal law.

[15] *cf* J Stewart, 'The End of "Modes of Liability" for International Crimes' (2012) 25 *Leiden Journal of International Law* 165.

[16] Article 21(1)(c) of the Rome Statute assigns 'general principles of law derived from state laws of legal systems in the world' the role of a secondary source of law in the ICC. Consequently, the survey of domestic legal systems asserts the foundation of complicity as a general principle of law.

[17] Stewart (n 15) 165, 204.

[18] For example, 'indirect co-perpetration' used by the ICC stems from the German legal thought.

Chapter four investigates how the International Criminal Tribunal for the Former Yugoslavia (ICTY), the International Tribunal for Rwanda (ICTR), the Extraordinary Chambers in the Courts of Cambodia (ECCC) and the Special Court for Sierra Leone (SCSL) use complicity in their case law. It also touches upon the 'competing' concepts designed to address crimes with multiple accused. This overview reaches the conclusion that there are some gaps and inconsistencies in the understanding of complicity by these judicial bodies. The problematic aspects include the lack of sufficiently defined standard of causation and loose connection between the facts of the case, the elements of the substantive crimes and the legal requirements of liability modes.

Chapter five discusses complicity in the context of the International Criminal Court (ICC). The Rome Statute of the ICC provides the most comprehensive article on individual criminal responsibility in the history of international criminal law.[19] It seems, however, that the ICC has until recently neglected complicity in favour of the certain forms of commission. It appears to have viewed commission as the most appropriate form of responsibility for dealing with mass crimes because it corresponds to the higher levels of culpability of the accused. Some arguments against linking culpability of the accused to the mode of participation are presented in this chapter.

Chapters four and five show the struggle of the ad hoc tribunals (the ICTY and the ICTR), the hybrid courts (the SCSL and the ECCC) and the ICC to find a mode of participation that accommodates crimes with multiple accused. These judicial bodies define to some extent the traditional modes of participation through their statutes and jurisprudence. The tendency is to extend or adjust traditional participation modes to 'fit' international cases.

Chapter six contains a comparative analysis of complicity in the law of state responsibility and in international criminal law. The limits of complicity in both fields are carefully spelled out in this chapter. The findings show strong links between the law of state responsibility and international criminal law. It appears that both fields of law are complementary in filling the impunity gaps, but there are limits to cross-fertilisation between the two domains.

Chapter seven explores the correlation between complicity and punishment. In some domestic legal systems, complicity, especially in the form of aiding and abetting, results in the mitigation of an accomplice's sentence compared to that of the principal perpetrator. No such rule exists in international criminal law. This is not to claim that the form of participation

[19] Article 25(3) of the Rome Statute of the International Criminal Court (ICC), of 17 July 1998, UN Doc A/CONF.183/9.

plays no role at sentencing at an international level; the mode of liability may or may not—depending on the facts of the case—assist in assessing the gravity of the offence for sentencing purposes. However, it is the totality of factors—and not a single parameter—that is the basis for the final determination of the appropriate punishment for the convicted person.

Finally, the concluding chapter eight situates complicity in a broader context of international criminal law. This chapter looks at the aims of international criminal law as well as its limitations. The purpose is to set the direction in which the law on individual criminal responsibility should evolve. It appears that international criminal law currently struggles with the multitude of different aims that it strives to achieve, some of which are conflicting. In the absence of a consensus on the dominant goal of international criminal justice, defining various legal concepts (complicity included) presents some difficulties. It is argued in this chapter that the main role of international criminal law is symbolic—it signifies an agreement about the values shared by international community as a whole. In line with this general function, international criminal law should be conceptualised as an exemplary justice mechanism that embraces the notion of fairness to the greatest extent possible. Consequently, the ambition should be to apply the principle of fair labelling and describe the conduct of the accused in the most precise terms. Complicity is an indispensable tool in this process.

2

Origins of Complicity: The Domestic Law Intake

INTRODUCTION

BACK IN 2000, Kai Ambos claimed that despite the fact that the concept of individual criminal responsibility for violations of humanitarian and human rights norms is universally recognised, the elements of this responsibility are not sufficiently discussed in the literature.[1] This gap has been remedied in the past 15 years with a significant amount of literature analysing and criticising the modes of liability in international criminal law.[2] What is still missing is a systematic reference to domestic criminal law, which would provide normative and philosophical grounds for various forms of criminal participation.

Examining the jurisprudence and the statutes of the ad hoc tribunals, hybrid courts and the ICC shows that international bodies extensively engage with complicity in its various forms and manifestations. However, there are still gaps in understanding its constituent elements and theoretical underpinnings.[3] This chapter lays the foundation for the rest of the volume by surveying a number of national laws on complicity.[4] The purpose of this exercise is twofold. First, it assists in a deeper understanding

[1] K Ambos, 'Individual Criminal Responsibility' in GK McDonald and O Swaak-Goldman (eds), *Substantive and Procedural Aspects of International Criminal Law* (The Hague, Martinus Nijhoff, 2000) 6.

[2] For an extensive analysis of the relevant literature and case law, please see Chs 4 and 5.

[3] The recent volumes by Jackson and Aust are an excellent contribution to the field. See M Jackson, *Complicity in International Law* (Oxford, Oxford University Press, 2015); HP Aust, *Complicity and the Law of State Responsibility* (Cambridge, Cambridge University Press, 2013).

[4] Many scholars in the field of criminal law recognise the value of resorting to a comparative analysis of national legal systems for the purposes of developing international criminal law. See, for example, G Fletcher, *The Grammar of Criminal Law* (Oxford, Oxford University Press, 2007) 340–41; A Eser, 'The Importance of Comparative Legal Research for the Development of Criminal Sciences' in R Blancpain (ed), *Law in Motion: Recent Developments in Civil Procedure, Constitutional, Contract, Criminal, Environmental, Family & Succession, Intellectual Property, Labour, Medical, Social Security, Transport Law* (The Hague, Kluwer, 1997) 496 and 505; P Roberts, 'Comparative Law for International Criminal Justice' in E Orucu and D Nelken (eds), *Comparative Law: A Handbook* (Oxford, Hart Publishing, 2007) 355–56. For the international law perspective, see LC Green, 'Comparative Law as a Source of International Law' (1967) 42 *Tulane Law Review* 52, 66.

of complicity, its foundations and functional core. Complicity is deeply rooted in domestic law and exists in one form or another in countries with both common and civil law traditions.[5] Second, the chapter supports a broader claim that systematic reference to domestic law is beneficial for the discipline of international criminal law because, if performed with sufficient methodological rigour, it may produce the principles recognised by the variety of states and thus enjoy the legitimising effect of being one of the recognised sources of international law. It also serves as an interpretative tool with respect to two other sources of law—treaty and custom.

One may immediately object that national laws are too disparate to serve the purpose of clarifying complicity (or any other general concept), let alone provide a basis for adducing the general principle of international law. This is the position advocated by James Stewart in his excellent essay 'The End of "Modes of Liability" for International Crimes'. Stewart argues that 'complicity's most objectionable characteristics are inherited from domestic exemplars' and by borrowing domestic doctrine, 'international courts incorporate the historical idiosyncrasies of national criminal systems'.[6] He admits that the reliance of international criminal justice practitioners on domestic law may be unavoidable at times, but it must be limited. This is a valid concern for international criminal law that borrowed heavily from domestic law, and often without much contextualisation.[7] Sporadic appropriation of national law doctrines is not the approach advocated in this book, however. At times, one or two individual systems are sufficient to clarify minor discrepancy in international (criminal) law, but with grand concepts, such as complicity, a comprehensive study of a selection of legal systems is key to its deeper understanding.

This chapter therefore uses a comparative inquiry to examine complicity at a domestic level. The first section shows the relevance of this study to international criminal law. It links the comparative method to the notion of the 'law recognised by civilized nations', a source of international law. The same section discusses the particulars of the methodology used in this chapter as well as major criticisms levied against using domestic law as a source of international criminal law. The next section examines the concept of complicity in domestic jurisdictions. This section attempts to strike a balance between exploring complicity in depth and providing an overview of the range of legal systems. Appendix I should be

[5] See *Prosecutor v Akayesu*, ICTR Case No 96-4-T, Trial Chamber Judgment, 2 September 1998, para 527; M Dubber, 'Criminalizing Complicity: A Comparative Analysis' (2007) 5(4) *Journal of International Criminal Justice* 977; G Fletcher, *Rethinking Criminal Law* (Boston, Little, Brown, 1978) 634–82.

[6] J Stewart, 'The End of "Modes of Liability" for International Crimes' (2012) 25 *Leiden Journal of International Law* 169, 190.

[7] D Robinson, 'Darryl Robinson Comments on James Stewart's "End of Modes of Liability"', *Opinio Juris* blog, http://opiniojuris.org/2012/03/21/ljil-robinson-comments-on-stewart.

read in conjunction with this chapter. It provides a schematic overview of complicity in 31 jurisdictions. The penultimate section of the chapter adduces some general principles associated with complicity resulting from the study of domestic law and evaluates their relevance at an international level. This section provides an interdisciplinary perspective on complicity, including the limitations of transplanting the concept from national law into the international field.

I. THE COMPARATIVE METHOD IN INTERNATIONAL CRIMINAL LAW

A. General Principles of Law as a Source of Law and Inspiration

Comparative studies of domestic legal systems assist in the discovery of one of the sources of international law, namely the 'general principles of law'. Article 38(1)(c) of the Statute of the International Court of Justice lists 'general principles of law recognized by civilized nations' as one of the sources of international law.[8] The expression 'general principles of law' has been given different meanings in the context of public international law.[9] Some academics consider that the expression refers primarily to general principles of international law and only subsidiarily to the principles embedded in municipal law.[10] Others, when speaking of 'general principles of law', choose to refer to legal principles recognised in national law.[11] A third group, which includes Lauterpracht and Kelsen, almost denies the status of the 'general principles of law' as an independent source of law. Lauterpracht writes:

> Experience has shown that the main function of 'general principles of law' has been that of a safety-valve to be kept in reserve, rather than a source of law of frequent application. As a rule, the two primary sources of law enumerated in Article 38—treaty and custom—have provided a sufficient basis for decision.[12]

Equally, there does not seem to be an agreement on how many countries need to recognise a certain principle in *foro domestico* in order for it

[8] P de Cruz, *Comparative Law in a Changing World*, 3rd edn (Abingdon, Routledge-Cavendish 2007) 26.

[9] M Shaw, *International Law* (Cambridge, Cambridge University Press, 2008) 99; B Cheng, *General Principles of Law as Applied by International Courts and Tribunals* (Cambridge, Cambridge University Press, 1987) 2; FO Raimondo, *General Principles of Law in the Decisions of International Criminal Courts and Tribunals* (Leiden, Martinus Nijhoff, 2008) 1.

[10] D Anzilotti, *Cours de Droit international* (Hudson, 1920–42) 611.

[11] Raimondo (n 9) 1.

[12] H Lauterpacht, *The Development of International Law by the International Court*, (Cambridge, Cambridge University Press, 1958) 166. *cf* Hans Kelsen, who argues that 'it is doubtful whether such as thing as 'general principles of law recognised by civilised nations exits at all'. H Kelsen, *The Law of the United Nations: A Critical Analysis of its Fundamental Problems* (London, Stevens, 1950) 533.

to qualify as a source of international law.[13] Hans Kelsen posed this question as early as 1950,[14] but the answer is not entirely straightforward even today. In the *Baumgarten* case, the United Nations (UN) Human Rights Committee satisfied itself with the 'recognition of the general principle by the community of nations' standard when determining whether killings and attempted killings of those crossing the East German border were criminal offences in the 1980s.[15] In Van Hoof's view, two conditions need to be satisfied in order for a principle to be considered a source of law: first, the principle needs to be accepted by *all* states in *foro domestico*; and, second, there needs to exist a third party decision, which calls for the application of this source of law.[16]

Unlike public international law, international criminal law provides some guidance as to the hierarchy of sources of law. Article 21(1)(c) of the Rome Statute of the ICC assigns 'general principles of law derived from state laws of legal systems in the world' the role of a secondary source of law in the ICC. The Rome Statute is thus more specific than the Statute of the International Court of Justice on the content and the role of the 'general principles of international law': the general principles under Article 21(1)(c) are to be a subsidiary source of law when a gap exists in international law. It is essential that the general principle is *representative* of the variety of nations; hence, there is no call for a direct transposition of a certain concept from a *single* domestic legal system to international law. In a similar vein, the jurisprudence of the ad hoc tribunals does not require universal acceptance of the rule by all the states when abstracting legal rules from national systems.[17]

The first judgment of the ICC in *Lubanga* proves two issues that are crucially important for this discussion: (i) the modes of responsibility in international criminal law require more interpretation based on a solid methodology; (ii) there is a gap in understanding of the role and purpose of the 'general principles of law' in defining the modes of responsibility at an international level.[18] While the majority of the *Lubanga* Trial Chamber denied resorting to domestic law in the context of international proceedings, they introduced, through the back door, the German domestic law

[13] Cheng (n 9) 25.

[14] Kelsen (n 12) 533.

[15] The Human Rights Committee held that 'the disproportionate use of lethal force was criminal according to the general principles of law recognized by the community of nations already at the time when the author committed his acts.' See the decision of the Human Rights Committee in *Baumgarten v Germany*, Communication No 960/2000, para 9.4.

[16] GJH van Hoof, *Rethinking the Sources of International Law* (Boston, Kluwer, 1983) 140–42.

[17] FO Raimondo, 'General Principles of Law, Judicial Creativity, and the Development of International Criminal Law' in S Darcy and J Powderly (eds), *Judicial Creativity at the International Criminal Tribunals* (Oxford, Oxford University Press, 2010) 52.

[18] *Prosecutor v Thomas Lubanga Dyilo*, ICC-01/04-01/06, Trial Chamber I, Judgment Pursuant to Article 74 of the Statute, 14 March 2012, para 976.

concept of 'control over crime'.[19] Simultaneously, while Judge Fulford in his separate opinion criticised the Chamber's decision to use the German theory, he believed the Chamber took this decision based on the 'general principles of law' under Article 21(1)(c) of the Rome Statute.[20]

The ICC and the international criminal tribunals have been somewhat reluctant in decisions and judgments to resort to principles derived from the multitude of domestic legal systems, preferring instead to adopt a narrower perspective found in a single or few domestic legal systems.[21] However, there are several instances in which the general principles of law have assisted judges in finding the appropriate legal standard.[22] In *Erdemović*, for example, Judges McDonald and Vohrah determined that duress is not a complete defence to charges of crimes against humanity and war crimes by surveying 30 national legal systems, including civil law systems.[23] Similarly, the Trial Chamber of the Extraordinary Chambers in the Courts of Cambodia analysed several national legal orders in order to resolve the continuing debate between the prosecution and the defence relating to the extended form of the joint criminal enterprise.[24] After having surveyed several national legal systems, the Trial Chamber concluded that this form of liability cannot be considered to have been a general principle of law between 1975 and 1979.[25]

The approach developed in this book is that domestic law—or, rather, the results collected from examining several national legal systems—informs the 'general principles of law'. The question arises whether and to what extent domestic law also assists in the interpretation of the 'orthodox sources' of international law enshrined in Article 38(1)(a) and 38(1)(b) of the Statute of the International Court of Justice, namely treaty and custom.[26] Arguably, one can best conceptualise the 'general principles of law' as an independent source of law *and* a framework for interpretation of the principles that already exist (often vaguely) in the two other sources of international law, namely custom and treaty.

[19] ibid.

[20] *Prosecutor v Thomas Lubanga Dyilo*, ICC-01/04-01/06, Separate Opinion of Judge Adrian Fulford to the Trial Chamber I, Judgment Pursuant to Article 74 of the Statute, 14 March 2012, para 10.

[21] For an extended discussion of this issue, see Raimondo (n 17).

[22] For more on the jurisprudence of international courts and tribunals resorting to general principles of law, see Raimondo (n 9) 71 et seq.

[23] *Prosecutor v Erdemović*, ICTY Case No IT-96-22-A, Appeal Judgment, 7 October 1997 ('*Erdemović* Appeal Judgment'), Joint Separate Opinion of Judge McDonald and Judge Vohrah, Judgment, paras 56–72.

[24] *Prosecutor v Ieng Sary et al*, ECCC, Case No 002/19-09-2007/ECCC/TC, Decision on Applicability of Joint Criminal Enterprise, 12 September 2011, paras 29, 37.

[25] ibid.

[26] For the expression 'orthodox sources' of international law, see RY Jennings, 'The Identification of International Law' in Bin Cheng (ed), *International Law, Teaching and Practice* (London, Stevens & Sons, 1982).

It appears that domestic laws may be used to interpret these two sources of law. However, they cannot be the sole 'informant' of the treaty provision or the rule of customary law. Treaties, being classical examples of written international law, should in theory regulate the matters they address with sufficient clarity, thus eliminating the need to consult other sources. In many instances, however, treaty provisions require further elaboration and clarification.[27] This is because they are always a product of diplomatic negotiations.[28] This in turn implies compromises, deliberate gaps and omissions, as well as reservations by some parties. A legitimate question that stems from this inconsistency was posed by Jennings: how can such a 'package deal' be reconciled with the progressive development of law?[29]

The use of domestic laws to inform and clarify treaty provisions can be one answer to this question. This is especially true in respect of international criminal law, which, unlike other branches of public international law, is ultimately based on national criminal law with some international flavour to it. Consequently, national legislation fills in gaps in the statutes of international criminal courts and tribunals.[30] In particular, the 'general part' of international criminal law, including rules on punishment and the attribution of liability, benefits from the study of the underlying concepts in domestic legal systems.[31] Complicity, as a collective term for the derivative modes of liability, falls under this umbrella.

When it comes to the custom, it appears that courts on some occasions use the results of comparative analysis to support the existence of rules of customary law.[32] However, custom is arguably a problematic source of law, especially when it comes to human rights obligations or provisions of international criminal law.[33] The difficulty arises on several levels: first, it is difficult to identify a custom based on the past behaviour of the state because a uniform approach to an issue is rare and states often engage in behaviour negating the proposed rule;[34] second, the courts often do not make a distinction between two constitutive elements of custom—state

[27] B Simma and P Alston, 'The Sources of Human Rights Law: Custom, *Jus Cogens*, and General Principles' (1988–89) 12 *Australian Yearbook of International Law* 82.

[28] Jennings (n 26) 5.

[29] ibid 5–7.

[30] Green (n 4) 65 elaborated on the gap-filling function of comparative law.

[31] See Fletcher (n 4) 340.

[32] M Akehurst, 'Custom as a Source of International Law' (1976) 47 *British Yearbook of International Law* 1, 9

[33] 'It is often difficult to determine what constitutes customary international law, who defines customary international law, and how firmly established a norm has to be to qualify as a customary international law norm.' *Hamdan v US*, USCA 11-1257 (2012) 23.

[34] Simma and Alston (n 27) 92–93.

practice and *opinio juris*;[35] finally, Kelsen also highlighted the self-fulfilling prophecy nature of a custom: it can hardly constitute 'evidence' of state practice because it is in itself a qualified practice of the states.[36] In light of these problems, Bruno Simma and Phil Alston, when discussing the nature of some human rights obligations, suggested looking elsewhere to explain their universally binding nature. Instead of updating the concept of custom, they proposed resorting to another source of law, namely the general principles of law.[37]

There is some evidence in the jurisprudence of the ad hoc tribunals that domestic criminal law also serves to prove the existence of a customary rule.[38] It is important, however, to maintain a distinction between the two sources of law: custom represents 'a general practice *among* States accepted by them as law' (emphasis added) and general principles of law have recognition *in* the municipal law of states.[39] Both custom and general principles of law rely on the element of recognition of a certain rule. However, the emphasis is different: custom centres around the recognition of a legal character of a certain rule through state practice, while the general principles of law rely on the *existence* of a certain principle domestically.[40]

From the perspective of international criminal law, there exists confusion surrounding the concept of customary international law in the jurisprudence of the ad hoc tribunals.[41] The two traditional elements of custom—state practice and *opinio juris*—take different forms and encompass different values in the context of international criminal law. Larissa van den Herik argued that the tendency to place extra emphasis on the *opinio juris* component of custom inherent to international law in general is further complicated by the fact that the ad hoc tribunals tend to be selective in the cases that they use to support custom, which in turn may lead to a biased outcome.[42] This trend is due to the specific nature of human rights and international criminal law; state practice takes a 'backseat' because it frequently supports the 'violation of the rule' rather than state compliance with it. As with the 'general principles of law', the evidentiary standard required for the existence of custom differs according to the situation.[43]

[35] L van den Herik, 'Using Custom to Reconceptualise Crimes against Humanity' in S Darcy and J Powderly (eds), *Judicial Creativity at the International Criminal Tribunals* (Oxford, Oxford University Press, 2010) 101.

[36] Kelsen (n 12) 533. See also Simma and Alston (n 27) 88–89.

[37] Simma and Alston (n 27) 98–99.

[38] *Prosecutor v Tadić*, ICTY Case No IT-94-1-A and IT-94-1-Abis, Third Sentencing Judgment, 26 January 2000, paras 214–20. See also van den Herik (n 35) 102.

[39] Cheng (n 9) 24–25.

[40] ibid.

[41] A Zahar and G Sluiter, *International Criminal Law: A Critical Introduction* (Oxford, Oxford University Press, 2008) 224.

[42] Van den Herik (n 35) 99 and 102.

[43] ibid 104.

It follows that domestic law serves an interpretative function in relation to custom and treaty. This is in addition to being a source of international law through the concept of the 'general principles of law'. One can highlight two further beneficial aspects of exploring domestic laws for the purposes of international criminal law: first, comparative investigation can serve as a tool for discovering 'best practices' around the world and incorporating them into international criminal law;[44] second, the study of domestic practices is a crucial step in the cross-fertilisation of domestic and international criminal law with the prospect of developing uniform approaches.

The interplay between the two fields of law no longer works as a one-way street: there is a striking recent trend of international criminal law enriching and altering state penal systems. For example, in the *Hamdan* case, the US Court of Appeal overturned Hamdan's conviction for material support of terrorism because it was not an international law crime at the time that Hamdan engaged in the relevant conduct.[45] This is in contrast with, for example, aiding and abetting terrorism.[46] In arriving at this conclusion, the court looked into the sources of international law—custom and treaty law provisions, including the Rome Statute of the ICC.[47] This cross-fertilisation is especially relevant in the context of the complementarity principle at the ICC, whereby national jurisdictions have primacy over the ICC, subject to their inaction, unwillingness or inability.[48]

B. Critique of the Comparative Method

There are different levels of criticism against using the results of comparative studies of domestic penal legislation in international criminal law. On a more general level, De Cruz raised concerns about the transferability of national law concepts into international law decisions. He stressed that the comparative method does not replace judicial functions, but rather facilitates, informs and clarifies them.[49] He advocated for the cautious use of the results of comparative studies in international law. This chapter underscores and embraces De Cruz's concern: direct transposition of the concepts from national law into international criminal law or downright analogies do not serve the purpose of uncovering the scope of complicity,

[44] Roberts (n 4) 355.

[45] *Hamdan v US*, USCA 11-1257 (2012) 27.

[46] ibid 26. Note: the US Court of Appeals treats 'aiding and abetting terrorism' as one substantive crime without distinguishing the mode of participation—aiding and abetting—and the crime itself. This is in contrast with the approach adopted in international criminal law.

[47] ibid 23–25.

[48] H Olasolo, *Essays on International Criminal Justice* (Oxford, Hart Publishing, 2012) 74–75.

[49] De Cruz (n 8) 25.

nor do they provide space for accommodating the specific features of international criminal law. At the same time, this caution shall not serve as a barrier to the exploration of national law.

When it comes to international criminal law specifically, Tallgren argued against drawing an analogy between international criminal justice and national law in light of the particular circumstances of criminality involved in the former.[50] She pointed towards an extraordinarily complex relationship between war, crime and criminology, and the interests protected by international criminal law differ from those protected by state criminal law.[51] In response to this general concern about the incomparability of domestic and international criminal law, one may argue that, indeed, these fields of law deal with crimes committed on different scales and under different circumstances. However, the principle of individual criminal responsibility unites both fields of law.

Finally, both Markus Dubber and James Stewart questioned the value of a comparative method in relation to complicity specifically. Dubber suggested, after having studied in some detail the concept of complicity in German and American law, that national legal systems should serve as no more than a mere signpost for the development of the concept of accomplice liability in international criminal law. This has to do with the need to strike a balance between a broader view of accomplice liability urged by the enormity of the crimes involved and a more narrow view of complicity based on considerations of the principle of legality.[52] It is hard to argue against the view that national law concepts should not be directly transported into the sphere of international criminal law.[53] Brownlie noted on this point that it would be incorrect to assume that tribunals mechanically borrow from national law; instead, they use elements of legal reasoning.[54] Nonetheless, international criminal law needs to refine its theory of individual criminal responsibility. One way of doing this is by exploring national legislation of different countries to discover the divergence or conformity of domestic legal systems in the field of criminal participation.[55] This exercise leads to one adducing certain principles of law that can assist in the formulation of international principles of individual criminal responsibility.

[50] I Tallgren, 'The Sensibility and Sense of International Criminal Law' (2002) 13(3) *European Journal of International Law* 571–72.

[51] ibid 575, 586.

[52] Dubber (n 5) 1001.

[53] For example, Judge Cassese opposed the mechanical transposition of national law concepts into international criminal law. See *Erdemović* Appeal Judgment (n 23) Separate and Dissenting Opinion of Judge Cassese.

[54] I Brownlie, *Principles of Public International Law* (Oxford, Oxford University Press, 2008) 16.

[55] For more on the development of law and the comparative perspective, see Green (n 4) 54.

Stewart's point is broader and relates to the utility of the modes of liability in international criminal law.[56] He maintains that international criminal law unjustifiably relies on domestic criminal law and inherits its problems when it comes to liability modes, whereas a better option is to develop the model suited for international criminality. Stewart argues that complicity, usually much praised for its fairness and consistency, suffers from the same shortcomings as much-criticised extended joint criminal enterprise and superior responsibility.[57] These shortcomings can be summarised as follows. First, the principle of culpability is violated when the elements of the crime do not match those of the mode of liability. For example, complicity may unjustifiably amplify culpability by allowing for a lower mental threshold than that required for the crime itself—it may be sufficient for the accused to foresee the possibility of a crime being committed in order to be held accomplice to a crime, whereas the perpetrator would need to possess an intent.[58] Second, there is no plausible explanation as to *why* we need to distinguish between perpetrators and accessories.[59] Finally, there are pragmatic considerations for simplifying the process of attribution of liability by collapsing various labels into one capacious notion of perpetration that is not static like the traditional forms.[60] Simplification will enhance the expressive function of international criminal law by focusing on the factual side of criminality rather than the 'legalese' hardly understood by the majority of people across the world. Thus, the solution offered by Stewart is abandoning complicity, together with all other modes of liability, in favour of a unitary account of perpetration that only requires a substantial causal contribution to the crime with a requisite mens rea. Meeting these two conditions shall be sufficient to render a person responsible.[61]

It is important to address each of the thoughtful points raised above, for they contradict the approach advocated in this book. First, I understand the principle of culpability as not requiring the modes of liability to match the crime; rather, it presupposes holding a person accountable for his contribution to the crime if it is done culpably. There are two sets of elements that the prosecution must prove: those related to the crime itself and those linked to the way in which an individual became involved in the crime.[62] It is perfectly reasonable to attach responsibility

[56] Stewart (n 6).

[57] These forms of liability are discussed in Ch 4.

[58] Stewart (n 6) 198.

[59] ibid 204.

[60] ibid 199, 215.

[61] ibid 207.

[62] See also G Werle and B Burghardt, 'Establishing Degrees of Responsibility: Modes of Participation in Article 25 of the ICC' in E van Sliedergt and S Vailiev (eds), *Pluralism in International Criminal Law* (Oxford, Oxford University Press, 2014) 304.

to someone who intends to contribute to the crime and merely foresees its occurrence as a possibility. What matters is that the underlying act is wrongful and that the assistance is provided on the basis of a choice available to an accomplice and in the absence of legal excuses.[63]

The reasons for distinguishing between perpetrators and accessories are dictated by the principle of fairness—it is not sufficient to discuss responsibility of the accused at the stage of sentencing.[64] In this regard, it is essential to establish the difference between the attribution of responsibility and wrongdoing.[65] Fletcher drew this distinction, pointing out that the question of wrongdoing is dealt with under the set of primary legal norms, prohibiting or requiring particular acts, while the question of attribution 'is resolved under an entirely distinct set of norms, which are directed not to the class of potential violators, but to judges and jurors, charged with the task of assessing whether individuals are liable for their wrongful acts'.[66]

There exists a tension between the normative theory of attribution, which views the process of attribution as a judgment about whether the accused can be fairly held accountable for his wrongful act, and the descriptive theory, which implies that there is some single feature of all criminal conduct that serves to link the actor to the wrongful act, thus justifying liability.[67] Fletcher noted that countries with an Anglo-American tradition have sought to suppress the normative aspect of accountability and pack the problems of attribution into the concept of responsibility by focusing on the status and capacity of the actor, while the German tradition has favoured the normative approach to attribution.[68]

Collapsing all modes of liability into one concept would go beyond the normative/descriptive attribution divide and would erase the line between attribution and wrongful conduct altogether. The unitary model suggested by Stewart focuses on the causal link between the perpetrator and the act. However, such an approach presupposes an extended view of causation.

Complicity is a field of attribution that falls outside the standard of causation in the narrow sense of this term. At first glance, it may seem illogical to infer the accomplice's culpability based on the actions of the principal when it is presumed that the principal's actions are fully voluntary and

[63] M Moore, *Placing Blame: A Theory of the Criminal Law* (Oxford, Oxford University Press, 1997) 404.
[64] JD Ohlin, 'LJIL Symposium: Names, Labels, and Roses', *Opinio Juris* blog, http://opiniojuris.org/2012/03/23/ljil-names-labels-and-roses.
[65] Fletcher (n 5) 491–92.
[66] ibid.
[67] ibid 492–95.
[68] ibid 496–97.

the accomplice may not be said to have caused these actions.[69] Kadish explained this phenomenon by the derivative (or indirect) nature of accomplice liability. He argued that an accomplice is culpable not because he caused certain events (as would be the case with the primary perpetrator) and not because he caused the perpetrator to commit a crime, but because the accomplice is to be blamed for the conduct of another person.[70]

Finally, simplifying the attribution of liability in international criminal law for practical reasons is not justified in my view. The expressive function of international criminal justice is based not only on the outcome, namely convictions, but also on the way in which the administration of justice is carried out. If the public sees the process as 'rushed' or unscrupulous, this may equally hurt the credibility of the final judgment.[71]

C. Methodology

The literature devoted to comparative law places great significance on methodology.[72] This is particularly relevant for the purposes of adducing certain principles to be later used as a source of international law. Thus, it is essential to justify the perspective of the comparative study, the scope of the study and the choice of legal systems. There are several issues to take into account when discussing complicity.

First, it is essential to understand the function of complicity before attempting to compare the concept across different legal cultures. Zweigert and Koetz suggest that the basic working hypothesis of all comparative studies is that of functionality, meaning that incomparable notions cannot be contrasted.[73] One way to verify the role of a particular legal concept is to establish the 'common core'—the highest common factor of an area of substantive law.[74] This chapter focuses on finding this common core for complicity by, first, describing the types of participants in the crime that can be found in different national legal systems and, then, by separating one mode of participation from the other. The study goes beyond the linguistic distinction between principals and accomplices[75] and tries to

[69] SH Kadish, 'Complicity, Cause and Blame: A Study in the Interpretation of Doctrine' (1985) 73(2) *California Law Review* 327.

[70] ibid 332. On the nature of derivative liability, see also Fletcher (n 5) 583.

[71] For more discussion on the goals of international criminal law, see Chs 7 and 8.

[72] K Zweigert and H Koetz, *An Introduction to Comparative Law*, 3rd edn (Oxford, Clarendon, 1998) 33.

[73] ibid 34.

[74] De Cruz (n 8) 26.

[75] Translation of the terms without exploring the meaning attached to them often leads to confusing results because different languages have different capacities to express various forms of liability. However, it follows from this study that the underlying rationale for distinguishing different participants in the crime is often the same.

establish the consequences of holding someone to be an accomplice to the crime, as opposed to finding him to be the perpetrator.[76]

The second important consideration is the number of countries to be examined. In this regard, it is worth underlining that the results of the study will form the basis of the notion of complicity as a 'general principle of law'. Consequently, it is vital to ensure a wide representation of countries in terms of numbers and geographical coverage. It is tempting to explore as many jurisdictions as possible. However, this is not practically feasible. Moreover, as explained below, many legal systems resemble each other—this reduces the number of domestic legal orders under scrutiny. Fabian Raimondo provided some practical guidance in adducing 'general principles of law'. He divided this process into two parts, namely a 'vertical move' and a 'horizontal move'. The 'vertical move' distils an underlying legal principle from the variety of national legal systems, while the horizontal move corroborates its acceptance by the generality of states.[77] An example of the 'horizontal move' is the study by Judges McDonald and Vohrah of the national law on duress in 30 jurisdictions in support of their separate opinion in *Erdemović*.[78] The present report on complicity is similar to *Erdemović* in that it examines briefly (in a table format) the concept in 31 jurisdictions. However, it is also supplemented and reinforced by the in-depth analysis of a select number of legal systems in line with Raimondo's 'vertical move'.[79]

Another notable methodological issue is the choice of legal systems to be compared.[80] On a more general level, Zweigert and Koetz suggest choosing representatives of the major parent legal systems as a rule of thumb: English and American law of the Anglo-Saxon family, French and Italian law as examples of the Romanistic family, German and Swiss law of the Germanic system, and, finally, Denmark and Sweden to showcase the Nordic system.[81] René David holds a similar view, although he grouped major legal families slightly differently: the Romano-Germanic family, the common law family and the socialist law family. He made it clear, however, that there are other systems situated outside of these three traditions or that share only a part of their concepts and practices.[82] Raimondo noted that basing the selection on legal families' criteria might lead to a certain bias. He proposed utilising a test based on equitable geographical

[76] *cf* Stewart (n 6) 186.

[77] Raimondo (n 17) 52.

[78] *Erdemović* Appeal Judgment (n 23) Joint Separate Opinion of Judge McDonald and Judge Vorah, paras 40, 55–72, as cited in Raimondo (n 17) 54–55.

[79] See Appendix I.

[80] Zweigert and Koetz (n 72) 40; De Cruz (n 8) 25.

[81] Zweigert and Koetz (n 72) 41.

[82] R David and JEC Brierley, *Major Legal Systems in the World Today: An Introduction to the Comparative Study of Law* (London, Stevens, 1985) 22.

distribution to 'even out' the legal systems under consideration.[83] Regardless of the general cataloguing, there is agreement among academics that the suitability of any classification depends on the subject matter of the research and the perspective (regional or worldwide).[84]

When it comes to criminal law, Fletcher's analytical structures of thinking about criminal offence are useful for the purposes of a comparative exercise. Fletcher identified *bipartite, tripartite* and *quadripartite* systems.[85] The common law countries, as well as France and Francophone countries, adhere to the bipartite mode. This system distinguishes between actus reus and mens rea. Smith and Hogan held actus reus to be made up of conduct (which includes acts or omissions) and sometimes its consequences, as well as the circumstances in which the conduct took place.[86] An example of the 'circumstances' would be the lack of the consent of the rape victim.[87] For the crime to attract criminal liability, actus reus must be committed with the requisite state of mind. The term 'mens rea' denotes the state of mind, intent or recklessness required by the specific crime. The Rome Statute of the ICC adopted the bipartite system in that it distinguishes between 'material elements' and 'intent or knowledge'.[88]

The quadripartite system is a framework developed in the communist literature on criminal liability.[89] It features the following categories: the subject of the offence, the object of the offence, the subjective side of liability and the objective side of liability. The subjective and objective sides are similar to mens rea and actus reus. The subject of the offence is the person liable for violating the criminal norm and the object is the social harm caused by the offence.[90] This system is unlikely to persist at an international level because of the general demise of the Soviet legal family in the post-communist period.[91]

Finally, the tripartite system denotes the German way of thinking about the offence. This approach surfaces in the German- and Spanish-speaking countries, as well as in the Far East (for example, Japan).[92] Conduct only attracts criminal liability if it satisfies the definition of the offence, is wrongful and blameworthy.[93] The three elements incorporate the notions of justification and excuses that exist as separate categories in the bipartite and quadripartite systems. Killing a person in self-defence satisfies the

[83] Raimondo (n 17) 55.
[84] David and Brierley (n 82) 21.
[85] Fletcher (n 3) 43.
[86] JC Smith and B Hogan, *Criminal Law*, 10th edn (London, Butterworths, 2002) 30.
[87] ibid 31.
[88] Rome Statute, art 30(1).
[89] Fletcher (n 4) 47.
[90] ibid 47–48.
[91] ibid 48.
[92] ibid 54.
[93] ibid 51.

definition of the offence, but is not wrongful because it is justified; stealing under duress is wrongful, but is not blameworthy because it is excused.[94]

When one moves to the specific level of criminal participation, there is an additional consideration for selecting the case studies. Some jurisdictions, such as Italy, Austria and Poland, adhere to the 'unitary perpetrator model', while the majority of other states recognise 'the differential participation model'.[95] The 'unitary perpetrator model', also referred to as the model of 'individual agency', characterises every person who contributes to the carrying out of a crime in whatever way as the author of the offence, without distinguishing, at least at the statutory level, between direct perpetrators and accomplices.[96]

The 'differential participation model' sets perpetratorship apart from mere participation. The underlying rationale behind this model is that causal contributions to the commission of the offence vary in terms of weight and closeness.[97] Thus, it would be unfair to treat all persons involved in the same way.[98] There are three implications of the 'differentiated participation model'. First, this approach creates the possibility for sanctioning perpetrators and accessories in a different way by allowing more lenient punishment for accomplices or by excluding the liability of accomplices for less serious crimes.[99] However, this does not mean that every country following this model provides for such a distinction at the level of legislation. Second, this model connects the principal and the accessory in that the liability of the latter depends on the principal act and is consequently 'derivative' or 'accessorial' in nature. This is in contrast with the 'unitary model', in which each causal contributor to the crime is separately accountable for his own actions.[100] The unitary model adheres to a looser standard of causality in that any contribution that has effect on the crime is sufficient to establish the link between the individual and the offence. Finally, differentiated model presupposes that the accomplices are responsible for their assistance and the acts of the principals are not imputed to them.[101]

Based on the above discussion, this chapter strives to strike an uneasy balance between being comprehensive in line with the 'vertical move'

[94] ibid 52.

[95] A Eser, 'Individual Criminal Responsibility (Article 25)' in A Cassese et al (eds), *The Rome Statute of the International Criminal Court: A Commentary* (Oxford, Oxford University Press, 2002) 781–83; E van Sliedregt, *The Criminal Responsibility of Individuals for Violations of International Humanitarian Law* (The Hague, TMC Asser Press, 2003) 61–62.

[96] Eser (n 95) 781.

[97] For an analysis of causation in criminal law, please see Ch 4.II.B.

[98] Eser (n 95) 782.

[99] ibid.

[100] ibid 783. See also E van Sliedregt, *Individual Criminal Responsibility in International Law* (Oxford, Oxford University Press, 2012) 65.

[101] M Jackson, *Complicity in International Law* (Oxford, Oxford University Press, 2015) 22.

and representative in line with the 'horizontal move'. There is an in-depth analysis of the samples of various parent legal families: Germany of the Germanic legal system; France and Italy, which showcase the Romanistic family; Russia for Soviet law; the US and England as the examples of the common law; and, finally, India and China, which belong to the category of mixed or 'other' legal systems in the world. These countries also neatly reflect different ways of thinking about the criminal offence as discussed by Fletcher. Finally, Italy represents the 'unitary perpetrator model', while all other countries are the adherents of the 'differential participation model'.

Appendix I contains a table containing a survey of the modes of participation in 31 legal systems around the world. It supplements the in-depth analysis of various legal systems discussed in the following section. The table in Appendix I covers a wide geographical area and corresponds to Raimondo's 'horizontal move' in that it verifies the existence of common trends across jurisdictions. The table systemises crime participants for each country and reflects any sentencing considerations that attach to finding someone complicit in a crime as opposed to having directly perpetrated it. The table refers, at times, to conspiracy—a distinct offence somewhat similar to complicity—in order to mark the borders of complicity.

II. COMPLICITY IN DOMESTIC LAW

A. Complicity in Germany

The German Penal Code retained its conceptual structure, despite having been regularly amended since its initial adoption in 1871.[102] German criminal law relies heavily on legal doctrine and is based on the application of logic and well-developed methods of interpretation. German law is thus deductive in nature in that it favours coherence and overarching principles to the greatest extent. This is in contrast with the inductive common law approach, which relies primarily on the facts of the particular case.[103] The deductive approach informs the German Penal Code—an instrument that attaches conceptual importance to differentiating among various actors involved in the commission of the crime.

[102] M Dubber and K Heller, 'Introduction' in M Dubber and K Heller (eds), *The Handbook of Comparative Criminal Law* (Stanford, Stanford University Press, 2011) 6.

[103] M Bohlander, *The German Criminal Code: A Modern English Translation* (Oxford, Hart Publishing, 2008) 1–2.

The following crime participants can be identified based on the provisions of the German Penal Code:

— a primary perpetrator (*unmittelbarer Täter*) is an actor who commits the criminal act himself;[104]
— a co-perpetrator (*Mittäter*) is a person who commits the offence jointly with others;[105]
— an indirect perpetrator (*mittelbarer Täter*) is a principal who commits the offence through another (as per the German definition);[106]
— an instigator (*Anstifter*) is 'any person who intentionally induces another to intentionally commit an unlawful act';[107]
— a facilitator (*Gehilfe*) is 'any person who intentionally assists another in the intentional commission of an unlawful act'.[108]

In German law, the offences have to be committed with intent unless otherwise provided for by law.[109] There are three forms of intent: (1) *dolus directus* or direct intent; (2) *dolus directus* of the second degree; and (3) *dolus eventualis* (or 'advertent recklessness' in common law).[110] Direct intent refers to the carrying out of the acts and omissions by the offender with the knowledge that these actions will bring about the material elements of the crime and the desire or purposeful will (intent) for this to happen.[111] *Dolus directus* of the second degree means awareness that the crime will be the almost inevitable outcome of the acts or omissions of the accused—the actual will is not necessary.[112] *Dolus eventualis* consists of the knowledge of the risk or likelihood that the effect will occur and the will to bring it about, at least in the form of the acceptance.

Modern German criminal law relies heavily on the doctrine of *Tatherrschaft* in determining the line that separates principals from accessories. *Tatherrschaft* could be translated as 'control over crime' or, as Fletcher put it, 'hegemony over the act'.[113] Accessory is defined negatively as someone who does not have control over the execution of the crime.[114] Claus Roxin, an influential German criminal law scholar, devised this doctrine in the 1960s as a compromise between two competing liability theories, the

104 German Penal Code, art 25(1).
105 ibid, art 25(2).
106 ibid, art 25(1).
107 ibid, art 26.
108 ibid, art 27(1).
109 ibid, art 15.
110 K Hamdorf, 'The Concept of a JCE and Domestic Modes of Liability for Parties to a Crime' (2007) 5 *Journal of International Criminal Justice* 214.
111 W Schabas, *The International Criminal Court: A Commentary on the Rome Statute* (Oxford, Oxford University Press, 2010) 475.
112 ibid.
113 Fletcher (n 5) 656.
114 ibid.

objective theory and the subjective theory, both of which have fallen out of favour with German legal scholars.[115]

The objective theory holds only those who have partially or entirely committed the offence, described in the special part of the penal code, as perpetrators. All others are instigators and aiders.[116] The subjective theory, on the other hand, distinguishes between perpetration and mere participation based on the internal cognitive processes of the individual, such as will, motives and intentions. There is a division within the subjective theory between those who consider that the factor distinguishing perpetration and participation is individual will and those who stress the importance of acting in one's own interest or someone else's interest.[117]

Since the end of the nineteenth century, German courts have consistently taken the subjective approach. The great majority of German academics criticised the courts' subjective approach due to its lack of rational criteria in distinguishing between perpetrators and accessories.[118] The case of *Stashynsky*, decided by the German Supreme Court (Bundesgerichtshof or BGH) in 1962,[119] demonstrates the weakness of the subjective approach. Stashynsky was a KGB agent who in 1957 murdered two exiled Soviet dissidents on the direct orders of the head of the KGB. In 1961, he fled to West Berlin, where he was apprehended and tried for murder. The court sentenced him to eight years' imprisonment for merely aiding the head of the KGB, who was perceived as the real principal. This ruling of the court was widely criticised for being too lenient. This outcome was a consequence of the court's result-oriented approach.[120] Roxin's theory of a perpetrator who 'dominates' the execution of the criminal offence—in cases when a person does the relevant act himself, jointly with others or uses another person as his tool—supplied the BGH with a much-longed-for ingredient of objectivity. The legislature welcomed this approach by incorporating it into Article 25 of the German Penal Code in the late 1960s.[121]

The other case to inspire Roxin to develop his theory of crimes as part of organised structures was the *Eichmann* case decided by the District Court of Jerusalem in the early 1960s.[122] According to Roxin, it is in fact the

115 Dubber (n 5) 982.

116 C Roxin, *Täterschaft und Tatherrschaft*, 6th edn (Berlin, de Gruyter, 1994) 34. The ICC adopted elements of Roxin's approach to criminal participation. See Ch 5.I.A.

117 Roxin (n 116) 51.

118 T Weigend, 'Perpetration through an Organization: The Unexpected Career of a German Legal Concept' (2011) 9 *Journal of International Criminal Justice* 94–95; M Bohlander, *Principles of German Criminal Law* (Oxford, Hart Publishing, 2009) 162.

119 BGHSt18, 87, as cited in Bohlander (n 118) 162.

120 Bohlander (n 118) 162.

121 Weigend (n 118) 95.

122 C Roxin, 'Crimes as Part of Organized Power Structures' *Goltdammer's Archiv für Strafrecht* (1963) reproduced in (2011) 9(1) *Journal of International Criminal Justice*, 193. See also *Attorney-General of the Government of Israel v Adolf Eichmann*, Criminal Case 40/61, District Court of Jerusalem, 11 December 1961.

structure of an apparatus that continues to operate—unconcerned with the loss of any particular individual—that distinguishes the behaviour of those behind the scenes from instigation and turns it into perpetration.[123] The Jerusalem court first established Eichmann's responsibility as an accomplice to the general crime of the 'Final Solution'.[124] However, the court did not content itself with finding the traditional liability mode in respect of Eichmann's deeds. Instead, it held that the specific nature of crimes involved warrants specific approach to responsibility:

> In such an enormous and complicated crime as the one we are now considering, wherein many people participated at various levels and in various modes of activity—the planners, the organizers and those executing the acts, according to their various ranks—there is not much point in using the ordinary concepts of counselling and soliciting to commit a crime. For these crimes were committed en masse, not only in regard to the number of the victims, but also in regard to the numbers of those who perpetrated the crime, and the extent to which any one of the many criminals were close to, or remote from, the actual killer of the victim, means nothing as far as the measure of his responsibility is concerned. On the contrary, in general, the degree of responsibility increases as we draw further away from the man who uses the fatal instrument with his own hands and reach the higher ranks of command, the 'counsellors' in the language of our Law.[125]

Thus, Eichmann was treated not just as a mere implementer but also, with regard to his subordinates, as the one giving orders.[126] This complex interrelationship between the participants in the crime inspired Roxin's theory of perpetration through an organised power structure.

The doctrine of *Tatherrschaft* thus serves to differentiate between co-perpetrators and accomplices. As long as the participant is willing to influence the actual mode of commission and offers a contribution that has an impact on how the common agreement is shaped or enforced, he will be classified as a co-perpetrator.[127] The common plan is the foundation of the cooperation of the participants. Each of them must perceive his actions as furthering those of others and theirs as furthering his.[128] The court infers the intent from the objective participation in the execution of the crime and the interest of the individual members of the venture in its outcome.[129]

The effect of establishing the existence of co-perpetration is the attribution of the offences committed by each co-perpetrator to all other

[123] Roxin (n 122) 200.
[124] Judgment against *Adolf Eichmann* (n 122).
[125] ibid, No 197.
[126] Roxin (n 122) 200.
[127] Bohlander (n 118) 162.
[128] BGH NStZ 1988, 406 as cited in Bohlander (n 118) 163.
[129] BGHSt 47, 383; BGH StV 2003, 279; BHG NStZ-RR 2004, 40 as cited in Bohlander (n 118) 164.

perpetrators in this joint venture.[130] However, the mutual attribution has limits. The rule is that if one of the participants lacks a certain quality necessary for the particular offence or lacks the necessary mens rea,[131] he cannot be a joint principal of that offence. In this respect, the BGH has held that co-perpetrators will be liable for any acts that 'lie within a range of typical offences that one can expect to be committed given the circumstances of the case, namely if these [acts] will reach the aim of the other co-perpetrator to a similar extent, e.g. if one steals goods instead of money, if the goods can easily be sold'.[132]

At the same time, the deviation of a joint principal from a common plan cannot be attributed to the other participants.[133] The BGH refused to infer intent in the form of *dolus eventualis* in the cases when crimes committed by the co-perpetrator were outside the agreed plan. For example, A and B decide to rob a bank, and B carries a gun without telling A. A and B have to run from the police and B shoots a policeman, C, who dies. In this case, A will not be liable for murder.[134]

German law recognises two types of secondary participation, instigating and facilitating, which both have to be intentional (at a minimum in the form of *dolus eventualis*)[135] and dependent on an unlawful act committed by the principal. The instigator has to 'cause' another to commit an unlawful act.[136] The causal link is established based on whether the instigator's acts significantly increase the likelihood of the principal committing the offence.[137] With regard to the aider, the standard linking the act of the aider and the offence is lower. The German courts are of the view that it is sufficient that the aider furthers the actions of the principal.[138] There is a limited dependence of the accessory liability on the principal offence: the principal need not be criminally liable for the act. It is sufficient that the act is unlawful.[139] This peculiarity makes the line between indirect perpetration and accessory liability murky. The determination of the appropriate liability mode depends on the degree of control that the instigator or aider exercise over the actions of the principal.[140]

130 Bohlander (n 118) 163.
131 ibid, 165.
132 BGH, Monatsschrift fuer Deutsches Recht (1966) 197, as cited in Hamdorf (n 110) 216.
133 BGH NStZ 1997, 82, as cited in Bohlander (n 118) 165.
134 See *Reichsgericht* RGSt 44, 321, as cited in Hamsdorf (n 110) 215.
135 BGH NJW 1998, 2835, as cited in Bohlander (n 118) 169.
136 'Causing' here may be understood in a broader sense of the word. See Ch 4.II.B for a discussion on causation.
137 Bohlander (n 118) 168–69.
138 RGSt 58, 113; BGHSt2, 130; BGH NJW 2001, 2410, as cited in Bohlander (n 118) 172.
139 Bohlander (n 118) 168.
140 Roxin (n 122) 196. For a critical perspective on the degree of control, see Ch 5.I.A and Weigend (n 118) 100.

Finally, German law recognises some kind of criminal conspiracy: 'a person who declares his willingness or who accepts the offer of another or who agrees with another to commit or abet the commission of a felony shall be liable under the same terms'.[141] Withdrawal from the plan or an earnest attempt to prevent the completion of the crime suffices to exempt such a participant from liability.[142]

B. Complicity in France

French criminal law, unlike civil law, is not strongly influenced by the Roman law tradition. Its structure has developed from medieval roots in royal law.[143] The first French Penal Code was adopted in 1791. It borrowed heavily from the ideas of Enlightenment and, in particular, the ideas of Cesare Beccaria.[144] The second Penal Code came into existence in 1810 and was commonly referred to as the 'Napoleonic Code'. In 1992, France adopted its third Penal Code after unsuccessful attempts to reform the Napoleonic Code.[145] French criminal law relies heavily on three basic principles: the principle of legality requiring codification of conduct that is subject to criminal law; the requirement of a 'material' criminal act, as opposed to a mere intention; and the 'mental responsibility' of the actor—the law does not punish individuals lacking mental capacity.[146]

The French Penal Code recognises only two participants in crime: perpetrator (*auteur*) and accomplice (*complice*). The perpetrator commits the prohibited act. The accomplice either: (1) facilitates its preparation or commission by aid and assistance; or (2) incites the commission of an offence by means of a gift, promise, threat, order, or an abuse of authority or powers, or gives the directions to commit it.[147] In French law, the instigator is an accomplice and he does not occupy a separate place in the system of crime participants.[148]

The criminal liability of accomplices presupposes that the underlying act is objectively punishable. French authors refer to this phenomenon as 'borrowed criminality' (*emprunt de criminalité*). This means that the accomplice's actions derive their criminality from the existence of the

[141] StGB, arts 30(2) and 31.
[142] ibid.
[143] J Bell, S Boyron and S Whittaker (eds), *Principles of French Law* (Oxford, Oxford University Press, 2008) 201.
[144] GA Bermann and E Picard, *Introduction to French Law* (Dordrecht, Kluwer Law International, 2008) 104.
[145] Dubber and Heller (n 102) 5.
[146] Bermann and Picard (n 144) 106.
[147] French Penal Code, arts 121.4–121.7.
[148] Bermann and Picard (n 144) 118.

principal offence.[149] For example, in *Schieb and Benamar*, Schieb tried to procure Benamar to murder Schieb's wife. Schieb paid Benamar sums of money and supplied him with a gun. Benamar took the money and the gun, but then told a friend, who informed the police. Benamar claimed he never intended to kill Schieb's wife. The court acquitted both defendants of attempted murder, finding that Schieb cannot be an accomplice since there was no attempt.[150] Under French law, incitement is addressed to a specific person with the view of inducing him to execute a particular offence, and the advice is followed by an effect. Consequently, Schieb was not held liable for incitement where Benamar had not committed any acts in furtherance of the offence.[151] Complicity exists, on the other hand, in cases where the perpetrator cannot be punished because he is insane or a minor. It does not exist when there is a legitimate reason why the perpetrator did not commit an offence, or, in other words, the perpetrator's conduct is excused by law.[152]

In principle, the act of complicity must be positive and intentional and must occur at the time of the offence. However, Bell notes that the courts do not follow the strict approach when it comes labelling certain act as a 'positive act' or determining the time when complicity occurred.[153] For example, in *Coutant*, the court found that the failure of a company's board member to report the fraudulent actions of the chairman amounted to active collusion and renders the board member complicit.[154]

The mens rea of complicity under French consists of the knowledge of the intended crime and the intention to assist (meaning there cannot be aiding and abetting negligent offences). In *Paemelabre*, the court failed to infer complicity in the unlawful slaughter of animals solely based on the fact that a man drove a truck containing pigs to a place where they were slaughtered and afterwards removed the dead animals' carcasses.[155]

The performance of the actus reus of the offence is the line that divides co-perpetrators and accomplices under French law. The co-perpetrators perform the actions, which constitute an offence, while the accomplices carry out ancillary acts with the view of assisting the offence.[156] However, this distinction does not lead to differentiated punishment. The accomplice is punished as a primary actor.[157]

149 ibid 230.
150 Crim 25 October 1962, D 1963.221, as cited in Bell, Boyron and Whittaker (n 143) 231–33.
151 Bell, Boyron and Whittaker (n 143) 233.
152 ibid 231.
153 ibid 232.
154 Crim 29 January 1936, DH 1936.134, as cited in Bell, Boyron and Whittaker (n 143) 215.
155 Crim 1 December 1944, D 1945.162, as cited in Bell, Boyron and Whittaker (n 143) 232.
156 Bell, Boyron and Whittaker (n 143) 233.
157 French Penal Code, art 121.6.

Complicity in French law makes it possible to attach responsibility in the situations where a group of people is involved in the commission of the offence, but where it is not possible to identify the primary offender. In this scenario, it is possible to convict all as accomplices to the most serious offence committed by the member of the group without identifying the exact perpetrator.[158]

Complicity under the French Penal Code is a liability mode and not an offence. French law is also equipped with specific substantive offences tackling participation by several accused. These offences are called collective offences (*infractions collectives*) and they involve a plurality of persons.[159] Examples of such offences are 'plotting to execute an attack' (*complot*) or 'criminal association' (*association de malfaiteurs*) established with a view to the preparation for the crime. In both cases, the steps need to be taken in furtherance of the agreement.[160] The concept of the *association de malfaiteurs* served as the inspiration in devising the concept of criminal organisations at Nuremberg.[161] French law as recently amended penalises 'participation in a group formed or an understanding reached for the perpetration of one of the felonies specified in Articles 211-1, 212-1 and 212-2 (genocide, crimes against humanity and war crimes), when evidenced by one or more overt acts.[162]

C. Complicity in England

Despite efforts at codification, the criminal law of England still relies heavily on the common law and judicial decisions, especially when it comes to the general part of criminal law.[163]

The principle of individual autonomy underlies the concept of complicity as a form of responsibility in English law. Ashworth clarifies that at the heart of the principle of autonomy lies the idea for respect of individuals as rational, choosing persons[164] who are 'sovereigns of their own actions'.[165] Consequently, the decision to support another in the commission of the crime and the realisation of this decision in the form of assisting is culpable and deserves a criminal sanction.[166] This is in line with the derivative

[158] Crim 19 May 1978, D 1980.3 as cited in Bell, Boyron and Whittaker (n 143) 233.
[159] Bermann and Picard (n 144) 118.
[160] French Penal Code, arts 412-2 and 450-1.
[161] ibid, arts 265–68. See van Sliedregt (n 95) 105.
[162] French Penal Code, art 212-3, para 1.
[163] A Ashworth, 'UK Criminal Law' in Dubber and Heller (eds) (n 102) 532.
[164] A Ashworth, *Principles of Criminal Law*, 2nd edn (Oxford, Clarendon, 1995) 83.
[165] Kadish (n 69) 330.
[166] Ashworth (n 164) 409.

view of complicity adopted in English law.[167] It may seem that complicity casts its net too wide by not requiring that the act of the accomplice caused the principal to act. However, Ashworth points out that the loose conduct requirements of complicity are narrowed by more stringent fault requirements—a small act of assistance may suffice, but only if done with intent to assist or encourage the commission of the principal's crime.[168]

English law recognises two types of parties to a crime: principals and accomplices.[169] The principal under English law is someone whose act is the most immediate cause of the actus reus.[170] English law allows the holding of two or more persons as co-principals (co-perpetrators) if each of them satisfies some part of the conduct element of substantive crime and if each of them has the necessary mental element.[171] If two persons attack the third person and the combined effect of their blows kills the victim, they are both guilty of murder as co-perpetrators because they both caused the actus reus.[172] Indirect perpetration manifests itself in English law in the doctrine of 'innocent agency'. An innocent agent brings about the actus reus without being a participant in the crime due to infancy or insanity. The indirect perpetrator will be the one whose act is the most immediate cause of the innocent agent's act.[173]

Unlike civil law, the common law does not maintain a distinction between different types of accessories.[174] The accomplice in English law (sometimes called 'an accessory' or a secondary party) is anyone who aids, abets, counsels or procures a principal.[175] Accomplices in English law are punished as a principal offender in accordance with the principle of equal punishment.[176]

'Procuring' implies bringing about an offence, such as by deceiving another so that the other commits an offence.[177] This is the only term of

[167] KJM Smith, *A Modern Treatise on the Law of Criminal Complicity* (Oxford, Clarendon, 1991) 3.

[168] Ashworth (n 164) 409. Smith noted in the same vein that 'the more limited the causal requirement the stronger the claim for a closer connection between the accessory's mental state and the principal's action … because an accessory, particularly the one not present at the commission of the offence, is one stage removed or detached form active criminality, the opportunity and ability to reflect on the consequences of actions is liable to be greater'. Smith (n 167) 153–54.

[169] See generally Smith and Hogan (n 86) ch 8.

[170] ibid 142.

[171] Ashworth (n 164) 411.

[172] *Macklin and Murphy's Case* (1838) 2 Lew CC 225.

[173] Smith and Hogan (n 86) 142.

[174] Fletcher (n 5) 644.

[175] Ashworth (n 164) 410. See also the Accessories and Abettors Act 1861, as amended by the Criminal Law Act 1977, s 65(4).

[176] Accessories and Abettors Act 1861. See also Smith (n 167) 73; HLA Hart and T Honoré, *Causation in the Law* (Oxford, Oxford University Press, 1985) 379.

[177] Ashworth (n 163) 539.

the four that implies some form of causal relationship between the act of procurement and the execution of the offence.[178] The remaining three categories do not require such a causal connection.[179] The word 'counsels' presupposes that the accused is responsible if he *persuades* the principal to commit an offence not by threats or bribes, but by pointing out the advantages of the proposed course of action or by giving advice to the principal offender.[180] Abetting involves some encouragement of the principal to commit the offence.[181] There must be some connection between abetting or counselling and the execution of the crime, but it does not have to be causal in a sense of being *conditio sine qua non* for the crime.[182]

Abetting and counselling may require a meeting of minds of the secondary party and the principal. In contrast, aiding does not seem to require either a causal link or the agreement with the primary perpetrator. Aiding implies intentionally providing means and opportunity for the principal to act.[183] Encouragement, which is distinct from providing an opportunity, may also amount to 'aiding'. For example, the presence of the accused at the time when the offence is committed may have an encouraging effect on the principal.[184] Unlike abetting or counselling, assistance may be unwanted and unexpected.[185]

Complicity requires proof of intention, not purpose, and *dolus eventualis* (or 'adverted recklessness') may be sufficient.[186] The test of specificity of accessorial knowledge is whether the offence committed was within the contemplated range of offences; if not, then was it of the same type as any of those offences contemplated?[187]

The distinction between the co-principals and accessories is often a subtle one.[188] Presumably it is based on the causality principle and common agreement. If the offender causes the actus reus of the offence and was in agreement with the other co-principals, he is deemed to be a perpetrator. If the acts of the accused amount to simply assisting or encouraging the commission of the crime, he is the secondary party.[189]

178 Smith and Hogan (n 86) 145; Ashworth (n 164) 422.

179 The term 'causal connection' is used in this section in the strict sense of the word, implying a 'but-for' relationship between the conduct of the accused and the harm that it caused. For more discussion on the broad notion of causation in complicity, including the position of English law, see Ch 4.II.B.

180 Hart and Honoré (n 176) 380.

181 Ashworth (n 164) 414.

182 *Wilcox v Jeffery* [1951] 1 All ER 464, as cited in Ashworth (n 164) 416.

183 *R v Laverty* [1970] 3 All ER 432, as cited in Hart and Honoré (n 176) 385.

184 *R v Coney* (1882) 8 QBD 534, as cited in Hart and Honoré (n 176) 386.

185 Smith and Hogan (n 86) 147.

186 *Blakeley and Sutton v Chief Constable of West Mercia* [1991] RTR 405, as cited by Ashworth (n 163) 539.

187 Smith (n 167) 167–69, referring to *Maxwell v DPP* [1978] 1 WLR 1350 and *R v Bainbridge* (1960) 1 QB 129.

188 Smith and Hogan (n 86) 143.

189 ibid 145.

From the perspective of English law, Ashworth notes that most complicity cases involve some kind of agreement. However, historically it was unclear whether common purpose, or joint enterprise, amounted to an additional form of complicity liability (beyond aiding, abetting, counselling or procuring) or if it was simply attached to each of them. The English courts used the doctrine to address the question of an unexpected turn of events.[190] The courts, relying on the *Chan Wing-Siu* case,[191] held the member of the joint enterprise responsible if the jury was satisfied that the defendant contemplated that there was a real possibility that one member of the joint enterprise might go beyond the agreement. Therefore, the basis of liability for secondary participation, developed in *Chan Wing-Siu*, was premised on a defendant's realisation of the risk that the principal will act with the required mens rea and his acceptance of that risk. Marianne Giles suggested that such liability follows from the 'principle of implied authorisation'.[192] Consequently, the basis of liability was *subjective* foresight of a significant possibility of the conduct.

The recent *R v Jogee* case decided by the UK Supreme Court in February 2016 clarified the status of the joint enterprise in English law and changed the direction set by *Chan Wing-Siu*.[193] The Court explained that speaking of the 'joint enterprise' as a secondary liability is a misuse of the expression because the term merely refers to the situation when two or more people are engaged in a crime together. However, the question of the secondary liability arises if crime B is committed during the course of crime A. In this case, the Supreme Court held that *Chan Wing-Siu* incorrectly lowered the threshold for the mental element required of the secondary party from 'intent to assist or encourage the principal to commit the crime' to a mere foreseeability of the crime potentially being committed.

The Supreme Court concluded that *Chan Wing-Siu* took the wrong turn by erroneously treating the *foresight* of crime B as its automatic authorisation. This is so because the mental element for the secondary liability is always the *intent to assist or encourage* the principal crime. The difference may be in the specificity of the crime in question—sometimes assistance is given to a specific crime and sometimes it is given to a range of crimes, one of which is committed. The correct approach is to treat foresight of crime B as evidence of intent to assist rather than express authorisation of the crime. The Supreme Court noted that its decision does not automatically lead to the reversal of the past convictions, but rather calls for a case-by-case reconsideration when substantial injustice has been done. In its view,

190 Ashworth (n 164) 429. See also Smith and Hogan (n 86) 162.

191 *Chan Wing-Siu v The Queen* (1985) AC 168.

192 M Giles, 'Complicity: The Problems of Joint Enterprise' (1990) *Criminal Law Review*, 383, 383–93.

193 *R v Jogee* [2016] UKSC 8 and *Ruddock v The Queen* (Jamaica) [2016] UKPC 7.

if a person joins in a crime which any reasonable person would realise involves a risk of harm, and death results, this person is guilty at least of manslaughter.[194]

It is worth noting that *R v Jogee* reversing implied authorisation for the acts following from the agreement as an acceptable mental element for secondary parties is not entirely unexpected. English law has changed several times on the required mental element of the participants of the joint enterprise.[195] Prior to *Chan Wing-Siu*, the test used to be a stricter *objective* test of foreseeability with a strong element of prior agreement or 'authorisation'.[196] This was discussed, for example, in *Anderson and Morris*, where it was decided that: 'If one of the adventurers goes beyond what has been tacitly agreed as part of the common enterprise, his co-adventurer is not liable for the consequences of that unauthorized act [and] it is for the jury in every case to decide what was done in part of a joint enterprise, or went beyond it and was in fact an act unauthorized by that joint enterprise.'[197]

D. Complicity in the US

The US criminal law originally started as the 'common law' of England as adopted by the American colonies in the eighteenth century, but has evolved continuously since.[198] First, the courts and, later, the legislature developed criminal law at the state and federal levels. Nowadays almost every state has a criminal code as a primary source of law, while the courts merely interpret it.[199] A large portion of the states introduced or reformed their criminal codes on the basis of the 1962 Model Penal Code (MPC), promulgated by the American Law Institute as a part of the major criminal law revision.[200]

The MPC defines each crime participant:

- A direct perpetrator who personally engages in the proscribed conduct;[201]
- An indirect perpetrator who causes an innocent or irresponsible person to engage in the proscribed conduct;[202]

[194] ibid.

[195] Van Sliedregt (n 95). See also Hamdorf (n 110) 221.

[196] Van Sliedregt (n 95) 104.

[197] *R v Anderson and Morris* (1966) 2 QB 110.

[198] PH Robinson, 'Comparative Summary of American Criminal Law' in Dubber and Heller (eds) (n 102) 564.

[199] ibid.

[200] ibid 565.

[201] Model Penal Code, s 2.06(1).

[202] ibid, s 2.06(2)(a).

- An accomplice who, with the purpose of promoting or facilitating the commission of the offence,
  - Solicits such other person to commit it;[203]
  - Aids or agrees or attempts to aid such other person in planning or committing it;[204]
- Having a legal duty to prevent the commission of the offense, fails to make proper effort so to do.[205]

The MPC draws a fundamental distinction between someone who commits an offence 'by his own conduct' and someone whose criminal liability derives from 'the conduct of another person for which he is legally accountable'.[206] Consequently, the perpetrator satisfies the objective conduct requirement through his own conduct or the conduct of an innocent agent, while the accomplice satisfies the objective element of an offence through the perpetrator's conduct by facilitating it via solicitation, aiding or failing in a legal duty to prevent the commission of the offence.

From the wording of the MPC, it follows that mere knowledge of the crime is not sufficient to satisfy the fault requirement for complicity; it is essential that an accomplice intends to participate in it.[207] This is not to say that the US courts never applied a lower standard to establish fault. In *Backun v US*,[208] the court upheld the seller's conviction for complicity in the interstate transportation of stolen merchandise based on his mere knowledge that the goods were stolen and the buyer would go to the other state to sell them. The judge in this case did not require that the seller 'had a stake in the outcome of the case' or specifically desired the buyer to leave the state. A different approach was adopted in *US v Peoni*,[209] where the court held that the complicity doctrine requires the defendant to 'in some sort associate himself with the venture, that he participate in it as something that he wishes to bring about, that he seek by his action to make it succeed'.[210] The MPC upheld the higher standard of the *Peoni* case, which is now widely accepted as the predominant test for the accomplice's guilty state of mind in the US.[211]

The conduct requirement for complicity under the MPC is less stringent than the fault requirement. The accomplice's assistance need not

203 ibid, s 2.06(2)(c) and (3)(a)(i).
204 ibid, s 2.06(2)(c) and (3)(a)(ii).
205 ibid, s 2.06(2)(c) and (3)(a)(iii).
206 ibid, s 2.06(1).
207 ibid, s 2.06(2)(3)(a) provides that an accomplice acts with 'the purpose of promoting or facilitating the commission of the offence'. The same standard had been previously confirmed in *US v Nye & Nissen*, 336 US 613 (1947).
208 *Backun v US* 112 F 2d 635 (4th Cir 1940).
209 *US v Peoni* 100 F 2d 401, 402 (2d Cir 1938).
210 ibid.
211 R Weisberg, 'The Model Penal Code Revisited: Reappraising Complicity' (2000) 4 *Buffalo Criminal Law Review* 239.

be necessary for the successful completion of the offence, nor need it be substantial, the least degree of assistance sufficing.[212] Moral encouragement qualifies as assistance.[213] The accomplice can be prosecuted even though the direct perpetrator has not been prosecuted or convicted, provided the fact of commission of the offence is proven.[214] Recent case law has summarised the requirements for complicity as a two-prong test: 'first, there must be evidence that the person intended to aid or promote the underlying offence, and second, there must be evidence that the person actively participated in the crime by soliciting, aiding, or agreeing to aid the principal'.[215]

All crime participants—accomplices included—are treated as principals for punishment purposes under the Section 2 of Title 18 of the United States Code.[216] Consequently, the distinction between crime participants has no impact on the sentence.[217] This is so because the centrepiece of the US system of criminal participation is the principle of individual culpability. According to Dubber, the MPC drafters—who laid the basis for the criminal codes of most states—embraced the peno-correctional vision of criminal law that prioritised deterrent punishments over proportionate punishments. The individual assessment of culpability, ie, dangerousness of the offender, was central to this approach. Accordingly, what mattered for punishment purposes was the abnormal dangerousness of an individual rather than the way in which he was involved in the offence.[218] The approach whereby accomplices and principals are punished alike is consistent with the traditional common law, although rooted in a different rationale.[219] The case law confirms that the accomplice is subject to the same punishment as the principal.[220]

In contrast with complicity, which is not a distinct crime but a means of committing an offence,[221] conspiracy exists in both English and American

[212] *People v Durham* (1969) 70 Cal 2d 171, 185; *Commonwealth v Murphy* 844 A 2d 1228, 1234 (Pa 2004); *Commonwealth v Gladden* 665 A 2d 1201, 1209 (Pa Super 1995).

[213] Robinson (n 198) 577.

[214] Model Penal Code, s 2.06(7).

[215] *Commonwealth of Pennsylvania v Rega*, 933 A 2d 997 (2007).

[216] 18 USC para 2 (2012) reads as follows: 'Principals: (a) Whoever commits an offense against the United States or aids, abets, counsels, commands, induces or procures its commission, is punishable as a principal; (b) Whoever willfully causes an act to be done which if directly performed by him or another would be an offense against the United States, is punishable as a principal.' See also United States Sentencing Commission, Guidelines Manual, para 2.X2.1 (December 2012), which states that the offence level for aiding and abetting is the same level as that for the underlying offence.

[217] Weisberg (n 211) 225.

[218] Dubber (n 5) 987–89.

[219] ibid.

[220] NJ Super AD 2001, 767 A 2d 976, 337 N J Super 493.

[221] *US v Roan Eagle* 867 F 2d 436, 445 (8th Cir 1989); *US v Causey* 835 F 2d 1289, 1291 (9th Cir 1987). See also Weisberg (n 211) 224.

law as a distinct offence, consummated upon entering into the agreement to commit criminal acts. Conspiracy also generates a standard for holding each conspirator complicitous in the crimes of fellow conspirators, but unlike complicity, which is a category of accessorial liability, conspiracy functions as a test of what it means to be a co-perpetrator.[222] Conspiracy typically requires an agreement between two or more conspirators that at least one of them will commit a substantive offence.[223] Modern American codes have adopted a unilateral conspiracy requirement, which permits the conspiracy liability as long as the person agrees with another person, without regard for whether the other person is returning the agreement. An overt act performed in furtherance of the agreement is typically also required to maintain the conviction.[224]

In *Pinkerton v US*, the US Supreme Court held that each member of a conspiracy can be liable for substantive offences carried out by co-conspirators in furtherance of the conspiracy, even when there is no evidence of their direct involvement in—or even knowledge of such offences—provided they were 'reasonably foreseen as a necessary or natural consequence of the unlawful agreement'.[225] The practical outcome of the *Pinkerton* rule is that conspiratorial complicity destroys the distinction between accomplices and perpetrators, since the effect of finding membership in the conspiracy is to make the defendant a co-perpetrator of substantive offences committed in furtherance of the conspiracy.[226]

E. Complicity in Italy

The Italian Penal Code of 1930 extends liability to all participants of the criminal offence.[227] This is in line with the unitary approach to participation in crime discussed above.[228] The idea is that each form of participation is autonomous and depends on the respective role of an individual participant. The responsibility is distinguished on the basis of the facts of the case; the difference between the perpetrator and the accomplice is predetermined by the objective characteristics of the case.[229]

Article 110 of the Penal Code reads as follows: 'When more than one person participates in the same offence, each of them shall be subject to the punishment prescribed, except as provided in the following articles.'

[222] Fletcher (n 5) 646.
[223] Model Penal Code, s 5.03(1).
[224] Robinson (n 198) 579–80.
[225] *Pinkerton v US* (1946) 328 US 640.
[226] Fletcher (n 5) 674.
[227] A di Amato, *Criminal Law in Italy* (Alphen aan den Rijn, Wolters Kluwer, 2011) 109.
[228] See section II.C.
[229] G Fiandaca and E Musco, *Diritto Penale, Parte Generale* (Zanichelli Editore, 2005) 450.

The all-encompassing term 'participation' (*concorso di persone*) expresses the notion that any involvement whatsoever on the part of an actor in any offence establishes his connection to the crime.[230] Participation, as envisaged by Article 110, embraces all the acts of the co-participants. Thus, the acts of each co-participant are their own acts, which are attributed to all the others. The latter statement is true only if two conditions are met:

— an objective condition: there must be a causal link between the acts and the criminal result; and
— a subjective condition: each participant must be aware of the final purpose of all the actions. In other words, each participant must deliberately and consciously give his contribution—material or intellectual—to the commission of the crime (that is sought by everyone).[231]

Thus, for a person to qualify as a party to crime in Italy, it is sufficient that the person willingly contributes to the commission of the offence with the general knowledge about the factual situation and that his input constitutes necessary support for carrying out the crime.[232] The contribution need not be *conditio sine qua non* for carrying out the crime.[233]

The adoption of the unitary approach to criminal participation does not preclude doctrine and judgments from discussing the ways in which the persons become involved in crimes. The contribution may take different forms. Doctrine distinguishes between (co-)perpetrators (*autore* or *coautori*) and accomplices (*complice*).[234] The difference between the two lies in the fact that co-perpetrators take the decision to carry out the offence, while accomplices aim at the realisation of the decision taken by others. The accomplice's willingness to carry out an offence manifests itself in instigating (*sollecitare*) co-perpetrators to make a decision to commit a crime or in facilitating the commission of the offence.[235] Nonetheless, regardless of the form of the contribution, the judge is still required to establish the causal link between the contribution and the offence. The judge must identify the specific way in which the contribution manifested itself.[236]

As discussed above, the Italian system is based on a 'monist' or unitary theory of crime, rejecting at the level of attribution of responsibility different degrees of participation, primary and secondary parties, accomplices, etc.

[230] U Sieber, *Participation in Crime: Criminal Liability of Leaders of Criminal Groups and Networks, A Comparative Analysis* (Berlin, Freiburg, 2006) 13.

[231] CCC, 1st division, no 8084, 4 July 1987.

[232] *Codice penale: annotato con la giurisprudenza,* S Beltrani, R Marino, R Petrucci (eds) (Napoli, Simone, 2003) ('Codice penale annotato') 429

[233] CCC, 1st division, no 8084, 4 July 1987.

[234] Codice penale annotato 429; CCC, 2nd division, no 5522, 12 May 1992.

[235] ibid.

[236] CCC, Sezioni Unite, no 45276, 24 November 2003.

This implies that the end result is caused by the combination of the actions of various actors and is imputable to each of the co-participants who have contributed to the crime. In principle, the equal treatment of the participants in the crime leads to their equal punishment. Nonetheless, Italian penal law found some way to adjust the sentences based on the mode of participation using the provisions on the mitigating and aggravating circumstances.[237] For example, Article 112 of the Italian Penal Code allows for an increase in penalty if the number of offenders contributing to the crime is more than five or for those who exercised authority, direction and supervision that led others to commit the crime. Similarly, Article 114 of the Italian Penal Code provides for the decrease in a sentence in cases of minimal contribution to the commission of the offence.

As a general rule, Italian penal law does not penalise the agreement and incitement to commit a criminal offence if it is never committed.[238] Conspiracies to commit certain crimes constitute an exception to this rule and are punishable as such.[239]

F. Complicity in Russia

The new Russian Penal Code was adopted in 1996 and entered into force on 1 January 1997.[240] It is the fourth Penal Code in the history of Russia, following the Penal Codes of 1922, 1926 and 1960. The new Penal Code represents a progressive legislative development and is aimed at abandoning the ideological overtones that characterised the Penal Codes of the Soviet era. The 1996 Penal Code does, however, retain the quadripartite approach to offence featuring the four categories—the subject of the offence, the object of the offence, the subjective side of liability and the objective side of liability—typical of communist legal theory.[241]

The Penal Code recognises the following types of crime participants:[242]

— a perpetrator
  — a primary perpetrator 'directly or 'at first hand' commits the criminal act;
  — a co-perpetrator 'directly' or 'at first hand' participates in the commission of the offence together with other perpetrators;

[237] Codice penale annotato 430.
[238] Italian Penal Code, art 115.
[239] See, for example, art 304 of the Italian Penal Code, which punishes conspiracies to commit crimes against the state.
[240] Russian Penal Code, art 33(2).
[241] See section II.C above.
[242] Russian Penal Code, art 33.

— an indirect perpetrator is 'the person who committed the offence by using other persons, not subject to criminal responsibility due to their age, insanity or other factors'.[243]

— an organiser is someone who 'organized the crime or directed its execution, as well as the person who created an organized group or criminal organization, or supervised them';[244]

— an instigator is 'a person who induced another to commit a crime through persuasion, bribery, threat or any other means';[245]

— an aider is 'a person who assisted in the commission of the offence by supplying counsel, directions, information or the means for the commission'.[246]

The Penal Code labels all modes of participation listed above as 'complicity'. However, a more accurate translation of this umbrella term would be 'co-participation' (*souchastije*). The commentaries to the Penal Code discuss the 'subjective' and the 'objective' features of co-participation.[247] The objective side of co-participation implies that two or more persons take part in the commission of the offence and that their acts are complementary of each other and cause a certain effect to occur. The subjective side of co-participation is intent in the form of *dolus directus* (direct intent) or *dolus eventualis* (indirect intent). The co-participants need to be 'subjects' of the offence, namely sane individuals who have reached the age of maturity.[248] There exist two forms of co-participation: simple co-participation involves co-perpetration, while complex co-participation implies different roles assigned to different actors.[249]

The core difference between perpetratorship and other modes of criminal involvement lies in the fact that the (co-)perpetrator (*soispolnitel*) always performs the objective side of the offence or a part thereof, whereas none of the other crime participants perform the objective side of the offence.[250] This line is not always clear-cut, especially in complex crimes. For example, in the case of *D*, the Supreme Court had to qualify the contribution of D to the theft. D—on the basis on the prior agreement—brought other crime participants to the flat, broke the door of the flat and, later, disposed of the stolen goods. The Court decided that the role of D in the theft is significant enough to render him a co-perpetrator and not a mere aider.[251]

243 ibid, art 33(2).
244 ibid, art 33(4).
245 ibid.
246 ibid, art 33(5).
247 Commentary on art 32 of the Russian Penal Code in A. Checkalin (ed) *Kommentarii k Ugolovnomu Kodeksu Rossii*, (Yuright, 2006); N. Gromov (ed), *Kommentarii k Ugolovnomu Kodeksu Rossii* (Moskva, Gross Media, 2007).
248 ibid.
249 Commentary on art 32 of the Russian Penal Code in Chekalin (n 247).
250 Ruling of the Plenum of the Supreme Court of Russia No 1, dated 27 January 1999, cl 10.
251 Bulletin of the Supreme Court of Russia, 1997, No 11, at 20.

In addition to aiding and instigating—the traditional modes of accessorial liability found in many legal systems around the world—Russian law recognises an additional form of participation in crime, namely, 'organising'. The commentary to the Penal Code considers organising the most dangerous form of co-participation in crime because the organiser is usually the leader who coordinates all other participants and represents the 'soul of the group'.[252] Organisers are sometimes wrongly convicted as perpetrators, as in the case of *N and T*. In this case, the two accused agreed to murder N's wife and hired M to carry out the crime. The accused—N and T—brought the victim to the forest, where M strangled her. N and T were first convicted as co-perpetrators, but the Supreme Court later ruled that they were organisers and not perpetrators, as they did not perform the objective side, or actus reus, of the offence.[253]

Instigating is a somewhat similar activity to organising a crime. The difference between the two lies in the fact that an instigator induces the offender-to-be to commit a crime, while the organiser works with those who have already decided to engage in criminality.[254] An instigator always aims at convincing a person to commit a specific crime (not any crime) and there is always a causal link between the acts of the instigator and the crime committed. The law requires the same causal link between the aider's acts and the result.[255]

Instigators and organisers are considered more dangerous than aiders; as such, the latter category is usually punished less severely.[256] However, there is no explicit provision in the Penal Code reducing the penalty for aiders. The principle is that each participant is punished in accordance with the level of his contribution, taking into account the intensity of his criminal activities that were aimed at achieving a common criminal result.[257]

Russian law is similar to German law in that it punishes conspiracy only in the form of an agreement to commit a felony (and not in relation to minor offences). The commission of an offence with a prior agreement is also an aggravating factor at sentencing.[258] Under Russian law, the co-perpetrators are not liable for the so-called 'excess of the perpetrator', when the principal commits crimes not intended by the other members.[259]

[252] Commentary on art 33 of the Russian Penal Code in V. Lebedev (ed) *Kommentarii k Ugolovnomu Kodeksu Rossii*, (Moskva, Yuright, 2005).

[253] Bulletin of the Supreme Court of Russia, 1997, No 4, at 14.

[254] Commentary on art 33 of the Russian Penal Code in Chekalin (n 247).

[255] Commentary on art 33 of the Russian Penal Code in Lebedev (n 252).

[256] ibid, commentary on art 34.

[257] ibid.

[258] Articles 30(2) and 35(7) of the Russian Penal Code.

[259] ibid, art 36.

G. Complicity in India

Macaulay's Indian Penal Code of 1860 draws its inspiration from three sources: English criminal law, the French Penal Code and Edward Livingston's Benthamite draft Louisiana Penal Code.[260] The Indian Penal Code draws a crucial distinction between a person committing an offence and a person who 'abets the doing of a thing'. The entire Chapter 5 of the Indian Penal Code is devoted to abetment. The Indian Penal Code provides for three types of abettors:[261]

— An instigator—a person who, by wilful misrepresentation or by wilful concealment of a material fact which he is bound to disclose, voluntarily causes or procures, or attempts to cause or procure, a thing to be done.
— A conspirator—a person who engages with one or more other person or persons in any conspiracy for the doing of that thing, if an act or illegal omission takes place in pursuance of that conspiracy.
— An aider—a person who, either prior to or at the time of the commission of an act, does anything in order to facilitate the commission of that act, and thereby facilitates the commission thereof.

Indian law treats abetment as an offence in its own right that in principle is not dependent on the person actually committing an offence.[262] While this holds true for the cases of abetment by instigation and abetment by conspiracy, the courts have held that aiding requires that the act aided was committed.[263]

The actus reus of abetment by instigation amounts to provoking, inciting, urging on or bringing about by persuasion the commission of the crime. It is essential that the instigation relates to a specific act. The fact that a husband had mistreated his wife, who later committed a suicide, is not enough to constitute an abetment of suicide.[264] There must be proof of direct or indirect acts of incitement leading to the commission of a particular offence.[265] The actus reus of abetment by conspiracy entails two parts—engaging in the conspiracy and an illegal act or omission following from such conspiracy. Abetting by aiding involves facilitating the

[260] Dubber and Heller (n 102) 6.

[261] Section 107 of the Indian Penal Code.

[262] Explanation 2 to art 108 of the Indian Penal Code; S Yeo, 'Comparative Summary of Indian Criminal Law' in M Dubber and K Heller (eds) (n 102) 296.

[263] *Jamuna Singh v State of Bihar* AIR 1967 SC 553.

[264] *Kishori Lal v State of MAT* AIR 1999 SCW 1115; *Sohan Raj Sharma v State of Haryana* AIR 2007 SCW 1464.

[265] *Ranganayaki v State by Inspector of Police* AIR 2003 SC 1505.

commission of the offence. Mere presence near the scene of the crime is not sufficient to attract the liability of the aider.[266]

With regard to the mens rea, the abettor must have intended that the actual perpetrator carry out the conduct abetted and must have known that such conduct amounted to a crime.[267] 'Intention' in these circumstances seems to be interpreted broadly to incorporate knowledge—the commentary to the Indian Penal Code provides that there is no abetment without knowledge *or* intention.[268] The mere giving of aid without knowing that the offence is being committed does not amount to intentional aiding.[269] For example, it is essential to prove that the accused knew that the actual murderer intended to commit the murder—mere presence of a person while another is committing the offence is not sufficient.[270] What is clear is that mere negligence on the part of a person who facilitated the commission of an offence by another is not abetment.[271] The law does not require that the actual perpetrator has the requisite intent or state of mind for the offence. The direct perpetrator can be innocent.[272]

The distinction between abettors and principals does not affect the punishment—both those who are deemed to have committed the offence and those who abetted are punished for the offence actually committed.[273]

Abettors are liable for the result, namely for the effect that occurred as an outcome of the abetment regardless of the abettor's intention, provided he was aware of the likelihood of causing the result by his actions.[274] By the same token, the abettor is liable for the act done, even if it is different from what he intended, provided that the act done was a probable consequence of the abetment.[275] In this regard, the Indian Penal Code uses the example of the child who is instigated to put poison in the food of one person, but accidentally gives the poison to another person. The instigator is nevertheless liable.[276]

266 *Harji v State of Rajasthan* 1978 Raj LW 1.

267 *Mohd Jamal v Emperor* AIR 1930 Sind 64.

268 *Law of Crimes: Exhaustive Commentary on Indian Penal Code, 1860* ('Commentary on the Indian Penal Code'), Justice VV Raghavan (ed) (New Dehli, India Law House, 5th edn, 1999, vol 1) (ss 1–300) citing *Mahomad Janab*, AIR 1930 Sind 64; 30 Cr LJ 1077, 269.

269 *Ram Nath*, 26 Cr LJ 362; AIR 1925 All 230, as cited Commentary on the Indian Penal Code (n 268) 273.

270 *In re, Nenur Ram Reddi*, 17 Cr LJ 175; AIR 1917 Mad 351, as cited in the Commentary on the Indian Penal Code (n 268) 269.

271 Commentary on the Indian Penal Code (n 268) 272.

272 Explanation 3 to art 108 of the Indian Penal Code.

273 Indian Penal Code, s 109.

274 ibid, s 113.

275 ibid, s 111.

276 ibid.

H. Complicity in China

Criminal law has always been an important branch of law in the Chinese legal system.[277] Historically, criminal law was dominant in China because it was used as an instrument of the ruling class.[278] Nonetheless, except for several discrete regulations, there had never been a penal code in China before the commencement of the legal reconstruction following the death of Mao Zedong. The Criminal Law of the People's Republic of China (PRC) was adopted in 1979 and was one of the first laws enacted as a part of the legal reconstruction.[279]

Chinese criminal law resembles Soviet law and adopts the quadripartite framework of thinking about the offence.[280] The subject is the person who is capable of bearing criminal responsibility; the subjective aspect is that crimes must be committed intentionally, unless otherwise provided by law; the objective aspect includes an act of an offence, a harmful consequence and causation between them; finally, the object amounts to the social values violated by the offence.[281]

Article 25 of the Criminal Law of the PRC stipulates: 'A joint crime is an intentional crime committed by two or more persons jointly.' The following categories of actors can take part in the joint crime:

— a principal offender is one who organises and leads a criminal group in conducting criminal activities or plays a principal role in a joint crime—he is responsible for all the crimes he participated in, organised, or directed;[282]
— an accomplice is one who plays a secondary or supplementary role in a joint crime;[283]
— someone who is compelled or induced to participate;[284]
— an instigator.[285]

Knowledge of the circumstances of the offence is a mandatory prerequisite to attract the liability of any of the joint participants. If knowledge cannot be proved, the offender is not liable.[286] The provisions describing

[277] J Chen, *Chinese Law: Towards an Understanding of Chinese Law, its Nature and Development* (Dordrecht, Kluwer Law International, 1999) 167.
[278] W Chenguang and Z Xianchu, *Introduction to Chinese Law* (Petaling Jaya, Sweet & Maxwell Asia, 1997) 107.
[279] ibid 108.
[280] See section I.C above.
[281] Chenguang and Xianchu (n 278) 110–14.
[282] Criminal Law of the PRC, art 26.
[283] ibid, art 27.
[284] ibid, art 28.
[285] ibid, art 29.
[286] *He Liannu* (1991) China LR 348.

crime participants include indications on the punishment appropriate for this form of participation, demonstrating the importance that Chinese law places on distinguishing different types of offenders for sentencing purposes. The Criminal Law of the PRC prescribes that accomplices and persons coerced into participating shall either receive a more lenient sentence, in contrast with that received by the principal offender, or be totally exempt from the punishment.[287] Instigators are punished in accordance with the role they played in the commission of the crime. An accomplice's sentence is mitigated when the crime has not been carried out. In cases of instigation of underage persons, the sentence is more severe.[288]

The case of *Dai Jun and Others* demonstrates the disparity in sentences given to the perpetrators and the accomplice. In *Dai Jun and Others*, the three defendants robbed a tourist. The first defendant, recognised by the court as an accomplice, kept watch, while the other two, labelled as joint perpetrators, injured the tourist, with one defendant using a stone and the other a knife. The accomplice received three years' imprisonment, while the other two defendants received 15 years' imprisonment and the death penalty respectively.[289]

The Criminal Law of the PRC provides for a variety of criminal enterprise, namely the criminal gang, which it defines as 'a more or less permanent crime organization composed of three or more persons for the purpose of jointly committing crimes'.[290] The criminal gang does not amount to conspiracy as it does not constitute a separate offence, but it does provide for a form of liability similar to that of joint perpetration.[291] The leader of the gang bears criminal responsibility for all crimes committed by the gang.

III. LESSONS LEARNED FROM COMPARATIVE STUDIES

A. Trends in Domestic Legal Systems: In Search of a Common Dimension

The analysis of complicity in domestic jurisdictions resulted in a fully fledged study of all modes of participation recognised by the respective domestic legislation.[292] This is so because it is difficult to separate

[287] Criminal Law of the PRC, arts 27 and 28.
[288] ibid, art 29.
[289] *Dai Jun and Others* (1991) 1 China LR.
[290] Criminal Law of the PRC, art 26.
[291] Chenguang and Xianchu (n 278) 115–16.
[292] This section relies on the findings from section II above and Appendix I.

complicity from other modes of participation. Semantic peculiarities also frequently impede a clear understanding of the term 'complicity' until it is placed in the appropriate context. Fletcher's view of complicity as falling outside the standard of causation has been adopted as the starting point of the study. Both Fletcher and Kadish emphasise the derivative, or indirect, nature of accomplice liability.[293] Following the analysis of various jurisdictions, it appears reasonable to suggest that most jurisdictions adopt a broader view of causation in respect of complicity.

The reason for going beyond the paradigm traditionally associated with complicity is that in many jurisdictions, the difference between perpetrators and accomplices is often not set in stone; it shifts depending on the level of the offender's contribution, the type of crime and the general approach to criminal involvement adopted in the respective jurisdiction. At times, the actions of accomplices have a direct effect on the crime. Therefore, Stewart's claim that domestic legal systems presuppose the static idea of the modes of liability does not seem to hold if one scrutinises each individual system.[294] It is equally fair to say that the standard of causation is a fluctuating concept.[295] Following the analysis of various national legal orders, it cannot be said that only those offenders whose acts *do not* have a causal connection to the crime are accomplices. Complicity is multidimensional. In many instances, there is some causal connection, especially in cases of incitement or leadership. For example, in German law, an instigator's acts have to increase the likelihood of the commission of the offence. 'Procuring' under English law implies a causal relationship between the act of procurement and the execution of the offence. Italian law provides that there must be some causal link between the acts of any crime participant and the criminal result.

The distinction between perpetrators and accomplices varies depending on many factors. In search of a general theory of complicity, this chapter looks for some common approaches to the differentiation of crime participants. German law separates perpetrators from accomplices based on the semi-objective doctrine of 'control over the crime'. Under Russian and French law and the US MPC, a perpetrator always performs the objective side of the offence or a part thereof, while all other crime participants do not. English law places most weight on causality—the principal is the one who causes the crime to occur. The Italian doctrine holds as co-perpetrators those who take the decision to carry out the crime, and holds as the accomplices those who aim at the realisation of the decision

[293] See Ch 4.II.B.
[294] Stewart (n 6) 199.
[295] *cf* ibid 203.

taken by others. Norway does not endorse the difference between the attribution of liability and the particular crime.[296] Modes of participation form part of the description of the substantive offences in the Norwegian Penal Code. Indian law treats 'abetment' as an offence in its own right, which in principle is not dependent on the person actually committing an offence.

Such a divergence of approaches to criminal participation requires distinguishing the constituent elements of the offence and the constituent elements of the mode of liability used in conjunction with this offence. In cases where the offence is committed solely by the primary perpetrator (the principal), it is not necessary to examine his mode of liability separately because his conduct fully satisfies the actus reus for the defined crime and he acted with the requisite mens rea. In Norway, it would be sufficient to stop at this point also with regard to other modes of participation because the mode of liability is already enshrined in the description of the substantive offence. However, in all other jurisdictions, when discussing various forms of complicity, one needs to distinguish the actus reus and mens rea of the substantive crime committed by the principal and *the way* in which the accomplice was involved in this act. Consequently, there exists a separate set of requirements for the various forms of complicity.

Thus, one should not be guided purely by the accepted terms and their translations in search of the boundary distinguishing complicity from its counterparts. Linguistics has its limitations, and often the term that is translated from different languages as 'complicity' would refer to different types of conduct in the respective jurisdictions. For example, the translation of the Penal Code of Bosnia and Herzegovina refers to joint perpetrators as 'accomplices'. By the same token, Indonesian law places instigator ('provoker') in the category of principals. Consequently, it is necessary to understand the anatomy of each form of criminal involvement accepted in the respective jurisdiction, the constituent elements of this mode of participation, the general principles of attribution of liability and the mechanisms whereby criminal responsibility attaches to substantive crime.

Despite the disparities evident from the comparison of national orders, there exist elements of criminal participation that are common to most legal systems:

— All of the legal systems reviewed in this study acknowledge complicity in one form or another,

[296] In Norway, modes of participation are not listed in the general part of the code; rather, they form a part of the description of specific offences in the special part of the code. See Appendix I for a summary of the Norwegian criminal participation model.

— The functional value of complicity can be reduced to the common formula: complicity determines the circumstances when one party (accessory) by virtue of prior simultaneous activity or association is held criminally responsible for another's (the perpetrator's) wrongful behaviour,[297]
— Criminal liability of accomplices presupposes that the underlying act is objectively punishable. This does not imply that the primary perpetrator has to be punished by law as he may be exempt from criminal liability due to infancy or insanity, or his actions may be excused,[298]
— Most legal systems provide for different types of accomplices, even if it is not specially mentioned in their criminal law. Italy, for example, adheres to the 'unitary perpetrator' model, but the doctrine still distinguishes between those who take the decision to commit an offence and those who help in the realisation of this offence through facilitation or instigation, which happen to be the most common types of complicity,
— The distinction between unitary and differentiated models of criminal participation is not set in stone: while formally French legal system falls under the latter category, French law makes it possible to convict a group of offenders acting jointly as accomplices if it is impossible to identify the primary offender—a position that is close to the unitary approach. In contrast, Polish law upholds the unitary model by stipulating that 'each person co-operating in the perpetration of a prohibited act shall be liable within the limits of his intent or a lack of it, irrespective of the liability of others co-operating in the perpetration', carefully distinguishing already at the level of the Criminal Code among different crime participants,
— In addition to 'instigator' and 'facilitator' (or 'aider'), some legal systems have additional types of accomplices. Russian, Georgian and Italian law recognise an 'organiser' as a menacing figure leading the group. India, Bangladesh and United Arab Emirates place 'conspirators' in the category of accomplices. China, on the other hand, introduced 'someone coerced to participate'—usually a less culpable offender compared to all the other crime participants. Polish law punishes those who ordered the execution of the crime or directed it. However, these two participants are placed in the 'perpetrator' category,
— A total of 16 out of 31 reviewed jurisdictions provide for sentencing discounts for some types of accomplices. Typically, the law stipulates

[297] Smith (n 167) 1–2: 'Due to this very general function, the opportunities for extreme complexities have been considerable.'
[298] France, Germany, Italy and the US. *cf* India and Bangladesh.

that only minor contributions qualify for a more lenient sentence. For example, the legislation of Latin American countries provides for a sentencing discount only for those accomplices whose aid was *not* indispensable for the commission of the crime.[299] It is noteworthy that only Chinese law envisages a discretionary sentencing reduction for instigators. Other jurisdictions regard instigation as extremely dangerous.[300] Some accomplices are treated even more severely than the perpetrators. For example, Italian law provides for the increase in punishment for those who 'lead others to cooperate'.

— The most influential factor in determining the sentence of accomplices across jurisdictions appears to be the principle of individual culpability.[301] Many penal codes provide for the punishment of each crime participant according to his guilt or for the result he intended, regardless of the outcome.[302]
— The mental element for complicity is not static and depends on the circumstances of the case. For example, *dolus evenutalis* may be sufficient in England and Germany.
— Most legal systems covered in this study envisage legal solutions for cases with multiple accused. Penalising group participation as substantive crime of conspiracy is one response of the legislature to organised criminality. For example, Albanian law punishes the creation and participation in a criminal organisation, terrorist organisation, armed gang or structured criminal group. Other responses to mass crimes include the mutual attribution of acts of the accused under the doctrine of co-perpetration (Germany), punishing the person who 'masterminded' the offence as a principal (Japan), holding individuals accountable as organisers (Russia), attributing all crimes committed by the criminal gang to the leader of this gang (China) and increasing the severity of punishment for leaders (Italy).

B. Applicability of the Findings to International Criminal Law

The summary of the general trends in the previous sub-section shows that, despite the visible disparity of the legal systems in setting the boundary between complicity and perpetration, common grounds as well as a common functional core of complicity can be identified.[303] The summary

[299] Argentina, Bolivia and Venezuela.
[300] India and Russia.
[301] Austria, Georgia, Poland, Russia and the US.
[302] Argentina, Bosnia and Herzegovina, Bulgaria and the UAE.
[303] *cf The Prosecutor v Mathieu Ngudjolo Chui* ICC-01/04-02/12-4, Trial Chamber II, Concurring Opinion of Judge Christine van den Wyngaert to Judgment Pursuant to Article 74 of

also shows that there exists more than one solution offered by different legal systems for crimes committed by several accused or by an accused who did not physically perform the actus reus of the offence.

International criminal courts and tribunals frequently prefer 'custom-made' forms of responsibility in addressing collective criminality. The ad hoc tribunals employ the doctrine of the joint criminal enterprise, adapted primarily from the English law, while the ICC reinvented the German law theory of (in)direct co-perpetration.[304] It is remarkable that in international law, both theories have been extended beyond what they were originally intended to mean in their original domestic jurisdictions. The joint criminal enterprise in English law and the theory co-perpetration based on 'control over crime' in German law are both limited to cases where crimes have been envisaged by co-participants. International criminal law arguably takes a step further and extends liability, pursuant to these specifically crafted doctrines, to cases where the crimes were committed outside of the scope of the agreement as its consequence.[305]

An alternative to inventing new modes of participation to accommodate international criminality would be to explore the traditional forms of criminal responsibility accepted in the majority of legal orders. Looking at a range of domestic legal systems could assist in refining and improving the part of international criminal law that deals with criminal participation. Reliance on the variety of legal orders, as opposed to just one, is valuable for two main reasons—legitimacy and accuracy. First, grounding the doctrine of criminal participation in 'general principles of law derived from state laws of legal systems in the world' increases the perceived legitimacy of international criminal law, especially in countries outside the Western world. There are currently 121 states parties to the Rome Statute. This fact alone supports a comparative inquiry into different domestic legal systems as it makes it possible to adduce principles representative of the legal systems from the various regions of the world. Through this exercise, legal doctrine becomes a reliable source of international law pursuant to Article 21(1)(c) of the Rome Statute. Second, the synergy of legal systems allows us to identify the best solutions for a variety of complex legal and factual situations arising from international criminality.

Thus, there is no need to rush into adopting a concept devised by the domestic law of one single country. It appears wiser to learn what various legal systems have to offer, identify some common trends and utilise the mechanisms that best address the nature of international wrongdoing.

the Statute, 18 December 2012, para 17. Judge Van den Wyngaert refers to the 'the radical fragmentation of national legal systems when it comes to defining modes of liability'.

[304] For more details, please see Chs 4 and 5.

[305] ibid.

Comparing different jurisdictions is already a reasonable exercise in itself because it gives a perspective and a deeper understanding of the rationales behind the doctrine of criminal participation.

There are some concerns associated with using the comparative method with the prospect of developing international law in general, and international criminal law in particular.[306] One of the main sources of unease is the impossibility of directly transplanting domestic concepts into international law. This is a valid concern. However, there is no problem in general in relying on the principles enshrined in a multitude of legal orders, provided the methodology is rigorously defined and the limitations of international criminal law are accounted for.[307] Despite the unique nature of international criminality,[308] the principle of individual criminal responsibility guides the process of attribution of responsibility in both domestic and international criminal law. This principle also embodies the phenomenon of organised criminality and multi-party crimes at the level of domestic law, which offers many solutions addressing group participation in the crimes and varying degrees of indirect participation.

Complicity as a traditional mode of liability, once defined and delineated from the neighbouring concepts, can be an indispensable tool in dealing with the accused removed from the scene of the crime. There is a general concern in international criminal law that holding someone as an accomplice to a certain crime, as opposed to a primary perpetrator, does not reflect the inherent gravity of the crimes committed by the accused.[309] However, as has been shown in the comparative sections of this chapter, domestic law does not often treat accomplices as less culpable parties to the crime. If an accomplice receives mitigation in punishment, this is usually due to his minimal contribution to the crime rather than the label attached to his behaviour. Instigators and organisers are treated at least as severely as the principals. Thus, labelling certain conduct as 'complicity' does not automatically imply a lesser degree of responsibility.

One of the major strengths of complicity in comparison with the other forms of responsibility designed to address international criminality is that it offers a more nuanced approach to criminal participation: under one

[306] See section I.B above.

[307] For a discussion on limitations of international criminal law, see Ch 8.I.

[308] For a detailed study of the unique features of international criminality, see M Heikkilä, *Coping with International Atrocities through Criminal Law: A Study into the Typical Features of International Criminality and the Reflection of These Traits in International Criminal Law* (Turku, Åbo Akademi University Press, 2013).

[309] S Manacorda and C Meloni, 'Indirect Perpetration versus Joint Criminal Enterprise: Concurring Approaches in the Practice of International Criminal Law' (2011) 9(1) *Journal of International Criminal Justice* 161. *cf Prosecutor v Taylor* SCSL-03-1-T, Sentencing Judgment, 30 May 2012 ('*Taylor* Sentencing Judgment') para 40. For more discussion on sentencing, see Ch 7.

heading—'complicity'—there exist several sub-modes of participation. The other strong point is its firm grounding in academic literature and domestic legal philosophy, both of which are useful interpretative tools in the complex factual situations that characterise international criminal law.

CONCLUSION

Complicity is a traditional form of criminal liability. Each legal system reviewed in this chapter defines complicity in one way or another and attaches certain consequences to finding someone an accomplice in a crime. Complicity comprises of different subcategories, including aiding and instigating. In cases where several accused are removed from the scene of the crime—a typical international criminal law scenario—it can be difficult to distinguish complicity from co-perpetration. However, the main problem is not the distinction itself, but rather providing a comprehensive definition of both modes of responsibility. Therefore, complicity, once properly described, is an excellent tool for international criminal law. The definition of complicity, as well as of all other forms of criminal participation, shall preferably rely on principles derived from a range of legal systems. This is essential for two reasons. First, any legal concept developed methodologically with the view of the 'general principles of law recognized by civilized nations' has a more solid foundation as a source of international law than a concept borrowed from just one single legal system. Second, exploring the variety of legal systems makes it possible to discover the best solutions for the complex factual and legal situations that undeniably mark international criminal law.

3

The Evolution of Complicity as a Construction for Dealing with Collective Criminality

INTRODUCTION

THIS CHAPTER EXPLORES the evolution of the principle of individual criminal responsibility for violations of international law, which began developing at Nuremberg with the establishment of the International Military Tribunal (IMT).[1] The Nuremberg Charter attached to the London Agreement was one of the first international legal instruments targeting persons as opposed to states.[2] Article 6 of the Charter established the jurisdiction of the IMT over persons acting in the interests of the European Axis countries 'as *individuals* or as *members of organisations*' (emphasis added).[3] Control Council Law No 10, passed a few months later, provided a framework for the subsequent prosecution of war criminals in the occupied Germany.[4] The Charter of the International Military Tribunal for the Far East (IMTFE)[5] followed the lead of the Nuremberg Charter by focusing on Far Eastern war criminals.[6] These instruments represented a new development in public international law: piercing the veil of the state in the sphere of war crimes.[7] The shift to individual criminal

[1] United Nations, *Agreement for the Prosecution and Punishment of the Major War Criminals of the European Axis* ('London Agreement'), 8 August 1945, 82 UNTC 280.

[2] Charter of the International Military Tribunal annexed to the London Agreement of 8 August 1945 for the Prosecution and Punishment of Major War Criminals of the European Axis, 82 UNTS 279 ('Nuremberg Charter').

[3] ibid, art 6.

[4] Control Council Law No 10, Punishment of Persons Guilty of War Crimes, Crimes against Peace and against Humanity, 20 December 1945, Official Gazette of the Control Council for Germany, No 3, Berlin, 31 January 1946, art II.2.

[5] Charter of the International Military Tribunal for the Far East of 19 January 1946, as amended 26 April 1946 ('Tokyo Charter').

[6] ibid, art 6.

[7] Andrew Clapham describes the Nuremberg trials as a paradigm shift, going beyond the obligations of states and attaching duties to individuals. See A Clapham, 'Issues of Complexity, Complicity and Complementarity: From Nuremberg Trials to the Dawn of the Next International Criminal Court' in P Sands (ed), *From Nuremberg to the Hague: The Future of International Criminal Justice* (Cambridge, Cambridge University Press, 2003) 33.

responsibility for international crimes was easier on paper than in practice and entailed the challenges discussed below.

Since its inception, international criminal law has struggled with the problem of attributing responsibility for mass atrocities. The main difficulties are the enormity of crimes in question, the collective nature of criminal activity that involves many individuals at different levels of state hierarchy and the strong organisational element involved in the commission of international crimes.[8] The newly developed principle of individual criminal responsibility for the violations of international law struggled with the complexity of the offences in question. The famous pronouncement of the IMT, 'Crimes against international law are committed by men, not by abstract entities',[9] stands in contrast with the constructions developed by this tribunal to capture the collective nature of crimes committed by Nazi Germany—conspiracy, criminal organisation and inference of guilt based on the official position of the accused in the apparatus of power. Likewise, the judgment of the IMTFE relied heavily on the notion of conspiracy and the group responsibility of members of the government for violations of the law of war.[10]

Complicity as a traditional criminal law concept for attributing criminal responsibility to those who do not physically perpetrate the crime is at the heart of this tension stemming from the need to declare individual guilt while capturing the collective nature of wrongdoing.[11] Doudou Thiam, the Special Rapporteur of the International Law Commission (ILC) assigned with drafting the Code of Crimes against the Peace and Security of Mankind, insightfully pointed out that in the context of international crimes, the 'traditional moulds are broken' and 'the classic dichotomy

[8] The former IMTFE judge Röling underlined the complexity of the matter by calling international crimes 'system criminality'. See E Van Sliedregt, *Individual Criminal Responsibility in International Law* (Oxford, Oxford University Press, 2012) 20. A Nollkaemper developed the notion of system criminality to include the wide variety of actors. See A Nollkaemper and H Van der Wilt, *System Criminality in International Law* (Cambridge, Cambridge University Press, 2009).

[9] *France et al v Göring et al*, Judgment of 1 October 1946 ('Nuremberg Judgment'), 41 American Journal of International Law 333 1947, at 221.

[10] *US and Others v Araki, Sadao and Others*, judgment of 12 November 1948, in J Pritchard and SM Zaide (eds) *The Tokyo War Crimes Trial*, Vol. 22 ('Tokyo Judgment'), at 48, 445–46. See N Boister, 'The Application of Collective and Comprehensive Criminal Responsibility for Aggression at the Tokyo International Military Tribunal' (2010) 8 *Journal of International Criminal Justice* 425–47.

[11] In this regard, the ICTY Trial Chamber correctly noted that the principle of individual criminal responsibility implies that even those who do not physically commit the crime in question are still liable for other forms of participation. See *Prosecutor v Delalic et al*, ICTY Case No IT-96-21-T, 16 November 1998 ('*Čelebići* Trial Judgment'), para 319.

of principal and accomplice, which is the simplest schema, is no longer applicable because of the plurality of actors'.[12]

The purpose of this chapter is to situate complicity in the context of international criminal law by providing a historical overview of the doctrine's development. The contours of complicity in international criminal law can only be drawn against this historical background. There are two additional reasons for looking into the past. First, from the strictly legal perspective, the historical analysis provides evidence as to the formation of custom in the meaning of Article 38(1)(b) of the Statute of the International Court of Justice. Custom is a notoriously ambiguous source of international law when it comes to defining human rights obligations and international criminal law provisions,[13] and the historical analysis assists in dispelling some of the uncertainties associated with the existence or absence of a certain customary rule (in this case complicity). Second, the development of complicity reveals tensions characteristic of international criminal law in general, allowing for deeper insight into this field of law.

One can identify three main avenues along which complicity historically evolved as a concept: the Nuremberg and Tokyo trials, the subsequent trials of war criminals before the Nuremberg Military Tribunals and domestic courts, and, finally, the efforts of the ILC in codifying the Nuremberg principles and drafting the Code of Crimes against the Peace and Security of Mankind.[14] This chapter will follow the chronological development of complicity along these three avenues, while focusing on the tensions associated with the concept of complicity that run throughout history. The first section of the chapter will look at the means of addressing collective criminality during the Nuremberg and Tokyo proceedings. Section II will explore how accomplice liability evolved at the crossroads of domestic and international law in the course of the subsequent prosecutions of the former Nazis.[15] Section III will discover the work of the ILC in defining complicity for the purposes of international criminal law. Finally, section IV will elaborate on the tensions that shaped complicity over time.

[12] Doudou Thiam, Special Rapporteur, *Eighth Report on the Draft Code of Crimes against the Peace and Security of Mankind*, UN Doc A/CN.4/430 and Add 1, para 23, at 30.

[13] B Simma and P Alston, 'The Sources of Human Rights Law: Custom, *Jus Cogens*, and General Principles' (1988–89) 12 *Australian Yearbook of International Law* 82, 91–92.

[14] The Draft Code of Crimes against the Peace and Security of Mankind adopted by the International Law Commission in 1996, Report of the ILC to the General Assembly, Forty-Eighth Session, U.N. GAOR, 51st Session, Suat No 10 UN A/51/10 (1996).

[15] William Schabas noted that the war crimes case law provides many examples of prosecution of accomplices, including some directly related to the Nazi genocide. W Schabas, 'Enforcing International Humanitarian Law: Catching the Accomplices' (2001) 83 *International Review of the Red Cross* 842, 443.

I. CONSPIRACY VERSUS COMPLICITY AT NUREMBERG AND TOKYO

It is important to remember that the Nuremberg and Tokyo Charters were the products of a political compromise between the Allied powers.[16] A number of conflicts, mostly rooted in national variations, characterised the London Conference where the Nuremberg Charter was adopted. The US Chief Prosecutor at Nuremberg, Robert H. Jackson, stressed, among other things, the ideological dissimilarities between the Soviet and the Western European legal traditions, and the differences between the common law adversarial proceedings and the continental inquisitorial criminal trial.[17] The wording of the Tokyo Charter was based largely on that of the Nuremberg Charter, with some changes necessitated by the different circumstances of the Far East.[18] Thus, the Tokyo Charter embraced many of the ambiguities of its Nuremberg prototype. The political and legal concessions made at the birth of international criminal law affect the way in which we view subsequent proceedings.

A. Conspiracy as a Method of Dealing with Collective Criminality

The struggle among legal traditions coupled with various extra-legal considerations did not stop at the stage of the drafting of the IMT and IMTFE Charters. Framing the charges and, in particular, defining the link between the accused and the crime were highly influenced by the Anglo-Saxon concept of conspiracy. The first count of the IMT indictment—general conspiracy incorporating all actions of the accused deemed to be criminal from the formation of the Nazi Party in 1919 to the end of the war in 1945—was the solution proposed by Prosecutor Jackson on the basis of the memorandum by the US military lawyer Murray Bernays.[19] Count one of the Nuremberg indictment contained a charge of conspiracy to commit

[16] Richard Overy noted that the British delegation initially insisted on summary executions for the perpetrators of war crimes, while the Soviets and the Americans were in favour of trial in front of the military tribunal, but with different understandings of what the trial entailed (the Soviet authorities regarded the trial as a show trial). The final list of the defendants to be prosecuted before the IMT also represented a series of compromises: the Allied powers assembled an eclectic list of persons who represented the dictatorial regime in different capacities. See R Overy, 'The Nuremberg Trials: International Law in the Making' in P Sands (ed), *From Nuremberg to the Hague: The Future of International Criminal Justice* (Cambridge, Cambridge University Press, 2003).

[17] R Jackson, 'Nuremberg in Retrospect: Legal Answer to International Lawlessness' (1949) XXXC *American Bar Association Journal* 813–16 and 881–87, reproduced in G Mettraux (ed), *Perspectives on the Nuremberg Trial* (Oxford, Oxford University Press, 2008) 358–59.

[18] N Boister, *The Tokyo International Military Tribunal: A Reappraisal* (Oxford, Oxford University Press, 2008) 21–26.

[19] Nuremberg Judgment (n 9) 222; Overy (n 16) 14–16; van Sliedregt (n 8) 22.

crimes against peace, war crimes, and crimes against humanity, as defined in Article 6 of the Nuremberg Charter. This Article called for individual criminal responsibility for the following acts:

> (a) crimes against peace: namely, planning, preparation, initiation or waging of a war of aggression, or a war in violation of international treaties, agreements or assurances, or participation in a common plan or conspiracy for the accomplishment of any of the foregoing;
> (b) war crimes: namely, violations of the laws or customs of war. Such violations shall include, but not be limited to, murder, ill-treatment or deportation to slave labour or for any other purpose of civilian population of the occupied territory, murder or ill-treatment of prisoners of war or persons on the seas, killing of hostages, plunder of public or private property, wanton destruction of cities, towns or villages, or devastation not justified by military necessity;
> (c) crimes against humanity: namely, murder, extermination, enslavement, deportation, and other inhumane acts committed against any civilian population, before or during the war; or persecutions on political, racial or religious grounds in execution of or in connection with any crime within the jurisdiction of the Tribunal, whether or not in violation of the domestic law of the country where perpetrated.
>
> Leaders, organizers, instigators and accomplices participating in the formulation or execution of a common plan or conspiracy to commit any of the foregoing crimes are responsible for all acts performed by any persons in execution of such plan.

Continental lawyers at Nuremberg objected to the grand conspiracy charge and rejected the idea of conviction without proof of the specific crimes perpetrated by the defendants.[20] As a result of this disagreement, the IMT felt compelled to narrow the scope of the charge in two respects. First, it rejected the prosecution's idea of a single conspiracy capturing all the criminal conduct of the defendants and instead held that the evidence establishes the existence of many separate plans. The tribunal declined to accept Hitler's *Mein Kampf* as the evidence of a common plan:

> Conspiracy is not defined in the Charter. But in the opinion of the Tribunal the conspiracy must be clearly outlined in its criminal purpose. It must not be too far removed from the time of decision and of action. The planning, to be criminal, must not rest merely on the declarations of a party program, such as are found in the 25 points of the Nazi Party, announced in 1920, or the political affirmations expressed in *Mein Kampf* in later years.[21]

Second, the IMT distinguished between conspiracy to commit acts of aggressive war as a substantive crime flowing from Article 6(a) of the

[20] Overy (n 16) 19.
[21] Nuremberg Judgment, 222.

Nuremberg Charter and conspiracy in the sense of Article 6(c) aimed at establishing the responsibility of persons participating in a common plan. The IMT proceeded with charges under count one only in relation to the substantive crime of conspiracy to wage aggressive war.[22] As a result of curtailing the conspiracy charge, three of the defendants—Franz von Papen, Hjalmar Schacht and Hans Fritsche—were acquitted on all four counts of the indictment.[23] The IMT entered convictions for this charge only in relation to seven defendants, who were 'informed and willing participants of German aggression'.[24]

One of the greatest opponents of conspiracy at Nuremberg—the French judge Donnedieu de Vabres—criticised this legal doctrine as being specific to common law and unknown to German and French law.[25] De Vabres insisted that the last paragraph of Article 6(c) of the Nuremberg Charter adopts the French notion of complicity and endorses the principles of ordinary criminal law.[26] He explained that the charge of conspiracy stems from the same social necessity to capture the acts of a multitude of individuals that is present in both continental and English law. The technical means of addressing this legal problem in continental law are, however, different. French law uses the notion of complicity or accessory participation in relation to the intended crime. The French point of view is subjective in that it captures the moral or psychological element connecting separate conducts which aim at the same result, namely the commission of the common crime. In contrast, the English notion of conspiracy focuses on the external objective indicators of the existence of a common plan. De Vabres thought that the French counterpart of conspiracy—complicity—is more consistent with modern doctrines that insist on the idea of individualised punishment.[27]

In addition to conspiracy, the IMT used another concept to address the issue of collective criminality. The tribunal declared certain organisations that existed in the Nazi Germany to be criminal. These organisations were the Leadership Corps of the Nazi Party, the SS, the Gestapo, the General Staff and the High Command.[28] The idea behind this pronouncement was that the declaration by the IMT of the criminality of a group would have

[22] ibid 223–24.

[23] Overy (n 16) 28.

[24] For example, Rudolf Hess, Nuremberg Judgment (n 9) 276.

[25] H. Donnedieu de Vabres, 'Le process de Nuremberg devant les principes modernes du Droit Penal International [The Nuremberg Trial and the Modern Principles of International Criminal Law]' (1947) 70 *Recueil des Cours de l'Academie de droit international de la Haye* 477–582, reproduced in Mettraux (n 17) 242–51.

[26] Mettraux (n 17) 250.

[27] ibid 243. De Vabres, however, acknowledged the tempting nature of conspiracy as a charge giving to the Hitlerian enterprise 'the cover of a romantic prestige that is not without seductive appeal'.

[28] Nuremberg Judgment (n 9) 223–24.

the definitive authority of *res judicata* in the subsequent prosecutions of members of these organisations.[29]

The wording of Article 5 of the Tokyo Charter was very similar to that of Article 6 of the Nuremberg Charter. Article 5 provided for individual criminal responsibility for the following acts:

(a) crimes against peace: Namely, the planning, preparation, initiation or waging of a declared or undeclared war of aggression, or a war in violation of international law, treaties, agreements or assurances, or participation in a common plan or conspiracy for the accomplishment of any of the foregoing;
(b) conventional war crimes: Namely, violations of the laws or customs of war;
(c) crimes against humanity: Namely, murder, extermination, enslavement, deportation, and other inhumane acts committed against any civilian population, before or during the war, or persecutions on political or racial grounds in execution of or in connection with any crime within the jurisdiction of the Tribunal, whether or not in violation of the domestic law of the country where perpetrated. Leaders, organizers, instigators and accomplices participating in the formulation or execution of a common plan or conspiracy to commit any of the foregoing crimes are responsible for all acts performed by any person in execution of such plan.

The Tokyo prosecution team, like the Nuremberg prosecutors, opted for the all-encompassing count of conspiracy (count one), but also supplemented it with a number of subsequent counts, breaking down the grand conspiracy into constituent parts. The reason for these extra counts was to secure convictions if the umbrella charge failed, as happened at Nuremberg.[30]

The IMTFE prosecution extended conspiracy over a period of over 18 years and defined its objective in broad terms of securing 'the military, naval, political, and economic domination of East Asia and the Pacific and Indian Oceans, and for all countries and islands therein and bordering thereon'.[31] However, in contrast with the Nuremberg judgment, which rejected the existence of grand conspiracy, the first broad count of the Tokyo indictment proved to be successful, rendering the subsequent sub-conspiracy counts redundant. The majority judgment supported the broad interpretation of conspiracy to wage aggressive war—all of the defendants, except General Iwane Matsui and Foreign Minister Mamoru Shigemitsu, were convicted on count one as 'leaders, organizers, instigators, or accomplices' in the conspiracy.[32] The IMTFE established that 'the

[29] Nuremberg Charter (n 2) arts 9–11; De Vabres in Mettraux (n 17) 253; Van Sliedregt (n 8) 23.
[30] Boister (n 18) 207.
[31] ibid, Tokyo Judgment (n 10) 48,421.
[32] Tokyo Judgment (n 10) 49,773. See G Ireland, 'Uncommon Law in Martial Tokyo' (1950) 4 *Year Book of World Affairs* 80; Boister (n 18) 217–19.

conspiracy existed for and its execution occupied a period of many years' and: 'All of those who at any time were parties to the criminal conspiracy or who at any time with guilty knowledge played a part in its execution are guilty of the charge contained in Count I.'[33]

The charge of conspiracy to wage an aggressive war stemmed from the provision of Article 5(a) of the Charter. The IMTFE interpreted this provision as covering five different substantive crimes: planning, preparation, initiation, waging aggressive war, and participation in a common plan or conspiracy for the accomplishment of any of the foregoing.[34] Therefore, the tribunal treated conspiracy, as well all the other ways of engaging in war listed under the same heading, as a separate substantive crime and not as a mode of participation. In the view of the IMTFE, the last sentence of Article 5(c) related exclusively to sub-paragraph (a), which referred to conspiracy as a crime.[35] Thus, just like the Nuremberg Tribunal, the IMFTE rejected the view that the Charter criminalised conspiracy to commit war crimes or crimes against humanity.[36]

The IMTFE also found that the charge of conspiracy subsumed the actions of the original conspirators or later adherents directed towards planning and preparing for its fulfilling. This merger rendered it unnecessary to enter convictions for planning and preparing aggressive wars.[37] More importantly for this discussion, the judgment did not attempt to distinguish the substantive crimes and modes of liability in the context of both sub-paragraphs (a) and (c) of the Tokyo Charter: conspiracy was treated as a substantive offence, yet its function in attributing guilt to all those who took part in the conspiracy resembled the notion of the joint criminal enterprise.[38]

The decision of the IMTFE to adopt the notion of grand conspiracy quickly attracted criticism from contemporaries.[39] One of the main arguments against conspiracy was the non-transferability of the concept from domestic to international law.[40] Gordon Ireland noted back in 1950 that conspiracy is elastic and its elasticity stems from the authority of the state to administer criminal equity based on the need to prevent and suppress

[33] Tokyo Judgment (n 10) 49,770; Boister (n 18) 223.
[34] Tokyo Judgment (n 10) 48,447.
[35] ibid 48,450.
[36] ibid.
[37] ibid 48,448. The Tokyo Tribunal dismissed 45 counts of the indictment, leaving valid only 10, which included the grand conspiracy (count 1); waging the war of aggression against China, the US, the British Commonwealth, the Netherlands, France, the Soviet Union and Mongolia (counts 27, 29, 31, 32, 33, 35 and 36, respectively); ordering, authorising and permitting violations of the laws of war (count 54); and deliberately and recklessly disregarding the legal duty to secure the observance of the laws of war (count 55). See Ireland (n 32) 61.
[38] For an extended discussion of the concept of the joint criminal enterprise, see Ch 4.I.C.
[39] S Horwitz, 'The Tokyo Trial' (1950) 465 *International Conciliation* 475, 553.
[40] Ireland (n 32) 81–82.

crimes.[41] The safeguard against stretching conspiracy too far is the opt-out provision: the participant can withdraw from the agreement by adequate notice without entailing responsibility for the overt acts subsequently undertaken.[42] The IMTFE did not develop a similar opt-out provision in relation to the defendants, making them collectively responsible for the crimes committed during the whole period of the existence of conspiracy, regardless of the time when each became part of the agreement and their respective contributions. This approach amounted to administering guilt by association.

Just like the French judge at Nuremberg, the IMTFE French judge, Henri Bernard, insisted on the broader use of complicity. His point of view was that the Japanese Emperor should have been punished as a principal author of the Pacific War and all of the defendants standing trial at Tokyo could only be considered his accomplices.[43] Judge Pal (India) in his dissent also criticised the prominent place that conspiracy occupied in the Tokyo indictment and held that 'conspiracy by itself is not at all a crime in international life'.[44] From the substantive point of view, he disagreed with the existence of conspiracy, with its alleged criminal purpose for domination of the territories and with the fact that the defendants were members thereof.[45]

B. The Sentencing Policy

The IMT judgment was divided into three distinct parts: the first part outlined in detail the factual circumstances of Germany's aggression against several countries; the second part followed the indictment and discussed the charges against the defendants; and the third and final part dealt with reasons for declaring the guilt or innocence of the 22 accused standing trial.[46] This part did not attempt to 'label' the behaviour of the accused with any legal terms. There is no analysis as to the elements of crimes or the necessary legal requirements for the commission of these crimes. This part simply discussed the position of the accused in the Nazi regime and the specific events in which the accused took part.

Without distinguishing the modes of liability of the accused, the sentences in the judgment reflect to some extent the degree of their participation. For example, Reich Marshall Hermann Göring received a death

41 ibid.
42 ibid.
43 Dissenting Opinion of Judge Bernard, at 22, reproduced in part in Ireland (n 32) 64, fn 22.
44 Dissenting Opinion of Judge Pal, at 991, reproduced in part in Ireland (n 32) 100.
45 ibid 990.
46 Nuremberg Judgment (n 9) 272 et seq.

sentence. He is described as the most prominent individual in the Nazi regime after Hitler. He developed the Gestapo and created the first concentration camps. He commanded one of the major attacks on Poland and signed a directive concerning the maltreatment of Polish workers in Germany. Therefore, his high position of authority and first-hand participation in the atrocities committed by the Nazi regime justified, in the view of the IMT, the imposition of ultimate punishment. It is peculiar that the IMT characterised Göring's admissions regarding the use of slave labour as 'complicity' in the crime. One can infer, however, that the IMT used this term loosely, referring to Göring's association with the crime rather than the mode of participation. Similarly, Reich Foreign Minister Joachim von Ribbentrop was sentenced to death because of his significant diplomatic role in activity that ultimately led to the attack on Poland and his active assistance in carrying out certain criminal policies, particularly those involving the extermination of Jews.

In contrast, Konstantin von Neurath, the subsequent Minister of Foreign Affairs and Reich Protector of Bohemia and Moravia, was only sentenced to 15 years' imprisonment because his participation in the crimes committed by Nazi Germany was mostly limited to attending conferences and negotiations. Moreover, he intervened with the Security Police for the release of Czechoslovaks detained for protesting against German occupation. Similarly, the Supreme Commander of the Navy, Karl Dönitz, received only 10 years' imprisonment in recognition of his limited participation in Hitler's plans. He appeared to have known about the concentration camps, but his active involvement amounted to a single instance of waging unrestricted submarine warfare upon all British merchant ships—contrary to the Naval Protocol of 1936—whereby he ordered the murder of survivors of all shipwrecked vessels, whether enemy or neutral.

Despite the fact that the offenders' role in the commission of crimes was to some extent acknowledged in the judgment, the sentencing policy of the IMT attracted wide criticism. Some scholars were dissatisfied with the fact that the IMT imposed the death sentence for crimes against humanity and not for planning aggressive wars.[47] Others criticised the Nuremberg Tribunal for adhering to an excessively high standard of proof in relation to the 'conspiracy' count of the indictment.[48]

The Tokyo judgment comes to over 1,000 pages, substantially longer than its Nuremberg counterpart (less than 200 pages). Notwithstanding

[47] Q Wright, 'The Law of the Nuremberg Trial' (1947) 41 *American Journal of International Law* 38.

[48] This criticism mostly relates to the acquittal of Von Papen, the former Vice Chancellor in Hitler's Cabinet. Von Papen put Hitler in power in 1932 and 1933. However, the IMT held that it has not been proved beyond a reasonable doubt that Von Papen knew about Hitler's purpose when he put him into power. See N Birkett, 'The Issues of the Nuremberg Trial' in Mettraux (n 17) 305.

the difference in length, the Tokyo judgment essentially followed the same fact-based approach adopted at Nuremberg, explaining at extraordinary length the circumstances of Japan's military domination and aggression,[49] but devoting remarkably little space to the individual contribution of each of the accused.[50] This discrepancy showcased the collective guilt approach adopted by the Tokyo Tribunal.

The sentences rendered by the Tokyo Tribunal were harsher than those handed down by the IMT: out of the 28 senior figures of the Japanese government and military standing trial in Tokyo, seven were sentenced to death, 16 to life imprisonment, two (Shigemitsu and Toco) to imprisonment of seven and 20 years, respectively, two defendants died during the trial, while one was declared insane.[51] These sentences were more homogeneous than those issued at Nuremberg, making it even more difficult to distinguish between the level of culpability and the nature of the contribution of each particular accused. The position occupied by the defendant within the government and military apparatus often served as an indication of his participation in a common plan.

For example, the IMTFE convicted and sentenced to life Sadao Araki, Japan's Minister of War between 1931 and 1934, as a 'prominent leader' of conspiracy to wage aggressive war and 'an energetic proponent of the Army policy of political domination at home and of military aggression abroad'.[52] Similarly, General Kenji Dohihara, who had spent 18 years in China, was sentenced to death due to his being 'intimately involved in the initiation and development of the war of aggression waged against China'. The tribunal noted that Dohihara acted in close concert with other military leaders, without however naming those individuals.[53]

In addition to the conspiracy charge, charges related to war crimes attracted a number of convictions in Tokyo.[54] Shunroko Hata, the Commander-in-Chief of the expeditionary forces in China from 1941 to 1944, was convicted and sentenced to life imprisonment for, inter alia, failing to secure the observance of the laws of war (count 55 of the indictment). The IMTFE attributed responsibility to Hata solely based on the fact that troops under his command committed atrocities in China over a long period of time, and he either knew of these things and took no steps to prevent their occurrence or he was indifferent.[55] The IMTFE thus adhered

[49] Ireland (n 32) 61.

[50] The part of the judgment dealing with individual verdicts is less than five per cent of the whole judgment.

[51] Tokyo Judgment (n 10) 49,854.

[52] ibid 49,774.

[53] ibid 49,777.

[54] ibid 49,772.

[55] ibid 49,784.

to a very relaxed mens rea standard.[56] The duty to prevent war crimes was also extended to government officials.[57] The IMTFE held that the Minister of Foreign Affairs, Mamoru Shigemitsu, as a member of the government, was responsible for the welfare of prisoners and it was incumbent on him to investigate the situation and press the matter, if necessary to the point of resigning, in order to acquit himself of a responsibility.[58] Shigemitsu was sentenced only to seven years' imprisonment, which could indicate that the tribunal regarded him as less culpable than his military counterparts.

II. DOMESTIC LAW VERSUS INTERNATIONAL LAW DURING THE SUBSEQUENT TRIALS

Domestic law continued to play an important role in shaping international criminal law during the criminal trials of war criminals that followed the Nuremberg IMT. These trials relied on the two sets of rules relating to criminal responsibility: provisions implementing Control Council Law No 10 and national criminal law.[59] The rules enacted in the British and American zones were based on Control Council Law No 10, while other states, such as France and Norway, relied exclusively on their domestic law in trying war criminals.[60] Even those states that relied on Control Council Law No 10 drew heavily on their domestic law in determining the main criminal law concepts.

A. The British Approach

The British way of dealing with multiple perpetrators of war crimes was to charge them with 'being concerned in' committing a specific war crime.[61] This charge stemmed from the traditional English criminal law notion of common design.[62] Framing the charges along the lines of common design exposed the ambiguities inherent to English law, which is

[56] K Ambos, 'Individual Criminal Responsibility' in GK McDonald and O Swaak-Goldman (ed), *Substantive and Procedural Aspects of International Criminal Law* (The Hague, Martinus Nijhoff, 2000) 15.

[57] Judge Pal criticised in his dissent the extension of this duty to government officials: 'as members of the government, it was not their duty to control troops in the field … [they] were certainly entitled to rely on the competency of such high ranking officers in this respect'. Judge Pal Dissent, Tokyo Judgment (n10) 102.

[58] Tokyo Judgment (n 10) 49,831.

[59] Van Sliedregt (n 8) 30–31.

[60] ibid.

[61] *The Parties to Crimes: Rules Relating to Complicity,* Law Reports prepared by the UN War Crimes Commission, 15 LRTWC 49 (1949), at 49.

[62] Van Sliedregt (n 8) 33.

unclear as to whether 'common design' is an additional form of accomplice liability (beyond aiding, abetting, counselling or procuring), or if it is simply attached to each of them, serving as a legal construction of addressing the unexpected turn of events.[63] For example, in the case of Franz Schonfeld and Nine Others, the British Military Court in Essen faced the task of determining whether several members of the German Security Police were concerned in the killing of three unarmed members of the Allied air force, who were hiding in the house provided by members of the Resistance. Instead of effectuating the arrest, the defendants shot the pilots.[64] The court convicted four of the defendants and acquitted the remainder.[65] The evidence clearly established that the actual shooting was carried out by only one of the defendants, but the court convicted three more individuals of the same crime based on their actual or constructed presence at the scene of the crime (entering the pilots' house together with the direct perpetrator). All four persons convicted of war crimes were sentenced to death.

The precise basis for conviction in *Schonfeld* is unclear.[66] The Judge Advocate made several conflicting observations. First, he held that if the object of the visit to the house was initially lawful, ie, to arrest the pilots, the three others were not guilty of the charge of 'being concerned with the killing' that resulted from one of them starting to shoot. They are innocent so long as they did not aid or abet the direct perpetrator. Second, if the three men aided and abetted the shooter, they would be guilty. Finally, if the rule regarding 'common design' were found to be applicable, the others present would be guilty of murder whether or not they aided or abetted the offence.[67]

Notwithstanding some contradictions, the most significant finding in *Schonfeld* was that the responsibility of the three defendants present at the scene of the crime depended on the guilt of the actual perpetrator, regardless of whether the principle of common design applied or whether only the rules on aiders and abettors were applicable.[68] It is noteworthy that the UN War Crimes Commission in its report on the case highlighted that British courts did not attempt to try the war criminals under English law,

[63] A Ashworth, *Principles of Criminal Law*, 2nd edn (Oxford, Clarendon, 1995) 429. See also J Smith and B Hogan, *Criminal Law* (London, Butterworths, 2002) 162.

[64] *UK v Franz Schoenfeld and Nine Others* (1949) 11 LRTWC 64 (British Military Court), 64.

[65] ibid 67.

[66] R Skilbeck, 'Case Note' in A Cassese (ed), *The Oxford Companion to International Criminal Justice* (Oxford, Oxford University Press, 2009) 905.

[67] The Judge Advocate went on to explain the difference between various modes of participation in English law: accessory before the fact is always absent from the scene of the crime; a principal in the first degree is an actual perpetrator, and a principal in the second degree is present at the commission of the offence and aids and abets its commission. *UK v Franz Schoenfeld* (n 64) 69–70.

[68] ibid 70.

but rather used it to frame the charges against the accused in the absence of the relevant international law provisions. The Commission attempted to further legitimise the approach of the British courts by noting that 'it would not be hard to show that, for instance, the rules of English law regarding complicity in crimes, which are frequently quoted in war crime trials before British Military Courts, will be "found in substance in the majority" of systems of civilized law'.[69]

The term 'concerned in the killing' was further clarified in the case of Werner Rohde and Eight Others decided by the British Military Court in Wuppertal. Judge Advocate in this case held that:

> [T]o be concerned in a killing it was not necessary that any person should actually have been present ... If two or more men set out on a murder and one stood half a mile away from where the actual murder was committed, perhaps to keep guard, although he was not actually present when the murder was done, if he was taking part with the other man with the knowledge that other man was going to put the killing into effect then he was just as guilty as the person who fired the shot or delivered the blow.[70]

In this case, the court convicted several officials working at the Stuthof/ Natzweiler camp of killing four captive women prisoners. The roles of the accused varied, but none was charged with actually killing the women concerned: the medical officer at the camp admitted to giving lethal injections; the prisoner working in crematorium acknowledged preparing the oven for the occasion; while another accused, a functionary at the camp, followed the order to bring the harmful drug and overheard the conversations relating to the execution of the four women prisoners.[71] In contrast with *Schoenfeld*, the *Rohde* tribunal differentiated between the contributions of 'those concerned in killing' at sentencing: the medical officer was sentenced to death, while the prisoner who prepared the oven and the functionary who delivered the drug were sentenced to five and four years' imprisonment, respectively.[72]

B. The US Approach

The US military tribunals operating at Nuremberg relied on the modes of participation listed in the provision of Article II(2) of the Control Council Law No 10, which reads as follows:

> Any person without regard to nationality or the capacity in which he acted, is deemed to have committed a crime as defined in paragraph 1 of this Article, if

[69] ibid 72.
[70] *UK v Rohde et al* (1948) 15 LRTWC 51 (British Military Court, Wuppertal), 56.
[71] ibid 55.
[72] ibid 51. See also *The Parties to Crimes: Rules Relating to Complicity* (n 61).

> he was (a) a principal or (b) was an accessory to the commission of any such crime or ordered or abetted the same or (c) took a consenting part therein or (d) was connected with plans or enterprises involving its commission or (e) was a member of any organization or group connected with the commission of any such crime or (f) with reference to paragraph 1 (a) if he held a high political, civil or military (including General Staff) position in Germany or in one of its Allies, co-belligerents or satellites or held high position in the financial, industrial or economic life of any such country.

The critical modes of participation in the US trials were those involving secondary liability contained in clauses (b)–(e).[73] Despite the explicit reference to various forms of liability in these clauses, the tribunals never systematically distinguished between principals and accessories to a crime, primarily due to the adherence of the Control Council Law No 10 to the unitary model of perpetration, which does not distinguish between perpetration and complicity[74]—any participant was 'deemed to have committed a crime'.

The *Justice* case, brought by the US Military Tribunal against judges and officials of the German Ministry of Justice, is a good example of the application of the unitary approach to participation.[75] The tribunal put all the crime participants on an equal footing by declaring that 'the person who persuades another to commit murder, the person who furnishes the lethal weapon for the purpose of its commission, and the person who pulls the trigger are all principals or accessories to the crime'.[76]

The *Justice* indictment alleged that the accused, 'acting in concert with each other and with others, unlawfully, wilfully and knowingly were principals in, accessories to, ordered, abetted, took a consenting part in, and were connected with plans and enterprises, involving the commission of war crimes and crimes against humanity'.[77] These acts included, inter alia, the denial of the judicial process, the extension of the discriminatory German laws to non-German territories for the purpose of extermination of Jews and participation in the execution of Hitler's Night and Fog Decree, whereby the civilians accused of crimes of resistance were spirited away for secret trials.[78]

The tribunal followed the 'concerted approach' of the indictment in laying down two essential elements for proving the guilt of the defendant: first, knowledge on the part of the defendant of the offence charged as

[73] K Heller, *The Nuremberg Military Tribunals and the Origins of International Criminal Law* (Oxford, Oxford University Press, 2011) 251.

[74] Ambos (n 56) 17.

[75] *US v Alstötter et al* (1948) 6 LRTWC 1, 62.

[76] ibid. See also Schabas (n 15) 441.

[77] *US v Alstötter* (n 75) 2.

[78] ibid 3–4.

supported by evidence; and, second, his connection with the commission of that offence.[79] The nature of this connection to the crime varied on a case-by-case basis. The case of the defendant Joel exemplifies the tribunal's treatment of responsibility issues. Joel, in his capacity as a chief prosecutor, was in charge of the Night and Fog prosecutions and was tasked with supervising all prosecutors in his office.[80]

The core evidence against Joel consisted of the correspondence, mentioning the Night and Fog plan, of which he was either the author or the recipient. Thus, it could not be said that the accused was directly responsible for the death or ill-treatment of specific persons.[81] Nonetheless, his high rank did not absolve him of responsibility for the large-scale enterprises carried out by the Ministry of Justice where he knew of those schemes.[82] The question of personal knowledge was therefore one of the most critical issues at trial.[83] The court established Joel's complicity 'as having aided, abetted, participated in, and having been connected with, the Night and Fog scheme or plan'.[84] He was convicted of war crimes, crimes against humanity and membership in a criminal organisation (the SS and the SD), and was sentenced to 10 years' imprisonment.[85]

In the *Pohl* case, the US tribunal explicitly warned against assuming criminality, or even culpable responsibility, based on the official titles of the defendants.[86] The *Pohl* tribunal also clarified the actus reus required to sustain a conviction under Article II(2) of the Control Council Law No 10 because by itself mens rea—mere knowledge—was not a sufficient basis for conviction. The *Pohl* case concerned the responsibility for war crimes and crimes against humanity of SS officers managing concentration camps through the Economic and Administrative Main Office (WVHA) of the SS.[87] The tribunal acquitted the chief of the WVHA's audit department, Vogt, based on the lack of any positive action from his side: despite having the general knowledge of the existence of concentration camps, he never took any positive action that would have established his 'consent'

[79] ibid 84. See also *The Parties to Crimes: Rules Relating to Complicity,* (n 61) 54.
[80] *US v Alstötter* (n 75) 21–22.
[81] ibid 87.
[82] ibid.
[83] *The Parties to Crimes: Rules Relating to Complicity,* (n 61) 55.
[84] *US v Alstötter* (n 75) 86.
[85] ibid 76.
[86] *US v Pohl et al* 5 LRTWC, at 176–77. See also Heller (n 73) 252.
[87] K Gustafson, 'Case Note' in Cassese (n 66) 876–77. It should be noted the US tribunals followed the precedent set by the IMT and the IMTFE in rejecting the count of conspiracy to commit war crimes and crimes against humanity. The *Justice* and *Pohl* indictments contained a charge of conspiracy to commit war crimes and crimes against humanity, and in both cases the US tribunal refused to exercise jurisdiction in relation to this charge because it had not been defined as a separate offence in either the Nuremberg Charter or the Control Council Law No 10.

in the commission of crimes.[88] The tribunal clarified that the term 'being connected with' and 'taking a consenting part in' a crime in the meaning of Article II(2) of the Control Council Law No 10 means more than having knowledge of it: 'it means something more than being in the same building or even being in the same organization with the principals or accessories ... There is an element of positive conduct implicit in the word "consent"'.[89] Thus, Vogt's work could not, in the view of the tribunal, have been considered any more criminal than that of the bookkeeper who made up the reports which he audited.[90]

C. The French Approach

In dealing with group crime, the French courts relied almost exclusively on complicity.[91] In the trial of Gustav Becker, Wilhelm Weber and Eighteen Others, the Permanent Military Tribunal at Lyon convicted the former German customs officers in French Savoy for the illegal arrest and ill-treatment of French citizens, which resulted in the death of the three victims later in Germany. Two of the accused were convicted as perpetrators, while the remaining 17 were convicted as their accomplices.[92] The court stipulated: 'It is a principle of penal law that accomplices are held responsible in the same manner as actual perpetrators, and this principle is recognized in the field of war crimes as it is in that of common penal law.'[93] In addition to illegal arrest and ill-treatment, the court found all of the defendants guilty of causing death without intent to inflict it.[94] The tribunal found the accused responsible as they were instrumental to the death inflicted on the victims by the German perpetrators regardless of whether the injuries sustained in France were the direct cause of the subsequent death of the victims in Germany.[95]

The Permanent Military Tribunal in Strasbourg differentiated between different crime participants in Robert Wagner and Six Others.[96] The case was brought against Wagner, who was the head of the civil government in Alsace during the German occupation, and a number of other high-ranking administrative and judicial officials of the region for orchestrating the judicial murder of a group of Alsatians in the so-called Ballersdorf

88 *US v Pohl* (n 86) 41.
89 ibid.
90 ibid42.
91 Van Sliedregt (n 8) 35.
92 *France v Becker et al* (1948) 7 LRTWC 67 (Permanent Military Tribunal at Lyon), 70.
93 ibid.
94 ibid 67.
95 ibid 70.
96 *France v Wagner et al* (1948) 3 LRTWC 23 (Permanent Military Tribunal at Strasbourg), 23.

trial. The victims were intercepted trying to cross the border with Switzerland and were subsequently tried and sentenced to death by the Special Court in Strasbourg, which operated in violation of the most elementary rules of German law.[97] All of the accused, with the exception of Grüner, who was charged with premeditated murder, were charged with complicity in the crime.[98] Hence, the tribunal had to establish the relationship of each accused to the crime. The court held, inter alia, that Wagner had been an accomplice in the murders that followed as a result of the sham trial by virtue of him abusing his power or authority and by dictating or ordering the sentence to be awarded by the Special Court.[99] Gädeke was found guilty as an accomplice because he had transmitted Wagner's order to pass the sentence of death to the Court.[100] The Permanent Military Tribunal in Strasbourg sentenced all the defendants to death, with the exception of one, who was acquitted.[101] Huber was found complicit in the murders on the ground of his bending under pressure from Wagner and pronouncing the death sentences in the Ballersdorf trial.[102]

A few decades later, in 1992, the French courts continued to use complicity in connection with international crimes. In *Touvier*, the courts examined the notion of complicity in crimes against humanity.[103] The case revealed a complicated interrelationship between the mode of participation and the substantive crime. In 1943 and 1944, Paul Touvier served as a high-ranking militia officer in occupied Vichy France. He gave instructions for the shooting of seven Jewish prisoners at Rillieux following the announcement of the assassination of the Minister of Propaganda of the Vichy government, Philippe Henriot, by members of the Resistance. Touvier did not deny being implicated in the affair, but insisted that his role was limited in that he ceded to the inevitable. By ordering the execution of the seven prisoners, he attempted to limit more large-scale reprisals by the occupying authorities following Henroit's assassination.

The court held that Touvier had indeed played a limited role in the murder of the prisoners, but the instructions he had given in relation to the seven prisoners constituted sufficient evidence to establish his complicity in murder by assistance and instructions.[104] The problematic aspect was that under French law, further proceedings in the case of an ordinary murder were barred by the statute of limitations. Crimes against humanity were not subject to this rule, but in order to secure a finding of complicity

[97] ibid 31.
[98] *The Parties to Crimes: Rules Relating to Complicity,* (n 61) 57.
[99] *France v Wagner* (n 96) 40.
[100] ibid 41.
[101] ibid 42.
[102] ibid.
[103] *Touvier*, 100 ILR (Fr. Cour de Cassation 1992), 338 et seq.
[104] ibid 347.

in crimes against humanity, it was necessary to show that Touvier acted with specific intent to take part in the execution of a common plan by committing inhumane acts in a systematic manner in the name of a state that practised a policy of ideological supremacy.[105] The court of first instance held that the Vichy state could not be described as having practised a policy of ideological supremacy; hence, it could not be established that Touvier had specific intent serving a state practising such a policy.[106] This finding was reversed on appeal on the ground that Touvier's decision to execute the prisoners had been taken with the approval of the local Gestapo, an organisation declared to be a criminal organisation by the IMT.[107] Eventually, Touvier was convicted of complicity in crimes against humanity.[108]

D. Corporate Complicity

In addition to government officials, the British and the US military courts also heard cases against private individuals who worked for corporations involved in the commission of crime.[109] The trials of industrialists in the aftermath of the Second World War, albeit focusing on the individual responsibility of businessmen, were the closest that international criminal law ever came to corporate complicity in international crimes.[110]

In the *Zyklon B* case, the British Military Court in Hamburg examined the complicity of German industrialists in the murder of interned allied civilians by means of poison gas.[111] The court convicted the owner of the firm supplying the poison gas to concentration camps and the firm's procurement officer, who was described as second-in-command, of war crimes and sentenced to death.[112] The court acknowledged that the case dealt with commercial transactions by private individuals. However, 'any civilian who is an accessory to a violation of the laws and customs of war

105 ibid 352.

106 ibid.

107 ibid 363.

108 V Thalmann, 'Case Note' in Cassese (n 66) 957.

109 For further discussion on corporate complicity in international crimes, see Schabas (n 15).

110 The issue of whether the ICC should have responsibility not only over individuals but also over legal entities divided the Preparatory Committee charged with drafting the Rome Statute. In the absence of consensus on this issue, the draft Statute submitted to the Rome Conference did not include any provisions on corporate responsibility. *Report of the Preparatory Committee on the Establishment of an International Criminal Court*, A/CONF 183/2 ('Report of the ICC Preparatory Committee'), 31, fn 71. See also P Saland, 'International Criminal Law Principles' in R Lee (ed), *The International Criminal Court: The Making of the Rome Statute: Issues, Negotiations, Results* (The Hague, Kluwer Law International, 1999) 193–94.

111 *UK v Tesch et al* ('*Zyklon B* Case') (1947) 1 LRTWC 93 (British Military Court) 93–101. For a discussion of this case, see Schabas (n 15) 441.

112 *Zyklon B* Case (n 111) 102.

is himself also liable as a war criminal'.[113] The firm's gassing technician, on the other hand, was acquitted. The Judge Advocate emphasised that the technician's knowledge of the purposes for which the gas was supplied was not sufficient to establish his guilt because his subordinate position in the firm was such that he could neither influence the transfer of gas to Auschwitz nor prevent it.[114]

Other trials involving businessmen included *Flick*,[115] *IG Farben*,[116] and *Krupp Trials*,[117] all of which were heard by the US military tribunals.[118] In the *Krupp* trial, several officials of the Krupp corporation, including Alfried Krupp, were found guilty of having employed, contrary to the provisions of international law, prisoners of war, foreign civilians and concentration camp inmates under inhumane conditions in work connected with the conduct of war.[119] The *Krupp* tribunal insisted that the laws and customs of war are equally binding on private individuals and on government officials and military personnel, albeit with a difference in the degree of guilt, depending on the circumstances. It held:

> Officers, directors, or agents of a corporation participating in a violation of law in the conduct of the company's business may be held criminally liable individually therefor. So, although they are ordinarily not criminally liable for corporate acts performed by other officers of agents, and at least where the crime charged involves guilty knowledge or criminal intent, it is essential to criminal liability on his part that he actually and personally do the acts which constitute the offence or that they be done by his direction or permission. He is liable where his scienter or authority is established, or where he is the actual present and efficient actor.[120]

The sentences in *Krupp* case were rather lenient, possibly reflecting the lesser degree of guilt as noted by the tribunal; they ranged from three to 12 years' imprisonment.[121]

III. DEFINING THE CONTOURS OF COMPLICITY: THE ILC'S CONTRIBUTION

Courts were not the only bodies responsible for the development of international criminal law in general and modes of responsibility in particular.

113 ibid 103.
114 ibid 102.
115 *US v Friedrich Flick et al* (1948) 6 LRTWC 1217–21.
116 *US v Carl Krauch et al* (1948) 8 LRTWC 1169.
117 *US v Alfried Krupp et al* (1948) 10 LRTWC 69.
118 *The Parties to Crimes: Rules Relating to Complicity* (n 61) 59.
119 *US v Alfried Krupp* (n 117) 70.
120 ibid 150.
121 ibid 70.

By Resolution 177 (II) of 21 November 1947, the UN General Assembly decided to entrust the ILC with a twofold task: first, to formulate the principles of international law recognised in the Charter of the Nuremberg Tribunal and the Nuremberg Judgment; and, second, based on those principles, to prepare a draft Code of Crimes against the Peace and Security of Mankind (hereinafter the Draft Code).[122] In fulfilling its mandate, the ILC contributed significantly to understanding the scope and the meaning of complicity in international criminal law.

The first part of the mandate—the adoption of the Nuremberg principles—was accomplished in 1950.[123] Principle VII reads as follows:

> Complicity in the commission of a crime against peace, a war crime, or a crime against humanity as set forth in Principle VI is a crime under international law.[124]

It is clear from the wording that the Commission regarded complicity as a substantive offence. The ILC referred to the last paragraph of Article 6 of the Nuremberg Charter as establishing responsibility for complicity. However, the comment on Principle VII shows that the Commission failed to distinguish responsibility for conspiracy to wage aggressive war as a substantive crime and complicity as a mode of responsibility. In this comment, the ILC questions the Nuremberg Tribunal's finding that the last paragraph of Article 6 of the Charter does not add a new and separate crime to those already listed, but establishes the responsibility of persons participating in a common plan. The ILC saw a contradiction in this argument because the IMT found several defendants guilty of war crimes and crimes against humanity for giving orders rather than actually perpetrating the crime.[125] This reasoning reveals a failure to distinguish between the substantive crime and the way in which individuals were involved in the crime.

The second part of the ILC's mandate—preparing the Draft Code—proved to be more fruitful in defining forms of responsibility. The first Draft Code was adopted by the ILC in 1954 and contained only a brief account of acts that constitute offences against the peace and security of mankind.[126] This first version of the Code did not provide any definition of complicity. Article 2 of the Code listed acts that constituted offences against peace and security of mankind, and subheading 13 of this Article

[122] UN Doc A/RES/177(II).

[123] Adopted by the International Law Commission at its second session in 1950, *Yearbook of the International Law Commission*, 1950, vol II.

[124] ibid 377. Principle VI stipulated that the planning, preparation, initiation or waging of a war of aggression or a war in violation of international treaties, agreements or assurances, as well as participation in a common plan or conspiracy for the accomplishment of any of these acts, constituted crimes against peace.

[125] ibid at 377–78, paras 125–27.

[126] Adopted by the Commission at its sixth session, in 1954, *Yearbook of the International Law Commission, 1954, vol. II*, paras 54, 151.

listed conspiracy, complicity, direct incitement and attempt to commit any of the offences defined in the preceding paragraphs of the Article as acts constituting offences against peace and security of mankind. Thus, complicity was treated as a substantive offence, without further elaboration as to its content.

Following the adoption of the 1954 Draft Code, active work on the document was suspended for several decades and only resumed in the 1980s. Doudou Thiam was appointed as the ILC's Special Rapporteur charged with preparing the document[127] and identified the gap in international criminal law in attributing responsibility for the crimes committed by a plurality persons.[128] He attempted to fill this gap by investigating the notion of complicity in domestic and international law and delimiting its scope.

Thiam explored domestic law and found that the scope of the concept and its content varied from country to country: complicity may include physical acts (aiding and abetting, provision of means) and intellectual or moral assistance (counsel, instigation, orders). In some countries, those who provide intellectual assistance are labelled as 'indirect perpetrators', while in others they are labelled as 'originators'.[129] Moreover, the boundary between the concepts of perpetrator, co-perpetrator and accomplice shifts depending on the legislation in question.[130] Thiam stressed that the matter is further complicated when one attempts to assign the actors to one category or another and to determine the precise role played by each in the context of international law:

> Reduced to its simplest terms, complicity [in domestic law] involves two actors: the physical perpetrator of the offence (thief, murderer etc.), called the principal, and the person who assists the principal (by aiding, abetting, provision of means etc.), who is called the accomplice. But this simple schema does not reflect the complex reality of the phenomenon of complicity in the context of the topic under consideration.[131]

When it came to complicity in international law, Thiam acknowledged the need for a broad definition of criminal participation corresponding to the complexity of international justice. He pointed out that the concept of criminal participation encompasses not only the traditional concept of

[127] The Commission, from its thirty-fifth session, in 1983, to its forty-second session, in 1990, received eight reports from the Special Rapporteur. See the *Report of the International Law Commission on the Work of its Forty-Third Session*, 29 April–19 July 1991, UN Doc A/46/10, 80.

[128] Doudou Thiam, Special Rapporteur, *Fourth Report on the Draft Code of Offences against the Peace and Security of Mankind*, UN Doc A/CN.4/398 and Corr 1-3, paras 61, 89.

[129] Doudou Thiam, Special Rapporteur, *Eighth Report on the Draft Code of Crimes against the Peace and Security of Mankind*, UN Doc. A/CN.4/430 and Add 1, paras 7–13, 29.

[130] *Fourth Report* (n 128) paras 99, 64.

[131] *Eighth Report* (129) para 22, 30.

complicity, but also that of conspiracy (*complot*), which he dealt with in separate sections of his report. He thus drew a clear line between complicity and conspiracy.[132] Finally, he explicitly raised a point as to the place of complicity within the draft code, and whether it belonged to the section dealing with general principles of law or whether it should be placed in the part on specific offences.[133] He framed his inquiry as one of methodology, but in essence, it amounted to establishing the nature of complicity as a mode of participation or as substantive crime.

Based on the work of Special Rapporteur, the ILC adopted a new version of the Draft Code in 1991[134] and a further version in 1996.[135] The 1991 Draft Code provided for the first time a definition of complicity as 'aiding, abetting or providing the means for the commission of a crime against the peace and security of mankind'. The ILC also clarified that complicity is a form of participation and thus belongs in the chapter dealing with the general principles of law.[136] The final version of the Draft Code of Crimes against the Peace and Security of Mankind, adopted by the ILC in 1996, elaborated on the forms of liability even further by providing a list of the modes of criminal participation accompanied by a detailed description attached to each liability type.[137] Article 2(3) of the 1996 Draft Code holds an individual responsible if he:

(a) intentionally commits such a crime;
(b) orders the commission of such a crime which in fact occurs or is attempted;
(c) fails to prevent or repress the commission of such a crime in the circumstances set out in article 6;
(d) knowingly aids, abets or otherwise assists, directly and substantially, in the commission of such a crime, including providing the means for its commission;
(e) directly participates in planning or conspiring to commit such a crime which in fact occurs;
(f) directly and publicly incites another individual to commit such a crime which in fact occurs;
(g) attempts to commit such a crime by taking action commencing the execution of a crime which does not in fact occur because of circumstances independent of his intentions.

The Draft Code of Crimes against the Peace and Security of Mankind became more or less superfluous following the adoption of the Rome Statute, but it still serves as evidence of customary international law and has

132 ibid, para 26, 31.
133 ibid, para 6, 28.
134 *Report of the International Law Commission* (n 127).
135 *Report of the International Law Commission on the Work of its Forty-Eighth Session*, 6 May–26 July 1996, UN Doc A/51/10.
136 ibid, para 3, 98.
137 *Report of the International Law Commission* (n 135).

been used by the ICTY and the ICTR in various judgments.[138] Additionally, Article 2 of the Draft Code addressing the modes of responsibility eventually served as a basis for the negotiation of the relevant provision of the Rome Statute of the ICC.[139]

IV. HISTORICAL TRENDS

The historical account contained in this chapter has shown that complicity evolved across three main tensions inherent to international criminal law: domestic versus international law; collective wrongdoing versus individual criminal responsibility; and substantive crimes versus forms of participation. Each of these contradictions helped to shape the definition and the content of complicity in international criminal law.

When it comes to the first contradiction of national and international law, it is important to remember that from the very beginning, international criminal law was significantly influenced by domestic penal law systems.[140] The drafters of the Nuremberg Charter came from different legal and political cultures. The need to compromise shaped not only the language of the constituent documents, but also the charges against the accused and the final judgments. The US concept of 'conspiracy' was the chosen instrument of reflecting the collective nature of crimes at both Nuremberg and Tokyo.

Complicity, as an alternative mechanism for addressing system criminality, never arose in the Nuremberg and Tokyo judgments, notwithstanding the fact that Article 6(c) of the Nuremberg Charter and Article 5(c) of the Tokyo Charter specifically provided for the liability of accomplices participating in the execution of a common plan or conspiracy to commit any of the aforementioned crimes. However, the separate and dissenting opinions of individual judges from different jurisdictions reflected divergent views on the issue. These separate voices serve as the best indicators of the complexity of the legal landscape of the time. Complicity surfaced in the opinions of the French judges, primarily because of the importance of this mode of responsibility in France. Judge de Vabres of the IMT insisted that complicity would have been a more appropriate form of dealing with group criminality because of its wider acceptance in the variety of legal

[138] This is especially true of early jurisprudence. See, eg, *Prosecutor v Tadić*, ICTY Case No IT-94-1-T, Trial Judgment, 7 May 1997 ('*Tadić* Trial Judgment'), paras 647–49; *Prosecutor v Furundžija*, ICTY Case No IT-95-17/1-T, Trial Judgment, 10 December 1998 ('*Furundžija* Trial Judgment'), paras 227–32; *Prosecutor v Akayesu*, ICTR Case No 96-4-T, Trial Chamber Judgment, 2 September 1998 ('*Akayesu* Trial Judgment'), para 475. For more discussion, see I Brownlie, *Principles of Public International Law* (Oxford, Oxford University Press, 2008) 589.

[139] Saland (n 110) 198.

[140] Horwitz (n 39) 540.

systems and its focus on the subjective indicators of individual culpability, rather than external evidence of common agreement.

The subsequent proceedings against former Nazis were conducted under the Control Council Law No 10 and the national penal laws of the trying states. France, for example, used its domestic criminal law during these prosecutions. Thus, it is not surprising that French courts relied almost exclusively on the complicity–perpetratorship dichotomy when determining the modes of responsibility of the accused. However, prosecutions in the British and American zones pursuant to rules based on the Control Council Law No 10 were also highly 'domesticated'. The British courts used the national concept of 'common design' to determine whether the accused were 'concerned in' committing the specific war crimes, while the courts located in the US zone adhered to the common law 'concerted approach' to criminal participation and focused on the link between the accused and the crime on a case-by-case basis. Finally, the work of the ILC on defining the modes of responsibility for the Draft Code of Crimes against the Peace and Security of Mankind was predicated on the exploration of domestic legal systems. Special Rapporteur Thiam looked at complicity in various jurisdictions in an attempt to define the concept in international law.

There is one concluding observation in relation to the role of domestic law in shaping complicity in international criminal law, which is the frequency with which the first war crimes courts referred to the wide domestic acceptance of a certain rule in order to secure its international legitimacy. For example, the IMT alluded to the 'criminal law of most nations' in support of the rule that following the unlawful order does not absolve the defendant from responsibility.[141] The UN War Crimes Commission held that British rules regarding complicity in crimes are found in substance in the majority of legal systems.[142] This trend shows the historical importance of the general principles of law recognised by civilised nations as a source of international criminal law.[143]

The second tension between individual criminal responsibility and collective wrongdoing stems from the need for some 'medium' between the crime and the offender in international criminal law. This is because very few men standing trial for mass crimes directly order or perpetrate certain offences. The ILC Special Rapporteur emphasised the difficulty of applying the traditional domestic law principal–accomplice dichotomy to international offences. He acknowledged that the latter require a broader definition of complicity to cover the complexity of the legal context associated with international crimes.

[141] Nuremberg Judgment (n 9) 221.
[142] *UK v Franz Schoenfeld* (n 64) 72.
[143] For more discussion about complicity as a general rule of international law, see Ch 2.II.

The Tokyo Tribunal settled for conspiracy as a tool designed to capture collective criminality. Conspiracy declared the agreement to commit mass atrocities criminal without the need to prove underlying offences. The leadership position was determinative, in the eyes of the IMTFE judges, of whether the accused belonged to a conspiracy or was responsible for the crimes committed under his supervision. The IMT relied on conspiracy to a lesser extent than its Tokyo counterpart. The Nuremberg response to the problem of attribution of responsibility for the acts committed by distant others was to focus on the factual contribution of the accused to the common plan and his official position within the Nazi hierarchy. The IMT therefore avoided a legalistic discussion about the modes of participation of each accused.

The prosecutions of the former Nazis by national authorities in the aftermath of the IMT signified a shift from the fact-based approach to criminal participation of Nuremberg and Tokyo to a more nuanced and developed body of law regarding the ways in which the defendant was involved in a crime. These trials were driven, to a large extent, by national law. Thus, many ambiguities characteristic of the domestic legal systems affected the way in which various modes of participation were used. For example, the British court in *Schonfeld* struggled to distinguish participation in the common design and aiding and abetting. It referred to the theory of actual or constructive presence at the scene of the crime, which was used by the traditional English law doctrine to establish a boundary between the two forms of participation. Notwithstanding the reference to this theory in the judgments, the British courts failed to consistently apply it in cases like *Rohde* or *Schonfeld* and instead settled for a half-hearted compromise.

The US military tribunals adopted the unitary model of criminal participation, thereby placing all modes of responsibility on an equal footing. However, this did not mean that the judges paid no attention to the way in which the defendants became involved in the crimes. On the contrary, the US courts elaborated on the fault and conduct requirement of criminal participation. For example, the *Justice* case stressed the importance of the personal knowledge of the accused, while *Pohl* guarded against assuming criminality solely on the basis of official capacity. The *Pohl* tribunal also highlighted the importance of positive action in establishing a defendant's consent to the commission of the crimes. By focusing on legal requirements of responsibility, the US tribunals sitting at Nuremberg distanced themselves from the approach adopted at Nuremberg and Tokyo.

The trials of industrialists in the aftermath of the war are yet another example of the tension stemming from the complexity of crimes in question. Corporations represent the middle ground between the state and the person. As demonstrated in the *Krupp* case, for example, these corporations are perfectly capable of committing violations of international law. However, the attribution of responsibility for these violations to a particular individual within the firm is challenging. Nonetheless, the US and British courts undertook this task and acknowledged the responsibility of firms' officers for breaching the laws and customs of war.

The third tension between complicity as a mode of participation and complicity as a substantive crime flows directly from the collective nature of the offences in question. The distinction between the wrongdoing and the manner in which individuals become involved is not always clear in international criminal law. One can trace how judicial reasoning evolved in this regard. The first international criminal tribunals hardly referred to the form of liability of each accused, despite their being explicitly mentioned in the Nuremberg and Tokyo Charters. The Nuremberg and Tokyo judgments did not explicitly distinguish between primary perpetrators and other crime participants, and instead adopted a rather fact-based approach to attributing responsibility.[144] Kai Ambos noted that 'the Nuremberg approach can be called pragmatic rather than dogmatic'.[145] One can find two explanations for this peculiarity: first, the lack of theoretical framework during the first international criminal trials; and, second, the adoption of an inchoate offence of 'conspiracy', rather than various forms of complicity, as a method of capturing the collective nature of crimes.

The ILC first codified complicity in the commission of a crime against peace, a war crime or a crime against humanity as a substantive crime under international law.[146] Arguably this was the result of the lack of a distinction between the modes of participation and the substantive offences at Nuremberg. The ILC's position regarding complicity changed only with the adoption of the 1991 Draft Code of Crimes against the Peace and Security of Mankind, which recognised that complicity is a mode of participation and belongs to the section on general principles of law. The same 1991 Draft Code provided the definition of complicity for the first time since the beginning of the ILC's work on the issue in the early 1950s. This shift, leading to a deeper and more nuanced understanding of complicity, was likely the result of the scrupulous work on the issue by the ILC's Special Rapporteur in the 1980s. The other reason for this change of attitude towards complicity was the legacy of the post-IMT prosecutions war criminals. These trials rejected the fact-based approach of Nuremberg and Tokyo and stressed the importance of defining the link between the accused and the crime. The final 1996 Draft Code contained a detailed list

[144] E van Sliedregt, *The Criminal Responsibility of Individuals for Violations of International Humanitarian Law* (The Hague, TMC Asser Press, 2003) 39; Ambos (n 56) 8–9.

[145] Ambos (n 56) 8.

[146] Principle VII of the Nuremberg Principles adopted by the International Law Commission at its second session, in 1950, *Yearbook of the International Law Commission*, 1950, vol. II.

of the modes of criminal participation, paving the way for the relevant provisions of the Rome Statute.

The historical journey in this chapter reveals several notable trends related to the concept of complicity: the development of the legal requirements for complicity while moving away from the fact-based approach of Nuremberg and Tokyo; the introduction and abandonment of the notion of conspiracy as a substantive offence in international criminal law; the introduction and abandonment of the concept of corporate complicity in war crimes; and, finally, the constant struggle to attribute personal guilt for collective wrongdoing. This latter trend is arguably the most important in understanding the evolution of complicity. While it is never easy to capture personal guilt amid mass atrocities, it is possible. Complicity as a mechanism for dealing with collective criminality is deeply rooted in both domestic and international criminal law and, notwithstanding the many ambiguities that characterise this concept, still serves the purposes of allocating individual criminal responsibility.

4

Complicity in the Jurisprudence of the Ad Hoc Tribunals and Hybrid Courts

INTRODUCTION

AFTER SOME DECADES of inactivity, international criminal justice was reinvigorated with the creation of the ICTY pursuant to the Security Council Resolution 827.[1] Its establishment was prompted by the UN Commission of Experts investigating the violations of international humanitarian and human rights law in the territory of the former Yugoslavia.[2] The Commission cautiously suggested in its interim report either setting up an international tribunal that would combine national jurisdictions under the universality principle, akin to the IMT, or the establishment of an ad hoc tribunal authorised by the Security Council.[3] The latter option was preferred.[4] Roughly one year later, the ICTR came into existence with the mandate to punish those responsible for the atrocities committed in the Rwandan genocide and to put an end to such crimes.[5]

Due to the fact that the ICTY and the ICTR (the 'ad hoc tribunals') were established under very different circumstances from their Nuremburg and Tokyo predecessors, their creation marked a new era in the development of international criminal law. The IMT and the IMTFE were the result of a political comprise reached by the victorious states. In the aftermath of the Second World War, there was a practical necessity to 'do something' about the aggressors. While the solution eventually chosen by the Allied powers was to try them in a court of law, other options, including the executions or shows trials, were considered.[6] In contrast, the ad hoc tribunals were not established by the winning powers, but by the international community,

[1] SC Resolution 827 (1993) of 25 May 1993.

[2] SC Resolution 780 (1992) of 6 October 1992.

[3] Interim report of the Commission of Experts established by Resolution 780 (1992) (S/25274), 26 January 1992, paras 73–74.

[4] SC Resolution 808 (1993) of 22 February 1993.

[5] SC Resolution 955 (1994) of 8 November 1994.

[6] R Overy, 'The Nuremberg Trials: International Law in the Making' in P Sands (ed), *From Nuremberg to the Hague: The Future of International Criminal Justice* (Cambridge, Cambridge University Press, 2003) 10.

and not as a postscript to a war, but as a mechanism of ceasing the ongoing violence and preventing further atrocities. These functions were in addition to the traditional goal of a criminal justice system of bringing those responsible to justice, itself a challenging objective when pursued in the midst of a conflict. The ICTY and the ICTR therefore represented an enormous aspiration on the part of the international community.

In contrast with the ad hoc tribunals, introduced during the respective conflicts, the hybrid courts combining the features of an international and a domestic court, namely the Special Court for Sierra Leone (SCSL) and the Extraordinary Chambers in the Courts of Cambodia (ECCC), were established in the aftermath of hostilities.[7] The SCSL was established shortly before the end of the Sierra Leonean civil war,[8] while the ECCC did not begin operations until almost three decades had passed since the end of the bloody Khmer Rouge regime.[9] The ambitions of these two courts are nonetheless comparable to those of the ad hoc tribunals: ensuring accountability, promoting peace and contributing to national reconciliation.[10]

The aspirations of the modern international criminal justice had a direct bearing on the way in which law was formulated in the early judgments of the ICTY and the ICTR, including the doctrines of individual criminal responsibility. The desire to simultaneously achieve a plethora of objectives and deliberately avoid theoretical problems, such as those arising out of the interpretation of the sources of international criminal law, frequently led to unsatisfactory results.[11] The last chapter of this book provides a critical assessment of the purposes of international criminal law and suggests possible trajectories for their further refinement. This exercise is an attempt to bring coherence to the discipline in general and the law of complicity in particular.

The present chapter has a different purpose in mind. It aims at defining complicity, its scope and aims in the jurisprudence of the ad hoc tribunals

[7] This chapter will not cover the work of the Special Tribunal for Lebanon for two main reasons: first, it was conceived as a purely domestic court, albeit with some international elements; and, second, it is still at the early stages of its operation. See SC Resolution 1757 (2007) of 30 May 2007.

[8] SC Resolution 1315 (2000) of 14 August 2000.

[9] The Law on the Establishment of Extraordinary Chambers in the Courts of Cambodia for the Prosecution of Crimes Committed during the Period of Democratic Kampuchea ('ECCC Law'), *Reach Kram NS/RKM/0801/12* as amended in 2004 by *NS/RKM/1004/006*.

[10] SC Resolution 1315 (2000) of 14 August 2000; UN GA Resolution regarding the situation of human rights in Cambodia, 27 February 1998 (A/RES/52/135).

[11] On the lack of a clear objective, see M Damaška, 'What is the Point of International Criminal Justice?' (2008) 83 *Chicago-Kent Law Review* 329. On collective responsibility, see AM Danner and JS Martinez, 'Guilty Associations: Joint Criminal Enterprise, Command Responsibility and the Development of International Criminal Law' (2005) 93 *California Law Review* 75; G Boas, JL Bischoff and NL Reid, *International Criminal Law Practitioner Library International Criminal Procedure* (2 vols) (Cambridge, Cambridge University Press, 2007) 17–22; S Powles, 'Joint Criminal Enterprise: Criminal Liability by Prosecutorial Ingenuity and Judicial Creativity?' (2004) 2 *Journal of International Criminal Justice* 606.

and hybrid courts. The work of these institutions can be conceptualised as an intermediate step in the development of international criminal law linking the military tribunals of the post-Second World War era and the permanent body of international criminal justice—the International Criminal Court (ICC). However, the 'step' is enormous. In the last two decades, international criminal law has become the symbol of the international community's efforts to address political violence as it has unfolded in different parts of the world.[12] It is also possible to view the existence of the ad hoc tribunals and hybrid courts as a separate vector of the development of international criminal law independent from the ICC, given the fact that the circumstances of their creation and the aspirations of these institutions are not identical. However, regardless of how one perceives them, the ICTY, the ICTR, the SCSL and the ECCC contributed immensely to the definition and evolution of the law on individual criminal responsibility.

The first section of the chapter discusses the elements of different forms of responsibility in the jurisprudence of the ad hoc tribunals and hybrid courts. The purpose is twofold: first, to define various forms of complicity and to separate them from 'commission'; and, second, to analyse some problematic and contentious issues pertaining to the law on individual criminal responsibility. This section does not comprehensively cover all forms of responsibility as defined in the jurisprudence of the ad hoc tribunals and hybrid courts, but builds on excellent recent works dealing with the issue,[13] selecting those aspects that are crucial for defining and understanding complicity in all of its complexity.[14] The second section of this chapter discusses four problems characteristic of international criminal justice that hinder a coherent and just application of the concept of complicity. This exercise is intended to determine how best to deal with the complicity doctrine in international criminal law. When properly defined and employed, different forms of complicity make it possible to accurately describe the conduct of the accused and attach responsibility for the particular act, thereby avoiding the finding of collective guilt that is often produced by newly invented doctrines, such as joint criminal enterprise.

[12] D Luban, 'After Honey Moon: Reflections on the Current State of International Criminal Justice' (2013) 11 *Journal of International Criminal Justice* 505.

[13] The past decade saw an increased interest in the legal requirements for the modes of liability in international criminal law—a trend to be applauded. Kai Ambos argued in 2000 that the elements of individual criminal responsibility are not sufficiently discussed in the literature, despite this concept being universally recognised. Only recently have the technical issues received more profound treatment in the literature. See K Ambos, *Treatise on International Criminal Law, Volume I: Foundations and General Part* (Oxford, Oxford University Press, 2013) 103. *cf* K Ambos, '*Nulla Poena Sine Lege* in International Criminal Law' in R Haveman and O Olusanya (ed), *Sentencing and Sanctioning in Supranational Criminal Law* (Antwerp, Intersentia, 2006) 6.

[14] E van Sliedregt, *Individual Criminal Responsibility in International Law* (Oxford, Oxford University Press, 2012); G Mettraux, *International Criminal and Ad Hoc Tribunals* (Oxford, Oxford University Press, 2005); Boas, Bischoff and Reid (n 11).

I. FORMS OF PARTICIPATION IN THE STATUTES OF THE AD HOC TRIBUNALS AND HYBRID COURTS

A. Requirements of Individual Criminal Responsibility

The following provisions in the Statutes of the ICTY, the ICTR and the SCSL[15] and the ECCC Law[16] deal with matters of individual criminal responsibility.[17]

Article 7(1) ICTY Statute:

> A person who planned, instigated, ordered, committed or otherwise aided and abetted in the planning, preparation or execution of a crime referred to in articles 2 to 5 of the present Statute, shall be individually responsible for the crime.

Article 6(1) ICTR and SCSL:

> A person who planned, instigated, ordered, committed or otherwise aided and abetted in the planning, preparation or execution of a crime referred to in articles 2 to 4 of the present Statute, shall be individually responsible for the crime.

Article 29 of the ECCC Law:

> Any Suspect who planned, instigated, ordered, aided and abetted, or committed the crimes referred to in article 3 new, 4, 5, 6, 7 and 8 of this law shall be individually responsible for the crime.

The modes of participation are not defined in the Statutes[18] and the ECCC Law. The ICTY Appeals Chamber clarified that the Statute only provides an a priori jurisdictional framework *ratione personae*, and the existence of a particular form of liability as well as its legal requirements will be determined by customary international law.[19] This is in contrast to the Rome Statute of the ICC, which spells out the modes of participation in greater

[15] Statute of the International Criminal Tribunal for the Former Yugoslavia adopted on 25 May 1993, S/RES/ 827; Statute of the International Criminal Tribunal for Rwanda adopted on 8 November 1994, S/RES/955; Statute of the Special Court for Sierra Leone adopted on 14 August 2000, S/RES/1315.

[16] ECCC Law, art 29.

[17] Article 7(1) of the ICTY Statute; Article 6(1) of the ICTR and SCSL Statutes; Article 29 of the ECCC Law.

[18] Pocar noted in respect to the ICTY Statute that: 'The drafters of the Statute had explicitly declined to make it a self-contained criminal code. They instead granted the Tribunal jurisdiction over a set of very broadly defined crimes, the specific content of which was to be found in customary international law.' F Pocar, *Audiovisual Library of International Law*, available at www.un.org/law/avl/.

[19] *Prosecutor v Šainović et al*, ICTY Case No IT-99-37-AR72, Decision on Dragoljub Ojdanić's Motion Challenging Jurisdiction—Joint Criminal Enterprise, 21 May 2003 ('*Ojdanić* JCE Appeal Decision'), paras 9–10 (quoting the Report of the Secretary-General Pursuant to para 2 of Security Council Resolution 808 (1993), para 21). See also *Prosecutor v Delalic et al* ('*Čelebići* Appeal Judgment') ICTY Case No IT-96-21-A, Appeal Judgment, 20 February 2001, para 178, as cited by Mettraux (n 14) 270.

detail and assigns customary international law a secondary role vis-a-vis the provisions of the Rome Statute.[20]

In the absence of a definition in the Statutes and the ECCC Law, it is up to the ICTY, the ICTR, the SCSL and the ECCC to spell out the legal requirements for each mode of liability. In this process, it is important to distinguish the constituent elements of the offence and the legal requirements of the mode of responsibility used in conjunction with this offence.[21] The constituent elements of the offence are the objective element or actus reus and the subjective element or mens rea. Cassese defines 'actus reus' as a conduct (an act or omission contrary to a rule imposing specific behaviour) and 'mens rea' as a state of mind (a psychological element required by the legal order for the conduct to be blameworthy and consequently punishable).[22]

There exists a separate set of requirements for each form of individual criminal responsibility. Their purpose is to help the judge or the juror decide whether an individual's involvement in a crime entails criminal responsibility or not. In the literature and the judgments, the terms 'mens rea' and 'actus reus' are often used in relation to both the substantive offences and the mode of responsibility.[23] The goal of this book is to separate the two sets of elements. This aim is in line with an important tendency of international criminal law to view modes of participation and substantive offences as separate issues—a significant trend that has taken some time to evolve.[24] The terms frequently used in this book to refer to the elements of individual criminal responsibility (as opposed to the elements of the crime) are the 'legal requirements', consisting of a 'conduct requirement' and a 'fault requirement'.[25]

In cases of direct primary participation (ie, commission), the conduct and fault requirement of legal responsibility form 'mirror' the mens rea and actus reus of the substantive offence: the conduct of the principal fully corresponds to the elements of the crime. However, when it comes to more complex forms of commission, such as commission through the joint criminal enterprise, as well as different forms of complicity, the requirements of liability supplement the constituent elements of an offence. It is

[20] For a detailed discussion of the relevant provisions of the Rome Statute, see Ch 5.I.

[21] Various forms of liability have different conduct and mental requirements. See R Cryer, H Friman, D Robinson and E Wilmeshurst, *An Introduction to International Criminal Law and Procedure*, 2nd edn (Cambridge, Cambridge University Press, 2010) 361.

[22] A Cassese, *International Criminal Law*, 2nd edn (Oxford, Oxford University Press, 2008) 53.

[23] Boas, Bischoff and Reid (n 11) 4.

[24] See Ch 3.

[25] Despite the author's attempt to reserve the terms 'mens rea' and 'actus reus' for the substantive crimes and 'fault requirement' and 'conduct requirement' for modes of participation, the former set of terms still occasionally appear throughout this book in conjunction with modes of responsibility. This is so because many academic works and judgments refer to the constituent elements of the modes of responsibility as 'mens rea' and 'actus reus'.

essential to establish that the crime was committed and *the way* in which the accused was involved in it.

The first international criminal law judgment since Nuremberg—*Tadić*—pointed out this phenomenon. The Trial Chamber had to determine 'whether the conduct of the accused ... sufficiently connects the accused to the crime'.[26] In doing so, the judges drew a distinction between instances when the accused directly engaged in the actions alleged and cases where the accused did not directly commit some of the offences charged, but was present at the time of, or otherwise involved in, their commission.[27] The *Tadić* Trial Chamber consequently established a two-prong test to establish liability for complicity. The first element of the test is 'intent, which involves awareness of the act of participation coupled with a conscious decision to participate by planning, instigating, ordering, committing, or otherwise aiding and abetting in the commission of a crime'. To satisfy the second part of the test, the conduct of the accused must have contributed to the commission of an illegal act.[28]

B. The Scope of Complicity

The early *Tadić* interpretation of 'complicious conduct' introduced the broader understanding of complicity then subsequently applied by the ad hoc tribunals and the hybrid courts. It encompassed all forms of participation mentioned in Article 7(1) of the ICTY Statute.[29] Such a broad understanding of complicity can be explained by the legacy of the IMT and subsequent jurisprudence that formed the basis of the first ICTY

[26] See *Prosecutor v Tadić*, ICTY Case No IT-94-1-T, Trial Judgment, 7 May 1997 ('*Tadić* Trial Judgment'), para 673.

[27] The subsequent case law of the ICTY and the ICTR does not stress this subtle difference, with the exception of situations when conviction on appeal was revised: multiple Appeals Chambers permitted changing the mode of liability on appeal, reiterating that it does not amount to entering a new conviction. Judge Pocar noted the following instances of changing the mode of liability on appeal: *Prosecutor v Vasiljević*, ICTY Case No IT-98-32-A, Appeal Judgment, 25 February 2004 ('*Vasiljević* Appeal Judgment'), paras 132–35, 141–43, 147, 181–82; *Prosecutor v Krstić*, ICTY Case No IT-98-33-A, Appeal Judgment, 19 April 2004 ('*Krstić* Appeal Judgment'), paras 135–44, 266, 268; *Prosecutor v Simić et al*, ICTY Case No IT-95-9-A, Appeal Judgment, 28 November 2006 ('*Simić* Appeal Judgment'), paras 74–75, 84, 105, 114–18, 130–38, 148–59, 182–89, 300–30; *Prosecutor v D Milošević*, ICTY Case No IT-98-29/1-A, Appeal Judgment, 12 November 2009 ('*D Milošević* Appeal Judgment'), paras 275–82, 334; *Prosecutor v Rukundo*, ICTR Case No 2001-70-A, Appeal Judgment, 20 October 2010 ('*Rukundo* Appeal Judgment'), paras 39, 50–54, 175–77, 269–70; *Prosecutor v Blaskić*, ICTY Case No IT-95-14-A, Appeal Judgment, 29 July 2004. ('*Blaskić* Appeal Judgment'), paras 32–42, 659–70. See *Prosecutor v Gotovina and Markač*, ICTY Case No IT-06-90-A, Appeal Judgment, 16 November 2012 ('*Gotovina* Appeal Judgment'), Dissenting Opinion of Judge Pocar, para 33.

[28] *Tadić* Trial Judgment (n 26) paras 674 and 688.

[29] ibid, para 674.

judgment. As discussed in Chapter 3, pre-1993 case law adopted a rather fact-based unitary approach to the modes of responsibility. Thus, little clarity existed in this regard at the time when the *Tadić* judgment was drafted.[30] In *Krnojelac*, the ICTY Appeals Chamber addressed the *Tadić* approach by clarifying that the term 'accomplice' has different meanings depending on the context and may refer to a co-perpetrator or an aider and abettor.[31] The ECCC Trial Chamber delimited 'aiding and abetting' from the broader notion of complicity. This finding was made despite the French version of Article 29 of the ECCC law translating 'aiding and abetting' using the word 'complicité'. Given the fact that 'complicité' encompasses a broader conduct, a more accurate translation would have been 'aidé et encouragé'.[32] The conclusion about the shifting scope of complicity is corroborated by the separate declaration of Judge Keith to the *Genocide* judgment in which he examined various definitions of 'complicity' and came to the conclusion that 'complicity is *often* restricted to aiding and abetting' (emphasis added).[33]

International criminal law is rooted in domestic criminal law.[34] Relying on the survey of different domestic jurisdictions provided in Chapter 2 of this book, it is fair to say that complicity in international criminal law should be understood as embracing planning, instigating, ordering, aiding and abetting. This conclusion follows from the theoretical underpinning of complicity as a form of secondary participation, which is derivative in nature.[35] Various domestic law systems recognise different forms of complicity—aiding and abetting and instigating being the most common.[36]

[30] In a different part in the same judgment, the Trial Chamber used the term 'complicity' as a synonym to 'aiding and abetting'. *Tadić* Trial Judgment (n 26) para 688.

[31] *Prosecutor v Krnojelac*, ICTY Case No IT-97-25-A, Appeal Judgment, 17 September 2003 ('*Krnojelac* Appeal Judgment'), para 70.

[32] *Prosecutor v KAING Guek Eav alias Duch*, ECCC Case No 001/18-07-2007/ECCC/TC, Trial Judgment, 20 March 2012 ('*Duch* Trial Judgment'), para 532.

[33] *Case Concerning the Application of the Convention on the Prevention and Punishment of the Crime of Genocide (Bosnia and Herzegovina v Serbia and Montenegro)*, ICJ Reports 2007 ('*Genocide* Judgment'), Declaration of Judge Keith, 353.

[34] At the time of the conception of the ICTY, the idea seemed to be precisely to ground international criminal law in the two disciplines—public international law and domestic criminal law. The French jurists suggested finding the satisfactory balance between the principles of public international law on the one hand, and the principles of criminal law and criminal procedure on the other. See *Report of the Committee of French Jurists to Study the Establishment of International Criminal Tribunal to Judge the Crimes Committed in the Former Yugoslavia* ('*Report of the Committee of French Jurists*'), appended to the letter dated 10 February 1993 from the Permanent Representative of France to the United Nations addressed to the Secretary General, UN DOC S/25266, para 50(d).

[35] As Smith put it, 'complicity's function is to determine the circumstances when one party (an accessory) by virtue of prior simultaneous activity or association will be held criminally responsible for another's (the perpetrator's) wrongful behaviour'. He adds that English common law adopted and developed a derivative form of complicity. See KJM Smith, *A Modern Treatise on the Law of Criminal Complicity* (Oxford, Clarendon, 1991) 1–3.

[36] For a detailed analysis of complicity in the domestic legal systems, see Ch 2.

The idea is that an accomplice does not directly perpetrate the crime, but is nonetheless involved in its commission. 'Committing', on the other hand, signifies principal perpetration, whether directly or indirectly through an agent.[37] Broader and narrower notions of complicity shall be contextualised and treated as mere rhetorical tools. Consequently, all modes of participation listed in the statutes of the ad hoc tribunals and hybrid courts aside from 'committing' belong to the sphere of 'complicity'.[38]

There is an important point following from the derivative nature of complicity spelled out by Miles Jackson with which I agree: accomplices ought to be held responsible for their contribution rather than the principal's wrong. This vision supports preference for non-imputational complicity rules—those who assist, plan or instigate a certain offence must be held accountable for that act rather than the offence itself.[39] This view is consistent with the approach adopted by the majority of domestic legal systems under review in this volume. Most jurisdictions—including those adhering to the unitary model of participation, such as Italy—already spell out the contribution of the accused at the stage of attribution of responsibility. The US Model Penal Code (MPC) appears to be at odds with the majority in adopting an imputational view of complicity: it draws a fundamental distinction between someone who commits an offence 'by his own conduct' and someone whose criminal liability derives from 'the conduct of another person for which he is legally accountable'.[40] As a result, the MPC requires accomplices to act with a 'purpose', presumably to match the mental state of the perpetrator. This is an enhanced fault requirement compared to other jurisdictions. At the same time, the MPC allows for minimal contributions to the crime, therefore remedying a certain disbalance created by the heightened fault requirement.

Complicity should be distinguished from command responsibility regulated by distinct provisions of the Statutes and the ECCC Law. These norms allow for holding the superior responsible for the acts of his subordinate 'if he knew or had reason to know that the subordinate was about to commit such acts or had done so and the superior failed to take the necessary and reasonable measures to prevent such acts or to punish the perpetrators'.[41] The common feature of the accomplice and superior responsibility is that they both entail culpable commission by others. However, command

[37] For a theoretical discussion on the distinction between primary and secondary participation in domestic criminal law, see Ch 2.I.B.

[38] W Schabas, *The UN International Criminal Tribunals: The Former Yugoslavia, Rwanda and Sierra Leone* (Cambridge, Cambridge University Press, 2006) 305.

[39] M Jackson, *Complicity in International Law* (Oxford, Oxford University Press, 2015) 86.

[40] Model Penal Code, s 2.06(1).

[41] ICTY Statute, art 7(3); ICTR Statute, art 6(3); SCSL Statute, art 6(3); and ECCC Law, art 29(3). See the texts in Appendix I.

responsibility cannot be characterised as complicity.[42] The key conceptual distinction between the two is that the superior bears responsibility for his *own* culpable omission to act in the presence of such duty, while accomplice liability is derivative in nature and necessarily stems from the criminal conduct of another person.[43] For this reason, command responsibility has been referred to in *Orić* as responsibility *sui generis*.[44]

The ad hoc and hybrid courts and tribunals defined the legal requirements of various forms of liability on a case-by-case basis, relying on the existent customary international law.[45] The following subsections summarise their findings. Complicity in genocide is treated in a distinct section because it is a separate provision in the ICTY and ICTR Statutes (but not the SCSL Statute or the ECCC Law). 'Committing' is included in the description of the modes of liability for the purposes of better defining the contours of complicity.[46]

C. Committing

The term 'commit' in the jurisprudence of the ICTY, the ICTR, the SCSL and the ECCC implies direct commission and participation in the joint criminal enterprise.[47] The *Tadić* Appeal Chamber held that Article 7(1) of the ICTY Statute covers 'first and foremost the physical perpetration of a crime by the offender himself, or the culpable omission of an act that was mandated by a rule of criminal law'.[48] Despite this statement, only slightly more than a dozen of the accused standing trial at the ICTY, less than 20 per cent of all convictions, were convicted as direct perpetrators or co-perpetrators. The remainder of the convictions were founded on participation in the joint criminal enterprise, superior responsibility or various forms of complicity.[49] The SCSL or the ECCC produced no convictions for direct perpetration.[50]

[42] G Mettraux, *The Law of Command Responsibility* (Oxford, Oxford University Press, 2009) 39.

[43] 'Ordering' is the form of complicity that is arguably the closest to 'superior responsibility'. The former, unlike the latter, does not require a superior–subordinate relationship between the order giver and the perpetrator so long as it is demonstrated that there existed the authority to order. Responsibility of the order giver derives from the wrongful act of the principal rather than the formal link between the two participants in the crime.

[44] *Prosecutor v Orić*, ICTY Case No IT-03-68-T, Trial Judgment, 30 June 2006, para 293.

[45] See, for example, *Čelebići* Appeal Judgment (n 19) para 178.

[46] Smith (n 35) 64 noted that 'analysis of complicity's distinct *mens rea* and *actus reus* elements needs to be carried out within the complete framework of responsibility demands'.

[47] Van Sliedregt (n 14) 91.

[48] *Prosecutor v Tadić*, ICTY Case No IT-94-1, Appeals Chamber Judgment, 15 July 1999 ('*Tadić* Appeal Judgment') para 188. The SCSL and the ECCC followed the same approach. *Prosecutor v Brima, Kamara and Kanu*, SCSL-04-16-T, Trial Judgment, 20 June 2007 ('*AFRC* Trial Judgment'), para 762; *Duch* Trial Judgment (n 32) para 479.

[49] See Appendix II.

[50] ibid.

The ICTR jurisprudence on commission stands in contrast to that of other courts. It issued convictions for committing in a third of the cases it dealt with and assigned a less prominent role to the joint criminal enterprise.[51] This trend could be explained by the unique approach to 'commission' adopted by the ICTR. The Appeals Chamber in *Gacumbitsi* accepted the extended interpretation of this form of liability, holding that 'direct and physical perpetration' need not be confined to physical killing, but can also include other acts, such as 'directing' and 'playing a leading role in conducting and, especially, supervising'.[52] In accordance with this interpretation, the ICTR judges held that Sylvestre Gacumbitsi—the highest-ranking local administrative official in one of the municipalities in Rwanda—committed genocide through being physically present at the scene of the crime and personally directing the Tutsi and Hutu refugees to separate into different groups. The Chamber found these actions to be 'as much an integral part of the genocide as were the killings which it enabled'.[53] The subsequent paragraph of the judgment provides reasons for such a broad interpretation of commission, which is the conviction that other modes of participation—ordering, planning or instigating—do not, taken alone, fully capture the accused's criminal responsibility.[54] The appellate judges stated that by being present at the scene of the crime, Gacumbitsi did not 'merely 'instigate' the killings', but rather committed them.[55]

The Appeals Chamber in *Seromba* adopted the same approach to commission by holding that 'Athanase Seromba crossed the line separating aiding and abetting from committing genocide and became a principal perpetrator in the crime itself'.[56] The judges noted that Seromba, in his capacity as the local priest, exercised influence over the driver who drove a bulldozer into the church where 1,500 Tutsi were taking refuge.[57] The Appeals Chamber observed that Seromba's conduct 'was not limited to giving practical assistance, encouragement or moral support to the principal perpetrators of the crime, which would *merely* constitute the *actus reus* of aiding and abetting' (emphasis added).[58] The recent *Munyakazi* appeal judgment confirmed this broad interpretation of commission.[59]

[51] ibid.

[52] *Prosecutor v Gacumbitsi*, ICTR Case No 2001-64-A, Appeal Judgment, 7 July 2006 ('*Gacumbitsi* Appeal Judgment'), para 60.

[53] ibid.

[54] ibid, para 61.

[55] ibid.

[56] *Prosecutor v Seromba*, ICTR Case No 2001-66-A, Appeal Judgment, 12 March 2008 ('*Seromba* Appeal Judgment'), para 182.

[57] ibid, para 171.

[58] ibid, para 172. The word 'merely' denotes an implied hierarchy of the modes of participation accepted by the Appeals Chamber.

[59] *Prosecutor v Munyakazi*, ICTR Case No 97-36A-A, Appeal Judgment, 28 September 2011 ('*Munyakazi* Appeal Judgment'), paras 136–38.

Not all of the appellate judges supported this wide reading of commission. Judge Liu dissented in *Seromba* and *Munyakazi* on three main points: first, he noted that the *Gacumbitsi* interpretation of commission is reserved for genocide alone;[60] second, extended commission is somewhat superfluous because the joint criminal enterprise is the mode of liability covering commission without physical perpetration, so it must be pleaded instead of the commission;[61] and, finally, 'the expanded notion of commission not only embraces acts that technically amount to secondary forms of participation, but also extends to conduct that contributes to the commission of crimes of others'.[62] This interpretation resembles co-perpetration or indirect perpetration as possibly envisaged by the ICC, but not the ICTR Statute.[63]

It is noteworthy that the accused need not hold a position in the army or state apparatus to incur individual criminal responsibility under the jurisprudence of the ad hoc tribunals. Alfred Musema, the director of a tea factory, was involved in attacks against Tutsi refugees in the area surrounding his factory at the time when the Rwandan atrocities occurred. The ICTR prosecutors charged him with extermination, rape as a crime against humanity, genocide or, alternatively, complicity in genocide.[64]

The form of commission that Judge Liu alluded to when he criticised the extended form of commission in the ICTR jurisprudence is that of joint criminal enterprise. This form of liability is not explicitly mentioned in the ICTY, ICTR or SCSL Statutes or the ECCC Law, but has frequently been used by all of these courts to address situations where multiple accused are removed from the scene of the crime. The ICTY in *Tadić* developed three forms of the joint criminal enterprise:[65]

— The first category involves cases where all participants are acting pursuant to a common purpose and share the same criminal intent.
— The second category refers to instances of systemic ill-treatment in organised institutions, such as concentration camps.
— The third category, called the 'extended form' of the joint criminal enterprise, entails liability of the members of the group for the acts

[60] *Seromba* Appeal Judgment (n 56) Dissenting Opinion of Judge Liu, para 2; *Munyakazi* Appeal Judgment (n 59) Dissenting Opinion of Judge Liu, paras 2 and 5.

[61] *Seromba* Appeal Judgment (n 56) Dissenting Opinion of Judge Liu, para 6; *Munyakazi* Appeal Judgment (n 59) Dissenting Opinion of Judge Liu, para 4.

[62] *Seromba* Appeal Judgment (n 56) Dissenting Opinion of Judge Liu, paras 9–10; *Munyakazi* Appeal Judgment (n 59) Dissenting Opinion of Judge Liu, para 4.

[63] Even at the ICC, these concepts receive some critical appraisal. For the detailed discussion, see Ch 5.

[64] *Prosecutor v Musema*, ICTR Case No 96-13-T, Trial Judgment, 27 January 2000 ('*Musema* Trial Judgment'), paras 149, 168, 218, 220. The prosecution also charged Musema with violations of art 4 of the ICTR Statute (war crimes), but the Trial Chamber failed to establish the nexus between the acts of the accused the armed conflict. See *Musema* Trial Judgment, para 974.

[65] *Tadić* Appeal Judgment (n 48) paras 195–226, as discussed by Schabas (n 38) 309–10.

which occur as a 'natural and foreseeable consequence' of carrying out the common purpose.[66]

The conduct requirement of all three forms of the joint enterprise is as follows: (i) a common plan involving the commission of a crime; (ii) a plurality of persons; and (iii) an individual contribution of the accused to the execution of the plan.[67] The fault requirement differs depending on the type of the joint enterprise—intent to perpetrate for the first type, personal knowledge of the system of ill-treatment and the intent to further the system for the second type.[68] The third type of the joint criminal enterprise requires the intention to participate and further the criminal activity or the criminal purpose of the group, and to contribute to the joint criminal enterprise or to the commission of a crime by the group. The responsibility for a crime other than that agreed upon in the common plan arises only if, under the circumstances of the case: (i) it was foreseeable that such a crime might be perpetrated by a member of the group; and (ii) the accused willingly took that risk.[69]

Despite the acknowledgement in the jurisprudence that the joint criminal enterprise is a form of 'commission',[70] the legal requirements of the joint criminal enterprise are similar to those of certain forms of complicity, namely aiding and abetting.[71] This proximity prompted the ICTY Appeals Chamber to distinguish joint criminal enterprise from aiding and abetting. The main difference between the two forms of participation is that the aider and abettor *knowingly* commits acts *specifically directed* at assisting the perpetration of a particular crime, while members of the joint criminal enterprise perform acts *in some way directed* towards the furtherance of common design with the *intent* to pursue this design.[72] No proof of common plan is required for aiding and abetting.[73] In addition, the threshold for contribution to the specific crime pursuant to aiding and abetting appears to be higher than the contribution to the joint criminal enterprise.[74]

[66] *Tadić* Appeal Judgment (n 48) para 204.
[67] ibid, para 227.
[68] *Tadić* Appeal Judgment (n 48) para 228.
[69] ibid.
[70] *Vasiljević* Appeal Judgment (n 27) para 95; *Tadić* Appeal Judgment (n 48) para 188; *Krnojelac* Appeal Judgment (n 31) para 29; Mettraux (n 14) 288.
[71] Schabas (n 38) 319 even considers joint criminal enterprise as a form of participation or complicity.
[72] *Tadić* Appeal Judgment (n 48) para 229.
[73] ibid; *Duch* Trial Judgment (n 32) para 534.
[74] The Appeals Chamber in *Kvočka* held that there is no specific legal requirement for the accused to make a substantial contribution to the joint criminal enterprise. The significance of the accused's contribution is only relevant in terms of demonstrating that the accused shared the intent to pursue the common purpose. *Prosecutor v Kvočka*, ICTY Case No IT-98-30/1-T, Appeal Judgment, 28 February 2005 ('*Kvočka* Appeal Judgment'), para 97. See also *Gotovina* Appeal Judgment (n 27) para 149.

Van Sliedregt has traced the evolution of the application of the joint criminal enterprise.[75] It was initially created as a solution for small-scale enterprises and group criminality, such as in *Tadić* and *Furundžija*, but was later used to address the liability of senior political and military leaders in cases such as *Krajišnik*,[76] *Popović*[77] and *Nuon Chea*.[78] The ICTR Appeals Chamber in *Rwamakuba* expressly refuted the defence's claim that the doctrine of common purpose, as applied in post-Second World War cases, was limited to crimes with a large degree of specificity:

> The fact that certain prosecutions charged participation in small-scale plans involving few victims or in the operation of specific concentration camps does not suggest that customary international law forbade punishment for genocide committed through plans formulated and executed on a nationwide scale.[79]

As a result of the application to the large-scale enterprises, the scope of the common plan required to hold individuals responsible under this form of liability expanded significantly.[80] For example, the Appeal Chamber in *Krajišnik* ruled that the contribution to the joint criminal enterprise need not be criminal provided 'that it furthers the execution of the common objective or purpose involving the commission of crimes'.[81] This feature of the judgment is startling. The Appeals Chamber held that Krajišnik's main contribution to the joint criminal enterprise was in setting up and supporting the structures of the Serbian Democratic Party (SDS), an activity not criminal in itself, but instrumental to the commission of the crimes.[82]

The SCSL Appeals Chamber reasoned along the similar lines. In the *AFRC* case, in addition to the modes of responsibility expressly mentioned in Article 6(1) and 6(3) of the SCSL Statute, the prosecution charged the accused with participation in the joint criminal enterprise, the objective of which was to take any action necessary to gain and exercise political power and control over the territory of Sierra Leone, in particular the diamond mining areas.[83] Initially, the Trial Chamber found that the prosecution failed to define the criminal objective when determining the responsibility

[75] Van Sliedregt (n 14) 136.

[76] *Prosecutor v Krajišnik*, ICTY Case No IT-00-39-A, Appeal Judgment, 17 March 2009 ('*Krajišnik* Appeal Judgment').

[77] *Prosecutor v Popović et al*, ICTY Case No 05-88-T, Trial Judgment, 10 June 2010 ('*Popović* Trial Judgment').

[78] *Prosecutor v Ieng Sary et al*, ECCC, Case No 002/19-09-2007/ECCC/OCIJ, Closing Order, Office of the Co-Investigating Judges, 15 September 2010 ('*Ieng Sary* Closing Order'), para 1524.

[79] Decision on Interlocutory Appeal Regarding Application of Joint Criminal Enterprise to the Crime of Genocide, *Rwamakuba v Prosecutor*, Case No ICTR-98-4-AR72.4, 22 October 2004, para 25.

[80] Van Sliedregt (n 14) 136.

[81] *Krajišnik* Appeal Judgment (n 76) para 218, as cited in van Sliedregt (n 14) 137.

[82] ibid.

[83] *Prosecutor v Brima, Kamara and Kanu*, SCSL-04-16-A, Appeal Judgment, 22 February 2008 ('*AFRC* Appeal Judgment'), para 15.

of the accused and refused to consider the joint criminal enterprise as a mode of participation.[84] The Appeals Chamber subsequently overturned this particular finding, noting that 'the criminal purpose underlying the joint criminal enterprise can derive not only from its ultimate objective, but also from the means contemplated to achieve that objective'.[85] The Appeals Chamber then suggested that even though gaining and exercising political power over the territory of Sierra Leone may not be a crime in itself, the criminal actions taken by the AFRC to reach this goal qualify as a means to achieve the objective and hence themselves constitute a criminal objective.[86]

The concept of the joint criminal enterprise created much debate in academic circles and to some extent in the case law of the ad hoc tribunals.[87] The first line of criticism relates to the questionable legal status of the concept under the customary international law. In the *Milutinović et al* case, the defence of Dragoljub Ojdanić raised this point, claiming that the Appeals Chamber in *Tadić* misinterpreted the drafters' intentions by inferring the joint criminal enterprise from the ICTY Statute—the drafters would have explicitly mentioned this form of liability if they intended it to be applicable.[88] The appellate panel in *Milutinović et al* refuted this argument, holding that it was satisfied with the *Tadić* interpretation of the Statute, which provides, albeit not explicitly, for joint criminal enterprise as a form of liability because it has a basis in customary international law.[89]

The second major criticism of the joint criminal enterprise is the inconsistency between the theoretical concept and its practical application.[90] Harmen van der Wilt drew attention to the fact that 'the doctrine does not entirely dovetail with the gloomy reality of the modern bureaucracies that engage in systematic crime'.[91] The conceptual idea of the joint criminal enterprise is based on one subjective and one objective element: the subjective element is the agreement and the shared intent to pursue a common plan that aims at or includes the commission of criminal acts, while the objective is the accused's participation in that plan. The emphasis is, however, on the subjective element.[92] In the actual application of the

84 AFRC Trial Judgment (n 48) para 1639.
85 AFRC Appeal Judgment (n 83) para 76.
86 ibid, paras 81–84.
87 Van Sliedregt (n 14) 141.
88 *Ojdanić* JCE Appeal Decision (n 19) para 18.
89 ibid, para 21.
90 V Haan, 'The Development of the Concept of Joint Criminal Enterprise at the ICTY' (2005) 5 *International Criminal Law Review* 167.
91 H van der Wilt, 'Joint Criminal Enterprise: Possibilities and Limitations' (2007) 5(5) *Journal of International Criminal Justice* 91.
92 This importance of mens rea has been confirmed by the *Tadić* appeal when the Chamber has delineated the joint criminal enterprise from aiding and abetting based on the mens rea criteria. See *Tadić* Appeal Judgment (n 48) para 229.

concept, the judges seem to have reversed the importance of the objective and subjective elements of the joint criminal enterprise. While many Chambers set a higher standard for the objective element, requiring, in addition to participation, that the accused played an influential part within the joint criminal enterprise and that he was in a position of authority vis-a-vis the direct perpetrators,[93] they do not examine whether there existed a shared intent between the accused person and the direct perpetrator at all.[94] As Verena Haan noted, the ICTY deals with complex cases where numerous persons acted at various levels of authority. While there might have existed a common agreement to pursue a criminal plan among members of 'one level of authority', the persons acting at different levels of authority have most likely not been linked to the crime through a common agreement, but through hierarchical structures, such as military chains of command.[95]

The third major criticism relates to the scope of application of the joint criminal enterprise and, in particular, its extended version. Powles has observed that it is hard to see how someone guilty of participating in the third category of the joint criminal enterprise, ie, where the crime falls beyond the object of criminal enterprise, can be said to have actually 'committed' the crime in question when they do not possess the intention to actually commit the crime and may not even be aware of that crime before, during or even after it has actually been committed.[96] Danner and Martinez added that the prosecution may use this over-expansive form of responsibility in cases when there is not sufficient evidence to secure the conviction under a different form of responsibility, leading to a dangerous over-reliance on victim-oriented teleological interpretation that produces a result of 'guilt by association'.[97] The authors advocate an approach that is more sensitive to the concern that low-level perpetrators may be charged and convicted of large-scale mass crimes, even where they only played a minor role.[98]

On a conceptual level, it appears that the joint criminal enterprise constitutes a somewhat 'borderline' case, lying between complicity and the actual commission of an offence. On the one hand, the acts of the participants are attributed to all members of the group as if each participant has

[93] eg, *Prosecutor v Stakić*, ICTY Case No IT-97-24-T, Trial Judgment, 31 July 2003 ('*Stakić* Trial Judgment'), para 440; *Prosecutor v Krstić*, ICTY Case No IT-98-33-T, Trial Judgment, 2 August 2001 ('*Krstić* Trial Judgment'), para 607; *Prosecutor v Simić et al*, ICTY Case No IT-95-9-T, Trial Judgment, 17 October 2003 ('*Simić* Trial Judgment'), para 998.

[94] eg, *Krstić* Trial Judgment (n 93) para 612; *Tadić* Appeal Judgment (n 48) para 230; *Stakić* Trial Judgment (n 93) para 478.

[95] Haan (n 90) 196.

[96] Powles (n 11) 606–19.

[97] Danner and Martinez (n 11) 56.

[98] ibid 85.

committed these acts himself. In this sense, the joint criminal enterprise resembles some features of the national law concepts of co-perpetration and conspiracy.[99] The conspiratorial form of liability developed by the US Supreme Court in *Pinkerton* strongly resembles the extended form of the joint criminal enterprise as defined in *Tadić*.[100] It is noteworthy that the *Pinkerton* case has been widely criticised both in the US and abroad, and the rule has never been incorporated into the US MPC.[101]

On the other hand, certain members of the group do not directly perpetrate these acts and their liability is derivative. The concept of the joint criminal enterprise seems to be borrowed from English law, with the difference that in England, the joint enterprise is a creation designed to deal for the most part with an unexpected turn of events,[102] whereas in the jurisprudence of the ad hoc tribunals, it has become an independent, stand-alone mode of liability. Despite this functional difference, it could be fairly said that until recently, the approach of English law was consistent with extended joint criminal enterprise in international criminal law—both emphasised the risk-taking behaviour on behalf of the accused. The *Chan Wing-Siu* case decided in England in 1985 directed courts to hold members of the joint enterprise responsible for crimes falling outside of the scope of the agreement if these crimes were foreseeable.[103] Thirty years later, in 2016, the UK Supreme Court overturned this position, pointing out that accomplices must possess *at least* knowledge of the crime being committed, so mere foreseeability must be treated as evidence of their willing assistance. At the same time, they must not be convicted of crimes falling outside of the agreement as joint perpetrators, for this is a misuse of the term.[104]

D. Planning

'Planning' usually focuses on the responsibility of high-level civil and military commanders.[105] The Tokyo and Nuremberg Charters mentioned 'planning' in relation to crimes against peace only.[106] The ICTY, the ICTR

[99] For a comparative treatment of these forms of participation in domestic law, see Ch 2 and Appendix I.

[100] *Pinkerton v US* (1946) 328 US 640; van Sliedregt (n 14) 132.

[101] G Fletcher, *Rethinking Criminal Law* (Boston, MA, Little, Brown, 1978) 634 et seq.

[102] A Ashworth, *Principles of Criminal Law*, 2nd edn (Oxford, Clarendon, 1995); 429; See also JC Smith and B Hogan, *Criminal Law*, 10th edn (London, Butterworths, 2002) 162.

[103] *Chan Wing-Siu v The Queen* (1985) AC 168.

[104] *R v Jogee* [2016] UKSC 8; *Ruddock v The Queen* (Jamaica) [2016] UKPC 7.

[105] S Manacorda, 'Case Note' in A Cassese (ed), *The Oxford Companion to International Criminal Justice* (Oxford, Oxford University Press, 2009) 456.

[106] Nuremberg Charter, art 6(a); Tokyo Charter, art 5(a).

and SCSL Charters and the ECCC Law[107] include planning along with the other forms of complicity applicable to all crimes within the jurisdiction of the respective court or tribunal. The Rome Statute does not mention 'planning' in the forms of participation under Article 25(3).[108]

'Planning' implies 'that one or several persons contemplate designing the commission of a crime at both the preparation and execution phases'.[109] The Trial Chamber in *Akayesu* clarified that in order for a person to incur liability under the heading of 'planning', the crime that had been planned must have been executed.[110] This clarification distanced planning from the notion of conspiracy, which is similar to planning in that it criminalises preparatory steps for the commission of the crime. The difference between the two concepts is that conspiracy is an inchoate offence, completed once the preparatory steps are undertaken, while planning is a form of responsibility dependent on the commission of the crime towards which it is directed.

To attract responsibility for planning, the person other than the planner, who is considered an actual perpetrator, must be acting in furtherance of a plan.[111] Thus, there must be a connection between the plan and the crime, it being sufficient that planning was a factor substantially contributing to criminal conduct.[112] In other words, the level of involvement of the accused in the planning of the crime must have been sufficiently 'substantial'.[113] The SCSL Appeals Chamber gave important practical guidance in assessing whether the accused's acts amount to a substantial contribution to attract liability for planning; it has to be done on a case-by-case basis in the light of evidence as a whole.[114]

[107] The ECCC Trial Chamber highlighted that from the modes of responsibility mentioned in art 29 of the ECCC Law, only planning and superior responsibility were not covered by the general provisions of the domestic criminal code applicable at the time of the commission of the crimes by Khmer Rouge. 'Planning' was, however, criminalised by specific provisions of this code, meaning criminalization of such conduct was foreseeable to the accused. *Duch* Trial Judgment (n 32) para 474.

[108] 'Planning' resembled the contentious notion of 'conspiracy' that the drafters of the Rome Statute attempted to avoid. See Ch 5.I.D.

[109] *Prosecutor v Akayesu*, ICTR Case No 96-4-T, Trial Chamber Judgment, 2 September 1998, para 480; *Prosecutor v Blaskić*, ICTY Case No IT-95-14-T, Trial Judgment, 3 March 2000 ('*Blaskić* Trial Judgment'), para 279; *Prosecutor v Sesay, Kallon and Gbao*, SCSL-04-15-T, Trial Judgment, 2 March 2009, para 268. In *Kordić and Čerkez*, the Appeals Chamber adopted a slightly different definition, later reproduced by the ECCC: 'The *actus reus* of "planning" requires that one or more persons design the criminal conduct constituting one or more statutory crimes that are later perpetrated.' See *Prosecutor v Kordić and Čerkez*, ICTY Case No IT-95-14/2-A, Appeal Judgment, 17 December 2004 ('*Kordić and Čerkez* Appeal Judgment'), para 27; *Duch* Trial Judgment (n 32) para 518.

[110] *Akayesu* Trial Judgment (n 109) para 473.

[111] *Blaskić* Trial Judgment (n 109) para 278.

[112] *Kordić and Čerkez* Appeal Judgment (n 109) para 26.

[113] *Prosecutor v Bagilishema*, ICTR Case No 95-1A-T, Trial Judgment, 7 June 2001 ('*Bagilishema* Trial Judgment'), para 30; Mettraux (n 14) 280.

[114] *Prosecutor v Taylor*, SCSL-03-1-A, Appeal Judgment, 26 September 2013, para 550; *Prosecutor v Sesay, Kallon and Gbao* ('*RUF* Case'), SCSL-04-15-A, Appeal Judgment, 26 October 2009, para 769.

The fault requirement for this mode of responsibility entails the intent to plan the commission of a crime or, at a minimum, the awareness of the substantial likelihood that a crime will be committed in the execution of the acts or omissions planned.[115] The ECCC found Nuon Chea responsible for planning the movement of population out of Phnom Penh—a plan that resulted in the commission of crimes against humanity, such as murder and persecution. Nuon Chea and other members of the Central and Standing Committees designed a plan to forcibly transfer the population of Phnom Penh with the knowledge that such activity in the past had caused discriminatory violence and suffering. The Trial Chamber was satisfied that NUON Chea intended, or at a minimum was aware of the substantial likelihood, that crimes would be committed upon the execution of the plan for the mass evacuation of people.[116]

The *Dragomir Milošević* case illustrates the importance of an individual assessment of the mode of liability together with the facts. In this case, the Appeals Chamber acquitted the accused of responsibility for planning the campaign of sniping and shelling of civilians in Sarajevo because the evidence as to whether he orchestrated each and every incident, which he allegedly planned, was lacking.[117] While the conviction for planning failed, the appellate judges found the same facts to constitute a sufficient basis to support a conviction for ordering.[118] The Appeals Chamber found that the accused personally ordered the deployment and distribution between different brigades of air modified bombs, a highly inaccurate weapon with a high explosive force. He also ordered the construction of launchers for these weapons.[119]

Planning a crime also serves as an aggravating factor when sentencing the actual perpetrator.[120]

E. Instigating

'Instigation' presupposes 'urging, encouraging, or prompting' another person to commit a crime.[121] Instigation can take the form of a positive act or an omission so long as it can be established that the accused's conduct

[115] *Kordić and Čerkez* Appeal Judgment (n 109) paras 29, 31; *D Milošević* Appeal Judgment (n 27) para 268; *Prosecutor v Nuon Chea and Khieu Samphan*, ECCC Case No 001/18-07-2007/ECCC/TC, Trial Judgment, 7 August 2014 ('*Chea et al* Trial Judgment') para 882.

[116] *Chea et al* Trial Judgment (n 115) paras 880, 882.

[117] *D Milošević* Appeal Judgment (n 27) para 268.

[118] ibid, para 273.

[119] ibid, para 272.

[120] Mettraux (n 14) 280.

[121] *Prosecutor v Semanza*, ICTR Case No 97-20-T, Trial Judgment, 15 May 2003 ('*Semanza* Trial Judgment'), para 381, *Akayesu* Trial Judgment (n 109) para 482; *Orić* Trial Judgment (n 44) para 270; *Kordić and Čerkez* Appeal Judgment (n 109) para 27; *Krstić* Trial Judgment (n 93) para 601.

had an effect on the perpetrator.[122] It is not necessary that these actions be perpetrated in public or take any particular form.[123] Several Trial and Appeals Chambers have held that there must be a causal relationship between the act of instigation and the commission of the crime.[124] This statement is qualified by the explanation that the contribution of the accused does not need to be a *conditio sine qua non* for the crime to occur; it is sufficient to show that his conduct was a contributing factor to the conduct of the other person(s).[125]

The requirement of a causal relationship between the act of instigation and the commission of the crime stands in contrast to the requirements for the other forms of complicity—planning, ordering, and aiding and abetting—that do not require such a causal relationship according to the wording adopted by the ad hoc tribunals.[126] This disparity shows some lack of understanding of the appropriate standard of causation for complicity.[127] Arguably the *sine qua non* test is not applicable to complicity because any form of complicity entails influencing the voluntary conduct of another person. As such, it cannot be reasonably said that an accomplice is a necessary prerequisite for harm caused by the primary perpetrator; rather, he affects the behaviour of the principal.[128] Likewise, causation in the strict sense of the word appears to be applicable only to the events happening in the physical world and not to the actions of others. The causal chain is broken when interrupted by the free choice of an individual, even one acting under an accomplice's influence.[129] Consequently, singling out 'instigation' as the only form of complicity requiring a causal relationship to the crime appears to be unreasonable. Instigation, like all other forms of complicity, affects the freely chosen acts by other individuals—primary perpetrators. It cannot be said that that an act of an instigator (or, equally, an aider and abettor, planner or order giver) *causes* the crime to occur in the same way as the primary perpetrator brings about the offence in the real world. Causation may be extended to complicity, but its content must be modified.

[122] *Blaskić* Trial Judgment (n 109) para 270; *Duch* Trial Judgment (n 32) para 522.

[123] *Prosecutor v Akayesu*, ICTR Case No 96-4-A, Appeal Judgment, 1 June 2001 ('*Akayesu* Appeal Judgment'), paras 478–82; *Blaskić* Trial Judgment (n 109) para 270.

[124] *Blaskić* Trial Judgment (n 109) para 278; *Bagilishema* Trial Judgment (n 113) para 30; *Semanza* Trial Judgment (n 121) para 381.

[125] *Kordić and Čerkez* Appeal Judgment (n 109) para 27; *Prosecutor v Kvočka*, ICTY Case No IT-98-30/1-T, Trial Judgment, 2 November 2001 ('*Kvočka* Trial Judgment'), para 252; *Prosecutor v Kordić and Čerkez*, ICTY Case No IT-95-14/2-T, Trial Judgment, 26 February 2001 ('*Kordić and Čerkez* Trial Judgment'), para 387; van Sliedregt (n 14) 104.

[126] *Prosecutor v Furundžija*, ICTY Case No IT-95-17/1-T, Trial Judgment, 10 December 1998, para 233; *Simić* Appeal Judgment (n 27) para 85; *Blaskić* Appeal Judgment (n 27) para 48.

[127] Mettraux (n 14) 281.

[128] For a discussion of causation in complicity, see section II.B below.

[129] SH Kadish, 'Complicity, Cause and Blame: A Study in the Interpretation of Doctrine' (1985) 73(2) *California Law Review* 334.

The *Orić* Trial Chamber seems to have adopted a broad view on the question of causation in cases of complicity. It held that the commission of the crime may depend on a variety of activities and circumstances, and it suffices to prove that the conduct of the accused was a substantially contributing factor.[130] The Trial Chamber made a noteworthy distinction between aiding and abetting and instigating. Persuasion or a strong encouragement by an instigator may contribute to the final determination of the principal perpetrator to commit a crime, while further encouragement or moral support in cases when the principal has definitely decided to commit a crime 'may *merely*, though still, qualify as aiding and abetting' (emphasis added).[131] However, this interpretation of the difference between aiding and abetting and instigating does not seem to find support in international jurisprudence. The *Orić* Trial Chamber further clarified: 'not any contributing factor can suffice for instigation, as it must be a substantial one, on the other hand, it need not necessarily have direct effect, as prompting another to commit a crime can also be procured by means of an intermediary'.[132]

When it comes to the fault requirement, it is necessary that the accused directly intended to provoke the commission of the crime[133] or was aware of the substantial likelihood that the commission of a crime would be a probable consequence of his acts.[134] The Trial Chamber in *Orić* clarified that the intention has two components: a cognitive element of knowledge and a volitional element of acceptance.[135] The first element is present when the accused is aware of the influencing effect of his actions on the principal perpetrator and is aware of, and agrees to, the intentional completion of the principal crime.[136] The second volitional element of intent is met when the instigator accepts the occurrence of the crime with the knowledge the commission of the crime will more likely than not result from his conduct.[137]

130 *Orić* Trial Judgment (n 44) para 274.

131 ibid, para 271 See also van Sliedregt (n 14) 105.

132 *Orić* Trial Judgment (n 44) para 276.

133 *Kordić and Čerkez* Trial Judgment (n 125) para 387.

134 *Kvočka* Trial Judgment (n 125) para 282; *Akayesu* Trial Judgment (n 109) para 482; *Prosecutor v Simeon Nchamihigo*, ICTR, Case No 2001-63-A, Appeal Judgment 18 March 2010 ('*Nchamihigo* Appeal Judgment'), para 62.

135 *Orić* Trial Judgment (n 44) para 279. See also van Sliedregt (n 14) 104.

136 ibid.

137 ibid.

F. Ordering

'Ordering' entails 'a person in a position of authority using that position to convince another to commit an offence'.[138] Ordering requires a positive act from the person in the position of authority.[139] The authority may be reasonably implied from the circumstances.[140] The issue of the probative value of the inferences was at stake in the *Galić* appeal case, in which the Appeals Chamber held that an omission cannot constitute an act of ordering per se, but failures to act may form circumstantial evidence to prove the mode of liability of ordering.[141] Thus, Galić's responsibility for ordering the shelling of civilians in the occupied Sarajevo was not inferred from the fact that he failed to act and his omission constituted an order. Instead, his multiple failures to act in response to the attacks over a period of 23 months served as circumstantial evidence for the mode of liability of ordering.[142] In contrast, in *Kalimanzira*, the Appeals Chamber answered in the negative the question of whether the assistance in providing armed reinforcements substantially contributing to the overall attack served as circumstantial proof that the accused ordered the attack.[143] It concluded that despite the fact that Kalimanzira had authority over the attackers and thus had the possibility to order the attack, it was not the only reasonable inference following from the surrounding circumstances.[144]

The ECCC found that Nuon Chea together with Pol Pot exercised ultimate decision-making power over the Party; thus, he used his authority to instruct lower-level Khmer Rouge cadres and soldiers to commit crimes of murder, extermination, political persecution and the other inhumane acts of forced transfer and attacks against human dignity.[145] In contrast, the co-accused in the same case—KHIEU Samphan—was not found to be responsible under the heading of 'ordering' because the Trial Chamber did not find evidence that he issued orders implemented by others. KHIEU

[138] *Akayesu* Trial Judgment (n 109) para 483 as cited in Mettraux (n 14) 270; *Prosecutor v Đorđević*, ICTY Case No IT-05-87/1-T, Trial Judgment, 23 February 2011 ('*Đorđević* Trial Judgment'), para 1871; *Prosecutor v Galić*, ICTY Case No IT-98-29-A, Appeal Judgment, 30 November 2006 ('*Galić* Appeal Judgment'), para 176; *Duch* Trial Judgment (n 32) ECCC, para 527.

[139] *Galić* Appeal Judgment (n 138) para 176; *Blaskić* Appeal Judgment (n 27) para 660.

[140] *Đorđević* Trial Judgment (n 138) para 1871; *Prosecutor v Brđanin*, ICTY Case No 99-36-T, Trial Judgment, 1 September 2004 ('*Brđanin* Trial Judgment'), para 270.

[141] *Galić* Appeal Judgment (n 138) para 177.

[142] *Prosecutor v Galić*, ICTY Case No IT-98-29-T, Trial Judgment, 5 December 2003, para 749; *Galić* Appeal Judgment (n 138) para 177.

[143] *Prosecutor v Kalimanzira*, ICTR Case No 05-88-A, Appeal Judgment, 20 October 2010 ('*Kalimanzira* Appeal Judgment'), paras.208 and 213.

[144] ibid, paras.211 and 213.

[145] *Chea et al* Trial Judgment (n 115) para 884.

Samphan was not part of the military structure, so he did not have the sufficient military authority to instruct others to commit crimes.[146]

Neither the form of the order (explicit or implicit) nor its legality is a decisive factor attracting the liability for ordering a crime.[147] With regard to the fault requirement, the person ordering must have the same state of mind as that required for the crime that he orders.[148] In addition, it is necessary that the order giver is aware of the substantial likelihood that a crime would be committed as a consequence of the execution or implementation of the order.[149] ICTY and ICTR case law is not clear on whether responsibility follows from the order that was not implemented or an instigation that failed.[150] If one adopts the view of complicity as derivative in nature, it seems that the underlying offence has to occur or at least be attempted.[151]

'Ordering' is the form of complicity that is especially similar to superior responsibility.[152] The difference between these two forms of responsibility is that no formal superior–subordinate relationship is required for a finding of 'ordering' so long as it is demonstrated that the accused possessed the authority to order.[153] This is in contrast to superior responsibility, which is only applicable if the superior has effective control over the persons committing underlying violations, in the sense of having the ability to prevent and punish these violations.[154] The Appeals Chamber in *Semanza* stressed the formality of the super–subordinate relationship as the distinguishing factor between the two forms of responsibility—all that is required for 'ordering' is the implied existence of a superior–subordinate relationship.[155] The *Gacumbitsi* Appeal Chamber further confirmed this statement by holding that the superior–subordinate relationship under Article 6(3) of the ICTR Statute is characterised by effective control.[156] It is peculiar that in the case law of the ICTR, 'ordering' is

[146] ibid, para 1005.

[147] *Blaskić* Trial Judgment (n 109) para 281; see also Cassese (n 22) 230; Mettraux (n 14) 282.

[148] *Brđanin* Trial Judgment (n 140) para 270.

[149] *Đorđević* Trial Judgment (n 138) para 1872; *Brđanin* Trial Judgment (n 140) para 270; *Blaskić* Appeal Judgment (n 27) para 42; *Duch* Trial Judgment (n 32) para 528.

[150] Van Sliedregt (n 14) 106.

[151] Van Sliedregt and Cryer support conceptualising ordering in such a way as to require the execution of the order. See van Sliedregt (n 14) 106; Cryer et al (n 21) 379.

[152] ICTY Statute, art 7(3); ICTR Statute, art 6(3); SCSL Statute, art 6(3); and ECCC Law, art 29(3).

[153] *Kordić and Čerkez* Trial Judgment (n 125) para 388.

[154] *Prosecutor v Delalić et al* ('*Čelebići* Trial Judgment') ICTY Case No IT-96-21-T, 16 November 1998, para 387; *Prosecutor v Kunarac*, ICTY Case No IT-96-23-T& IT-96-23/1-T, Trial Judgment, 22 February 2001 ('*Kunarac* Trial Judgment'), para 399.

[155] *Prosecutor v Semanza*, ICTR Case No 97-20-A, Appeal Judgment, 20 May 2005 ('*Semanza* Appeal Judgment'), para 361.

[156] *Gacumbitsi* Appeal Judgment (n 52) para 182; van Sliedregt (n 14) 106.

treated as a mode of participation inferior to 'committing'. The *Gacumbitsi*, the Appeal Chamber held:

> [The accused] did not simply 'order' or 'plan' genocide from a distance and leave it to others to ensure that his orders and plans were carried out ... Rather, he was present at the crime scene to supervise and direct the massacre, and participated in it actively ... and this constitutes 'committing' genocide.[157]

G. Aiding and Abetting

The early judgments of *Tadić* and *Furundžija* interpreted 'aiding and abetting' by relying heavily on the case law produced by the post-Nuremberg war crimes trials and the ILC Draft Code.[158] These interpretations proved to be authoritative, with subsequent judgments merely clarifying the elements set out by *Tadić* and *Furundžija*.[159]

An aider or abettor is one who provides 'practical assistance, encouragement, or moral support' to the principal.[160] These actions must have had a substantial effect on the perpetration of a crime.[161] The *Tadić* Trial Chamber borrowed this element of aiding and abetting from the formulation of the ILC Draft Code, which called for the criminal responsibility of the individual who 'knowingly aids, abets or otherwise assists, directly and substantially, in the commission of such a crime'.[162] The ILC Commentary does not define 'substantially', but does provide a hint—assistance of the accomplice must facilitate the commission of a crime in some *significant* way.[163] Based on these considerations, the *Tadić* Chamber clarified that a substantial contribution requirement presupposes a contribution that in fact has an effect on the commission of the crime.[164] Later jurisprudence underlined that determining whether an act or omission had a substantial effect on the commission of a crime is a fact-based inquiry.[165] This statement underlines the practical difficulty of measuring the effect of the contribution.

[157] ibid, para 61.

[158] Boas, Bischoff and Reid (n 11) 307; van Sliedregt (n 14) 121.

[159] Boas, Bischoff and Reid (n 11) 303–04.

[160] *Furundžija* Trial Judgment (n 126) para 235; *Prosecutor v Delalić et al (Čelebići)* ICTY Case No IT-96-21-A, Appeal Judgment, 20 February 2001, para 35; *Tadić* Appeal Judgment (n 48) para 229; *Duch* Trial Judgment (n 32) ECCC, para 533.

[161] *Furundžija* Trial Judgment (n 126) para 223, 224, 249; *Blaskić* Appeal Judgment (n 27) para 48 as discussed by Mettraux (n 14) 284; Cassese (n 22) 188.

[162] ILC Draft Code 1996, art 2(3)(d).

[163] ILC Commentary to the Draft Code 1996, at 21, para 11.

[164] *Tadić* Trial Judgment (n 26) para 688.

[165] *Prosecutor v Mrkšić and Šljivančanin*, ICTY Case No T-95-13/1-A, Appeal Judgment, 5 May 2009 ('*Šljivančanin* Appeal Judgment'), para 200; *Prosecutor v Popović et al*, ICTY Case No 05-88-T, Appeal Judgment, 30 January 2015 ('*Popović et al* Appeal Judgment'), para 1741.

The *Furundžija* Chamber further elaborated on the effect of assistance, holding that the acts of the accomplice need not 'bear a causal relationship to, or be a *conditio sine qua non* for, those of the principal'.[166] This finding underlines the derivative nature of aiding and abetting: an accomplice can only influence the conduct of the principal perpetrator to a certain extent, as the final decision to commit or not to commit a crime rests with the perpetrator and not with the accomplice.[167]

There is a slight semantic difference between the terms 'aiding' and 'abetting'. Aiding has been described by international criminal tribunals as meaning 'giving somebody assistance', whereas 'abetting' stands for 'facilitating the commission of an act by being sympathetic thereto'.[168] The contribution of the aider or abettor may be provided at any stage of a criminal process, including planning, preparation and execution.[169]

Assistance may occur before, during or after the commission of the crime.[170] However, ex post facto aiding and abetting only falls within the scope of this provision if there was a prior agreement between the principal and the person who subsequently aids and abets at the time of the planning, preparation and execution of the crime.[171] Assistance may take the form of either a positive act or an omission. Indeed, mere presence at the scene of the crime could constitute aiding and abetting where 'it is demonstrated to have significant encouraging effect on the principal offender'.[172] Aiding or abetting may manifest itself in a culpable omission 'provided this failure to act had a decisive effect on the commission of the crime and that it was coupled with the requisite *mens rea*'.[173] However, the *Blaškić* Appeals Chamber stressed that the circumstances of a given case

[166] *Furundžija* Trial Judgment (n 126) para 233. See also *Prosecutor v Simić et al*, ICTY Case No IT-95-9-A, Appeal Judgment, 28 November 2006, para 85; *Blaskić* Appeal Judgment (n 27) para 48; Boas, Bischoff and Reid (n 11) 318.

[167] It seems that the judges in this instance use 'causation' in a narrow sense of the word, meaning causing events in the physical world. Complicity is linked to the voluntary acts of individuals rather than directly to the physical events. Causation may be the term applicable to complicity, but its scope must be understood as extended. Thus, when Sliedregt discussed different formulas in respect of the 'causation requirement' of aiding and abetting—namely 'substantial effect or 'substantial contribution'—she presumably referred to causation in a broader sense as applicable to complicity. Van Sliedregt (n 14) For more discussion on causation, see section II.B.

[168] *Kvočka* Trial Judgment (n 125) para 254; *Akayesu* Trial Judgment (n 109) para 484.

[169] *Tadić* Trial Judgment (n 26) para 677.

[170] *Blaskić* Appeal Judgment (n 27) para 48; *Prosecutor v Aleksovski*, Trial Judgment, ICTY Case IT-95-14/1-T, 25 June 1999 ('*Aleksovski* Trial Judgment'), para 62.

[171] *Prosecutor v Blagoević and Jokić*, ICTY Case No IT-02-60, Trial Judgment, 17 January 2005 ('*Blagoević* Trial Judgment'), para 731. See also W Schabas, *The International Criminal Court: A Commentary on the Rome Statute* (Oxford, Oxford University Press, 2010) 435.

[172] *Prosecutor v Vasiljević*, ICTY Case No IT-98-32-T, Trial Judgment, 29 November 2002 ('*Vasiljević* Trial Judgment'), para 70; *Furundžija* Trial Judgment (n 126) para 232.

[173] *Blaskić* Trial Judgment (n 109) para 284.

determine whether an omission may constitute the actus reus of aiding and abetting.[174]

In *Furundžija*, the position of the accused as a local commander led the judges to conclude that he was guilty of aiding and abetting rape by virtue of merely being present in the room because his position of authority had an encouraging effect.[175] In the *Šljivančanin* case, in the view of the Appeals Chamber, the failure of the accused to prevent the implementation of the unlawful order satisfied all the requirements for a conviction for aiding and abetting murder by omission.[176] The judges in this case held that, regardless of the fact that Šljivančanin no longer exercised de jure authority over the military police, his duty to protect the prisoners of war required him to order the police not to withdraw from the hospital where the prisoners were kept.[177] The Appeals Chamber employed largely inferential analysis suggesting that 'had he ordered the military police not to withdraw, these troops may well have, in effect, obeyed his order to remain there'.[178] In *Popović et al*, the judges found that the local commander Vinko Pandurević substantially contributed to the murder of the prisoners by failing to transfer them to a safe location.[179] In this instance, what mattered was the availability of means to protect prisoners, and both Chambers rejected as speculative Pandurević's argument that his intervention would have made no difference.[180]

With regard to the fault requirement, it is not necessary that the accomplices share the mens rea of the principal perpetrator,[181] it being sufficient that he knows of the essential elements of the crime, including the mens rea of the actual perpetrator, and takes 'the conscious decision to act in the knowledge that he thereby supports the commission of the crime'.[182] Furthermore, it must be shown that the aider and abettor 'knew (in the sense he was aware) that his own acts assisted the commission of the specific crime in question by the principal offender'.[183] The aider and abettor need not know the precise crime that was intended and which in the event was committed—awareness that one of a number of crimes will probably

[174] *Blaskić* Appeal Judgment (n 27) para 47.
[175] *Furundžija* Trial Judgment (n 126) para 275.
[176] *Šljivančanin* Appeal Judgment (n 165) paras 101–103.
[177] ibid, paras 92 and 98.
[178] ibid, para 93.
[179] *Popović et al* Appeal Judgment (n 165) para 1745.
[180] ibid, para 1744.
[181] *Furundžija* Trial Judgment (n 126) para 245; *Vasiljević* Appeal Judgment (n 27) para 102; *Blaskić* Appeal Judgment (n 27) para 49.
[182] *Kunarac* Trial Judgment (n 154) para 392; *Orić* Trial Judgment (n 44) paras.286–88. See also van Sliedregt (n 14) 122–23; Boas, Bischoff and Reid (n 11) 321.
[183] *Vasiljević* Trial Judgment (n 172) para 71; *Prosecutor v Aleksovski*, ICTY Case IT-95-14/1-A, Appeal Judgment, 24 March 2000 ('*Aleksovski* Appeal Judgment'); *Furundžija* Trial Judgment (n 126) para 245.

be committed is sufficient.[184] Vinko Pandurević during the *Popović et al* appeal argued that this test implies the accused knowing that at least one of the crimes will be committed. The Appeals Chamber disagreed, noting that the correct standard is merely the awareness that one of *a number* of crimes will likely be committed.[185]

One may suggest that by not requiring precise knowledge about the crime to be committed, the judges are inappropriately lowering the fault requirement for aiding and abetting to the level of recklessness or risk-taking.[186] However, it appears practically impossible to demand accomplices to possess the exact knowledge about the future crime committed by someone else. Accepting individual action as autonomous has implications: it is only fair to demand the accomplice to intend to assist *and* have the awareness that one of a range of offences might be committed as a result. The second leg of the fault requirement is enhanced by the need to prove intent to support the crime.

When it comes to the specific intent crimes, such as genocide and persecution, the position is that the aider and abettor does not need to share the intent of the principal perpetrator, but does need to be aware of it.[187] Judge Shahabuddeen in his partial dissenting opinion in *Krstić* highlighted the difference between the intent of the perpetrator and the intent of the aider and abettor in relation to the crime of genocide—the former intends to commit genocide, while the latter intends to provide means by which the perpetrator, if he wishes, can realise his intent to commit genocide.[188]

In the view of some Trial and Appeals Chambers, the fact that the aider and abettor may not have shared the intent of the principal offender generally lessens his culpability for sentencing purposes.[189] However, a number of considerations usually affect the judges' reasoning at sentencing—the mode of participation of the accused being just one of them.[190]

The last remark in this section is on the novel interpretation of the conduct requirement of aiding and abetting as containing the element of the

[184] *Furundžija* Trial Judgment (n 126) para 246.

[185] *Popović et al* Appeal Judgment (n 165) paras 1749, 1751.

[186] J Stewart, 'The End of "Modes of Liability" for International Crimes' (2012) 25 *Leiden Journal of International Law* 169, 193.

[187] *Krstić* Appeal Judgment (n 27) para 140; *Vasiljević* Appeal Judgment (n 27) para 142; *Krnojelac* Appeal Judgment (n 31) para 489. See also Boas, Bischoff and Reid (n 11) 325.

[188] *Krstić* Appeal Judgment (n 27) Partial Dissenting Opinion of Judge Shahabuddeen, para 66, as cited in Boas, Bischoff and Reid (n 11) 320.

[189] *Vasiljević* Appeal Judgment (n 27) paras 181–82; *Krstić* Appeal Judgment (n 27) para 268; *Prosecutor v Kajelijeli*, ICTR Case No 98-44A-T, Trial Judgment, 1 December 2003, para 963.

[190] To that effect, the *Šljivančanin* Appeals Chamber acknowledged the practice of treating aiding and abetting as a lower form of liability that attracts a lesser sentence. However, the Chamber clarified that the gravity of the underlying crimes remains an important consideration in order to reflect the totality of the criminal conduct. *Šljivančanin* Appeal Judgment (n 165) para 407.

'specific direction'. This contentious point, which emerged in the ICTY jurisprudence in 2013 and was subsequently abandoned, stirred up a lot of debate as to the correct legal test for an accomplice liability in international criminal law.[191]

The origins of the 'specific direction' issue can be found in the early ICTY jurisprudence. According to the ILC, the contribution of an aider and abettor need not only be 'substantial', as discussed above, but also 'direct'.[192] The ILC Commentary does not explain the exact meaning of 'direct' contribution. This particular qualifier has caused some confusion in the case law of the ad hoc tribunals from their creation. The *Tadić* Trial Chamber seems to have embraced this requirement, treating the accused as culpable where his participation 'directly and substantially affected the commission of the offence'.[193] However, in *Furundžija*, the court rejected the term 'direct' in qualifying the proximity of the assistance and the principal act as misleading because 'it may imply that assistance needs to be tangible, or to have a causal effect on the crime'.[194]

The issue of the direction of the contribution by the accused resurfaced in early 2013 when the ICTY Appeals Chamber returned to the question in *Perišić*, when it interpreted the actus reus of aiding and abetting as requiring that the assistance is specifically directed towards the crimes.[195] The justification for this additional element was the need to address the situations where the accused's individual assistance is remote from the actions of principal perpetrators or when such assistance could be used for both lawful and unlawful activities.[196] In such circumstances, the Chamber reasoned, it is necessary to establish 'a *direct link* between the aid provided by an accused individual and the relevant crimes committed by principal perpetrators' (emphasis added).[197] In line with this restrictive formulation of accessory liability, the Appeals Chamber overturned Perišić's conviction for aiding and abetting the Army of the Republika Srpska (VRS) in his capacity as Chief of the Yugoslav Army General Staff. This was notwithstanding the fact that Perišić, as the most senior figure in the Yugoslav Army, knowingly provided logistical and personnel assistance to the VRS, which was committing crimes in Sarajevo and Srebrenica.[198]

[191] For an extended discussion, see M Aksenova, 'The Specific Requirement for Aiding and Abetting: A Call for Revisiting Comparative Criminal Law' (2015) 4(1) *Cambridge Journal of International and Comparative Law* 88.

[192] ILC Commentary to the Draft Code 1996, at 21, para 11.

[193] *Tadić* Trial Judgment (n 26) para 692. Consequently, the *Tadić* Appeal Chamber later used the 'specific direction' criterion to delimit aiding and abetting and participation in the joint criminal enterprise. See *Tadić* Appeal Judgment (n 48) para 229.

[194] *Furundžija* Trial Judgment (n 126) para 232.

[195] *Prosecutor v Perišić*, ICTY Case No 04-81-A, Appeal Judgment, 28 February 2013, para 44.

[196] ibid, paras 44 and 73.

[197] ibid, para 44.

[198] ibid, paras 2, 62 and 68.

The rationale for the acquittal in *Perišić* was the Chamber's reluctance to find that the accused's assistance was specifically directed towards supporting the criminal activities and not just geared towards the general war effort.[199] In particular, the VRS was conceptualised as 'an army fighting a war' rather than an organisation whose actions were criminal per se.[200] The judges thus concluded that since not all of the VRS's activities were criminal in nature, the policy of providing assistance to the VRS's general war effort did not, in itself, demonstrate that assistance facilitated by Perišić was specifically directed to aid the crimes.[201]

The *Perišić* appellate panel justified its explicit consideration of the 'specific direction' issue on two main grounds. First, the judges claimed that they did not diverge from, but merely clarified the *Tadić* formula for aiding and abetting, which already contains the contentious element.[202] In so deciding, the *Perišić* Appeals Chamber had to dismiss a previous pronouncement made in the *Šljivančanin* Appeal judgment that '"specific direction" is not an essential ingredient of the actus reus of aiding and abetting'.[203] The *Perišić* Appeals Chamber found feeble arguments to support the dismissal of the *Šljivančanin* definition: it held that in *Šljivančanin*, the reference to the 'specific direction' was erroneously made in the context of the mens rea element of aiding and abetting, and not the actus reus where it rightfully belonged. Second, the Chamber held that the issue was mentioned only in passing and therefore did not amount to 'careful consideration' that warrants a departure from the previous case law.[204]

By arguing that the 'specific direction' element has been part of the previous jurisprudence and the *Šljivančanin* judgment rejecting it does not alter this practice, the *Perišić* Appeals Chamber avoided the situation whereby it would have to furnish 'cogent reasons in the interests of justice' for departing from the previous precedents.[205] The established rule is that the Appeals Chamber should follow its previous decisions for the reasons of legal certainty and predictability, unless the previous decision has been decided on the basis of a wrong legal principle or the judges were ill-informed about the applicable law.[206]

The second reason for expressly considering the specific direction in *Perišić* was the alleged lack of treatment of the issue in the jurisprudence of the ad hoc tribunals. This peculiarity was explained 'by the fact that prior convictions for aiding and abetting entered or affirmed by the Appeals

[199] ibid.
[200] ibid, para 53.
[201] ibid.
[202] ibid, paras 27, 32.
[203] *Šljivančanin* Appeal Judgment (n 165) para 159.
[204] *Perišić* Appeal Judgment (n 195) paras 33, 34.
[205] *Aleksovski* Appeal Judgment (n 183) para 107.
[206] ibid. paras 107–08.

Chamber involved relevant acts geographically or otherwise proximate to, and thus not remote from, the crimes of principal perpetrators'.[207] This is to some extent tenuous because comparable cases have been before the ICTY Appeals Chamber in the past. For example, in *Brđanin*, the accused—a leading political figure in the Autonomous Region of Krajina and the President of the Crisis Staff—was found guilty of aiding and abetting due to the decisions he took in his official capacity having a substantial effect on the commission of the charged acts. Due to his general leadership role, Brđanin's proximity to the specific crimes is questionable. However, a discussion about the specific direction does not appear in this judgment.

The 'specific direction' test also appeared in the *Stanišić and Simatović* trial judgment.[208] The accused in this case organised and directed a special unit within the Serbian state security service, which they knew committed crimes of murder, deportation, forcible transfer, and persecution.[209] However, the Trial Chamber fell short of declaring this unit a criminal organisation, despite the fact that it operated covertly and was engaged in numerous crimes.[210] The extensive involvement of the accused with the operation of the unit led the judges to conclude that their contributions assisted the commission of the crimes by the unit members.[211] Yet, the fact that the accused were not physically present in the field during operations resulted in the finding that their assistance may have been directed towards the legitimate military objective of establishing and maintaining Serb control and not the criminal goals.[212]

Perišić and *Stanišić and Simatović* were reversed shortly afterwards. Both the SCSL and the ICTY revisited the issue of the specific direction as an element of aiding and abetting a few times following the contested judgments. First, the SCSL in the *Taylor* appeal judgment rejected the requirement of specific direction.[213] The Appeals Chamber concluded that the definition of the actus reus of aiding and abetting under customary international law is established by the substantial effect on the crimes, not the particular manner in which such assistance is provided.[214] The *Taylor* appellate panel found the acts of the accused to have a substantial effect on the commission of the crime, thereby establishing a sufficient causal link. It therefore saw no reason to depart from the settled principles of law and introduce the novel element of the specific direction in the definition

[207] *Perišić* Appeal Judgment (n 195) para 38.
[208] *Prosecutor v Stanišić and Simatović*, ICTY Case No IT-03-69-T, Trial Judgment, 30 May 2013 ('*Stanišić and Simatović* Trial Judgment'), para 2360.
[209] ibid, paras 2318, 2323.
[210] ibid, paras 1421, 1423.
[211] ibid, para 2359.
[212] ibid, para 2360.
[213] *Taylor* Appeal Judgment (n 114) para 486.
[214] ibid, para 475.

of actus reus of aiding and abetting.[215] The judges further noted that the question of physical proximity between the accused and the crimes may be relevant on a case-by-case basis, but it is not a legal requirement.[216] The *Taylor* Appeals Chamber stressed that the element of specific direction discussed in *Perišić* could be inferred from the *Tadić* appeal judgment, which purported to distinguish aiding and abetting liability from the joint criminal enterprise liability rather than establish the elements of aiding and abetting under customary international law.[217]

Second, the appeal judgment rendered by the ICTY in *Šainović et al* in early 2014 also reversed the direction of the *Perišić* Appeals Chamber.[218] The defence team of Vladimir Lazarević in the *Šainović et al* case contested his conviction for aiding and abetting deportation and forcible transfer on the basis of the lack of determination by the Trial Chamber as to whether his alleged acts and omissions were specifically directed to assist the commission of these crimes.[219] The majority of the Appeals Chamber disagreed with the pronouncement in *Perišić* that the previous jurisprudence of the ICTY does not diverge on the issue of the specific direction.[220] On the contrary, the *Šainović et al* judges concluded that there is a clear divergence on the matter between the *Perišić* and the *Šljivančanin* appeal judgments.[221] The *Šainović et al* judges solved the legal conundrum by assessing where the law stands on the issue of the specific direction.[222] Jurisprudence of the ad hoc tribunals and post-Second World War cases begged for the conclusion that specific direction is not an element of aiding and abetting liability under customary international law or the Statute of the ICTY.[223] The Appeals Chamber also made brief a reference to national law, correctly stating that the variations among national jurisdictions do not make it possible to deduce a common principle on the issue at hand.[224]

The rejection of the 'specific direction' requirement in the case law of the ICTY was confirmed by two recent appeal judgments: *Stanišić and Simatović* and *Popović et al.* In the latter case, the defence of Vinko Pandurević argued that purposeful assistance is an essential part of aiding and abetting liability, regardless of whether it is incorporated into the mens rea or actus reus. The Appeals Chamber refuted this claim,

[215] ibid, para 490.
[216] ibid.
[217] ibid, para 475.
[218] *Prosecutor v Šainović et al*, ICTY Case No IT-05-87-A, Appeal Judgment, 23 January 2014 ('*Šainović et al* Appeal Judgment'), para 1649.
[219] ibid, para 1617.
[220] *cf* ibid, Dissenting Opinion of Judge Tuzmukhamedov, paras 43, 47.
[221] ibid, para 1621.
[222] ibid, para 1622.
[223] ibid, para 1649.
[224] ibid, para 1644.

holding that it has been established that the 'specific direction' is *not* an element of aiding and abetting liability under customary international law.[225] The most recent appeal judgment in *Stanišić and Simatović* overturned the acquittals in this case and ordered a retrial because the Trial Chamber had erred in two major respects: first, it did not examine in sufficient detail the nature of the agreement required to prove the existence of the joint criminal enterprise; and, second, it erroneously required that the acts of the aider and abettor be specifically directed towards assisting the commission of the crime.[226]

The recent rejection of 'specific direction' as an element of aiding and abetting liability in *Taylor*, *Šainović et al*, *Stanišić and Simatović* and *Popović et al* is to be applauded for a number of reasons. The enhanced version of aiding and abetting purports to bridge the temporal and/or spatial gap between the accomplice and the principal perpetrator. This is unnatural for aiding and abetting; the form of liability that targets precisely the situations where the accused is removed from the scene of the crime. The revised standard may have led to gaps in responsibility, where culpable assistance with a substantial effect on the crime does not attract liability due to a simple lack of physical proximity between the crime and the assistance.

There are a number of other problems with the element that has been correctly abandoned. First, it lacks foundation in the jurisprudence of the ad hoc tribunals. The requirement of the specific direction, creatively inferred from the wording of the *Tadić* appeal judgment, appears to have been taken out of context, and there is case law rejecting 'specific direction' as an element of aiding and abetting.[227] The *Tadić* Appeals Chamber used the 'specific direction' criterion for aiding and abetting in order to contrast it with acts in some way directed towards the furtherance of common design.[228] Thus, the emphasis was not on the physical proximity of the accomplice's aid to the offence in question, but rather on the existence of the crime-specific relationship between the aider and abettor and the principal perpetrator. This is in contrast to the group-specific situation, which is characteristic of the joint criminal enterprise.

[225] *Popović et al* Appeal Judgment (n 165) paras 1756, 1758.

[226] *Prosecutor v Stanišić and Simatović*, ICTY Case No IT-03-69-A, Appeal Judgment, 9 December 2015 ('*Stanišić and Simatović* Appeal Judgment'), paras 90, 106.

[227] *Šljivančanin* Appeal Judgment (n 165) para 159; *Prosecutor v Blagoević and Jokić*, ICTY Case No IT-02-60-A, Appeal Judgment, 9 May 2007 ('*Blagoević* Appeal Judgment'), para 189; *Furundžija* Trial Judgment (n 126) para 232. Judge Liu argued to this effect in his partially dissenting opinion: 'Given that specific direction has not been applied in past cases with any rigor, to insist on such a requirement now effectively raises the threshold for aiding and abetting liability.' *Perišić* Appeal Judgment (n 195) Partially Dissenting Opinion of Judge Liu, para 3.

[228] *Tadić* Appeal Judgment (n 48) para 229.

Second, the additional criterion conflates assistance with performing part of the actus reus of the offence itself and brings aiding and abetting dangerously close to commission. The former, in contrast with the latter, need not be the direct cause of the crime.[229] Third, the specific direction requirement is superfluous and does not have an independent standing of its own. One can view it either as an implied element of substantial contribution, in a sense of the accomplice's actions having some impact on the conduct of the principal and thus, being *directed* towards the crime, or as part of the accused's *mens rea* for aiding and abetting, which is knowledge. If the accused knew about the crime and still provided assistance, then logically his acts are directed towards the offence.[230]

Finally, the requirement that the aid is specifically directed towards the crime and not just to the establishing military control or other fighting objective—even in the circumstances when the assistance is provided with the knowledge and facilitates the commission of offences—brings to the surface an uncomfortable question that goes beyond the legal technicalities of a particular liability mode: what are the conditions that turn the 'general war effort' into a 'crime' attracting individual criminal responsibility? Also, what is the standard of behaviour that we expect from the senior leadership in the context of war?

H. Complicity in Genocide

Article 4(3)(e) of the ICTY Statute and Article 2(3)(e) of the ICTR Statute, which deal with the substantive crime of genocide, criminalise, inter alia, complicity in genocide. These provisions create an overlap with those articles that provide for different forms of complicity as a form of individual criminal responsibility.[231]

Boas summarised three approaches adopted by different Trial Chambers when addressing the relationship between the two provisions.[232] The first approach, adopted by the *Akayesu* Trial Chamber, was to treat aiding and abetting genocide and complicity in genocide as

[229] Judge Liu noted: 'If specific direction is indeed part of the *actus reus* of aiding and abetting liability, it could be argued that there is little difference between aiding and abetting and certain forms of commission.' *Perišić* Appeal Judgment (n 195) Partially Dissenting Opinion of Judge Liu, fn 9.

[230] Judges Meron and Agius, in their joint Separate Opinion in *Perišić*, packed the 'specific direction' element under the fault requirement of aiding and abetting, stating that 'whether an individual specifically aimed to assist relevant crimes logically fits within our current *mens rea* requirement'. *Perišić* Appeal Judgment (n 195) Joint Separate Opinion of Judges Meron and Agius, paras 2–3. See also *Perišić* Appeal Judgment (n 195) Partially Dissenting Opinion of Judge Liu, fn 7.

[231] ICTY Statute, art 7; ICTR Statute, art 6.

[232] Boas, Bischoff and Reid (n 11) 291 et seq.

having distinct physical and mental elements. Aiding and abetting genocide consisted in a failure to act or refraining from action, combined with the accused possessing a genocidal intent, while complicity in genocide required that the accused engage in an overt act with the mere knowledge of the actual perpetrator's intent.[233] The second approach, adopted in *Stakić* and *Semanza*, held that aiding and abetting genocide and complicity in genocide are identical.[234] Finally, the most authoritative approach is that of *Krstić* Appeals Chamber, which held that 'complicity' and 'accomplice' may encompass conduct broader than that of aiding and abetting. The court characterised Krstić's conduct as that of aiding and abetting genocide.[235] The Appeals Chamber did not require an aider and abettor to possess a specific intent; mere knowledge of the intent of the physical perpetrator sufficed.[236]

It appears that the most reasonable way of delineating these two overlapping norms is to distinguish them functionally: 'complicity in genocide' shall be regarded as a substantive offence because it is located in an article dealing with the crime of genocide, while various modes of liability in Articles 7 and 6 of the ICTY and ICTR Statutes serve the different purpose of attaching liability and characterising the conduct of the accused. The consequence of the functional approach is to treat the substantive crime provision on complicity in genocide as embracing all forms of participation in the actus reus and mens rea of the offence itself. The *Krstić* approach endorses the functional distinction between complicity in genocide as a substantive crime and complicity in genocide as a mode of responsibility and a crime.

II. PROBLEMS WITH BUILDING A COHERENT ACCOUNT OF COMPLICITY

The above discussion concerned the legal requirements for modes of liability in international criminal law. It seems that the judges of the ad hoc tribunals and the hybrid courts often resort to predetermined formulas to discuss the ways in which the accused are involved in crimes. Different forms of complicity are frequently utilised by the ad hoc tribunals and hybrid courts: a table demonstrating the correlation between liability modes and sentencing provided in Appendix II of this book shows that

233 *Akayesu* Trial Judgment (n 109) paras 485, 538, 548, as cited in Boas, Bischoff and Reid (n 11) 294.

234 *Semanza* Trial Judgment (n 121) para 394; *Stakić* Trial Judgment (n 93) para 31, as cited in Boas, Bischoff and Reid (n 11) 294.

235 *Krstić* Appeal Judgment (n 27) para 139, as cited in Boas, Bischoff and Reid (n 11) 297.

236 ibid, para 140.

situations of instigating, ordering, aiding and abetting, and planning arise in approximately one-third of the ICTY cases and approximately two-thirds of the ICTR cases. The SCSL employed the joint criminal enterprise in one case and various forms of complicity as well as superior responsibility in the other cases, while the ECCC chose to refer to all available forms of participation aside from 'committing' in its first and second judgments, although the second judgment placed most emphasis on the joint criminal enterprise.[237]

The joint criminal enterprise, commission, extended commission and superior responsibility are the alternative legal tools used by courts to address international criminality, sometimes alongside and sometimes instead of complicity. This section reflects on four problems preventing coherent application of the liability doctrines, in particular complicity, in international criminal law.

A. Fragmentation

An overview of the jurisprudence of the ad hoc tribunals and hybrid courts shows that each body applying international criminal law adopts its own approach to the modes of participation. The ECCC seems to adhere to the unitary model of participation and resembles the Nuremberg prototype. Its judgments assessed the conduct of the accused under every mode of liability available under the ECCC Law aside from committing.[238] The ICTY frequently used the concept of the joint criminal enterprise to address collective criminality, while the ICTR adopted its own notion of commission, namely the extended one.

Various forms of complicity also frequently make an appearance in the jurisprudence of the ad hoc tribunals and the hybrid courts, but the way in which they are applied to the facts are entirely different. The ICTR often employs several modes of responsibility to address the same conduct, whereas the ICTY and the SCSL are more selective, in that they usually prefer a particular form of responsibility.[239] Even within one institution, the legal standards differ from case to case. The ICTY extended aiding and abetting to include liability for omission. It convicted Šljivančanin as an aider and abettor for failing to prevent the implementation of an unlawful order in the absence of any formal position of authority. It then

[237] See Appendix II; *Chea et al* Trial Judgment (n 115) ss 15 and 16; D Cohen, M Hyde and P van Tuyl, 'A Well-Reasoned Opinion? Critical Analysis of the First Case against the Alleged Senior Leaders of the Khmer Rouge (Case 002/01)', WSD HANDA CENTER for Human Rights and International Justice, Stanford University (EastWestCentre.org 2015) 6.

[238] *Duch* Trial Judgment (n 32) paras 486, 516, 521, 526, 531, 537, 549.

[239] See Appendix II.

dramatically restricted aiding and abetting liability by introducing the requirement of 'specific direction' in *Perišić* and *Stanišić and Simatović.*

The recent *Taylor* and *Šainović et al* and *Popović et al* appeal judgments, which reject the specific direction requirement as an element of the actus reus of aiding and abetting, are the most vivid examples of the fragmentation of international criminal law. The rejection of the specific direction requirement by the SCSL and the ICTY is a double-edged sword. On the positive side, it upholds the appropriate standard of complicity for the purposes of international criminal law. The negative side is the lack of coherence and coordination between different courts and tribunals applying international criminal law.[240] The discipline is becoming highly fragmented as it is pulled apart by a multitude of considerations, many of which are extra-legal.

Why do we need coherence in international criminal law? Why not allow each international judicial body to adopt its own set of rules? The answer to this question is threefold. First, differential treatment of offenders across various courts and tribunals violates the principle of the equality of punishment. This principle is at the heart of the retributive rationale adopted as one of the guiding principles by international criminal justice.[241] As Kant framed it, the punishment should be commensurate to whatever undeserved evil one inflicts on another person.[242] In modern retributive thinking, the measuring is done according to the principle of proportionality—the sentence must be proportionate to the gravity of criminal conduct.[243] The idea behind this principle is that individuals should be treated as rational beings capable of making choices, and it is the choice to offend that is punished, not the individual himself; consequently, the punishment must be commensurate to the evil inflicted.[244] In Dworkinian terms, individuals have a right to equal concern and respect in the administration of the political institutions that govern them.[245] Acceptance of the differential treatment of offenders in international criminal law requires, at a minimum, some adjustments to the retributive punishment

[240] Judge Tuzmukhamedov disagreed with the majority in *Šainović et al* on exactly this point. He argued that the case at hand did not merit consideration of the 'specific direction' issue for factual reasons—Lazarević's assistance was not remote. He also maintained that the reasons of legal certainty, stability and predictability required the majority to furnish cogent reasons for deviating from the *Perišić* judgment. See *Šainović et al* Appeal Judgment (n 218) Dissenting Opinion of Judge Tuzmukhamedov, paras 43, 45, 47.

[241] For a detailed discussion of the retributive rationale in domestic and international criminal law, see Ch 7.

[242] I Kant, *The Metaphysics of Morals* (Cambridge, Cambridge University Press, 1991 [1797]) 141.

[243] A von Hirsch, 'Proportionate Punishment: A Desert Perspective' in A von Hirsch, A Ashworth and J Roberts (eds) *Principled Sentencing*, 3rd edn (Oxford, Hart Publishing, 2009) 117.

[244] Ashworth (n 63) 26.

[245] R Dworkin, *Taking Rights Seriously* (Cambridge, Mass, Harvard University Press, 1977)180.

rationale extensively cited as one of the main sentencing goals in international criminal law.[246]

The matter is further complicated if one focuses on a particular legal concept: that of complicity. The law of complicity distorts the principle of the equality of punishment on a conceptual level, making it ever more important to maintain a uniform approach to the matter. The common law position illustrates this bias of complicity. Common law translates the principle of the equality of punishment for all parties into treating principal perpetrators and accomplices alike.[247] Reconciling this principle with complicity's derivative nature required many changes and refinements in English law, including the adoption of the broad notion of presumed causality for complicity.[248] While these modifications allowed for the principle of the equality of punishment in English law, the matter is by no means free from controversy.

Second, there is a pragmatic reason militating against fragmentation. The judgments in the area of international criminal law are often criticised for being too lengthy and requiring significant time and financial input. One way to improve the efficiency is to facilitate a better dialogue between different international courts and within each institution. For example, it appears that both the *Taylor* and the *Šainović et al* Appeals Chambers undertook essentially the same exercise of trying to determine whether specific direction as an element of aiding and abetting is part of customary international law. It seems reasonable, for the purposes of judicial efficiency, to promote cross-referencing and collaboration across the field with the view of reducing the extra workload for individual Chambers.

The final reason for maintaining some level of internal coherence in international criminal law arises from the need to preserve the principle of legality. This fundamental principle, sometimes expressed by the maxim *nullum crimen sine lege* or the 'rule of law', has both procedural and substantive implications.[249] The specific aspects of the principle of legality that are eroded by fragmentation are the principle of maximum certainty in defining offences (also termed 'fair warning') and the principle of 'fair labelling', concerned with providing a fair representation of the nature and the magnitude of the law breaking.[250] The reason for maintaining the distinctions is again the principle of proportionality—one of the aims of criminal law is to provide a proportionate response to offending by accurately describing the criminal conduct.[251]

[246] For a discussion on the adjustments that international criminal law should make in relation to the domestic punishment goals, see Ch 7.II.C.
[247] Smith (n 35) 73.
[248] ibid 90.
[249] Ashworth (n 63) 67.
[250] ibid 73, 86.
[251] ibid 86.

These principles in domestic law do not exist unchecked, but are balanced by current pragmatic and political considerations.[252] Ashworth noted that the principle of legal certainty runs counter to the policy of social defence, a position that some vagueness in criminal law is beneficial because it allows the enforcement authorities and the judiciary to deal flexibly with new variations in misconduct without awaiting the legislature.[253] The principle of fair labelling is balanced by the considerations of increasing efficiency in the administration of criminal justice—fewer and broader categories of offence make it easier to secure convictions and lead to the reduction in spending on the court system.[254]

The examples provided are from the domestic system of criminal justice. International criminal law has yet to define its objectives, as well as the policy considerations that shape judicial reasoning in an international context. How can procedural fairness be balanced with the completion strategy? How can mass atrocities be made to 'fit' individual indictments? How can economic efficiency be maintained? How can the line be drawn between a 'general war effort' and a war crime?[255] These are some of the problematic questions with policy implications. It is difficult to answer these while international criminal law still searches for its identity and purposes.[256] Without an understanding of what this field of law aspires to achieve, it is difficult to conceptualise how the policy considerations counterbalance different aspects of the principle of legality in the context of international criminal law. Fragmentation should be avoided to the maximum extent possible, pending the resolution of the general problems of policy and purposes. Undermining coherence requires more justification than is currently provided.

B. Unclear Standard of Causation

The jurisprudence emanating from the ad hoc tribunals and hybrid courts appears ambiguous when it comes to defining the standard of causation for complicity. The fact that some chambers held that instigation, in contrast with aiding and abetting, ordering and planning, requires a causal

[252] ibid 67.
[253] ibid 75.
[254] ibid 89.
[255] It seems that one emerging trend is the pragmatic approach to war, which manifests itself in the acceptance of the inevitability of some level of wrongdoing during the hostilities. The recent ICTY acquittals in *Gotovina, Perišić* and *Stanišić and Simatović* have this consideration in common. See *Gotovina* Appeal Judgment (n 27); *Perišić* Appeal Judgment (n 195); *Stanišić and Simatović* Trial Judgment (n 208).
[256] D Robinson, 'The Identity Crisis of International Criminal Law' (2008) 21(4) *Leiden Journal of International Law* 925. For more discussion on the purposes and limitations of international criminal law, see Ch 8.

link between an act of instigation and the commission of a crime exemplifies the lack of clarity in this sphere.[257]

The classification by Sanford Kadish of the consequences of human actions is helpful in understanding causation in the context of complicity. Kadish explained that a person's actions might result in two outcomes: first, they may lead to the subsequent chain of events governed by the laws of nature, as for example with setting a house on fire by lighting a match; and, second, the consequence of a person's action may also consist in actions of other people, in the situations of instigation, persuasion, etc.[258] In the first case, responsibility follows for the harm that is *caused* by the freely chosen action, while in the second instance, the basis of responsibility is whether help or persuasion renders an accomplice accountable for another's actions and their effect.[259] Kadish wrote:

> [W]hether I am to be blamed for the other person's action would not be assessed by asking whether I caused his action in the same sense that his lighting the match caused the fire. Rather, my responsibility would be determined by asking whether my persuasion or help made me accountable for the other person's actions and what they caused.[260]

Causation *stricto sensu* manifests itself only in the first case, when the events happen in the natural world, through its two components: the 'cause in fact' requirement and the 'proximate' or 'legal' cause requirement.[261] The first requirement refers to causation in the scientific or factual sense and the dominant test for the cause in fact is the 'sine qua non' or 'but-for' test, which implies that the defendant's action was a necessary condition for the harm to occur.[262] The second, legal, requirement of causation is evaluative in nature and involves determining whether the defendant is culpable of causing certain harm based on a number of policy considerations; protected social interests, foreseeability, deterrence and directness of the contribution.[263] The synergy of these two requirements allows us to establish causation in the narrow sense of the word. However, the process is not a clear-cut exercise: the unified view of causation conceives causation as a matter of *degree*—one thing can be more of a cause of a certain event than another.[264] Consequently, even establishing causation in the physical

257 See section I.E above.
258 Kadish (n 129) 334.
259 ibid 334.
260 ibid 332. On the nature of derivative liability, see also Fletcher (n 101) 583.
261 M Moore, 'Causation in the Criminal Law' in J Deigh and D Dolinko (eds), *The Handbook of Philosophy of Criminal Law* (Oxford, Oxford University Press, 2011) 169.
262 ibid 170.
263 ibid 170, 179–85.
264 M Moore, *Placing Blame: A Theory of the Criminal Law* (Oxford, Oxford University Press, 1997) 359.

world, between the harm and the perpetrator, requires some flexibility and an evaluative assessment.

In the second scenario discussed by Kadish, the causal chain is interrupted by the freely chosen acts of others.[265] It is therefore not necessary to establish that the crime would not have been perpetrated without the accused's involvement; the *sine qua non* test is not applicable in this situation.[266] The accomplice is only able to influence the conduct of the actual perpetrator, but he cannot be said to have caused the crime. This understanding of complicity is in line with its derivative nature. The secondary party incurs the liability by virtue of the violation of the law by the primary party to which the secondary party contributed.[267] Accomplice liability therefore depends on the liability of the primary perpetrator.[268] This is not to suggest that the language of causation is inapplicable to complicity. Kadish admitted that complicity and causation are cognate issues—'they fix blame for a result characterized by a but-for relationship to the actor's contribution, although complicity allows for a weaker version of that relationship'.[269] Furthermore, causation '*broadly conceived*, concerns the relationship between successive phenomena, whether they have the character of events or happenings, or of another person's volitional actions' (emphasis added).[270]

The key distinction is that causation in complicity is different from physical causation. It is essential that international judges stress and clarify this difference. Kutz conceptualised complicity as avoiding individual inquiries into causation by treating harm intended (as opposed to harm caused) as the basis of criminal responsibility.[271] For Kutz, the essential shift that complicity entails is from objective causation to the subjective intent; from actual harm to risk.[272] Gardner contended that 'the difference between principals and accomplices is a causal difference, i.e. a difference between two types of causal contribution, not a difference between a causal and a non-causal contribution'.[273] The link between an accomplice and the

[265] C Kutz, 'The Philosophical Foundations of Complicity Law' in J Deigh and D Dolinko (eds) *The Handbook of Philosophy of Criminal Law* (Oxford, Oxford University Press, 2011) 154.

[266] Kadish ((n 129) 357) explained: 'In causation, the requirement of a condition sine qua non assures this sense of success, since the requirement means that without the act the result would not have happened as it did. In complicity, however, a sine qua non relationship in this sense need not be established. It is not required that the prosecution prove, as it must in causation cases, that the result would not have occurred without the actions of the secondary party.'

[267] ibid 337.

[268] ibid.

[269] ibid 366.

[270] ibid 334.

[271] Kutz (n 265) 157.

[272] ibid.

[273] J Gardner, 'Complicity and Causality' in *Offences and Defences: Selected Essays in the Philosophy of Criminal Law* (Oxford, Oxford University Press, 2007) 58.

harm for Gardner lies in the subjective sphere of reasoning as to why one engages in criminal conduct—justifying one's wrongs by claiming that they make no impact is not cancelling them, but showing one committed them for a sufficient reason.[274]

According to KJM Smith, English law adopted the broad notion of causality for complicity doctrine as a compromise between the strict theoretical demands of causality and the limitations of proof.[275] Smith maintained that the problem stems from the need to distinguish causal roles of the principals and accessories on the basis of immediacy and directness of causal contribution to the actus reus.[276] The accessory contributes only indirectly by influencing the principal. This peculiarity, the distance of an accomplice from the actual harm and the practical difficulty of showing causation, prompted English courts to adopt the implicit rule of the presumed cause—a theoretical adjustment driven by policy demands for a wide-ranging coverage of complicity.[277] This rule embraces the limitations of causation in the context of complicity: an accomplice may not be said to have 'caused' the principal to act in the same way as the principal causes certain crime to occur in the physical world through his voluntary act.[278] This is so because interpersonal relations lack predictability; they lack the sequence of cause and effect.[279] At the same time, if the accomplice's acts have no effect on the crime, no liability follows.[280] Consequently, the operating basis of complicity, according to Smith, is not positively established causal contribution, but the 'assumed cause', which is the product of tension between what could feasibly be proved and the breadth of conduct that should be covered by complicity law pursuant to policy demands.[281]

The theoretical discussion about the nature of causation in the sphere of complicity leads to three conclusions that are pertinent to international criminal law. First, all forms of complicity, instigation included, share the same derivative basis, so they may not be distinguished on the basis of present or absent causal connection to the crime.[282] One may safely

274 ibid 73.
275 Smith (n 35) 87. For more on the modes of liability in English law, see Ch 2.II.C.
276 Smith (n 35) 89.
277 ibid.
278 Kadish (n 129) 326; Hart and Honoré (n 176) 388.
279 Smith (n 35) 83.
280 ibid 87.
281 ibid.
282 'Instigation' in domestic law appears to be a form of complicity that entails a stronger link between the instigator and the primary perpetrator than that between the aider and abettor and the primary perpetrator. For example, in Germany, the instigator increases the likelihood of the principal committing an offence, while aiding and abetting only furthers the acts of the principal in some way. Consequently, it is understandable why some international judges sought to highlight the significance of the influence of the instigator on the principal with strengthening the causal link between his act and the crime. For the domestic law take on the issue, see Appendix I.

assume that no causation in the strict sense of the word is required for any form of complicity. The standard of international criminal law that the relationship between the contribution of the accomplice and the crime does not need to be *sine qua non* is correct. However, it seems that this test does not belong with complicity at all because it deals with events happening in the natural world and cannot be strictly applied to the acts of other people in light of the presumption of the freedom of choice and individual autonomy.

Second, it is possible to construct a wider concept of causation so as to include the effect of accomplice's aid or influence on the voluntary act of the primary perpetrator. The artificial nature of the link between accessory's contribution and the crime follows from the distinct moral importance of the perpetrator's role, regardless of the scale of the accessory's contribution.[283] The process of expanding the ordinary meaning of causation requires further elaboration.

One way to conceptualise causality in the sphere of complicity is to focus on the distinction found in the domestic legal systems between unitary and differentiated participation. The unitary model presupposes that any involvement whatsoever on the part of an actor in any offence establishes his connection to the crime, while the differential model requires connecting the liability of accomplices to the conduct of the principal perpetrator.[284] Thus, the unitary model allows for more flexibility when it comes to the causation standard—any contribution to the crime establishes the connection. The peculiarity of this model is that the liability of each crime participant stands on its own; in other words, it is not derivative. It seems, however, that the ICTY, the ICTR and the SCSL recognise the derivative nature of complicity.[285] The ECCC's conception of the forms of participation in the *Duch* judgment is perhaps a step closer to the unitary model of participation: the ECCC judges adopted a factual approach to the evidence. They established the responsibility of Kaing Kek Iev, or Duch, for every liability mode available under the ECCC Law, aside from 'committing' on the basis of his position as the head of the extermination centre Toul Sleng (S-21). The ECCC Trial Chamber did not elaborate on the

[283] Smith (n 35) 81.

[284] A Eser, 'Individual Criminal Responsibility (Article 25)' in A Cassese et al (eds), *The Rome Statute of the International Criminal Court: A Commentary* (Oxford, Oxford University Press, 2002) 788. For a detailed discussion of the difference between the unitary and differentiated perpetrator models, see Ch 2.I.B.

[285] This conclusion follows from the fact that various forms of complicity are defined with reference to the act of the principal perpetrator. For instance, an aider or abettor is one who provides 'practical assistance, encouragement, or moral support' to the principal. *Furundžija* Trial Judgment (n 126) para 235.

specific crimes committed by Duch's subordinates, the prison staff, but focused on the responsibility of Kaing Kek Iev himself.[286]

There is room for constructed causation even within the differential participation model. It appears that the jurisprudence of the ad hoc tribunals requires that the contribution of the aider and abetter has a substantial effect upon the perpetration of the crime.[287] Likewise, planning or instigation must be a factor that contributes substantially to the conduct of another person committing the crime.[288] The terms 'substantial effect' or 'substantial factor' present some conceptual difficulties if one views the will of the principal as autonomous. How does one measure the effect of the aid or influence on the primary perpetrator if he is an independent moral agent?

One potential solution to this problem is shifting the focus from the actual harm caused by the accessory's actions to the risk that he took by providing assistance or encouragement to the principal. This is in line with the proposition by Kutz that the basis for the accomplice's responsibility is not the harm caused, but the harm intended.[289] This conceptualisation of complicity leaves room for the extended form of causation, which may be called the 'subjective' causation: what matters is the internal perception of the risk of harm by the accomplice and the actions that he undertakes to further his plans. This is a shift from the objective causation required for primary perpetration.[290] It seems reasonable that international judgments should focus more on the accomplice's state of mind and his culpable contribution to the crime rather than seeking an objective, close cause–effect relationship between the accessory and the crime. It is essential not to conflate conduct and fault requirements of complicity, for these should be assessed separately and balanced against each other. The suggested approach shifts the emphasis from the end result, the crime, to the accomplice, his conduct and his intentions. When evaluating the culpability of an accomplice, it is also essential to bear in mind the specific type of criminality involved in international offending—a criminality that stems from obedience rather than deviance.[291]

[286] For example, the finding on aiding and abetting is just one paragraph: 'In light of the Chamber's previous findings, it is clear that the practical assistance, encouragement and moral support provided by the Accused to his staff had a substantial effect on their perpetration of crimes at S-21 (Section 2.3.3.5). The Chamber further finds that the Accused was aware that his conduct assisted in the commission of these crimes. Moreover, having trained his staff to consider all detainees as enemies of the CPK (Section 2.3.3.5.2), the Accused was aware of the discriminatory intent of the perpetrators in committing these crimes.' *Duch* Trial Judgment (n 32) para 537.

[287] eg, *Blaskić* Appeal Judgment (n 27) para 48.

[288] eg, *Kordić and Čerkez* Appeal Judgment (n 109) paras 26–27.

[289] Kutz (n 265) 157.

[290] ibid.

[291] S Milgram, *Obedience to Authority: An Experimental View* (Tavistock, Pinter & Martin, 1974). For more discussion on the type of criminality involved, see Ch 8.

Third, causation is a matter of degree and not a 'yes' or 'no' question. Even the causal link between the primary perpetrator and the harm implies attributing *relative degrees* of significance. The event is usually caused by a number of factors and each of them contributes to its occurrence to some extent.[292] When it comes to complicity, the effect of the influence of the accomplice on the primary perpetrator is subject to even more relativity. Predicting the principal's behaviour in the absence of the contribution by the accomplice is a speculative exercise. Consequently, it is essential to undertake a case-by-case assessment of the connection between the accomplice and the crime. The *Taylor* Appeals Chamber correctly held that 'the causal link between the accused's acts and conduct and the commission of the crime is to be assessed on a case-by-case basis'.[293] Domestic law provides for similar indications: in *Maxwell*, the UK House of Lords strongly emphasised the desirability of indictments that indicate the true factual nature of the case presented against the defendant.[294] The rationale is that, because all forms of behaviour have a certain potential to produce an encouraging effect on the principal perpetrator, complicity is not determined by literal constructions. Its limits are conceptual and lie elsewhere in causal expectations and the fault requirement.[295]

The level of influence on the principal varies from case to case and from one form of complicity to another. An instigator who uses threats or lies to induce the commission of a crime is closer to 'causing' a crime in the actual sense of the word than an aider who merely provides the means that could allow the principal to commit an offence if he wished to do so.[296] It is difficult to assess the impact of accessory's contribution on the primary perpetrator and ultimately on the offence in the context of international criminal law due to the scale of criminality involved and significant spatial and temporal gap between the crime and factors contributing to it. This lack of proximity has to be compensated by enhancing the fault requirement or conduct requirement, depending on the circumstances of the case.[297]

The problem of the specific direction in the ICTY jurisprudence partially stemmed from the lack of the well-defined causation standard for complicity. The justification for the introduction of the 'specific direction' element in the actus reus of aiding and abetting is the need to expressly establish the link between the accomplice's contribution and the wrongdoing in cases when the accused is removed from the offence. The assumption is that

[292] Kutz (n 265) 156; Moore (n 261) 186.
[293] *Taylor* Appeal Judgment (n 114) para 391.
[294] *Maxwell v DPP* [1978] 1 WLR 1350, 1352, 1357 and 1360, as cited in Smith (n 35) 33.
[295] Smith (n 35) 33–34.
[296] Hart and Honoré (n 176) 388.
[297] For more discussion on balancing the two elements of complicity, see section II.C below.

the link is implied when the accomplice is physically close to the crime.[298] However, physical proximity is often a false friend for establishing this connection—even when an accomplice is present at the scene of the crime, he is not directly perpetrating it and his contribution to the offence is often inferred from the evidence.[299] The same conclusion follows from the fact that the causal link between the accomplice and the crime is constructed: the connection stems from the risk that the secondary party envisages and undertakes rather than the actual harm that his actions cause. Hence, it is the mental state of the accomplice that grounds his relationship to the offence rather than his conduct. If one accepts that distance is not essential for establishing the effect of accessory's contribution on the offence, then the whole *raison d'etre* for the specific direction fails. It is no longer necessary to compensate for the distance by adding additional requirements to the actus reus of complicity, ie, that aid is specifically directed towards the crime.

C. Mismatch between Facts, Law and Forms of Liability

In an ideal world, the facts of the case, the definition of substantive offences and the legal requirements of the liability modes function as a single unit.[300] The harmonious collaboration of these three elements leads to the fair assessment of conduct of the accused in the particular circumstances of the case. However, in real life, matters are never simple, especially in cases where responsibility is something to be *decided* rather than simply *discovered*.[301] Joel Feinberg pointed out that often the questions of legal responsibility cannot be simply 'read-off' the facts and solved in a mechanical fashion, for they require a normative assessment of the fault of the defendant, whether he made sufficiently important contribution to an outcome and a number of ulterior practical considerations that the judges must keep in mind when arriving to a certain conclusion.[302] This complex process is open to 'glitches'.

Due to the high complexity of issues presented in international courts and the evolving nature of international criminal law, international judgments are usually very voluminous, with the structure reflecting a clear

[298] *Perišić* Appeal Judgment (n 195) para 38.

[299] For example, Furundžija's contribution was inferred from his position of authority.

[300] This is not to suggest that other factors are not part of the overall assessment. Defences, for instance, also form part of the analysis, but are not discussed in this book. Sentencing and the aims of punishment (discussed in Ch 7) also appear to be detached from the rest of the discussion—they are usually found in a separate part of the judgment.

[301] J Feinberg, *Doing and Deserving: Essays in the Theory of Responsibility* (Princeton, Princeton University Press, 1974) 27.

[302] ibid 26–29.

division between 'the law', 'the facts' and 'the sentencing'. This rigidity in the way in which international judgments are constructed and the autonomous nature of each distinct part of the document sometimes leads to the 'missing links' between the mode of liability and the substantive offence, between the facts of the case and the legal definitions, or among all three elements. It follows from the description of the liability modes furnished in the previous section that the wording that one finds in the case law of international tribunals and hybrid courts is frequently mechanical. We observe an engagement with the forms of responsibility as the simple application of certain labels. These labels are often not linked to the actual facts of the case or to the substantive office.

The missing link between the substantive offence and the mode of responsibility is revealed in the lack of a distinction between the legal requirements of the liability modes, conduct requirement and fault requirement, and the actus reus and mens rea of the substantive crimes.[303] Historically, the interplay between the two sets of elements has not been straightforward. The IMT and the IMTFE did not distinguish them, instead opting for a fact-based approach to attributing responsibility. The later case law and the work of the ILC show more awareness of the issue, divorcing the mode of liability and the substantive offence to which this liability attaches.[304]

The interplay between the offence and the form of responsibility is essential in developing a comprehensive theory of individual criminal responsibility in international criminal law. Forms of participation and substantive offences consist of elements and, to secure conviction, the prosecution has to prove both sets of elements.[305] To further complicate matters, the prosecution must also establish the existence of the so-called *chapeaux* elements or the 'general' or 'preliminary' conditions characteristic of a certain type of offence (for example, the existence of an armed conflict for war crimes, or the widespread or systematic attack for crimes against humanity).[306] This complexity makes it difficult to link different elements in one judgment, leading to a situation where the ad hoc tribunals and the hybrid courts treat the definition of crimes and the modes of liability for crimes as separate questions, with the ICTY, the ICTR, the SCSL and the ECCC discussing the substantive crimes and the forms of individual criminal responsibility in different parts of the judgments.[307]

[303] See section I.A above.

[304] See Ch 3.IV.

[305] Appendix II to this book shows for each accused the mode of responsibility and the crimes for which he is convicted in separate columns.

[306] Mettraux (n 14) 30.

[307] A Zahar and G Sluiter, *International Criminal Law: A Critical Introduction* (Oxford, Oxford University Press, 2008) 220.

Complicity in genocide—a provision that exists in the ICTY and ICTR Statutes as a substantive offence—showcases the difficulties encountered by the ad hoc tribunals in distinguishing the legal requirements of liability forms and the elements of the substantive offence.[308] The inclusion of 'complicity in genocide' as a substantive crime in the ICTY and ICTR Statutes is problematic in its own right—it creates an overlap between Articles 7/4 and 6/2, respectively, dealing with various forms of complicity, and covering the offence of genocide, including 'complicity in genocide'. However, the point to be made here is that until the *Krstić* appeal judgment, which distinguished 'complicity in genocide' as a substantive offence from aiding and abetting genocide as a combination of the mode of liability and the substantive offence, there existed little clarity on the matter.[309] Arguably, the root of the problem—the existence of the two sets of requirements in respect of every incident that the prosecution has to prove—is still not sufficiently spelled out in the jurisprudence of the ad hoc tribunals and the hybrid courts.

The other frequently missing link is between the facts of the case and the legal labels attached to them. A critical report on the ECCC trial judgment in Case 002/01 issued by the East-West Center highlighted a number of deficiencies in the way in which evidence was treated in this case. In particular, the report argues that the Trial Chamber used untested statements as a basis for conviction under the theories of joint criminal enterprise and command responsibility, without any corroborating evidence relating to the conduct of the accused vis-a-vis specific criminal acts.[310] This concern is especially pressing with regard to complicity, which is a highly fluid legal concept that has no rigid definition.[311]

The legal requirements of various forms of complicity—the conduct requirement and the fault requirement—provide only the initial framework for the assessment in each individual case. The abstract formulas utilised by the ad hoc tribunals and hybrid courts in respect of various forms of complicity seem to allow a flexibility to place more emphasis on the level of contribution of the accused *or* his knowledge of the crime. *Furundžija* provides a good example of balancing the two elements in establishing the case of aiding and abetting rape. The accused witnessed the crime happening. Presence at the scene of the crime was a 'strong'

[308] See section I.H above.

[309] *Prosecutor v Krstić*, ICTY Case No IT-98-33-A, Appeal Judgment, 19 April 2004, paras 139–140.

[310] Cohen et al (n 237) vii, 17.

[311] Chapter 2 explains that the dividing line between complicity and perpetration shifts even within one legal system, depending on the facts of the case. Likewise, the scope of complicity is fluid.

indicator of Furundžija's culpable mental state; this allowed for a 'weaker' conduct requirement—his contribution was inferred from the position of authority.[312]

Thus, the two constituent parts of complicity are interconnected—they cannot be assessed independently—something that the *Perišić* Appeals Chamber tried to do by stressing that it will only focus on the actus reus of aiding and abetting.[313] A more solid approach in the view of the constructed nature of complicity appears to be balancing the fault and the conduct requirement based on the facts of the particular case. As Smith put it, 'complicity's derivative quality must convincingly reside *at least* in either *mens rea* or *actus reus* components ... diminution in demands on the *mens rea* side have repercussions for the causal element as part of the *actus reus*; and vice-versa' (emphasis added).[314]

The need to perceive the fault and conduct requirement of complicity as one mechanism is relevant for the discussion on specific direction as part of the actus reus of aiding and abetting. It seems that making the requirements for the conduct element more stringent, without simultaneously lessening the fault requirement or getting rid of the requirement that the contribution of the accused must be substantial, skews the construction of complicity. The *Taylor* appeal judgment hinted at a more balanced approach to the two elements of aiding and abetting by drawing on the example of the US MPC that requires 'purpose'—instead of a more widely accepted 'knowledge'—as a mental element for aiding and abetting because it allows for *any* contribution to crime to qualify as a conduct element instead of a significant or substantial contribution.[315]

In sum, a harmonious approach to all three elements—facts, description of the substantive offences and the modes of liability—is preferred. This is achieved by the different parts of the judgments speaking to each other. The process of attribution of responsibility can be made more transparent if the form of responsibility is not used as an instrument for reaching a certain result—conviction or acquittal—but rather as a lens through which the court assesses the circumstances of the case, without any predetermined bias. The legal formulas should be attached to the specific facts and an inferential analysis, such as that which led to the conviction in the *Šljivančanin* case, should be justified at all times.[316]

[312] *Furundžija* Trial Judgment (n 126) paras 273–74.

[313] *Perišić* Appeal Judgment (n 195) para 48: 'The Appeals Chamber also underscores that its analysis of specific direction will exclusively address *actus reus*.'

[314] Smith (n 35) 195.

[315] *Taylor* Appeal Judgment (n 114) para 447. Smith (n 35) pointed out that American jurisdictions requiring purposeful accessorial attitudes experience fewer problems with specificity. For a discussion of complicity in the US, see Ch 2.II.D.

[316] *Šljivančanin* Appeal Judgment (n 165) para 93. See section I.G above.

D. Problem with the Sources

One of the defence teams in *Milutinović et al* raised the question whether the *Tadić* Appeals Chamber was correct in inferring the joint criminal enterprise from the ICTY Statute.[317] This concern exemplifies the problem with sources in international criminal law. The first judgments of the ICTY, *Tadić* and *Furundžija*, relied extensively on the post-Second World War jurisprudence to establish the existence of a customary rule in international criminal law. However, the analysis in the previous chapter shows that the Nuremberg and Tokyo judgments, as well as the subsequent convictions of the Nazi perpetrators pursuant to Control Council Law No 10, were highly politicised and influenced by domestic law considerations.[318] International criminal law is not incidental, but is the product of a combination of factors that need to be accounted for.

Most of the considerations that shaped international criminal justice at the time of its conception are extra-legal. Shklar referred to the environment that led to setting up the IMT in the following terms: 'a very rare situation in which there is no law, no government, no political order, and people have committed acts so profoundly shocking that something must be done about them'.[319] In spite of this, the early ICTY judgments seem to ignore the context in which the precedents they are relying on came into existence. The first steps of the ICTY can be characterised by uncritical adherence to the post Second World War jurisprudence. Boas argues that the most worrying characteristic of *Tadić* is the methodology used to establish the rules of customary international law. International judgments pursuant to Control Council Law No 10 supporting in *Tadić* the existence of common purpose liability do not amount to state practice.[320]

Custom is a very problematic source of international criminal law: tribunals often avoid making a distinction between the two constituent elements of the custom—*opinio juris* and state practice. This is understandable because the discipline is very peculiar in that the state practice element of the custom often points to an undesirable outcome (ie, a violation).[321] In addition, the field of international criminal law is relatively

[317] See section 1.C above.

[318] See Ch 3.

[319] J Shklar, *Legalism: An Essay on Law, Morals and Politics* (Cambridge, Mass, Harvard University Press, 1964) 153.

[320] Boas, Bischoff and Reid (n 11) 21–22.

[321] *First Report on Formation and Evidence of Customary International Law by Michael Wood, Special Rapporteur*, 17 May 2013, UN Doc A/CN.4/663, para 70. See also L van den Herik, 'Using Custom to Reconceptualise Crimes against Humanity' in S Darcy and J Powderly (eds), *Judicial Creativity at the International Criminal Tribunals* (Oxford, Oxford University Press, 2010) 101.

new and is still evolving, making it difficult to assess whether a particular provision has crystallised as a custom or not.[322]

A certain discomfort with the customary nature of the modes of liability in international criminal law is discernible in the jurisprudence of both hybrid courts. The Co-investigative judges at the ECCC scrutinised the cases the cases that *Tadić* relied on in support of the three forms of the joint criminal enterprise.[323] The judges found sufficient support in the customary international law for the first and second forms of the joint criminal enterprise,[324] but not the third, extended, form.[325] The Trial Chamber confirmed these findings a year later and, after having reviewed the domestic legislation of several states, rejected the proposition that the extended form of the joint criminal enterprise finds support in another source of international law, namely the general principles of law.[326]

The SCSL in the *Taylor* appeal judgment showed its unwillingness to directly engage with custom. The *Taylor* Appeals Chamber attempted to circumvent the difficulty related to the fragmentation of international criminal law by framing the discussion about the specific direction not along the lines of shaping the custom, but as a rejection of the ICTY precedent that is only internally binding.[327] As Kevin Jon Heller pointed out, this reasoning is unconvincing.[328] International courts and tribunals operating in the field apply the sources of international law—treaty, custom and the general principles of law.[329] Their statutes do not expressly mention the specific direction requirement for complicity. The question is therefore whether it is a custom or a general principle. However, the *Perišić* Appeals Chamber was on equally feeble ground when it entered the discussion in the first place.[330]

In modern international criminal law, a uniform approach by different courts and tribunals to a particular issue may serve as the evidence of a

[322] *First Report on Formation and Evidence of Customary International Law by Michael Wood* (n 321) para 68.

[323] *Prosecutor v Ieng Sary et al*, ECCC, Case No 002/19-09-2007/ECCC/OCIJ, Decision on the Appeals against the Co-investigative Judges Order on Joint Criminal Enterprise, Pre-Trial Chamber, 20 May 2010 ('*Ieng Sary* PTC JCE Decision').

[324] ibid, paras 57–71.

[325] ibid, paras 75–83.

[326] *Prosecutor v Ieng Sary et al*, ECCC, Case No 002/19-09-2007/ECCC/TC, Decision on Applicability of Joint Criminal Enterprise, 12 September 2011 ('*Ieng Sary* TC JCE Decision'), paras 36–38.

[327] *Taylor* Appeal Judgment (n 114) para 476.

[328] KJ Heller, 'The SCSL's Incoherent—and Selective—Analysis of Custom', *Opinio Juris Blog*, 27 September 2013, http://opiniojuris.org/2013/09/27/scsls-incoherent-selective-analysis-custom.

[329] The ICC is possibly an exception because of the special regime created by art 21 of the Rome Statute. UN General Assembly, Rome Statute of the International Criminal Court, 17 July 1998, ISBN No 92-9227-227-6, www.refworld.org/docid/3ae6b3a84.html.

[330] See section I.G above.

consensus on a given topic and thus allow us to speak of the formation of a customary rule. For example, the *Taylor* and the *Šainović et al* Appeals Chambers certainly weakened (if not disposed of) the emerging customary rule requiring the 'specific direction' element as a part of the actus reus of complicity, even though the *Taylor* appellate panel was not willing to engage expressly with the issue, and while the analysis furnished in *Šainović et al* is not free from controversy when it comes to assessing what constitutes a custom in international criminal law: not all of the cases cited in support of the absence of the specific direction in customary international law dealt with aiding and abetting liability.[331]

Looking at the other source of international law, the general principles of law, it seems that the requirement that the aid is directed towards the specific offence, in the sense that the ICTY attributed to it in *Perišić*, also lacks support in the majority of domestic legal systems.[332] In this regard, the initiative of the *Šainović et al* Appeals Chamber to 'probe' this third source of international law in order to establish whether domestic law may be of assistance in resolving the 'specific direction' problem deserves credit.[333] The Chamber's substantive conclusion about the lack of the uniform rule in respect of this particular aspect of aiding and abetting also appears to be correct.[334] However, the methodology employed for assessing domestic law is far from clear. The judgment adopted a reductionist approach when grouping the countries together, without taking into account the specific features of different legal families and individual legal systems.[335] The overview of national case law is cramped together in three paragraphs and several lengthy footnotes.[336]

Chapter 2 of this book argues in favour of the more extensive use of the general principles of law as a source of international criminal law. The overview of the case law of the ad hoc tribunals and courts provided empirical support for this claim in demonstrating the weakness of custom as a foundation of the discipline. The acceptance of a certain rule in the majority of national legal systems resonates with the domestic law origin of international criminal law and helps to increase the perceived

[331] For example, the *Justice* case, referred to in para 1641 of the judgment, showcases a unitary model of participation rather than any form of accomplice liability. See Ch 3.II.B.

[332] J Stewart, '"Specific Direction" is Unprecedented: Results from Two Empirical Studies,' *EJIL Blog*, 4 September 2013, www.ejiltalk.org/specific-direction-is-unprecedented-results-from-two-empirical-studies.

[333] *Šainović et al* Appeal Judgment (n 218) para 1643.

[334] For a detailed discussion of different elements of aiding and abetting in national law, see Ch 2.II and Appendix I.

[335] For example, *Šainović et al* Appeal Judgment (n 218) para 1645.

[336] ibid, paras 1643–46.

legitimacy of international courts;[337] the population of the affected states is more likely to view international judgments as legitimate if the juridical concepts employed in these judgments correspond to what is accepted and understood in a given domestic legal system.[338]

CONCLUSION

This chapter has provided an overview of the forms of responsibility that have crystallised in the jurisprudence of the ad hoc tribunals and hybrid courts. The special focus was on the contentious issues in the application of various responsibility doctrines. Different forms of complicity appear to be commonly employed to address the wrongdoing of the accused removed from the scene of the crime. Complicity serves as an alternative to the extended commission as developed by the ICTR and the joint criminal enterprise, used by both international tribunals and hybrid courts. The chapter summarised four main challenges of international criminal law that prevent the coherent deployment of the complicity doctrine: fragmentation, the deficiency in understanding the appropriate causation standard for complicity, the frequent lack of cohesion between factual circumstances and the legal labels attached to them, and the unreliability of some sources utilised by international courts.

How does one achieve a more harmonious integration of complicity into international criminal law? As argued in this chapter, this process is impeded by the absence of well-defined goals of international criminal justice. It is difficult to shape legal concepts and determine their respective weight without answering the question of what international criminal law strives to achieve. The lack of clarity about goals leads to a lack of agreement on the so-called 'policy objectives' of international criminal law, those pragmatic considerations counterbalancing legal concepts in the domestic law context. The last chapter of the book attempts to define an overarching objective of international criminal law and show how a unifying goal may affect the legal definition of complicity.

In the absence of a consensus on its objectives, it is important that international criminal law relies on its domestic law origins when engaging with the modes of responsibility. The need to accurately describe the

[337] Report of the Committee of French Jurists appended to the letter dated 10 February 1993 from the Permanent Representative of France to the United Nations addressed to the Secretary General, UN DOC S/25266, para 50(d). For a discussion on the limitations of international criminal law as a product of two fields, public international law and domestic criminal law, see Ch 8.I.

[338] M Damaška, 'What is the Point of International Criminal Justice?' (2008) 83 *Chicago-Kent Law Review* 329, 350.

behaviour of the accused in the context of national law stems from the notion of fairness—the accused has a right to be judged based on his conduct in the specific case. In addition, he has the right to be properly informed about the charges against him so that he stands a chance of preparing his defence.[339] It appears that similar considerations ought to apply to international criminal law. The practical outcome of this approach is careful selection of the most appropriate mode of responsibility at the stage of charging and meticulous application of the legal requirements of this mode of responsibility to the particular case at issue.

[339] W Jordash and J Coughlan, 'The Right to Be Informed of the Nature and Cause of the Charges: A Potentially Formidable Jurisprudential Legacy' in S Darcy and J Powderly (ed), *Judicial Creativity at the International Criminal Tribunals* (Oxford, Oxford University Press, 2010).

5

Complicity and the Hierarchy of the Participation Modes at the International Criminal Court

INTRODUCTION

THIS CHAPTER EXAMINES complicity in the context of the International Criminal Court (ICC). Article 25(3) of the Rome Statute contains the most comprehensive description of the liability modes as they have appeared in the history of international criminal law. The forms of participation are organised in a systematic fashion under the subparagraphs (a)–(d) of Article 25(3). Aside from 'committing', contained in subparagraph (a) of the Article, all other liability modes listed in the Rome Statute fit within the notion of 'complicity'.[1] Notwithstanding the availability of various forms of complicity under Article 25(3) of the Rome Statute, the ICC, in its early case law, leaned towards expanding the notion of 'commission' to include a wide array of conduct.[2]

Since its very beginnings, the ICC favoured the concepts of direct and indirect co-perpetration by means of control over crime in attaching responsibility to the accused removed from the scene of the crime.[3]

[1] Commentaries to the 1996 ILC Draft Code that served as a basis for the relevant provision of the Rome Statute refer to all modes of participation with the exception of 'commission' as 'complicity'. Report of the ILC to the General Assembly, Forty-Eighth Session, UN GAOR, 51st Session, No 10 UN A/51/10 (1996), at 20, para 6. See also W Schabas, *The UN International Criminal Tribunals: The Former Yugoslavia, Rwanda and Sierra Leone* (Cambridge, Cambridge University Press, 2006) 305. Article 25(3)(e) is a contentious case because it embodies the crime itself rather than a mode of responsibility. Genocide does not need to be committed or attempted to attract responsibility under this provision.

[2] W Schabas, *The International Criminal Court: A Commentary on the Rome Statute* (Oxford, Oxford University Press, 2010) 427–28.

[3] *Prosecutor v* Thomas *Lubanga Dyilo*, ICC-01/04-01/06, Pre-Trial Chamber I, Decision on the Confirmation of Charges, 29 January 2007 ('*Lubanga* Confirmation of Charges Decision'); *Prosecutor v Germain Katanga and Mathieu Ngudjolo Chui*, ICC-01/04-01/07, Pre-Trial Chamber I, Decision on the Confirmation of Charges, 30 September 2008 ('*Katanga* Confirmation of Charges Decision'); *Prosecutor v Jean-Pierre Bemba Gombo*, ICC-01/05-01/08, Pre-Trial Chamber II, Decision Pursuant to Article 61(7)(a) and (b) of the Rome Statute on the Charges, 15 June 2009 ('*Bemba* Confirmation of Charges Decision').

These constructions were inferred from subparagraph (a) of Article 25(3) of the Rome Statute, which mentions commission of a crime 'as an individual, jointly with another or through another person'.[4] The control over crime theory, which has its origins in German legal thought, is a form of commission that extends principal liability to those persons who do not physically commit the offence, but nonetheless possess a certain degree of control over its commission.[5] Accessories, on the other hand, do not have such control.[6] The ICC used the idea of control over crime to create the form of participation that not only delimits the conduct that warrants criminal liability but also functions as a criterion for qualifying the degree of responsibility of the accused.[7]

The reason for neglecting complicity in favour of the other forms of commission in the early case law of the ICC could be explained by the structure of Article 25(3) of the Statute and the alleged hierarchy of the participation modes that it contains. The ICC, by siding with the German legal tradition and inferring direct and indirect co-perpetration from the wording of the relevant provision, has acknowledged, in its first pronouncements on the matter, that the hierarchy of the modes of participation is implicit in Article 25(3).[8] Consequently, the court felt compelled to utilise the 'stronger' concept of co-perpetration as opposed to the various forms of complicity enshrined in the subsequent paragraphs of Article 25(3) with the aim of stressing the magnitude of crimes falling within the jurisdiction of the ICC.[9] Accordingly, the first conviction of the ICC was under the doctrine of co-perpetration pursuant to Article 25(3)(a) of the Statute.[10]

This approach has been confirmed on appeal, which reinforced the distinction between principals and accessories, and emphasised that the

[4] For a problems with the methodological interpretation of the sources at the ICC, see L Sadat and J Jolly, 'Seven Canons of ICC Treaty Interpretation: Making Sense of Article 25's Rorschach Blot' (2014) 27 *Leiden Journal of International Law* 755.

[5] C Roxin, 'Crimes as Part of Organized Power Structures' (1963) *Goltdammer's Archiv für Strafrecht* 193, reproduced in (2011) 9 *Journal of International Criminal Justice* 191.

[6] G Fletcher, *Rethinking Criminal Law* (Boston, Little, Brown, 1978) 655. For a detailed description of this theory, see Ch 2.II.A.

[7] G Werle and B Burghardt, 'Indirect Perpetration: A Perfect Fit for International Prosecution of Armchair Killers?' (2011) 9 *Journal of International Criminal Justice* 88.

[8] For references to this hierarchy, see *Prosecutor v Thomas Lubanga Dyilo*, ICC-01/04-01/06, Trial Chamber I, Judgment Pursuant to Article 74 of the Statute, 14 March 2012 ('*Lubanga* Judgment'), paras 996–99; *Katanga* Confirmation of Charges Decision (n 3) paras 469–71; *Prosecutor v Mbarushimana*, Pre-Trial Chamber I, ICC-01/04-01/10, Decision on the Confirmation of Charges, 16 December 2011 ('*Mbarushimana* Confirmation of Charges Decision'), para 279. *cf Prosecutor v Germain Katanga*, ICC-01/04-01/07, Trial Chamber II, Judgment Pursuant to Article 74 of the Statute, 7 March 2014 ('*Katanga* Judgment'), para 1386; *Prosecutor v Germain Katanga*, ICC-01/04-01/07, Trial Chamber II, Minority Opinion of Judge van den Wyngaert to Judgment Pursuant to Article 74 of the Statute, 7 March 2014 ('Minority Opinion of Judge van den Wyngaert'), para 279.

[9] E van Sliedregt, *Individual Criminal Responsibility in International Law* (Oxford, Oxford University Press, 2012) 85.

[10] *Lubanga* Judgment (n 8) para 976.

former implies a higher degree of blameworthiness than the latter, all other things being equal.[11] The judges noted that the Pre-Trial and Trial Chambers correctly relied on the 'control over crime' theory for distinguishing those who have committed the offence and those who have contributed to the crimes of others. The distinctive feature of commission is the essential contribution made at any stage of offending, including preparation, planning and execution. The idea is that this type of indispensable input places the perpetrator in control of the crime regardless of his physical presence at the scene.[12]

Arguably, the ICC has yet to determine its relationship with the doctrine of co-perpetration as a means of control over crime. Despite the support of the concept by the *Lubanga* appeal judgment, the signs of disillusionment with this approach cannot go unnoticed. The first serious benchmark decision questioning this theory—as well as the alleged hierarchy of crimes within Article 25(3) of the Rome Statute—was the separate opinion of Judge Adrian Fulford attached to the *Lubanga* judgment.[13] The other important development in this regard was the demise of the very case that pioneered the notion of indirect co-perpetration at the ICC: *Katanga*. Months after the parties' closing arguments in this case, the Trial Chamber changed the legal characterisation of facts relating to Germain Katanga's mode of participation from indirect co-perpetration under Article 25(3)(a) of the Statute to complicity in the commission of a crime by a group of persons acting with a common purpose on the basis of Article 25(3)(d) of the Statute.[14] Katanga was ultimately convicted of murder, an attack against the civilian population and the destruction of property under this latter form of responsibility.[15] The trial judgment rejected the hierarchy of participation modes, but retained the control over crime theory.

The same decision that recharacterised Katanga's modes of liability also severed the charges against the co-accused in the case,[16] Mathieu Ngudjolo, who was subsequently acquitted due to a lack of evidence.[17] Judge

[11] *Prosecutor v Thomas Lubanga Dyilo*, ICC-01/04-01/06 A 5, Appeals Chamber Judgment on the Appeal of Mr Thomas Lubanga Dyilo against His Conviction, 1 December 2014 ('*Lubanga* Appeal Judgment'), para 462.

[12] ibid, para 469.

[13] *Prosecutor v Thomas Lubanga Dyilo*, ICC-01/04-01/06, Separate Opinion of Judge Adrian Fulford to the Trial Chamber I, Judgment Pursuant to Article 74 of the Statute, 14 March 2012 ('Separate Opinion of Judge Fulford').

[14] *Prosecutor v Germain Katanga and Mathieu Ngudjolo Chui*, ICC-01/04-01/07, Trial Chamber II, Decision on the Implementation of Regulation 55 of the Regulations of the Court and Severing the Charges against the Accused Persons, 21 November 2012 ('*Katanga* Severing Decision'), para 7.

[15] *Katanga* Judgment, para 1691.

[16] *Katanga* Severing Decision (n 14) para 59.

[17] *Prosecutor v Mathieu Ngudjolo Chui*, ICC-01/04-02/12-4, Trial Chamber II, Judgment Pursuant to Article 74 of the Statute ('*Ngudjolo Chui* Judgment of Acquittal'), 18 December 2012, para 503.

Christine van den Wyngaert submitted a powerful concurring opinion to the acquittal judgment, expressing her views on the interpretation of Article 25(3)(a) of the Statute, whereby she criticised 'indirect co-perpetration' inferred from this provision and argued against the hierarchy of the modes of participation under Article 25(3) of the Statute.[18]

The lack of confidence in 'indirect co-perpetration' as a mode of liability also surfaced in the arrest warrants against Laurent and Simone Gbagbo, the former President of Côte d'Ivoire and his wife. The Pre-Trial Chamber III charged them with indirect co-perpetration in crimes, but stipulated that the mode of liability 'may well need to be revisited in due course'.[19] Subsequently, the judges cautiously confirmed charges against Laurent Gbago under alternative forms of responsibility, thereby allowing a certain degree of flexibility in relation to forms of participation.[20] The same alternative charging strategy has been adopted in the *Ntaganda* and *Blé Goudé* confirmation of charges decisions.[21] The latest divergent approaches in respect of (in)direct co-perpetration based on control over crime could be explained by the strikingly contrasting positions on the general assumption underlying the excessive use of this doctrine. That is the premise that the modes of participation within Article 25(3) are ranked according to their degree of blameworthiness; thus, the mode of participation listed first—commission—best reflects the culpability of the offenders standing trial for mass crimes within the ICC's jurisdiction.[22]

The aim of this chapter is to explore complicity in relation to the competing concept of co-perpetration.[23] It questions the assumptions underlying the over-use of the latter and paves the way to a more extensive and accurate use of the former. Section I critically examines the forms of

[18] *Prosecutor v Mathieu Ngudjolo Chui*, ICC-01/04-02/12-4, Trial Chamber II, Concurring Opinion of Judge van den Wyngaert to Judgment Pursuant to Article 74 of the Statute, 18 December 2012 ('Concurring Opinion of Judge van den Wyngaert'), para 6.

[19] *Prosecutor v Laurent Koudou Gbagbo*, Pre-Trial Chamber III, ICC-02/11, Warrant of Arrest for Laurent Koudou Gbagbo, 23 November 2011, para 11; *Prosecutor v Simone Gbagbo*, Pre-Trial Chamber III, ICC-02/11-01/12, Warrant of Arrest for Simone Gbagbo, 29 February 2012, para 16.

[20] *Prosecutor v Laurent Gbagbo*, ICC-02/1-01/1, Pre-Trial III, Decision on the Confirmation of Charges against Laurent Gbagbo, 12 June 2014 ('*Gbago* Confirmation of Charges Decision'), paras 226–28.

[21] *Prosecutor v Bosco Ntaganda*, ICC-01/04-02/06, Pre-Trial II, Decision Pursuant to Article 61(7)(a) and (b) of the Rome Statute on the Charges of the Prosecutor against Bosco Ntaganda, 9 June 2014 ('*Ntaganda* Confirmation of Charges Decision'), paras 99–100; *Prosecutor v Charles Blé Goudé*, ICC-02/11-02/11, Pre-Trial III Decision on the Confirmation of Charges against Charles Blé Goudé, 11 December 2014 ('*Blé Goudé* Confirmation of Charges Decision'), para 10.

[22] eg, Sadat and Jolly (n 4).

[23] Some parts of the discussion in this chapter are replicated in M Aksenova, 'The Modes of Liability at the ICC: The Labels That Don't Always Stick' (2015) 15 *International Criminal Law Review* 629.

participation at the ICC, with a special emphasis on the role of complicity in the attribution of liability as opposed to the notion of '(in)direct co-perpetration'. Section II explores the question of the alleged hierarchy of liability modes implicit in Article 25(3) of the Rome Statute. It provides arguments against ranking the forms of responsibility in the Rome Statute. Some conclusions are drawn in the final section.

I. MODES OF PARTICIPATION AT THE ICC

The Rome Statute of the ICC represents the future of the international criminal law, as it was drafted after the creation of the ICTY and the ICTR and makes use of their experience when defining different modes of participation.[24] It also takes into account the Draft Code of Crimes against the Peace and Security of Mankind adopted by the International Law Commission in 1996.[25] There is general agreement that, at least on the face of it, Article 25(3) of the Rome Statute leans towards the differential participation model as opposed to a unitary approach.[26] The division between differential and unitary perpetration is inherent in domestic criminal law. The core of this distinction is that the unitary model makes the responsibility of a party independent from the liability of the principal perpetrator, while the differential model implies accessorial dependence of the accomplice on the principal act of the perpetrator.[27] Thus, the premise underlying the differential participation model is that liability of an accessory derives from the wrongful act of the principal. This model in domestic law usually indicates a reduced punishment for the accomplices, as they are considered less blameworthy than the principals.[28]

[24] E van Sliedregt, *The Criminal Responsibility of Individuals for Violations of International Humanitarian Law* (The Hague, TMC Asser Press, 2003) 65.

[25] Report of the International Law Commission on the Work of its Forty-Eighth Session, 6 May–26 July 1996, UN Doc A/51/10. For more discussion on the preparation of the Draft Code of Crimes against the Peace and Security of Mankind adopted by the International Law Commission in 1996, Report of the ILC to the General Assembly, Forty-Eighth Session, U.N. GAOR, 51st Sess, Suat No 10 UN A/51/10 (1996).

[26] A Eser, 'Individual Criminal Responsibility (Article 25)' in A Cassese et al (ed), *The Rome Statute of the International Criminal Court: A Commentary* (Oxford, Oxford University Press, 2002) 788; K Ambos, 'The First Judgment of the International Criminal Court (*Prosecutor v Lubanga*): A Comprehensive Analysis of the Legal Issues' (2012) 12 *International Criminal Law Review* 144. Van Sliedregt employs slightly different terminology. She discusses the ICC's preference for the 'normative model'. This model implies that the principal is the one most responsible in the sense of having a decisive influence over the commission of the crime. In essence, this normativity falls within the ambit of differential participation model as it is based on the idea of the increased blameworthiness of the perpetrator. See van Sliedregt (n 9) 71–73, 79.

[27] Eser (n 26) 788.

[28] See, for example, the German model, discussed in further detail in Ch 2.

Article 25(3) of the Rome Statute provides that a person shall be criminally responsible and liable for punishment for a crime within the jurisdiction of the Court if that person:

(a) Commits such a crime, whether as an individual, jointly with another or through another person, regardless of whether that other person is criminally responsible;
(b) Orders, solicits or induces the commission of such a crime which in fact occurs or is attempted;
(c) For the purpose of facilitating the commission of such a crime, aids, abets or otherwise assists in its commission or its attempted commission, including providing the means for its commission;
(d) In any other way contributes to the commission or attempted commission of such a crime by a group of persons acting with a common purpose. Such contribution shall be intentional and shall either:
  (i) Be made with the aim of furthering the criminal activity or criminal purpose of the group, where such activity or purpose involves the commission of a crime within the jurisdiction of the Court; or
  (ii) Be made in the knowledge of the intention of the group to commit the crime;
(e) In respect of the crime of genocide, directly and publicly incites others to commit genocide;
(f) Attempts to commit such a crime by taking action that commences its execution by means of a substantial step, but the crime does not occur because of circumstances independent of the person's intentions. However, a person who abandons the effort to commit the crime or otherwise prevents the completion of the crime shall not be liable for punishment under this Statute for the attempt to commit that crime if that person completely and voluntarily gave up the criminal purpose.

Unlike the Statutes of the ad hoc tribunals, the Rome Statute contains a separate provision establishing the general fault requirement for the crimes under the ICC jurisdiction. Article 30 of the Rome Statute embraces two forms of culpability: *dolus directus in the first degree* and *dolus directus in the second degree.* The former is the direct intent, while the latter refers to the awareness—an understanding that the crime will be almost inevitable outcome of the acts or omissions of the accused.[29] This article shall be read in conjunction with Article 25(3), which sets out the modes of responsibility. Article 30 reads as follows:

1. Unless otherwise provided, a person shall be criminally responsible and liable for punishment for a crime within the jurisdiction of the Court only if the material elements are committed with intent and knowledge.

[29] *Katanga* Judgment (n 8) paras 774, 775. See also Schabas (n 2) 475.

2. For the purposes of this article, a person has intent where:
   (a) In relation to conduct, that person means to engage in the conduct;
   (b) In relation to a consequence, that person means to cause that consequence or is aware that it will occur in the ordinary course of events.
3. For the purposes of this article, 'knowledge' means awareness that a circumstance exists or a consequence will occur in the ordinary course of events. 'Know' and 'knowingly' shall be construed accordingly.

The following subsections elaborate on the forms of participation embodied in Article 25(3)(a)–(d) of the Rome Statute. Incitement to commit genocide under subparagraph (e) is not discussed because it constitutes an inchoate crime rather than a mode of responsibility. This is so because of the derivative nature of complicity—the conduct in the form of incitement derives its criminality from the crime that is attempted or committed. In this case, however, the crime of genocide does not need to be attempted or occur in order to bring about responsibility under this subheading.[30] Criminalising the act of incitement to commit genocide could be explained by the extreme gravity of the crime of genocide that calls for additional preventative measures. The inclusion of this inchoate offence in the article dealing with modes of responsibility is unfortunate as it properly belongs in the section dealing with substantive offences.

Complicity after the fact is also not examined in the following sections as it is not covered by Article 25.[31] The reason for this is the lack of a nexus between the act of assistance and the crime necessary according to the derivative nature of complicity.[32] While the Draft Code of Crimes adopted two years before the Rome Statute included ex post facto assistance in the category of complicity, it stipulated that this assistance would have to be agreed upon *prior* to the perpetration of the crime.[33]

Another provision that is not discussed at length in this chapter is Article 28 of the Rome Statute. This provision contains a distinct form of responsibility, namely that of commanders and other superiors. Command responsibility shares some characteristics with accomplice liability in that

[30] K Ambos, 'Commentary to Article 25 of the Rome Statute' in O Triffterer (ed) *Commentary on the Rome Statute of the International Criminal Court: Observers' Notes, Article by Article* (Baden-Baden: Nomos, 1999, Second Edition, 2003)) 487. *cf* art 2(3)(f) of the Draft Code of Crimes (1996), which provides for responsibility of the individual who 'directly and publicly incites another individual to commit such a crime which in fact occurs'.

[31] Schabas (n 2) 435; Ambos (n 30) 491.

[32] Ambos (n 30) 491.

[33] Report of the ILC, 48th Session, at 21, para 12. The ICC case law appears to take the same approach. In *Mbarushimana*, the Chamber found that art 25(3)(d) liability can include contributing to a crime's commission after it has occurred, so long as this contribution had been agreed upon by the relevant group acting with a common purpose and the suspect prior to the perpetration of the crime. See *Prosecutor v Mbarushimana*, Pre-Trial Chamber I, ICC-01/04-01/10, Decision on the Confirmation of Charges, 16 December 2011, para 287.

it emphasises one's relationship or association with others.[34] However, the theoretical underpinnings of these two forms of liability are entirely different: responsibility under Article 28 arises from the formal link between the superior and the agent and not from the latter's wrongful conduct, as is the case with complicity.[35] The basis for command responsibility is thus the superior's culpable failure to act.[36]

A. 'Commits Such a Crime, Whether as an Individual, Jointly with Another or through Another Person...'

Until recently, subparagraph (a) of the Rome Statute gave rise to most ICC practice relating to criminal participation.[37] It covers the commission of the crime through perpetration, co-perpetration and indirect perpetration, also referred to as 'perpetration by means'. Co-perpetration implies a functional division of the criminal tasks between the different co-perpetrators, who are usually interrelated by the common plan.[38] Indirect perpetration means that the person who commits the crime can be used as an instrument by the indirect perpetrator.[39] Article 25(3)(a) provides for the liability of the indirect perpetrator regardless of the mens rea of the person who actually commits the offence.[40] This permits

[34] G Vetter, 'Command Responsibility of Non-military Superiors in the International Criminal Court' (2000) 25 *Yale Journal of International Law* 89, 98.

[35] ibid, 99.

[36] ibid, 100. 'Command responsibility' most closely resembles complicity in the form of 'ordering' under Article 25(3)(b) of the Rome Statute.

[37] *Lubanga* Judgment (n 8); *Katanga* Confirmation of Charges Decision (n 3); *Prosecutor v Mudacumura*, Pre-Trial Chamber II, ICC-01/04-01/12, Decision on the Prosecutor's Application under Article 58, 13 July 2012 ('*Mudacumura* Decision'); *Prosecutor v Abu Garda*, ICC-02/05-02/09, Pre-Trial Chamber I, Decision on the Confirmation of Charges, 8 February 2010 ('*Abu Garda* Confirmation of Charges Decision'); *Prosecutor v William Samoei Ruto, Henry Kiprono Kosgey and Joshua Arap Sang*, ICC-01/09-01/11-373, Pre-Trial Chamber II, Decision on the Confirmation of Charges Pursuant to Article 61(7)(a) and (b) of the Rome Statute, 23 January 2012; *Prosecutor v Abdallah Banda and Saleh Jerbo*, ICC-02/05-03/09, Pre-Trial Chamber I, Decision on the Confirmation of Charges, 7 March 2011 ('*Abdallah Banda* and *Saleh Jerbo* Confirmation of Charges Decision'); *Prosecutor v Al Bashir*, ICC-02/05-01/09, Pre-Trial Chamber I, Warrant of Arrest for Omar Hassan Ahmad Al Bashir, 4 March 2009 ('*Al Bashir* Arrest Warrant'); *Prosecutor v* Simone *Gbagbo*, ICC-02/11-01/12, Pre-Trial Chamber III, Warrant of Arrest for Simone Gbagbo, 29 February 2012 ('*Simone Gbago* Arrest Warrant'); *Prosecutor v Gaddafi*, ICC-01/11, Pre-Trial Chamber I, Warrant of Arrest for Saif Al-Islam Gaddafi, 27 June 2011 ('*Gaddafi* Arrest Warrant'); *Prosecutor v Hussein*, Pre-Trial Chamber I, ICC-02/05-01/12, Warrant of Arrest for Abdel Raheem Muhammad Hussein, 1 March 2012 ('*Hussein* Arrest Warrant').

[38] Ambos (n 30) 479.

[39] ibid.

[40] The initial Working Paper submitted by Canada, Germany, the Netherlands and the UK to the Preparatory Committee as part of work on the modes of responsibility provided for the commission 'through a person who is not criminally responsible'. ('Working Paper'), A/AC.249/1997/WG.2/DAT1, 14 February 1997. This formulation changed to 'through

the extension of criminal responsibility of indirect perpetrators beyond the cases of innocent agency.[41] Due to this peculiarity, the ICC Pre-Trial Chambers have been actively using the concept of co-perpetration when confirming charges in the situations with multiple accused removed from the scene of the crime.[42]

The discussion about the correct interpretation of co-perpetration and indirect perpetration within Article 25(3)(a) began in *Lubanga*. The origin of this development was the need to identify the criteria for distinguishing principals and accessories. The *Lubanga* Pre-Trial Chamber held that the objective approach to distinguishing the two categories focuses on the realisation of one of the objective elements of the crime, thus labelling as (co-)perpetrators only those who physically perpetrate the crime.[43] The subjective approach, on the other hand, places the emphasis on the state of mind of the offender—those who have the shared intent are considered perpetrators.[44] The Chamber further argued that neither the objective nor the subjective criterion distinguishing principals and accessories could be reconciled with Article 25(3)(a). The former approach unjustly restricts indirect perpetration to those performing the actus reus of the offence, while the latter approach is already embodied in Article 25(3)(d), thus differentiating it from the co-perpetration within the meaning of Article 25(3)(a).[45]

Consequently, the ICC came up with the third method of 'control over crime' for distinguishing between principals and accessories, which it said applies in 'numerous legal systems'.[46] This approach is based on the work of the German criminal law scholar Claus Roxin.[47] The *Lubanga*

another person regardless of whether that person is criminally responsible' in the Report of the ICC Preparatory Committee, DOCUMENT A/CONF.183/2, 14 April 1998, 31.

[41] *Katanga* Judgment (n 8) para 1398.

[42] *Katanga* Confirmation of Charges Decision (n 3) paras 480–86, 490, 500–14, 527–39; *Lubanga* Confirmation of Charges Decision (n 3) paras 328–33; *Prosecutor v William Samoei Ruto, Henry Kiprono Kosgey and Joshua Arap Sang*, ICC-01/09-01/11-373, Pre-Trial Chamber II, Decision on the Confirmation of Charges Pursuant to Article 61(7)(a) and (b) of the Rome Statute, 23 January 2012 ('*Ruto* Confirmation of Charges Decision'), paras 291–292.

[43] *Lubanga* Confirmation of Charges Decision (n 3) para 328.

[44] ibid, para 329. The *Lubanga* Pre-Trial Chamber attributed the subjective approach to the jurisprudence of the ICTY on the joint criminal enterprise or the common purpose doctrine. Van Sliedregt, however, points out that neither the ICTY nor the ICTR has ever used the terminology of subjective/objective approach. See van Sliedregt (n 9) 84.

[45] *Lubanga* Confirmation of Charges Decision (n 3) paras 333–35.

[46] *Katanga* Confirmation of Charges Decision (n 3) paras 502, 504. Thomas Weigend noted that the list of 'numerous' national jurisdictions that are claimed to be in favour of the concept of perpetration through an organisation is limited to five (Argentina, Chile, Germany, Peru and Spain), in one of which (Argentina) the Supreme Court had overturned a lower court judgment proposing this theory. See T Weigend, 'Perpetration through an Organization: The Unexpected Career of a German Legal Concept' (2011) 9 *Journal of International Criminal Justice* 105.

[47] For a detailed discussion of the theory, see Ch 2.II.A.

Pre-Trial Chamber largely replicated the German approach by arguing: 'The notion underpinning this third approach is that principals to a crime are not limited to those who physically carry out the objective elements of the offence, but also include those who, in spite of being removed from the scene of the crime, control or mastermind its commission by virtue of deciding whether and how the offence will be committed.'[48] In line with this approach, the principals are those who have control over the crime and, while being aware of this control, either: (1) physically carry out the crime (direct perpetration); or (2) control the will of those who carry out the objective elements of the offence (indirect perpetration); or (3) who have, along with others, control over crime by reason of the essential tasks being assigned to them (joint or co-perpetration).[49]

The long-awaited first ICC judgment in *Lubanga* corroborated the Pre-Trial Chamber's approach.[50] The Chamber followed the Pre-Trial Chamber's analysis of the scope of co-perpetration based on the control over crime theory and held that the prosecution must prove the following elements to secure Lubanga's conviction for 'direct co-perpetration':[51]

(i) an agreement or common plan between the accused and at least one other co-perpetrator that results in the commission the relevant crime in the ordinary course of events;
(ii) an essential contribution of the accused to the common plan;
(iii) an intent on the part of the accused to commit a crime or his awareness that this crime is the consequence of the implementation of the plan in the ordinary course of events;
(iv) awareness that the accused provides an essential contribution to the implementation of the common plan; and, finally,
(v) awareness of the factual circumstances that established the existence of an armed conflict and the link between these circumstances and the conduct of the accused.

The conclusion on the basis of this list of elements was that Lubanga did indeed satisfy the above-mentioned criteria to qualify as a direct co-perpetrator in the meaning of Article 25(3)(a) for the crimes he has been charged with, namely enlisting children under the age of 15, conscripting children under the age of 15 and using children under the age of 15 to actively participate in hostilities.[52] The Chamber established that the accused and his alleged co-perpetrators worked together and each of them

[48] *Prosecutor v William Samoei Ruto, Henry Kiprono Kosgey and Joshua Arap Sang*, ICC-01/09-01/11-373, Pre-Trial Chamber II, Decision on the Confirmation of Charges Pursuant to Article 61(7)(a) and (b) of the Rome Statute, 23 January 2012, para 330.

[49] ibid, para 332.

[50] *Lubanga* Judgment (n 8) para 976.

[51] ibid, para 1018.

[52] Rome Statute, art 8(2)(b)(xxvi) or 8(2)(e)(vii).

had made an essential contribution to the common plan that resulted in the enlistment, conscription and use of children under the age of 15 to participate actively in hostilities.[53] The court treated the second element of co-perpetration—essential contribution to the common plan—as an indicator of control over the crime or lack thereof. The Chamber clarified that only those 'to whom essential tasks have been assigned—and who, consequently, have the power to frustrate the commission of the crime by not performing their tasks' have joint control over the crime.[54] The threshold for the essential contribution was therefore set at the capacity to frustrate the commission of the crime by withdrawing the contribution. In the *Gbagbo* case, the Pre-Trial Chamber accepted as essential a contribution without which the crime would not have been committed or would have been committed in 'a significantly different way'.[55]

The *Lubanga* Appeals Chamber confirmed the findings of the Trial Chamber, upholding Lubanga's conviction.[56] However, the Appeals Chamber slightly modified the criteria for holding someone responsible as a co-perpetrator. First, the judges appear to have rightly stressed the link between the contribution of the co-perpetrator and the crime. This is in contrast with the Trial Chamber's insistence on the contribution to the common plan. The appeal judgment refers to the agreement solely as a framework for making an essential contribution capable of frustrating the commission of a *crime*.[57] Second, the Appeals Chamber used the 'control over crime' theory in a way that is somewhat different from that of the Trial Chamber. The latter used it as a method of distinguishing between principals and accessories in lieu of the objective or subjective approaches.

In contrast, the appellate panel accepted that the objective approach defined by the accused person's extent of contribution to the offence while having control over crime, also renders the contribution essential when a co-perpetrator is not involved at the execution stage.[58] Notably, the Appeals Chamber clarified that it was not applying control over crime theory as a source of law, thereby refuting mounting criticism about the lack of legal foundation of this doctrine in international law,[59] but merely sought

[53] *Lubanga* Judgment (n 8) para 1271.

[54] ibid, para 925.

[55] *Gbago* Confirmation of Charges Decision (n 20) para 232.

[56] *Lubanga* Appeal Judgment (n 11) para 529.

[57] ibid, paras 467, 469. See also Judge Christine van den Wyngaert annexed to *Blé Goudé* Confirmation of Charges Decision (n 21) para 8.

[58] *Lubanga* Appeal Judgment (n 11) para 469, with reference to Kai Ambos' position arguing that a normative concept of control offers a plausible explanation of the way in which co-perpetration may be effectuated by those absent from the scene of the crime. See K Ambos, *Treatise on International Criminal Law, Volume I: Foundations and General Part* (Oxford, Oxford University Press, 2013) 153.

[59] Sadat and Jolly (n 4) 784.

guidance from approaches developed in other jurisdictions while interpreting and applying Article 25(3)(a) of the Rome Statute.[60] However, this argumentation does not explain why the plain reading of Article 25(3)(a) would not be acceptable. Regretfully, the Appeals Chamber avoided a much-needed discussion of the methodology of interpreting legal sources in international criminal law.[61]

Finally, the appellate judges introduced the idea of normative assessment of the person's role as a cornerstone principle of determining his role as a co-perpetrator.[62] The process of normative assessment is not fully elaborated in the judgment, but what is clear is that it involves weighting the specific circumstances of each individual case in 'an evaluation of whether the accused had control over the crime, by virtue of his or her essential contribution to it and the resulting power to frustrate its commission'.[63] In line with this approach, the Appeals Chamber upheld the Trial Chamber's conclusions that Lubanga made an essential contribution to the crimes he was charged with on the basis of cumulative criteria, which included, inter alia, his involvement in the planning of military operations, visits to the training camps and speeches. The appellate panel rejected Lubanga's submissions that his lack of day-to-day control over military affairs in the region rendered his contribution inessential. The key determination was the *cumulative* effect of the accused's activities rather than any of them taken in isolation.[64] The Appeals Chamber further established that the question of whether the accused 'committed' a crime does not depend on his proximity to the crime or the directness of his input.[65]

With regard to the mental elements, the Trial Chamber concluded that Thomas Lubanga acted with the intent and knowledge necessary to establish the charges pursuant to Article 30 of the Rome Statute. He was aware of the factual circumstances that established the existence of the armed conflict, and the nexus between those circumstances and his own conduct, which resulted in the enlistment, conscription and use of children below the age of 15 to participate actively in hostilities.[66] The definition of the mental element in *Lubanga* raises some critical points. The Trial Chamber claimed that 'awareness that a consequence will occur in the ordinary course of events' involves consideration by the participants of the concepts of 'possibility' and 'probability', which are inherent to the notions of 'risk' and 'danger'.[67] This statement comes dangerously close

60 *Lubanga* Appeal Judgment (n 11) para 470.
61 See Sadat and Jolly (n 4) 759.
62 *Lubanga* Appeal Judgment (n 11) para 466.
63 ibid, para 473.
64 ibid, paras 473, 479, 488.
65 ibid, para 473.
66 *Lubanga* Judgment (n 8) para 1357.
67 ibid, para 1012. *cf Katanga* Judgment (n 8) para 775.

to accepting *dolus eventualis*, or inadvertent recklessness, as the applicable fault requirement at the ICC.[68] *Dolus eventualis* is the lowest form of culpability and appears to be beyond what the drafters of the Rome Statute envisaged for the crimes within the court's jurisdiction.[69]

Without openly embracing inadvertent recklessness, the *Lubanga* Trial Chamber utilised the evidence more appropriate for this standard rather than *dolus directus in the second degree*. It found that the accused's participation in a common plan to build an army for the purpose of establishing and maintaining political and military control over the Ituri region resulted, in the ordinary course of events, in the conscription and enlistment of boys and girls under the age of 15, and using them to participate actively in hostilities.[70] Among the facts supporting this conclusion were the accused's speeches addressed to the population and aimed at recruiting youngsters, his use of soldiers under the age of 15 as bodyguards and his close contact with a potential recruiter of children.[71] All of these facts do not seem to support the conclusion that the recruitment of children would have been an *inevitable* outcome in the ordinary course of events, but rather that there was a high risk of the crime occurring.[72]

The *Lubanga* appeal judgment took a praiseworthy step and corrected this discrepancy by pointing out that the term 'risk' should have been avoided when interpreting Article 30.[73] The Appeals Chamber found that the standard for the foreseeability of events within the meaning of Article 30 of the Rome Statute is 'virtual certainty'.[74] Despite having rejected the term 'risk' and reaffirming 'virtual certainty' as the applicable legal standard, the Appeals Chamber left the door open for some degree of probability in the evaluation of evidence pertaining to the accused's knowledge. The judges were satisfied that the issue at stake in *Lubanga* was not so-called 'low risk' that broadens the scope of Article 30 in an unacceptable fashion. In contrast, the events forming the basis of the assessment followed from a long-term plan, which presupposed that the co-perpetrators were

[68] For criticism, see Separate Opinion of Judge Fulford (n 13) para 15; Concurring Opinion of Judge van den Wyngaert (n 18) paras 36–38.

[69] For a detailed discussion on the accepted fault requirement before the ICC, see *Bemba* Confirmation of Charges Decision (n 3) paras 358–68.

[70] *Lubanga* Judgment (n 8) para 1351.

[71] *Lubanga* Judgment (n 8) paras 1277, 1278, 1356.

[72] The weak evidence supporting the fault requirement in *Lubanga* played an important role during the sentencing deliberations. The fact that Thomas Lubanga did not mean to conscript children, but was, rather, aware that this would occur in the ordinary course of events mitigated his sentence. Mr Lubanga received the relatively lenient punishment of 14 years' imprisonment. See *Prosecutor v Thomas Lubanga Dyilo*, ICC-01/04-01/06, Trial Chamber I, Decision on Sentence Pursuant to Article 76 of the Statute, 10 July 2012 ('*Lubanga* Sentencing Decision'), paras 52, 53 and 98. For more discussion on the sentencing policy of the ICC, see Ch 7.

[73] *Lubanga* Appeal Judgment (n 11) para 449.

[74] ibid, para 447.

aware that the consequences will occur in the ordinary course of events.[75] Accordingly, the appellate panel was convinced that the threshold set out in Article 30 of the Rome Statute was met—Lubanga was aware of the circumstances prevailing in Ituri, for instance, by being in close contact with the senior Union of Congolese Patriots (UPC) members involved in conscripting and enlisting children.[76] This conclusion appears to stretch the evidence beyond the declared standard of virtual certainty and back to the notion of risk.[77] Future jurisprudence will have to provide more guidance on this matter.[78]

The notion of control over crime has been further developed in *Katanga* and took the form of the so-called 'indirect co-perpetration'. The Pre-Trial Chamber upheld the idea of combining co-perpetration and indirect perpetration and held:

> There are no legal grounds for limiting the joint commission of the crime solely to cases in which the perpetrators execute a portion of the crime by exercising direct control over it. Rather, through a combination of individual responsibility for committing crimes through other persons together with the mutual attribution among the co-perpetrators at the senior level, a mode of liability arises which allows the Court to assess the blameworthiness of 'senior leaders' adequately.[79]

Consequently, the *Katanga* Pre-Trial Chamber created an elaborate structure made of the subjective and objective elements of indirect co-perpetration by combining the features of both doctrines, including the following:

(i) the suspect must be part of a common plan or an agreement with one or more persons;
(ii) the suspect and the other co-perpetrator(s) must carry out essential contributions in a coordinated manner which result in the fulfilment of the material elements of the crime;
(iii) the suspect must have control over the organisation;

[75] ibid, para 450.

[76] ibid, para 527.

[77] The evidentiary shortcomings are partly to be blamed for the contested fault requirement in *Lubanga*. Judge Ušacka criticised in her dissenting opinion the vagueness of the charges against Lubanga that resulted in the practice of charging in relation to 'patterns' of conscription, enlistment and use of children under the age of 15 rather than referring to individual cases. See *Prosecutor v Thomas Lubanga Dyilo*, ICC-01/04-01/06 A 5, Appeals Chamber Judgment on the appeal of Mr Thomas Lubanga Dyilo against His Conviction, Dissenting Opinion of Judge Anita Ušacka, 1 December 2014, paras 8, 11.

[78] Cryer noted the ambiguity of the requirement that the defendant is aware that the consequences will occur in the ordinary course of events. See R Cryer, H Friman, D Robinson and E Wilmeshurst, *An Introduction to International Criminal Law and Procedure*, 2nd edn (Cambridge, Cambridge University Press, 2010) 387.

[79] *Prosecutor v Germain Katanga and Mathieu Ngudjolo Chui*, ICC-01/04-01/07, Pre-Trial Chamber I, Decision on the Confirmation of Charges, 30 September 2008, para 492.

(iv) the organisation must consist of an organised and hierarchal apparatus of power;
(v) the execution of the crimes must be secured by almost automatic compliance with the orders issued by the suspect;
(vi) the suspect must satisfy the subjective elements of the crimes;
(vii) the suspect and the other co-perpetrators must be mutually aware and accept that implementing the common plan will result in the fulfilment of the material elements of the crimes; and
(viii) the suspect must be aware of the factual circumstances enabling him to exercise joint control over the commission of the crime through another person(s).[80]

The Pre-Trial Chamber found that both co-accused in the case—Germain Katanga and Mathieu Ngudjolo—satisfied the numerous conditions for indirect co-perpetration of crimes against humanity and war crimes committed during the attack on Bogoro village on 24 February 2003 and confirmed the charges.[81] The Chamber found grounds to believe that Katanga and Ngudjolo served as de jure and de facto commanders of the forces responsible for the attack on Bogoro.[82]

At the trial stage, however, indirect co-perpetration as a mode of liability proved to be unsuccessful in respect of both accused in the *Katanga* case. After the closing arguments of the parties and the participants, the Trial Chamber proceeded with severing the charges against Mathieu Ngudjolo[83] and subsequently acquitted him.[84] The judges were unable to find sufficient evidence that Ngudjolo served as a military commander, despite the important role he played in the region due to his high social status.[85] Furthermore, the Chamber did not establish that the accused gave military orders or attempted to secure their compliance.[86] Accordingly, at least two elements of indirect perpetration failed, leading to the acquittal of Ngudjolo.[87]

With respect to Katanga, the Trial Chamber chose to change the legal characterisation of his mode of liability from indirect perpetration on the basis of Article 25(3)(a), which failed to provide a basis for conviction, to complicity in the commission of a crime by a group of persons acting

[80] ibid, paras 495–539. See also *Ruto* Decision (n 37) para 292; *Prosecutor v Jean-Pierre Bemba Gombo*, ICC-01/05-01/08, Pre-Trial Chamber II, Decision Pursuant to Article 61(7)(a) and (b) of the Rome Statute on the Charges, 15 June 2009, paras 350–351.

[81] *Katanga* Decision (n 79) paras 573–80.

[82] ibid, paras 540–41.

[83] *Katanga* Severing Decision (n 14) para 9.

[84] *Prosecutor v Mathieu Ngudjolo Chui*, ICC-01/04-02/12-4, Trial Chamber II, Judgment Pursuant to Article 74 of the Statute, 18 December 2012.

[85] ibid, paras 491, 499, 501.

[86] ibid, para 502.

[87] ibid, para 110.

with a common purpose pursuant to Article 25(3)(d)(ii).[88] While a detailed investigation of the implications of this decision falls outside the scope of the present analysis, it is sufficient to note that legal the recharacterisation of the liability mode at such a late stage of proceedings divided the Chamber. The majority considered the legal recharacterisation of the mode of responsibility compatible with the rights of the accused because it did not alter, in the view of the majority, the narrative of facts described in the decision on the confirmation of charges.[89] Judge Van den Wyngaert dissented on this point.[90]

The *Katanga* trial judgment indeed acquitted Germain Katanga as an indirect perpetrator, while convicting him pursuant to Article 25(3)(d)(ii).[91] In this case, the Trial Chamber confirmed the allegations that the accused facilitated the supply of weapons used by the local Ngiti militia in an attack on the village of Bogoro—a stronghold of the UPC.[92] The Hema-dominated UPC constituted a legitimate military target, but, in addition to the military causalities, a number of civilians died during the attack on Bogoro. The majority regarded the operation in Bogoro as an attack against the civilian population.[93] The argument was that Ngiti militia, driven by the ethnic hatred against Hema, regarded the UPC and the Hema civilians as one single enemy; as such, the attack was primarily directed against the civilians.[94]

Prior to dealing with Katanga's responsibility under Article 25(3)(d)(ii),[95] the Trial Chamber clarified the elements of indirect perpetration pursuant to subparagraph (a) of the same article.[96] In analysing the provision, the Trial Chamber unanimously rejected the hierarchy of liability modes inherent in Article 25(3).[97] The judges correctly reasoned that neither the Rome Statute nor the Rules of Evidence and Procedure provide for a mitigation of punishment for the forms of responsibility other than 'commission', and there is no reason why an accomplice shall be accorded

[88] *Katanga* Severing Decision (n 14) para 7.

[89] ibid, paras 23, 32.

[90] *Prosecutor v Germain Katanga and Mathieu Ngudjolo Chui*, ICC-01/04-01/07, Trial Chamber II, Dissenting Opinion of Judge van den Wyngaert to Decision on the Implementation of Regulation 55 of the Regulations of the Court and Severing the Charges against the Accused Persons, 21 November 2012 ('Dissenting Opinion of Judge van den Wyngaert'), para 11. See also Minority Opinion of Judge van den Wyngaert (n 8).

[91] *Katanga* Judgment (n 8) paras 23, 32.

[92] ibid, paras 1147, 1671.

[93] *Katanga* Judgment (n 8) para 1150.

[94] ibid, para 1144. Judge van den Wyngaert challenged the logic of equating the UPC and Hema civilians as one enemy subject to attack. See Minority Opinion of Judge van den Wyngaert (n 8) paras 214, 255.

[95] Section I(D) below.

[96] ibid, paras 1381 et seq.

[97] *Katanga* Judgment (n 8) para 1387; Minority Opinion of Judge van den Wyngaert (n 8) para 279.

lesser guilt or receive a lighter penalty than a perpetrator.[98] Thus, there is a clear rift in the jurisprudence of the ICC when it comes to the question of hierarchy of the forms of participation in Article 25(3), with the *Lubanga* appeal judgment upholding the implicit value-based differentiation of the modes of liability.[99]

The majority in *Katanga* and the *Lubanga* Appeals Chamber are nonetheless united in their commitment to retaining the control over crime theory as a guiding principle for distinguishing perpetrators and accessories.[100] The justification for upholding the control over crime approach in *Katanga* was the need to give full effect to Article 25(3) in the light of the distinction between the perpetrators and the accomplices inherent in this provision.[101] The judges reiterated already familiar arguments concerning the inapplicability of the objective and subjective approaches for differentiating crime participants.[102] The exercise of giving full effect to Article 25(3) through the control over crime theory avoided both a plain reading of this provision—its language does not contain any trace of the theory in question,—and interpreting the article in accordance with the rules established in international law.

As in the *Lubanga* case, the judges in *Katanga* brushed away, unconvincingly, the arguments regarding the theory's recognition in various national legal systems or in the customary international law. Examining these sources of law would have likely resulted in the dismissal of the theory altogether.[103] The majority thus proceeded to define indirect commission on the basis of control over crime theory. The judges concluded that the indirect perpetrator exercises within the organisation control over crime committed through another person.[104] The organisation in question must be a 'power structure' characterised by the automatic compliance—the link between the superior and the actual perpetrators is of little importance, making latter interchangeable.[105] The indirect perpetrator must hold real authority within the organisation, including the power to decide whether or not to execute the crime.[106] Relying on this definition, the Trial Chamber acquitted Germain Katanga of the charges as indirect perpetrator upon finding that the Ngiti militia lacked the organisation to qualify as a 'power structure'. In addition, the evidence was not conclusive as to

[98] *Katanga* Judgment (n 8) paras 1386, 1387.
[99] *Lubanga* Appeal Judgment, para 462, citing Ambos (n 58) 146.
[100] ibid, paras 1382, 1388. *cf* Minority Opinion of Judge van den Wyngaert (n 8) para 281.
[101] *Katanga* Judgment (n 8) para 1395.
[102] ibid, paras 1391, 1392.
[103] See *Katanga* Judgment (n 8) para 1395. See also Sadat and Jolly (n 4) 784.
[104] *Katanga* Judgment (n 8) para 1406.
[105] ibid, para 1409.
[106] ibid, para 1411.

the exact nature of the relationships between the commanders and their subordinates.[107]

The *Lubanga* appeal judgment left undecided the question of whether 'indirect co-perpetration' is an independent mode of liability under the Rome Statute.[108] The Appeals Chamber acknowledged only three ways of commission expressly provided by Article 25(3)(a): individual, joint or through another person. However, it held in the footnote that: 'Views have also been expressed in the Court's jurisprudence that article 25(3)(a) of the Statute provides for a fourth form of commission liability, whereby a perpetrator may commit a crime jointly with another person, where that other person commits the crime through [yet] another person.'[109] This statement, together with the express admission by the appellate judges that a co-perpetrator does not need to personally carry out the incriminated conduct,[110] opened up the possibility of adopting a more coherent structure reflecting joint commission.

This path was taken in *Blé Goudé*, whereby judges chose to distance themselves from the German-inspired multilayered structure of indirect co-perpetration. They did so by pointing out that joint perpetrators may execute crimes directly or through another person.[111] In the latter case, it is only required to establish: the existence of a common plan to commit crimes (or resulting, in the ordinary course of events, in their commission); coordinated action by co-perpetrators having control over crime by virtue of their essential contributions; jointly exercised control over direct perpetrators whose will is subjugated; and the requisite intent and knowledge with respect to the crimes charged.[112] This refinement of the joint commission at the ICC is most welcome for it eliminates the unnecessary complexity introduced in *Katanga* and is closer to the plain reading of Article 25(3)(a).

B. 'Orders, Solicits or Induces the Commission…'

The Rome Statute does not include 'instigating' in subparagraph (b) of Article 25(3), but the Pre-Trial Chambers consistently held that all three terms mentioned in this provision—'ordering', 'soliciting' and 'inducing'—fall into the broader category of instigation or prompting another person

[107] ibid, para 1418.
[108] See also Partly Dissenting Opinion of Judge Christine Van den Wyngaert annexed to *Blé Goudé* Confirmation of Charges Decision (n 21) fn 3.
[109] *Lubanga* Appeal Judgment (n 19) para 464, fn 863.
[110] ibid, para 466.
[111] *Blé Goudé* Confirmation of Charges Decision (n 21) para 136.
[112] ibid, para 137.

to commit a crime.[113] Nonetheless, there are some distinctions among these forms of participation, despite significant overlap.

Ordering pertains to an individual who is in a position of authority and uses his authority to compel another individual to commit a crime.[114] Thus, ordering implies a superior–subordinate relationship between one who orders and the agent. Views have been expressed that 'ordering' belongs to the category of perpetration by means, covered by subparagraph (a) of the same article[115] or responsibility of commanders and other superiors under Article 28 of the Rome Statute.[116] However, it appears that 'ordering' occupies its own niche among the various forms of complicity listed in the Statute. Perpetration through another person is a form of direct liability, even when it employs the doctrinal constructions, such as 'control over crime', used to assign liability to the perpetrator. In contrast, ordering is derivative in the sense that it depends on the liability of the actual perpetrator.[117]

'Ordering' under subparagraph (b) differs from the liability of superiors pursuant to Article 28 because the legal requirements for proving these two forms of responsibility differ. In case of 'plain' ordering under Article 25(3)(b), one has to prove only the specific superior–subordinate relationship with the perpetrator, but not the offender's effective control and command over the forces required to attract responsibility under Article 28.[118] The extra burden of proving the superior's effective control is compensated by a lower threshold for the mental element under Article 28. Ordering as a form of complicity under Article 25(3)(b) has to comply with the general fault requirements set out in Article 30, namely intent and knowledge. In contrast, superior responsibility under Article 28 embodies specific fault requirement, which is looser than the general fault requirement, and includes *dolus eventualis*.[119]

In *Mudacumura*, the ICC provided its early interpretation of ordering.[120] The court relied on the jurisprudence of the ad hoc tribunals in defining

[113] *Prosecutor v Laurent Gbagbo*, ICC-02/1-01/1, Pre-Trial III, Decision on the Confirmation of Charges against Laurent Gbagbo, 12 June 2014, para 243; *Blé Goudé* Confirmation of Charges Decision (n 21) para 159.

[114] Report of the ILC, 48th Session, at 20, para 8.

[115] Ambos (n 30) 480.

[116] Eser (n 26) 797.

[117] Van Sliedregt (n 24) 107.

[118] Article 28(a): 'A military commander or person effectively acting as a military commander shall be criminally responsible for crimes within the jurisdiction of the Court committed by forces under his or her effective command and control, or effective authority and control as the case may be, as a result of his or her failure to exercise control properly over such forces.'

[119] Article 28(a)(i) and (b)(i) provides for the following standard in respect of superior responsibility: 'knew or, owing to the circumstances at the time, should have known' and 'knew, or consciously disregarded information'.

[120] *Mudacumura* Decision (n 37) paras 63 et seq; *Ntaganda* Confirmation of Charges Decision (n 21) paras 145 et seq.

the elements of ordering—the Pre-Trial Chamber held that to be responsible under Article 25(3)(b) of the Statute, it must be established that:

(i) the person is in a position of authority;
(ii) the person instructs another person in any form to either:
   a. commit a crime which in fact occurs or is attempted or
   b. perform an act or omission in the execution of which a crime is carried out;
(iii) the order had a direct effect on the commission or attempted commission of the crime; and
(iv) the person is at least aware that the crime will be committed in the ordinary course of events as a consequence of the execution or implementation of the order.

Accordingly, it was alleged that Mudacumura acted in a position of authority because he was the top military commander for the relevant period.[121] He instructed others to conduct a military campaign resulting in the commission of war crimes. For example, he approved of a general order to pillage civilian property to sustain the military efforts.[122] His orders had a direct effect on the crimes due to his position of authority and compliance with these orders was taken as evidence of their direct effect.[123] Finally, he: (i) was aware of the factual circumstances that established the existence of the armed conflict; and (ii) was at least aware that by issuing said orders, crimes would be committed in the ordinary course of events as a consequence of the execution of his orders.[124]

There are at least two problems with the Chamber's interpretation of ordering in *Mudacumura*. First, intent is nowhere to be found in the stipulation of elements of ordering and the analysis of Mudacumura's state of mind. The court appears to have abandoned the intent element of Article 30 of the Rome Statute, relying solely on the suspect's awareness of the situation. Moreover, his knowledge is inferred from the reports he allegedly received by virtue of his position. It is questionable whether such a low standard is acceptable for 'ordering', which, according to Article 30, requires the proof of intent to contribute and the knowledge of the consequences. This is in contrast to superior responsibility, which allows for a lower standard of fault.[125] In the case of superior responsibility, inferences could be drawn to some extent from the position of the accused. The other

[121] *Mudacumura* Decision (n 37) para 64.
[122] ibid, para 65.
[123] ibid, para 66. See also *Ntaganda* Confirmation of Charges Decision (n 21) para 149.
[124] *Mudacumura* Decision (n 37) paras 66–67.
[125] This position was later corrected and the fault requirement for ordering was brought in line with art 30. For example, the Pre-Trial Chamber found that Charles Blé Goudé: (i) meant to instigate pro-Gbagbo forces to carry out certain actions resulting in crimes; and

problem is that of the exact addressees of Mudacumura's orders. The Pre-Trial Chamber simply stated that he issued orders to the 'others'. However, the derivative nature of ordering requires at least some identification of those who were instructed to carry out the crimes.[126]

Soliciting and inducing in the Rome Statute largely correspond to instigation in the ICTY and ICTR Statutes.[127] As with ordering, they are covered by the general mental element of Article 30.[128] These two forms of participation differ from ordering in that they do not require the person to hold a position of authority vis-s-vis the perpetrator(s) of the crime.[129] Soliciting a crime means commanding, authorising, urging, inciting, requesting or advising another to commit a crime.[130] Inducing denotes bringing on or about, affecting, causing or influencing an act or course of conduct.[131] Inducing appears to be a broader term, covering soliciting, as the latter refers to a more specific conduct.[132]

The Pre-Trial Chamber in *Ntaganda* defined the elements of inducement with the reference to the case law of the ad hoc tribunals:[133]

(i) the person exerts influence over another person to either commit a crime which in fact occurs or is attempted or to perform an act or omission as a result of which a crime is carried out;
(ii) the inducement has a direct effect on the commission or attempted commission of the crime; and
(iii) the person is at least aware that the crimes will be committed in the ordinary course of events as a consequence of the realisation of the act or omission.

Based on the above test, the Chamber held that the orders issued by Bosco Ntaganda to his military unit and civilians to commit crimes against a different ethnic group showed that he exerted influence over the perpetrators by creating an environment, in which offending was encouraged. He did so by physically perpetrating crimes himself, using derogatory language and failing to repress offending by others.[134]

(ii) was aware that crimes would be committed in the ordinary course of events following his instigation. *Blé Goudé* Confirmation of Charges Decision (n 21) para 164. See also *Gbagbo* Confirmation of Charges Decision (n 113) paras 248–49.

[126] Responsibility is derivative if it is not stand-alone, but depends on the responsibility of the perpetrator. On the theory of derivative liability, see Fletcher (n 6) 581.

[127] Schabas (n 2) 432; van Sliedregt (n 24) 107.

[128] Eser (n 26) 797.

[129] *Gbagbo* Confirmation of Charges Decision (n 113) para 243; *Blé Goudé* Confirmation of Charges Decision (n 21) para 159; Eser (n 26) 796.

[130] *Black's Law Dictionary* 6th edn (St Paul, West Publishing) 1392.

[131] ibid 775.

[132] Ambos (n 30) 481.

[133] *Ntaganda* Confirmation of Charges Decision (n 21) para 153.

[134] *Ntaganda* Confirmation of Charges Decision (n 21) para 155.

Inducing as a mode of liability was also invoked in the *Harun* case.[135] The court found grounds to believe that Ahmad Harun—a former Minister of Interior in the government of Sudan—personally incited the militia to attack the civilian population on several occasions through delivering speeches and promising financial and governmental support to them. These actions resulted in looting of the villages.[136] The Pre-Trial Chamber established the fault requirement—intent and knowledge—on the basis of two factors: the content of Harun's speeches and his position of authority, by virtue of which he received regular reports on rebel and counterinsurgent activities.[137] The Chamber held that there were grounds to believe that Harun not only knew about the militia's methods of attacking civilians and pillaged villages, but also personally encouraged the commission of such illegal acts.[138]

C. 'Aids, Abets or Otherwise Assists in its Commission…'

The conduct requirement under subparagraph (c) significantly expands the usual brief reference to aiding and abetting in the Statutes of the ad hoc tribunals. This provision of the Rome Statute contains a variety of conducts under the umbrella term 'assists'—aiding, abetting and providing means for the commission of a crime. The qualifier 'otherwise' indicates that the list of possible forms of assistance presented in this article is not exhaustive. *Black's Law Dictionary* also treats aiding and abetting as a broad notion that includes all assistance rendered by words, acts, encouragement, support or presence, whether actual or constructive.[139] Article 25(3)(c) does not require the assistance to contribute substantially to the commission of a crime. This is surprising because the 'substantial effect' or 'substantial contribution' standard is widely accepted by the ICTY and the ICTR.[140] Moreover, the ILC Draft Code of

[135] *Prosecutor v Ahmad Harun and Ali Kushayb*, ICC-02/05-01/07, Pre-Trial Chamber I, Decision on the Prosecution Application under Article 58(7) of the Statute, 27 April 2007 ('*Harun* Decision'), para 78.

[136] ibid, para 90.

[137] ibid, para 92.

[138] ibid, para 93.

[139] *Black's Law Dictionary* (n 130) 68.

[140] *Prosecutor v Blaskić*, ICTY Case No IT-95-14-A, Appeal Judgment, 29 July 2004, para 48; *Prosecutor v Vasiljević*, ICTY Case No IT-98-32-A, Appeal Judgment, 25 February 2004, para 102; *Prosecutor v Tadić*, ICTY Case No IT-94-1, Appeals Chamber Judgment, 19 July 1999, para 229; *Prosecutor v Gacumbitsi*, ICTR Case No 2001-64-A, Appeal Judgment, 7 July 2006, para 140. The same standard has been adopted by the hybrid tribunals. See *Prosecutor v KAING Guek Eav alias Duch*, ECCC, Case No 001/18-07-2007/ECCC/TC, Trial Judgment, 20 March 2012, para 533; *Prosecutor v Brima, Kamara and Kanu* ('AFRC Case'), SCSL-04-16-A, Appeal Judgment, 22 February 2008, para 775. See also A Clapham, 'Issues of Complexity, Complicity and Complementarity: From the Nuremberg Trials to the Dawn of the Next

Crimes contained an even stricter standard of a 'direct and substantial' contribution.[141]

The practice is still unsettled as to whether the ICC adopted the 'substantial contribution' standard prevalent in the jurisprudence of the ad hoc tribunals. There were signs in the early decisions pointing in this direction.[142] The Chambers seemed to have inferred this level of contribution relative to the essential contribution required under subparagraph (a). In contrast, more recent cases do not use this test.[143] In *Blé Goudé*, the judges focused on the factual effect of the efforts of the former Minister of Youth and Sports, Charles Blé Goudé on the growing capacity of the pro-Gbagbo forces to commit the crimes.[144] Likewise, in *Bemba Gombo et al*, the Pre-Trial Chamber focused on the realistic input of each member of Mr Bemba's defence team in assessing whether there were reasons to believe they committed crimes against justice by corrupting witnesses in the related case against Mr Bemba. The conduct of the case manager who facilitated money transfers to the witnesses matched the requirements of Article 25(3)(c).[145]

Aiding and abetting is preceded by the words 'for the purpose of facilitating the commission of a crime'. Consequently, the fault requirement of aiding and abetting under the Rome Statute is enhanced compared to that of the ad hoc tribunals—the accused must have both knowledge of the crime and act with *the purpose of its facilitation*.[146] This requirement goes beyond the general mens rea standard of Article 30 of the Rome Statute because it introduces a form of specific intent.[147] It remains to be seen how the ICC interprets this requirement in the case law.

There is no scholarly agreement as to the place of aiding and abetting in Article 25(3). Ambos refers to it as the 'weakest form of complicity', while Eser contends that aiding and abetting is assistance that falls short of instigation under subparagraph (b), but goes beyond other contributions according to subparagraph (d). Werle insists that assistance is a mode of participation that illustrates secondary responsibility and a rather

International Criminal Court' in P Sands (ed), *From Nuremberg to the Hague: The Future of International Criminal Justice*, (Cambridge, Cambridge University Press, 2003) 56; W Schabas, 'Enforcing International Humanitarian Law: Catching the Accomplices' (2001) 83 *International Review of the Red Cross* 842.

141 ILC Draft Code 1996, art 2(3)(d).

142 Concurring Opinion of Judge van den Wyngaert (n 18) para 44; *Mbarushimana* Decision (n 33) para 279; *Lubanga* Judgment (n 8) para 997.

143 *Prosecutor v Jean-Pierre Bemba Gombo et al*, ICC-01/05-01/13, Pre-Trial Chamber II, Decision pursuant to Article 61(7)(a) and (b) of the Rome Statute, 11 November 2014 ('*Bemba Gombo et al* Decision'), para 35; *Blé Goudé* Confirmation of Charges Decision (n 21) para 167.

144 *Blé Goudé* Confirmation of Charges Decision (n 21) para 169.

145 *Bemba Gombo et al* Decision (n 143) para 76.

146 *Mbarushimana* Decision (n 33) para 281. *cf* Ambos (n 30) 483.

147 Schabas (n 2) 435–36; Ambos (n 30) 483.

low degree of individual guilt,[148] while Van Sliedregt argues against categorising liability and degrees of assistance, but rather treats them as overlapping.[149] The latter position best reflects the complex reality of a large-scale criminality.[150]

D. 'In Any Other Way Contributes to the Commission...'

Subparagraph (d) of the Rome Statute introduces a new category of criminal participation, namely 'contributing to the commission of a crime by a group acting with a common purpose'. This provision was modelled on the 1997 International Convention for the Suppression of Terrorist Bombings[151] and was inserted into the Rome Statute during the last stage of negotiations.[152] It replaced the earlier draft provisions on planning and conspiracy,[153] which gave rise to divergent views during the negotiations.[154] Thus, notwithstanding the wide acceptance of planning as a form of criminal responsibility in international criminal law,[155] neither planning nor conspiracy was included in the Rome Statute, paving the way for the novel category of criminal participation—'contribution to the commission of a crime'. This form of liability merits detailed analysis because it has the potential to replace (in)direction co-perpetration, which seems to be falling out of favour at the ICC. The conviction of Germain Katanga under Article 25(3)(d)(ii) exemplifies this trend.

[148] G Werle, 'Individual Criminal Responsibility in Article 25 Rome Statute' (2007) 5(4) *Journal of International Criminal Justice* 970.

[149] Ambos (n 30) 481; Eser (n 26) 798; van Sliedregt (n 24) 127;

[150] The ICTY jurisprudence appears to have adopted the view of liability modes as overlapping. See *Prosecutor v Krnojelac*, ICTY Case No IT-97-25-T, Trial Judgment, 15 March 2002 ('*Krnojelac* Trial Judgment'), para 173.

[151] Resolution adopted by the General Assembly on the report of the Sixth Committee (a/52/653) 52/164,15 December 1997, art 2(3).

[152] Document A/CONF.183/C.1/WGGP/L3.

[153] The earlier draft called for the criminal responsibility of a person who either: (i) Intentionally participates in planning or plans to commit such a crime which in fact occurs or is attempted; or (ii) Agrees with another person or persons that such a crime be committed and an overt act in furtherance of the agreement is committed by any of these persons that manifests their intent and such a crime in fact occurs or is attempted. See Working paper submitted by Canada, Germany, the Netherlands and the United Kingdom, A/AC.249/1997/WG.2/DAT1; Report of the ICC Preparatory Committee, DOCUMENT A/CONF.183/2, at 31.

[154] Report of the ICC Preparatory Committee, DOCUMENT A/CONF.183/2, at 31, fn 74.

[155] Article 2(3)(e) of the International Law Commission's 'Draft Code of Crimes against the Peace and Security of Mankind' (1996). See Charter of the Nuremberg International Military Tribunal, art 6; ICTY Statute, art 7(1); ICTR Statute, art 6(1).

The ICC practice so far established the following objective and subjective elements of the liability under Article 25(3)(d) of the Statute:[156]

(i) a crime within the jurisdiction of the Court is attempted or committed;
(ii) the commission or attempted commission of such a crime was carried out by a group of persons acting with a common purpose;
(iii) the individual contributed to the crime in any way other than those set out in Article 25(3)(a) to (c) of the Statute;[157]
(iv) the contribution shall be intentional; and
(v) shall either
  a. be made with the aim of furthering the criminal activity or criminal purpose of the group, where such activity or purpose involves the commission of a crime; or
  b. in the knowledge of the intention of the group to commit the crime.

The first criterion presupposes that the objective, the subjective and the contextual elements of the specific crimes are established.[158] There is a difference between the requirements of the liability modes and the elements of crimes, and this particular criterion emphasises this distinction.

The second condition relates to the commission of crime by the group. It is highly contested. In *Katanga*, the Trial Chamber used the concept of the joint criminal enterprise developed by the ad hoc tribunals in interpreting the notion of a group pursuant to Article 25(3)(d).[159] The judges held that while it is not necessary that the group pursues solely criminal aims, it is important that the participants of the group are aware that crimes will be committed in the ordinary course of events.[160] On the basis of these elements, the majority in *Katanga* proceeded to the conclusion that Ngiti militia was a self-contained group acting with the primary purpose of regaining Bogoro through the attack on Hema civilians.[161]

[156] *Katanga* Judgment (n 8) para 1620; *Prosecutor v Mbarushimana*, Pre-Trial Chamber I, ICC-01/04-01/10, Decision on the Prosecutor's Application for a Warrant of Arrest against Callixte Mbarushimana, 28 September 2010 ('*Mbarushimana* Arrest Warrant'), para 39; *Prosecutor v Muthuara et al*, ICC-01/09-02/11, Pre-Trial II, Decision on the Confirmation of Charges Pursuant to Article 61(7)(a) and (b) of the Rome Statute, 23 January 2012 ('*Muthuara* Decision'), para 421; *Ntaganda* Confirmation of Charges Decision (n 21) para 158.

[157] The formulation in *Katanga* provides for a 'significant contribution to a crime' test. *Katanga* Judgment (n 8) para 1620. The formulation in *Blé Goudé* omits quantification altogether and simply mentions 'contribution to the commission of … crime'. *Blé Goudé* Confirmation of Charges Decision (n 21) para 172.

[158] *Katanga* Judgment (n 8) para 1622.

[159] ibid, para 1625.

[160] ibid, para 1627; Minority Opinion of Judge van den Wyngaert (n 8) para 286.

[161] *Katanga* Judgment (n 8) paras 1654–59.

The majority inferred the common purpose from the way in which Bogoro was attacked—in the early morning hours when the civilians were still sleeping. The assault involved looting and destruction of property, and violence against the civilian population.[162] Judge van den Wyngaert dissented on this point, arguing that there was not sufficient evidence to establish the existence of the common purpose to attack the Hema civilians.[163] She maintained that it is plausible that the UPC—the legitimate military target—was the primary object of the attack.[164] She also questioned the majority's assumption that the attack on the UPC amounts to the attack on the entire Hema population, for it is one thing to regard them as an enemy, but quite another to deny them the right to exist.[165]

The group requirement was challenged on two other occasions. In *Muthaura*, the prosecution charged one of the accused—Mohammed Ali—with responsibility under Article 25(3)(d) for contributing to the commission of crimes in Kenya by instructing the Kenyan police and ensuring that their response to post-election violence was ineffective.[166] The Pre-Trial Chamber held that a prerequisite for Ali's criminal responsibility for crimes allegedly committed *through* the Kenyan police would have been the finding that the Kenyan police indeed carried out the objective elements of the crimes charged, but since the evidence in this regard was insufficient, the crimes could not be attributed to Ali.[167]

Likewise, in *Mbarushimana*, the majority was unable to conclude that the armed group in question—the Democratic Forces for the Liberation of Rwanda (FDLR)—indeed pursued the policy of attacking the civilian population in the Kivu region of the Democratic Republic of Congo.[168] This conclusion led the majority to believe that the FDLR does not constitute a 'group of persons acting with a common purpose' as required by Article 25(3)(d).[169] In contrast, maintaining the former President of Côte d'Ivoire Laurent Gbagbo in power at any cost, including through the use of violence against civilians, was deemed sufficient to establish common purpose in the *Gbagbo* and *Blé Goudé* cases.[170]

[162] ibid.
[163] Minority Opinion of Judge van den Wyngaert (n 8) para 208.
[164] ibid, para 225.
[165] ibid, paras 255–56.
[166] *Muthuara* Decision (n 156) para 422.
[167] ibid, paras 424–26.
[168] *Mbarushimana* Decision (n 33) para 291.
[169] ibid.
[170] *Gbagbo* Confirmation of Charges Decision (n 113) para 254; *Blé Goudé* Confirmation of Charges Decision (n 21) para 174. *cf* Dissenting Opinion of Judge Christine van den Wyngaert annexed to *Gbagbo* Confirmation of Charges Decision (n 113) para 5; Partly Dissenting Opinion of Judge Christine van den Wyngaert annexed to *Blé Goudé* Confirmation of Charges Decision (n 21) para 6.

In *Mbarushimana,* the defence raised another interesting point in relation to the group requirement: it argued that Article 25(3)(d) liability applies only to persons *outside* of the group acting with a common purpose.[171] The Chamber rejected this argument for two main reasons: first, adopting the essential contribution test for co-perpetration under subparagraph (a) and excluding from the ambit of paragraph (d) responsibility of group members making an non-essential contribution would unfairly absolve a group of offenders of responsibility; and, second, because of the enhanced mental element for aiding and abetting under the Statute—requiring the person to act with the purpose to facilitate the crime—Article 25(3)(d) is the only way to hold persons responsible for contributions made with knowledge but not necessarily intent. Thus, the court concluded that Article 25(3)(d) encompasses contributions from both members and non-members of the group.[172]

The third criterion—the level of contribution to the crime—is far from settled in the jurisprudence of the ICC. In *Mbarushimana,* the Pre-Trial Chamber felt that criminalising *any* contribution to the group crime under subparagraph (d) would be inappropriate because:

> Without some threshold level of assistance, every landlord, every grocer, every utility provider, every secretary, every janitor or even every taxpayer who does anything which contributes to a group committing international crimes could satisfy the elements of [Article] 25(3)(d) liability for their infinitesimal contribution to the crimes committed.[173]

At the same time, the judges referred to Article 25(3)(d) as a 'residual' form of accessorial liability, which is at the bottom of the value-oriented hierarchy of participation in a crime.[174] Thus, 'article 25(3)(d)'s contributions "[i]n any other way" must be less than that required for liability under article 25(3)(a)–(c)'.[175] Bearing in mind these conflicting considerations, the majority in *Mbarushimana* decided that a contribution to a commission of the crime acting with a common purpose must be at least significant. The Chamber drew its inspiration, when deciding on the appropriate threshold, from the jurisprudence of the ad hoc tribunals pertaining to the joint criminal enterprise.[176] It used the similarity between these two forms of liability as a justification for borrowing the joint criminal enterprise's 'significant contribution' requirement from the case law of the ICTY and

[171] ibid, para 272. See also *Katanga* Judgment (n 8) para 1631.
[172] *Mbarushimana* Decision (n 33) paras 273–74.
[173] ibid, paras 276–77.
[174] ibid, paras 278–79.
[175] ibid.
[176] ibid, para 283.

the ICTR.[177] In *Katanga*, the Trial Chamber established a formula for what the 'significant contribution' implies: it has to either affect the occurrence of the crime or the way in which it was committed.[178]

As to the methodology of determining the level of contribution, the judges in both *Katanga* and *Mbarushimana* rightly stressed that the assessment has to be done on a case-by-case basis, taking into account such factors as sustained participation after learning about group's criminality, efforts made to prevent criminal activity and the role of the accused vis-a-vis the crimes.[179]

Factually speaking, the judges concluded that Germain Katanga's contribution to the crimes committed in Bogoro was significant: his role in facilitating the supply of arms to the local Ngiti militia allowed it to gain a military advantage over the UPC and carry out its plan to attack the civilian population in Bogoro.[180] The weapons and ammunition arranged by Katanga ensured the success of the operation in Bogoro.[181] In contrast, the majority in *Mbarushimana* held that the accused, whose main responsibility was issuing press releases and who held no real authority within the FDLR, did not provide *any* contribution to the FDLR.[182] The Pre-Trial Chamber's decision declining to confirm charges against Mbarushimana has been confirmed on appeal and, while the majority of the Appeals Chamber saw no need to delve into an academic discussion related to the level of contribution required under Article 25(3)(d),[183] Judge Fernández de Gurmendi considered it necessary to address this point in her separate opinion.[184]

Judge Fernández de Gurmendi argued that Article 25(3)(d) does not envisage the minimum level of contribution to the crime.[185] She found

[177] Nonetheless, the judges stressed the important differences between the joint criminal enterprise and responsibility under art 25(3)(d): the nature of liability—principal or accessory; the requirement for the membership in the group or absence thereof; the contribution to the common purpose or crimes committed; and whether some form of intent or mere knowledge is sufficient. See *Mbarushimana* Decision (n 33) para 280. Views have been expressed that art 25(3)(d) explicitly addresses the concept of the joint criminal enterprise. See A Cassese, *International Criminal Law*, 2nd edn (Oxford, Oxford University Press, 2008) 211–13. See also *Tadić* Appeal Judgment (n 140) para 222.

[178] *Katanga* Judgment (n 8) para 1633.

[179] *Mbarushimana* Decision (n 33) para 284. See also *Katanga* Judgment (n 8) para 634.

[180] ibid, paras 1671, 1679.

[181] ibid, para 1676.

[182] ibid, paras 292, 295, 299.

[183] *Prosecutor v Mbarushimana*, Appeals Chamber, ICC-01/04-01/10 OA4, Judgment on the Appeal of the Prosecutor against the Decision of Pre-Trial Chamber I of 16 December 2011 Entitled 'Decision on the Confirmation of Charges', 30 May 2012 ('*Mbarushimana* Appeal Judgment'), paras 68, 70.

[184] *Prosecutor v Mbarushimana*, Appeals Chamber, ICC-01/04-01/10 OA4, Separate Opinion of Judge Silvia Fernández de Gurmendi, 30 May 2012 ('Separate Opinion of Judge Fernández de Gurmendi').

[185] ibid, para 9.

both the practice of attaching certain level of contribution to each liability mode and the 'import' of the 'significance contribution requirement' from the JCE jurisprudence of the ad hoc tribunals into Article 25(3)(d) unconvincing.[186] She correctly argued that the real issue is not the label of 'significance' ascribed to the contribution, but rather the so-called 'neutral contributions'.[187] Unfortunately, the opinion does not elaborate on the meaning of this term, but one may suggest that it refers to the contributions that could be used for the legitimate military activities and crimes alike.

Indeed, measuring the smallest possible input under Article 25(3)(d) appears highly problematic. The impact of the same assistance may vary depending on the circumstances of the case—providing the ammunition to the soldiers may be a decisive factor in their potential criminality or it may equally have no impact at all if they are already in possession of weapons. The same criticism applies to the general idea of quantifying various contributions of the accused depending on their respective forms of participation.[188]

As an alternative to measuring the least possible input under Article 25(3)(d), Judge Fernández de Gurmendi suggested focusing on the 'normative and causal' links between the contribution and the crime.[189] The factual situation in *Katanga*, whereby the accused facilitated the supply of weapons that could be used for criminal and non-criminal aims alike, prompted Judge van den Wyngaert to look for an instrument to assess such 'generic' contributions.[190] She proposed utilising the 'specific direction requirement'—the element of the actus reus of aiding and abetting recently introduced (and abandoned) in jurisprudence of the ad hoc tribunals—as such an instrument.[191] These recommendations regarding 'neutral' or 'generic' input share the emphasis on the link between the crime and the assistance rather than the amount of the contribution in question.

More recent confirmation of charges decisions were more sensitive to these considerations. In the *Gbagbo* case, the accused's contribution to post-electoral violence was assessed in a purely factual way: the Pre-Trial Chamber mentioned Laurent Gbago's activities in issuing orders, supporting the militia by providing them with weapons and participating in the meetings with high commanders.[192] In *Blé Goudé*, the judges simply noted the cumulative effect of the activities of Mr Blé Goudé and the way they contributed to the commission of crimes. In particular, the Chamber

186 ibid, paras 13, 14.
187 ibid, para 12.
188 See section II.C below.
189 Separate Opinion of Judge Fernández de Gurmendi (n 184) para 12.
190 Minority Opinion of Judge van den Wyngaert (n 8) para 287.
191 For a detailed discussion on the 'specific direction requirement', see Ch 4.1.G.
192 *Gbabgo* Confirmation of Charges Decision (n 20) para 255.

held that his instructions to the youth to participate in the repression of an anti-establishment rally 'constituted a *relevant immediate* contribution to the crimes' (emphasis added).[193] The adjectives 'relevant' and 'immediate' underline the effect of the contribution of the accused without purporting to quantify it in numerical terms.

It seems that the relationship between the assistance and the offence is an important aspect of accomplice liability and needs to be taken into account. Using the 'specific direction' test is particularly helpful for the purposes of Article 25(3)(d) due to the fact that this provision deals with the group that could be simultaneously engaged in criminal and non-criminal activities, and not just singular perpetrators, as is the case with aiding and abetting. However, any form of complicity presents a challenge for establishing a straightforward connection between the contribution and the offence because it falls outside the scope of the law on causation.[194] The link between the two elements is always cursory since it is interrupted by the freely chosen acts of other people—the immediate perpetrators. On this point, the majority in *Katanga* noted that it is not necessary to establish the direct link between the conduct of the accomplice and the resulting harm, nor it is required that the assistance is proximate to the crime.[195]

How can the connection between the contribution and the offence be reinforced if the directness of the aid and its distance to the crime are not dispositive? The answer could be in enhancing the scrutiny of the accused's mental state: generic assistance becomes culpable when there is knowledge about the crime as well as an understanding of the potential effects of the rendered help. Thus, the fault element appears to be central in determining the responsibility of accomplices.

The subjective element for Article 25(3)(d) responsibility consists of intentional contribution made either with the aim of furthering criminal activity of the group or knowledge of the intention of the group to commit the crime. Article 25(3)(d) liability represents an exception from the general rule on culpability stipulated in Article 30 of the Rome Statute.[196] Complicity as a 'contribution to the group' also differs from aiding and abetting under subparagraph (c) because it allows a lower fault requirement under both subclauses. The terms used in Article 25(3)(d) shall nonetheless be interpreted in the light of the general Article 30.[197]

The Trial Chamber in *Katanga* defined 'intentional contribution' for the purposes of both subparagraphs (i) and (ii) of Article 25(3)(d) as a

[193] *Blé Goudé* Confirmation of Charges Decision (n 21) paras 177–78.
[194] For a detailed discussion on causation, see Ch 4.II.B.
[195] *Katanga* Judgment (n 8) paras 1635, 1636.
[196] ibid, para 1637.
[197] Ambos (n 30) 485.

conscious and deliberate choice to engage in a certain behaviour with the knowledge that it contributes to the activities of the group.[198] The Pre-Trial Chamber in *Mbarushimana* contended that the 'intentionality' of the contribution must include an additional element linking the contribution to the crimes alleged.[199] However, it appears that this extra requirement is superfluous in the light of the two qualifying clauses that do the job of linking the contribution to the criminal activity of the group.

'Intentional contribution' should be read together with two specific clauses characterising the attitude towards group activity: the suspect or the accused should either aim to further the group's purpose to commit a crime or should know about the intention of the group to commit the specific crimes. Judge van den Wyngaert noted the distinction between subparagraph (i), which requires a more general understanding of the group's purpose by referring to '*a* crime', and a more specific knowledge under subparagraph (ii) referring to the '*the* crime'.[200] The majority in *Katanga* also correctly focused on the specificity of the knowledge of the accused for the purposes of Article 25(3)(d)(ii): knowing about the general criminal intent of the group was not deemed sufficient since the accused must be aware of the specific crimes that the group intends to commit and that they will occur in the ordinary course of events.[201]

The majority in *Katanga* regrettably transferred the conflated vision of military and criminal activities of the Ngiti militia into its analysis of the accused's mental state. Katanga's intent to contribute to the attack on Bogoro was established on the basis of his own testimony, despite the fact that the accused was referring to the attack on the UPC—a legitimate military target.[202] The Chamber further held that Katanga knew that the ammunition he supplied would be used during the attack. He was also aware that the methods of warfare *generally* implemented in the region included atrocities against civilians. Finally, he knew that the UPC was a Hema militia and he shared a strong anti-Hema sentiment.[203] Judge van den Wyngaert fairly raised concerns about the way Katanga's mental state was evaluated. She stressed that there was no evidence showing that his contributions were specifically directed to the crimes and not just reconquering Bogoro, or that he shared anti-Hema ideology.[204] The factual analysis of Katanga's mental state—like the assessment of Lubanga's fault—appears to be close to the standard of *dolus eventualis*, which is rejected by the ICC doctrinally.

[198] *Katanga* Judgment (n 8) para 1639.
[199] *Mbarushimana* Decision (n 33) para 288; *Katanga* Judgment (n 8) para 1637.
[200] Minority Opinion of Judge van den Wyngaert (n 8) para 288.
[201] *Katanga* Judgment (n 8) paras 1641, 1642.
[202] ibid, para 1682.
[203] ibid, paras 1685, 1688, 1689.
[204] Minority Opinion of Judge van den Wyngaert (n 8) paras 291, 304.

The *Lubanga* Trial Chamber referred to Article 25(3)(d) as a 'residual form of accessory liability, which makes it possible to criminalize those contributions that cannot be characterized as ordering, soliciting, inducing, aiding, abetting or assisting'.[205] This early interpretation of Article 25(3)(d) created some expectations that it would play a minor role in the jurisprudence of the ICC.[206] However, it seems that mounting discontent over (in)direct co-perpetration pushed the court towards this residual form of liability. This was because, in essence, Article 25(3)(a) and Article 25(3)(d) address the same type of situation—that of multiple offenders involved in the crime.[207] It has been established that the term 'common plan' under both provisions is functionally identical and must include an element of 'criminality'.[208] So far, the ICC has drawn a line between the two provisions, primarily based on the level of contribution necessary to attract liability, with Article 25(3)(a) embodying a higher threshold than Article 25(3)(d).[209] If one rejects the premise that the level of contribution is dispositive in determining whether responsibility is primary or accessory, and that Article 25(3)(d) is a 'lesser' form of responsibility, one may come to the conclusion that contributing to the commission of a crime by a group is a suitable form of responsibility in many instances.

II. HIERARCHY OF THE PARTICIPATION MODES

The judgments and decisions reviewed in the previous section demonstrate the difficulties the International Criminal Court encountered when interpreting Article 25(3). One of the biggest problems plaguing the interpretation of this article appears to be the complexity of establishing the fault requirement in the light of the demands of Article 30 of the Rome Statute. The other difficulty is the struggle to find a suitable form of responsibility that accurately reflects the culpability of the accused in the context of mass criminality. In order to overcome this difficulty, it is crucial to answer the question of whether the forms of participation within the Rome Statute are arranged in a hierarchical manner or otherwise.[210]

[205] *Lubanga* Decision (n 48) para 337. See also *Katanga* Decision (n 79) para 483, 'degrading' responsibility in art 25(3)(d) on the basis of its accessory nature.

[206] See, for example, Schabas (n 2) 436.

[207] *Katanga* Severing Decision (n 14).

[208] *Mbarushimana* Decision (n 33) para 271.

[209] *Lubanga* Judgment (n 8) para 996.

[210] There is no scholarly agreement on this issue. See H Olasolo, *The Criminal Responsibility of Senior Political and Military Leaders as Principals to International Crimes* (Oxford, Hart Publishing, 2009), 3–4; Ambos (n 26); Ambos (n 58) 147; Werle (n 148); *cf* van Sliedregt (n 9) 85; Weigend (n 46); Schabas (n 2) 424; Sadat and Jolly (n 4) 758.

The ICC raised the question of hierarchy on several occasions in its previous case law. In *Mbarushimana*, the judges referred to Gerhard Werle's argument that the modes of liability listed in Article 25(3) of the Rome Statute are arranged in accordance with a value-oriented hierarchy of participation in a crime under international law.[211] The *Katanga* Pre-Trial Chamber implicitly confirmed the existence of a hierarchy in the forms of participation, whereby more serious forms of participation subsume less serious forms of participation: this is evident from its decision to dismiss the alternative charge of accessorial liability for 'ordering' the commission of war crimes and crimes against humanity pursuant to Article 25(3)(b) as 'moot' upon finding sufficient grounds to believe that the accused are responsible as principals pursuant to Article 25(3)(a).[212] Further support for the hierarchy came from the subsequent change of the legal characterisation of Katanga's modes of liability from 'indirect co-perpetration' pursuant to subparagraph (a) to 'contribution to the commission of a crime by a group' on the basis of subparagraph (d). In the Trial Chamber's view, this change was not prejudicial to the rights of the accused, inter alia, because the elements of participation in a crime within the meaning of Article 25(3)(d) *are an integral part* of the material elements characterising the commission of a crime within the meaning of Article 25(3)(a).[213] This logic follows from the assumption that principal liability 'subsumes' accomplice liability.[214]

Finally, the *Lubanga* trial judgment established a pecking order between the perpetrator referred to in paragraph (a) and accessories mentioned in paragraphs (b)–(d).[215] The Chamber found that Article 25(3)(a) refers to the principal liability of someone committing a crime, as opposed to the secondary liability, which is dependent on the act of the perpetrator, enshrined in Article 25(3)(b) and (c).[216] The majority reasoning was that the level of contribution of the (co-)perpetrator has to be essential to properly express the blameworthiness of those persons who are most responsible for the most serious crimes of international concern.[217] The judges referred to Article 25(3)(d) as a 'residual form of accessory liability'.[218] The Appeals Chamber reinforced this approach: it argued, relying on Kai

[211] eg, *Mbarushimana* Decision (n 33) para 279.

[212] *Katanga* Confirmation of Charges Decision (n 3) paras 469–71. *cf Katanga* Judgment (n 8) para 1387.

[213] *Prosecutor v Germain Katanga and Mathieu Ngudjolo Chui*, ICC-01/04-01/07, Trial Chamber II, Decision on the Implementation of Regulation 55 of the Regulations of the Court and Severing the Charges against the Accused Persons, 21 November 2012, para 33.

[214] *cf* Dissenting Opinion of Judge van den Wyngaert (n 90) paras 42–43.

[215] *Lubanga* Judgment, paras 917–1018.

[216] ibid, para 998.

[217] ibid, para 999.

[218] *Lubanga* Decision (n 48) para 337. See also *Katanga* Decision (n 79) para 483, 'degrading' responsibility in art 25(3)(d) on the basis of its accessory nature.

Ambos' work, that the distinction between principal and accessory liability within Article 25(3) is not merely terminological—a person who commits an offence is more blameworthy than the one who contributes to the crimes of others.[219]

Despite its latest confirmation on appeal in *Lubanga*, the question of hierarchy in the ICC jurisprudence still appears to be far from settled. The *Katanga* Trial Chamber recently rejected the 'hierarchy of guilt' implicit in Article 25(3), but maintained that the distinction between principals and accomplices needs to be guided by the control over crime theory.[220] In addition to *Katanga*, the ICC witnessed some strong dissents on this matter. Judge Fulford in his separate opinion attached to the *Lubanga* judgment criticised the majority's approach to modes of liability on a number of grounds.[221] He disagreed with the majority in *Lubanga* that there is a need to establish a hierarchy between the modes of participation in the Rome Statute and also opposed the view that these modes of participation are mutually exclusive.[222] Article 25(3) also does not suggest, based on the plain or contextual reading of the provision, that the forms of participation are arranged in a hierarchical order. Distinguishing the forms of responsibility in line with the differential participation model does not imply any particular ranking.[223]

Judge van den Wyngaert also refuted the hierarchy of the modes of participation in her concurring opinion to the judgment of acquittal of Mathieu Ngudjolo.[224] She failed to see a difference in blameworthiness between the accessory liability, such as aiding and abetting or ordering, and the principal liability for commission.[225] Her main argument was that the guilt of the accused depends on the factual circumstances of the case rather than on abstract categories.[226]

Possibly the strongest indicator that the ICC is slowly moving away from prioritising commission over all other forms of participation is the emerging practice of charging several modes of liability in the alternative at the stage of the confirmation of charges. The practical purpose of this exercise to secure conviction must not overshadow changing attitudes towards various forms of complicity, which are regarded as viable alternatives to perpetration under Article 25(3)(a).

There are three arguments against the hierarchy of the forms of participation within the ICC framework. First, control over crime theory

[219] *Lubanga* Appeal Judgment (n 11) para 462; Ambos (n 58) 146–47.
[220] *Katanga* Judgment (n 8) paras 1387, 1393.
[221] Separate Opinion of Judge Fulford (n 13).
[222] ibid, para 6.
[223] Separate Opinion of Judge Fulford (n 13) para 8.
[224] Concurring Opinion of Judge van den Wyngaert (n 18).
[225] ibid, paras 22, 24.
[226] ibid, paras 24, 26.

underlying the hierarchy has no support in the Rome Statute and, even if it had, it is not the basis for reading a hierarchy of the modes of liability into the Statute. Second, Article 25(3) represents a move towards the differential participation model.[227] The forms of responsibility are thus distinguished in different subparagraphs of the article. However, this does not mean that they are *ranked* in a particular order. Finally, the level of the accused's contribution is not the criterion for drawing the line between different modes of participation.

A. 'Control over Crime' is Not a Basis for Hierarchy

Control over crime theory and the hierarchy of the participation modes are interrelated issues. The ICC has tied the liability under Article 25(3)(a) to the increased level of contribution and, in turn, to the increased degree of blameworthiness. Roxin's theory served to support this reading of Article 25(3)(a).[228] If one removes the assumption that the modes of responsibility are arranged in a hierarchical order reflecting the shifting culpability scale, then the control over crime theory becomes functionally obsolete for the purposes of the ICC. The court can simply apply the various forms of complicity provided in the remainder of the article to address the situations of the accused removed from the scene of the crime.

According to Article 21(1)(a) of the Rome Statute, the court shall apply, in the first place, the Statute, Elements of Crimes and its Rules of Procedure and Evidence. It is therefore important to determine whether the Statute supports Roxin's control over crime theory. In answering this question, one has to keep in mind Articles 31–32 of the Vienna Convention on the Law of Treaties, which provide guidance on treaty interpretation. Article 31 of the Vienna Convention sets the general rule that treaty interpretation involves the assessment of three elements: the text, context along with the object, and purpose of the treaty. These elements should be read together as one rule. There is no priority of one element over another.[229] Subsequent practice, mentioned in Article 31(3), is an additional element to be considered when interpreting a treaty.[230] Article 32 outlines supplementary means of interpretation—preparatory work (*travaux preparatoires*) and the circumstances of the treaty conclusion—to be utilised only if the meaning is not clear after the application of Article 31.[231]

227 See *Katanga* Judgment (n 8) para 1385.

228 Roxin (n 5).

229 A Aust, *Modern Treaty Law and Practice* (Cambridge, Cambridge University Press, 2000) 187.

230 ibid, 193.

231 I Sinclair, *The Vienna Convention on the Law of Treaties* (Manchester, Manchester University Press, 1984) 116.

Article 25(3)(a) does not mention the control over crime theory, but rather contains the traditional forms of criminal responsibility—perpetration, co-perpetration and perpetration by means.[232] The only peculiarity is the possibility of holding a person accountable as an indirect perpetrator even in cases where the agent, through whom the crime is committed, is criminally responsible. This is in contrast to the majority of domestic legal systems that call the act 'perpetration' only if the agent is innocent and is hence an 'instrument' in the hands of the perpetrator. Control over crime doctrine builds on this feature: the physical perpetrator may or may not be criminally responsible—it only matters that his will is suppressed. However, the similarity between innocent agency and control over crime theories does not automatically imply that the provision of the Rome Statute on perpetration shall be read in the light of Roxin's theory. The position of the *Lubanga* Appeals Chamber that it is not applying the theory as a source of law, but rather uses it as an interpretative tool permitting it to infer the most suitable form of responsibility does not appear entirely convincing.[233] The analysis of the jurisprudence demonstrates that the court has yet to elaborate on the methodology of dealing with the sources of law applicable at the ICC.[234]

To that end, Judge Fulford argued in his separate opinion that the German-based control over crime theory is not necessary to establish criminal responsibility for co-perpetration under Article 25(3)(a) of the Rome Statute; as such, the five-prong test requiring, inter alia, an essential contribution on behalf of the accused is superfluous.[235] The object and purpose of the Rome Statute embodied in its preamble—putting an end to impunity—does not justify the over-extension of liability.[236] The *Katanga* justification for retaining control over crime theory for the purposes of giving effect to the distinction between perpetrators and accomplices already implicit in Article 25(3) does not seem very convincing either.[237] The conduct and fault elements for each form of responsibility seem to be sufficiently defined in the Rome Statute.

Travaux preparatoires demonstrate the compromise reached by the experts from different countries, each holding positions based on their domestic laws.[238] Neither the Working Paper nor the Report of the Preparatory

[232] Concurring Opinion of Judge van den Wyngaert (n 18) para 14.

[233] *Lubanga* Appeal Judgment (n 11) para 470. See also *Lubanga* Judgment (n 8) para 976.

[234] See Sadat and Jolly (n 4).

[235] Separate Opinion of Judge Fulford (n 13) paras 16, 21. See also Minority Opinion of Judge van den Wyngaert (n 8) para 281.

[236] Concurring Opinion of Judge van den Wyngaert (n 18) para 16.

[237] *Katanga* Judgment (n 8) paras 1395.

[238] P Saland, 'International Criminal Law Principles' in R Lee (ed), *The International Criminal Court—The Making of the Rome Statute: Issues, Negotiations, Results* (The Hague, Kluwer Law International, 1999) 198.

Committee on the Establishment of an International Criminal Court indicates any preference for the German control over crime model or the intention of the parties to rank the modes of participation in order of blameworthiness.[239] The changes to the initial draft followed debates on criminal responsibility of legal entities, mens rea for aiding and abetting, and the definition of group crime (the current subparagraph (d) of Article 25(3)).[240] Neither control over crime theory nor the hierarchy of the modes of liability surfaces in the debates that shaped the article on individual criminal responsibility.

Customary law at the ICC does not play as prominent a role as in the jurisprudence of the ad hoc tribunals.[241] However, the court has referred to an international custom when interpreting the notion of 'common purpose' contained in Article 25(3)(d). The Trial Chamber in *Katanga* found it reasonable to rely on the jurisprudence of the ad hoc tribunals pertaining to the joint criminal enterprise.[242] Thus, it is worth mentioning that control over crime theory cannot be said to have materialised as a custom. The theory is supported only by the *Stakić* trial judgment of the ICTY and the *Eichmann* judgment of the Jerusalem court.[243] Arguably, these authorities alone do not establish the existence of a customary rule. Nor can it be said that control over crime theory is recognised by the majority of legal systems to constitute a third source of international law—a general principle of law.

Finally, it has been noted that the original control over crime theory is distinct from its international criminal law counterpart in at least two significant ways. First, the German version of the doctrine places strict limitations on mutual attribution, which does not happen in respect of any action by the joint principal not covered by the common plan and intent.[244] The contours of the joint agreement are more difficult to define in respect of mass atrocities. For this reason, it may often be preferable to focus on the contribution to the crime rather than the plan in the context of international criminal law. Moreover, the fault requirement at the ICC is not a guarantee against unjustified mutual attribution as the standard

[239] Working paper submitted by Canada, Germany, Netherlands and the United Kingdom to the Preparatory Committee, A/AC.249/1997/WG.2/DAT1, 14 February 1997. This formulation changed to 'through another person regardless of whether that person is criminally responsible' in the Report of the ICC Preparatory Committee, Document A/CONF.183/2, 14 April 1998, 31.

[240] Saland (n 238) 199.

[241] Article 21 of the Rome Statute ranks the sources of law to be applied by the ICC, giving priority to the Statute. See, eg, *Lubanga* Appeal Judgment (n 11) para 472.

[242] *Katanga* Judgment, para 1625; see also *Lubanga* Appeal Judgment (n 11) para 445.

[243] *Prosecutor v Stakić*, Trial Chamber, ICTY Case No IT-97-24-T, 31 July 2003, paras 468–98; *Attorney-General of the Government of Israel v Eichmann*, Israel Supreme Court Case 40/61, 1962.

[244] See Ch 2.II.A.

'awareness that a consequence will occur in the ordinary course of events' hints at a certain degree of probability.[245]

Second, the classical theory does not appear to imply a higher degree of guilt for the indirect perpetrator. The focus is not on the level of contribution of the accused, but on the power to exercise control in the hierarchical system.[246] Roxin admitted that the accessory's or the instigator's behaviour need not be less reprehensible than that of the perpetrator; rather, their lack of power to control can be one of the factors to be considered at sentencing.[247] German criminal law provides for sentencing discounts for accessories; hence, as became evident in the *Stashynsky* case,[248] the introduction of the 'control over crime theory' was largely motivated by the unfairly lenient sentences distributed to accomplices. This problem does not exist at the ICC. It seems that the reading of theory by the Trial Chamber in *Katanga* appears closest to the original: unlike its predecessors, the majority refused to link the theory with a higher degree of guilt.[249]

B. Modes of Responsibility: Distinguished But Not Ranked

Article 25(3) of the Rome Statute represents a move towards the differential participation model that distinguishes different forms of responsibility, but does not necessarily rank them. Sentencing is the main reason for grading modes of liability at the national level. For example, the legislation of Estonia, Finland, Germany and Indonesia provide for sentencing discounts for accessories as opposed to perpetrators.[250] The Rome Statute does not contain a similar sentencing provision. Article 78 of the Statute only directs the court to take into account factors such as the gravity of the crime and the individual circumstances of the convicted person.[251] Thus, the liability label is not dispositive in determining the level of culpability of the offender. The factual circumstances of the case play a more important role at sentencing.[252] The *Lubanga* Appeals Chamber upheld broad

[245] See, eg, *Lubanga* Appeal Judgment (n 11) para 527.
[246] Roxin (n 5) 202.
[247] *cf* Manacorda and Meloni argue that control over the crime approach satisfies the need to consider high-level commanders and senior civilian leaders as perpetrators (ie, principals) and accordingly to sentence their actions appropriately. S Manacorda and C Meloni, 'Indirect Perpetration versus Joint Criminal Enterprise: Concurring Approaches in the Practice of International Criminal Law' (2011) 9(1) *Journal of International Criminal Justice* 159.
[248] See Ch 2.II.B.
[249] *Katanga* Judgment, para 1386.
[250] See Appendix I.
[251] Article 78 of the Rome Statute, 'Determination of the Sentence'.
[252] Weigend (n 46); Cryer (n 78) 364.

judicial discretion when it came to penalty determinations.[253] Moreover, there is nothing in the Rome Statute or the *travaux preparatoires* to suggest that modes of liability are arranged in a particular order. One may be tempted to suggest that the lack of a value-based hierarchy of the modes of participation leads to the conclusion that a rigorous distinction between principals and accessories would be obsolete.[254] This is not entirely justified. There are solid reasons to differentiate modes of participation at an international level; however, this exercise need not result in assigning a greater degree of blameworthiness to a certain form.[255]

The need to separate modes of liability stems from three different fields informing international criminal law—domestic criminal law, transitional justice and human rights law.[256] From the domestic law perspective, the distinction between differential and unitary perpetration models is significant. Both theories honour the principle of individual culpability, whereby a person is punished only for his own conduct. However, the two systems arrive at the same result in different ways. Differential participation presupposes the derivative nature of accomplice liability in that it depends on the wrongful act of the principal perpetrator.[257] The underlying rationale behind this approach is that there is one offence and many crime participants—each having a different role. In contrast, pursuant to the unitary perpetrator model, the responsibility of a party to the crime is less (if at all) dependent on the responsibility of the principal. A plurality of persons implies a plurality of offences because the liability of each party stands on its own.[258]

The difference between the two systems is manifested in different pleading techniques and a different standard of causation. In the unitary participation model, any involvement whatsoever on the part of an actor in any offence establishes his connection to the crime,[259] while the differential model requires connecting the liability of accomplices to the conduct of the principal perpetrator. The Rome Statute has adopted the differential

[253] *Prosecutor v Thomas Lubanga Dyilo*, ICC-01/04-01/06 A4 A6, Appeals Chamber Judgment on the Appeals of the Prosecutor and Mr Thomas Lubanga Dyilo against the 'Decision on Sentence Pursuant to Article 76 of the Statute', 1 December 2014, para 40.

[254] J Stewart, 'The End of "Modes of Liability" for International Crimes' (2012) 25 *Leiden Journal of International Law* 165; Separate Opinion of Judge Fulford (n 13) para 9.

[255] *cf Lubanga* Appeal Judgment (n 11) para 462; Ambos (n 58) 147.

[256] For a discussion on framing international criminal law, see AM Danner and JS Martinez, 'Guilty Associations: Joint Criminal Enterprise, Command Responsibility and the Development of International Criminal Law' (2005) 93 *California Law Review* 75.

[257] Eser (n 26) 782.

[258] ibid, 788.

[259] U Sieber, 'Participation in Crime: Criminal Liability of Leaders of Criminal Groups and Networks, A Comparative Analysis' in *Expert Opinion by the Max Planck Institute for Foreign and International Criminal Law as Commissioned by the ICTY* (Freiburg, Max Planck Institute, 2006) 13.

participation model, and the dynamics of this model shall inform the interpretation of Article 25(3) of the Statute. In line with the derivative nature of liability inherent in this theory, the link between the accomplice and the principal perpetrator needs to be spelled out in greater detail.

The human rights aspect of international criminal law requires the role of the offender to be defined in precise terms.[260] This follows from the right of the accused to be properly informed about the nature of charges against him. This right, which is recognised as a fundamental human right in the major human rights instruments, is part of the broader notion of 'fairness' in criminal proceedings.[261] The European Court of Human Rights (ECtHR) has held that 'in criminal matters the provision of full, detailed information concerning the charges against a defendant is an essential prerequisite for ensuring that the proceedings are fair'.[262] In *Pélissier and Sassi*, the ECtHR looked specifically at the issue of changing the legal characterisation of facts. The French court of appeal had convicted the claimants of aiding and abetting criminal bankruptcy as opposed to the commission of criminal bankruptcy charged in the indictment. The court found a violation of Article 6(3)(a) of the European Convention on Human Rights based on the consideration that 'aiding and abetting did not constitute an element intrinsic to the initial accusation known to the applicants from the beginning of the proceedings'.[263] The court acknowledged that the elements of aiding and abetting are different from those of perpetration. Thus, the accused could have used different defence strategies if they knew they were being tried for aiding and abetting as opposed to principal perpetration.[264] The reason for the existence of the rule to be properly informed about the charges stems from the notion of the equality of arms that is essential to the rights of the defence and underlies the concept of fairness.[265] True equality of arms can only be achieved if the accused is properly informed about the charges and is able to defend himself accordingly.

[260] F Megret, 'Prospects for "Constitutional" Human Rights Scrutiny of Substantive International Criminal Law by the ICC, with Special Emphasis on the General Part' (paper presented at Washington University School of Law, Whitney R Harris World Law Institute, International Legal Scholars Workshop, Roundtable in Public International Law and Theory, 4–6 February 2010) cited by J Ohlin, 'Joint Intentions to Commit International Crimes' (2011) 11 *Chicago Journal of International Law* 693.

[261] ICCPR, art 14(3)(a); ECHR, arts 6(1) and 6(3)(a).

[262] *Mattoccia v Italy*, 23969/94, Judgment, ECtHR, 25 July 2000, para 59; *Pélissier and Sassi v France*, Judgment, ECHR, G Ch, 25 March 1999, paras 50–52. See also W Jordash and J Coughlan, 'The Right to Be Informed of the Nature and Cause of the Charges: A Potentially Formidable Jurisprudential Legacy' in S Darcy and J Powderly (eds), *Judicial Creativity at the International Criminal Tribunals* (Oxford, Oxford University Press, 2010) 287

[263] *Pélissier and Sassi v France*, Judgment, ECHR, G Ch, 25 March 1999, para 61.

[264] ibid, para 62.

[265] *Borgers v Belgium*, Judgment, 214 Eur Ct HR (ser A) (1999).

Finally, the transitional justice aspect of distinguishing between different modes of liability manifests itself in the need to avoid assigning collective guilt. International criminal trials are extremely complex as they involve multiple accused, the crime scenes are often spread out in time and space, and the evidence linking the accused to the particular offence is often insufficient or missing. In these circumstances, it may be tempting to circumvent the principles of individual criminal responsibility in the name of achieving justice for numerous victims of mass atrocities.[266] However, assigning guilt by association is a dangerous tendency. Addressing past atrocities and criminal law guarantees for the accused are not two competing considerations in international criminal law, but go hand in hand. This is because international criminal trials are evaluated by subsequent generations based on their adherence to the strict legal principles.[267] The Tokyo and Nuremberg Tribunals are good examples of how international proceedings can be labelled 'victors' justice' because of jurisprudential shortcomings. The whole purpose of international criminal trials may be defeated if the principles of criminal law are not observed. Thus, honouring the principle of fair labelling by distinguishing between different forms of individual criminal responsibility is key to maintaining the perceived legitimacy of international and hybrid courts and tribunals.

C. The Level of Contribution is Not the Criterion for Differentiating Modes of Responsibility

The third and final argument against the culpability scale of different participation forms relates to the device that the ICC employed in some cases to delineate one form from another. Responsibility of the accused is measured by the amount of his contribution to the crime: the sequence of modes of liability is based on the level of contribution. The ICC requires an *essential* contribution by the accused to the common plan, in the sense of an ability to frustrate the commission of the crime by not performing the tasks, under subparagraph (a),[268] a *substantial* contribution to the commission of a crime for aiding and abetting under subparagraph (c)[269] and a *significant* contribution to the commission of a crime by a group under

[266] To that effect, Mark Osiel even goes so far as to argue that the context of mass atrocities requires a reassessment of the individualistic categories in which criminal law customarily thinks and judges. See M Osiel, *Making Sense of Mass Atrocity* (Cambridge, Cambridge University Press, 2009) 21.

[267] Minority Opinion of Judge van den Wyngaert (n 8) para 311.

[268] *Lubanga* Judgment, para 925; *Lubanga* Appeal Judgment (n 11) para 473. See also Ambos (n 58) 153.

[269] *Mbarushimana* Decision (n 33) para 279; *Lubanga* Judgment (n 8) para 997.

subparagraph (d) of Article 25(3) of the Rome Statute.[270] The *Lubanga* Trial Chamber reinforced the hierarchy based on the level of contribution by calling the latter provision a 'residual' form of liability, which makes it possible to criminalise those contributions that cannot be characterised as ordering, soliciting, inducing, aiding, abetting or assisting.[271] The Pre-Trial Chamber in *Mbarushimana* adopted the same approach. It felt compelled on the basis of the hierarchy of participation modes to measure the magnitude of the accused's contribution[272]—an exercise that proved to be challenging and was duly criticised by Judge Fernández de Gurmendi.[273]

However, there is a flaw in the reasoning connecting the form of liability and the level of contribution because it is impossible to measure the precise degree to which the accused contributed to the crime in abstract terms. This concern might have prompted the *Lubanga* Appeals Chamber's reliance on a normative assessment of the role of the accused person in determining his respective role in offending.[274] The worry is particularly true in respect of an 'essential', or *conditio sine qua non*, contribution required for co-perpetration.[275] This prerequisite goes against the distinction between nature and will, which Kadish accurately pointed out: in the physical world, events inevitably follow one from another, but in the world of voluntary human action, the outcome is the result of a freely chosen expression of will.[276] This distinction underlies the conception of responsibility in criminal law because it employs the doctrine of causation for the realm of nature, and complicity for the realm of will. Causation translates into the events happening in the physical world, while complicity results in another person's voluntary action.[277] The explanation for this differentiation is that every person is presumed to have free will and it cannot be said that another person *caused* him to act. The principal freely chose to commit a crime.

For example, it can be fairly said that a burglar caused a burglary by breaking into a house and appropriating the valuables. However, his accomplice, who provided the truck to transport the stolen goods with the knowledge that the crime was being committed, cannot be said to have *caused* the

[270] *Mbarushimana* Decision (n 33) para 280.

[271] *Lubanga* Decision (n 48) para 337. See also *Katanga* Decision (n 79) para 483, 'degrading' responsibility in art 25(3)(d) on the basis of its accessory nature.

[272] *Mbarushimana* Decision (n 33) para 292.

[273] Separate Opinion of Judge Fernández de Gurmendi (n 184) para 12.

[274] *Lubanga* Appeal Judgment (n 11) para 473.

[275] Recent case law evidences a more relaxed interpretation of the essential contribution as the one without which 'the crimes would not have been committed or would have been committed *in a significantly different way*'. See *Gbago* Confirmation of Charges Decision (n 20) para 232, emphasis added.

[276] SH Kadish, 'Complicity, Cause and Blame: A Study in the Interpretation of Doctrine' (1985) 73(2) *California Law Review* 323.

[277] ibid.

burglary; his responsibility lies in the wrongful choice to assist the principal. Another example involving co-perpetrators would be two men simultaneously delivering blows to a third person. Both co-perpetrators cause grave bodily harm to the other person. This event is happening in the physical world. Thus, causation applies to cases that do not involve an intermediary between the crime and the offender—these are the classical cases of perpetration, co-perpetration and perpetration by means. The latter form of perpetration is something of an exception to the general causation rule because there is an intermediary between the crime and the principal. However, this intermediary is innocent in a classical form of indirect perpetration. Consequently, he lacks free will and becomes an instrument, in the physical sense of the word, in the hands of the primary perpetrator.

In case of the ICC-developed doctrines of indirect or direct co-perpetration, the agents committing crimes are usually criminally responsible. Therefore, it cannot be said that they are instruments in the hands of others; they retain their autonomy to choose the course of action. Contribution *sine qua non* presupposes that the acts of the perpetrator directly cause the crime to occur. However, if the intermediary, who possesses the ability to act voluntarily, commits a crime, he is the sole cause of this event in the physical world, while the person exercising influence over the agent is responsible for changing the latter's motivation or subjugating his will. Thus, the causal link is nearly impossible to construct in cases of indirect perpetration if one treats individuals as sovereigns of their own acts. For instance, the mayor of the city who publicly delivers hate speeches urging one ethnic group to take up arms against another ethnic group cannot be said to have *caused* the members of the former group to commit acts of persecution or genocide, but rather influenced their behaviour through incitement.[278] The cases of co-perpetration also present many difficulties in the context of mass atrocities, which necessarily involve multiple actors and aspects that affect the end result. In that vein, one cannot be entirely certain that the recruitment of children in the Ituri region would have been avoided in the absence of Lubanga's military involvement and speeches.

Some quantification of contribution to the crime is nonetheless possible and necessary, otherwise marginal input would render a person criminally responsible. This will bring about the unjust result of punishing only the guilty state of mind rather than the state of mind *and* the conduct.[279] However, it seems more appropriate to talk about establishing the nature of assistance and its relevance to the crime rather than simply measuring

[278] For an extended discussion on this, see Weigend (n 46).

[279] For an extended discussion on 'guilt by association', see *Ezokola v Canada (Citizenship and Immigration)* 2013 SCC 40, [2013] 2 SCR 678.

it in numerical terms. If one talks about complicity, two more factors from the realm of culpability have to be placed in the background of any consideration of an accomplice's input: his intent to contribute and the level of specificity of his knowledge about the crimes.

The facts of a particular case usually permit an evaluation as to whether the contribution had *some* effect on the commission of the crime. This appears to be a reasonable approach. The *Mbarushimana* Pre-Trial Chamber and the *Katanga* Trial Chamber took a step in this direction by noting that determination as to which contributions are significant requires a case-by-case assessment in the proper context.[280] However, it seems that the ICC is still in search of the right formula for evaluating the effect of accomplice's assistance on the crime. The *Mbarushimana* Chamber could not refrain from providing some indicators regarding what amounts to significant contributions. These included the role played by the suspect vis-a-vis the seriousness and scope of the crimes committed or the sustained nature of the participation after acquiring knowledge of the criminality of the group's common purpose.[281] These indicators are useful in assessing the input of the suspect or accused, but can just as well be used to determine the contribution that is 'essential' and 'substantial', and not necessarily 'significant'.

Consequently, the level of contribution has to be at a certain level in order to attract *any* liability, but it cannot serve as an instrument for grading modes of liability and establishing a hierarchy. Alternative recommendations may include reinforcing the analysis of the accused's mental state on the basis of sufficiently detailed evidence and assessing 'neutral' or 'generic' input, emphasising the link between the crime and the assistance rather than the amount of the contribution in question. In *Blé Goudé*, the judges highlighted the immediacy and relevance of the contribution in the light of the particular circumstances of the case.[282] This is a welcome development, for it shifts the focus from quantifying assistance to assessing its nature.

CONCLUSION

This chapter has outlined the main forms of participation accepted by the ICC. The Rome Statute, albeit the most detailed contemporary statement of the modes of responsibility in international criminal law, still calls for some further interpretation. The ICC initially adopted the German-based doctrine of co-perpetration by means of control over crime as a default

[280] *Mbarushimana* Decision (n 33) para 284. See also *Katanga* Judgment (n 8) para 634.
[281] *Mbarushimana* Decision (n 33) para 284.
[282] *Blé Goudé* Confirmation of Charges Decision (n 21) para 178.

mode of responsibility dealing with collective criminality. However, it appears that the fascination with the newly developed control over crime theory premised on the hierarchy of participation modes is fading away. The application of this form of liability creates conceptual and practical difficulties. There is no support for this doctrine in the Rome Statute, customary international law or the general principles of law. The doctrine operates on the basis of numerous highly theoretical criteria that are often difficult to apply to the facts.

Moreover, the particular requirement of the 'essential' contribution of the co-perpetrator to the crime committed by someone who is criminally responsible himself is at odds with the principle of free will. Contribution *sine qua non* presupposes that the acts of the perpetrator directly cause the crime to occur. However, if the crime is committed by the intermediary, who possesses the ability to act voluntarily, it cannot be said that the principal perpetrator caused the crime; rather, he influenced the agent, who, in turn, caused the result in the physical world. The better approach to contributions would be to assess them in the context of the case, without attempting to quantify the contributions and construct a ranking of responsibility modes based on this quantification.

Until recently, the ICC has used different forms of complicity—embodied in Article 25(3)(b)–(d)—scarcely and with reluctance. The explanation for this could be the alleged hierarchy of the modes of participation implicit in the Rome Statute. This assumption in turn created a pressure on the court to utilise the 'stronger' mode of participation—commission under Article 25(3)(a)—to reflect the gravity of the crimes in the jurisdiction of the ICC. The attitudes are slowly changing with the second conviction rendered by the court under Article 25(3)(d). Indeed, the supposition that the modes of participations are ranked is questionable because it is not supported by the Rome Statute or *travaux preparatoires*. The hierarchy does not follow from the original German control over crime doctrine or the sentencing provisions in the Statute, which do not distinguish between different liability modes for sentencing purposes. Thus, the form of liability—principal or accomplice—is not the deciding factor in assessing the degree of offender's blameworthiness. Rather, it is the combination of case-specific aspects that renders the accused more or less culpable.

The main conclusion of the above discussion is that co-perpetration must not be used to the detriment of other forms of liability enshrined in the Rome Statute. Different forms of complicity do not amount to a 'lesser' form of responsibility because the forms of participation are not ranked in the Rome Statute. Complicity can serve an important role in addressing the issue of collective criminality because it is designed specifically to deal with cases involving multiple accused. The key challenge seems to be not the choice of the liability mode *in abstracto*, but rather faithfully assessing the facts of the case against the legal requirements of the chosen form of criminal participation.

6

Complicity in International Criminal Law and Law of State Responsibility: A Comparative Analysis

INTRODUCTION

THERE IS AN emerging trend among academics and practitioners to view international crimes such as genocide, war crimes and crimes against humanity in their complexity, implying a multiplicity of actors at different levels, including states, organisations, corporations and separate individuals.[1] The responsibility of one actor does not exclude the responsibility of another, but rather complements it.[2] Nollkaemper, for example, employed the term 'system criminality',[3] which he described as the allocation of responsibility for international crimes to 'the level of the system, in its various manifestations, rather than to the individual level'.[4] This view challenges the traditional paradigm established by the Nuremberg Tribunal, whereby 'crimes against international law are committed by men, not by abstract entities'.[5] Similarly, during the negotiations of the Draft Code of Crimes against the Peace and Security of Mankind adopted by the International Law Commission (ILC) in 1996,[6]

[1] A Clapham, 'Issues of Complexity, Complicity and Complementarity: From the Nuremberg Trials to the Dawn of the Next International Criminal Court' in P Sands (ed), *From Nuremberg to the Hague: The Future of International Criminal Justice* (Cambridge, Cambridge University Press, 2003) 50; A Nollkaemper, 'Introduction' in A Nollkaemper and H van der Wilt (eds), *System Criminality in International Law* (Cambridge, Cambridge University Press, 2009) 4; C Harding, 'Human Action or State Action? Locating the Site of Supranational Criminality' in R Haveman and O Olunsanya (eds), *Sentencing and Sanctioning in Supranational Criminal Law* (Antwerp, Intersentia, 2006) 82–83; W Schabas, 'Enforcing International Humanitarian Law: Catching the Accomplices' (2001) 83 *International Review of the Red Cross* 842.

[2] LS Sunga, *The Emerging System of International Criminal Law* (Leiden, Martinus Nijhoff, 1997) 246; Nollkaemper (n 1) 8.

[3] This term was first introduced by Dutch scholar and judge BVA Roeling. See A Cassese, *International Criminal Law* (2nd edn Oxford University Press, 2008) 54.

[4] Nollkaemper (n 1) 3.

[5] ibid, quoting *France et al v Göring et al*, Judgment of 1 October 1946, 41 American Journal of International Law 333 1947, Part 22, at 447.

[6] Report of the ILC to the General Assembly, Forty-Eighth Session, UN GAOR, 51st Session, Suat No 10 UN A/51/10 (1996).

some countries expressed the hope that in the future, the provisions of the Draft Code would apply to all perpetrators, not just individuals, because, in their view, the difference between treating individuals and states is merely procedural.[7]

One possible consequence of this complex approach to the allocation of responsibility is that certain criminal law concepts, such as complicity, are applied to various actors, including states and individuals.

'Complicity' has many meanings depending on the context in which one uses it. From the theoretical perspective, Kutz described 'the domain of complicity' as 'cultural and legal practices, surrounding relations of an agent to a harm that are mediated by other agents'.[8] The *Oxford English Dictionary* defines 'complicity' as 'the fact or condition of being involved with others in an activity that is unlawful or morally wrong'.[9]

The law of state responsibility and international criminal law share the legal concept of 'complicity'. Previous chapters discussed in some detail the components of complicity in international criminal law[10] and domestic criminal law.[11] The aim of this chapter is to define the legal requirements of complicity in the law of state responsibility and contrast them with those of international criminal law. While a more detailed discussion will follow in the following sections, it is sufficient to note at this point that the legal requirements used for holding states and individuals complicit in a crime are very similar. In the memorandum submitted to the UK Parliament's Joint Committee on Human Rights (hereinafter the UK Parliament's Committee), Professor Sands suggests using the international criminal law test to determine UK's alleged complicity in torture.[12]

The main objective of the analysis in this chapter is to determine whether the level of approximation of the content of complicity in the two legal fields—international criminal law and the law of state responsibility—has reached the point where complicity as a legal term can be used interchangeably across the two disciplines. In other words, the chapter aims at establishing the limitations (if any) of comparing individual complicity to state complicity.

The analysis is based on four legal cases, two of which deal with state complicity (judgments delivered by the International Court of Justice

[7] NHB Jorgensen, *The Responsibility of States for International Crimes* (Oxford, Oxford University Press, 2000) 142.

[8] C Kutz, *Complicity: Ethics and Law for a Collective Age* (Cambridge, Cambridge University Press, 2000) 3.

[9] *OED Online*, http://oxforddictionaries.com/definition/complicity.

[10] Chapters 4 and 5.

[11] Chapter 2.

[12] Memorandum Submitted by Professor Philippe Sands QC to Joint Committee on Human Rights, http://www.publications.parliament.uk/pa/jt200809/jtselect/jtrights/152/152we22.htm.

(ICJ) and the UK domestic courts) and two with individual complicity in the context of international criminal law.[13] The selected judgments focus on the same substantive crimes—genocide and torture. This approach eliminates the divergence in substantive crimes and allows a comparison between state and individual complicity in the same type of offence. Such a method leads to a deeper understanding of the elements of complicity at both levels and illustrates the interplay between the primary (substantive) and secondary (framework) rules of international law.

This chapter builds on the analysis of complicity and its legal requirements in international criminal law provided in Chapters 4 and 5. The first section of this chapter provides an analogous description of complicity in the law of state responsibility. Section II focuses on state complicity in genocide and torture. The focal point of the discussion is two judgments from the sphere of state responsibility—*Genocide* and *Binyam Mohamed*. These judgments are contrasted with two international criminal law judgments dealing with similar crimes—*Furundžija* and *Akayesu*. Section III explores the similarities and differences of complicity in the law of state responsibility and in international criminal law. Conclusions as to the applicability of the concept to both fields of law are drawn in the final section of this chapter.

I. COMPLICITY IN THE LAW OF STATE RESPONSIBILITY

A. Historical Perspective

The Nuremberg and Tokyo trials and subsequent prosecutions of former Nazis provided abundant opportunity to shape the principles of individual criminal responsibility in international law.[14] The Nuremberg and Tokyo Charters were unquestionably international instruments resulting from political compromise. However, they embodied basic domestic criminal law principles with which the drafters, coming from different jurisdictions and political systems, were nonetheless familiar.[15] Prosecuting individuals for crimes, albeit international ones, was nothing new to the community of lawyers and the IMT and the IMTFE applied these principles during the proceedings. The main difference with domestic

[13] These cases exemplify the practical application of complicity in international criminal law and the law of state responsibility. The cases are selected with the narrow aim of contrasting the legal concept of complicity in two different fields of law. Admittedly, the review of the jurisprudence of the human rights courts could broaden the analysis presented in this chapter; however, this would go beyond the scope of the book. For a comprehensive treatment of complicity in the law of state responsibility, see H Aust, *Complicity and Law of State Responsibility* (Cambridge, Cambridge University Press, 2013).

[14] See Ch 3 for a detailed discussion of this.

[15] ibid.

prosecutions was the scale of offences and the complexity of the interrelationship between various actors.[16] Further trials of war criminals in the aftermath of the IMT and the IMTFE also relied on domestic criminal law to a large extent. Mechanisms for dealing with the collective aspect of crimes including complicity and conspiracy were therefore borrowed from national law and modified to suit international proceedings.

In contrast, state responsibility did not develop along the same lines.[17] As it was impossible to rely on domestic law, the rules for attributing responsibility to the state had to be created de novo. Beginning soon after the Second World War, the International Law Commission worked on a draft of Articles on State Responsibility for several decades.[18] Complicity of states was not part of the initial discussion by the ILC.[19] However, by 1978, it held that complicity in the sense 'of participation in the internationally wrongful act of another by providing "aid or assistance"' had gained acceptance in international law and, by 1996, the Law Commission considered the rule of 'refraining from assisting wrongdoing states' as a well-established practice.[20] In 2007, the ICJ confirmed the customary nature of this norm.[21]

Historical divergence in the development of state responsibility and individual criminal responsibility can be explained by the conceptual difference between these two forms of responsibility: state responsibility is governed by a separate set of secondary rules, which establish the consequences of the violation of primary rules located elsewhere—in international treaties or customary international law.[22] Aust highlighted the conceptual difficulty with such a distinction, especially when it comes to

[16] ibid.

[17] This is the case notwithstanding the comments by the ILC that 'the question of the criminal responsibility of States as well as that of individuals acting on behalf of the State … may be considered in conjunction with the codification of the principles of the Nuremberg Charter and judgment'. *Survey of International Law in Relation to the Work of Codification of the International Law Commission: Preparatory Work within the Purview of Article 18, Paragraph 1, of the International Law Commission*, Memorandum submitted by the Secretary-General, 1949, A/CN.4/1/Rev.1, at 56. See also Jorgensen (n 7) 27.

[18] The topic of state responsibility was selected for codification at the 6th meeting of International Law Commission on 20 April 1949. See *Yearbook of the International Law Commission, 1949*, vol I, 49–50, para 32.

[19] K Nahapetian, 'Confronting State Complicity in International Law' (2002) 7 *UCLA Journal of International Law and Foreign Affairs* 99, 102.

[20] Report of the ILC to the General Assembly, Thirtieth Session, UN GAOR, 33d Session, Suat No 10, UN Doc A/33/10 (1978), at 103, para 16; and Report of the ILC to the General Assembly, Forty-Eighth Session, UN GAOR, 51st Session, Suat No 10, UN Doc A/51/10 (1996), 72, para 2.

[21] *Case Concerning the Application of the Convention on the Prevention and Punishment of the Crime of Genocide (Bosnia and Herzegovina v Serbia and Montenegro)*, ICJ Rep 2007 (including Declarations of Judge Keith and Judge Bennouna), para 419. Aust came to the same conclusion after examining available state practice and *opinio juris*. See Aust (n 13) 97–191.

[22] A Gattini, 'A Historical Perspective: From Collective to Individual Responsibility and Back' in Nollkaemper and van der Wilt (n 1) 105.

complicity.[23] The distance between primary and secondary rules in the law of state responsibility generates uncertainty as to whether international law includes the rule against complicity or whether it is merely a secondary rule contained in the Articles on State Responsibility.[24] On the contrary, individual criminal responsibility is governed by a narrower set of norms, namely substantive and procedural criminal law.[25]

B. Legal Requirements of Complicity

The International Law Commission adopted the Articles on State Responsibility in 2001.[26] These contain at least one provision dealing with complicity. Article 16 provides:

> A State which aids or assists another State in the commission of an internationally wrongful act by the latter is internationally responsible for doing so if:
>
> (a) That State does so with knowledge of the circumstances of the internationally wrongful act; and
> (b) The act would be internationally wrongful if committed by that State.[27]

The ILC Commentary to Articles on State Responsibility discusses in full detail the two explicit and one implicit condition for state responsibility for aiding and assisting.[28] The first explicit requirement is knowledge of the circumstances of the internationally wrongful act.[29] The ILC Commentary is not, however, entirely clear on the necessary fault requirement: on some occasions, it mentions aid and assistance provided to another state with a *view to facilitating* the commission of an internationally wrongful act; on another occasion, the ILC speaks of the state organ *intending*, by aid and assistance, to facilitate the commission of a wrongful act;[30] while on a third occasion, it discusses the state being held responsible

[23] Aust (n 13) 51.
[24] ibid 91.
[25] ibid.
[26] Report of the ILC on the Work of its Fifty-third Session, Official Records of the General Assembly, Fifty-Sixth session, Supplement No 10, UN Doc A/56/10.
[27] Aust (n 13) 3 noted that despite the recognition of the customary status of this provision, the contours of this rule remain unclear.
[28] Report of the ILC on the Work of its Fifty-Third Session (23 April–1 June and 2 July–10 August 2001), Fifty-Sixth session, UN Doc A/56/10 ('ILC Commentary') 66. See also A Reinisch, 'Aid or Assistance and Direction and Control between States and International Organizations in the Commission of Internationally Wrongful Acts' 2010 7 *International Organizations Law Review*.
[29] ILC Commentary (n 28) 66.
[30] Aust (n 13) 239 argued in favour of 'intent' as being the correct standard for state responsibility for aiding and assisting because otherwise the provision would move very close to responsibility for lawful behaviour.

for assisting in human rights violations if it was *aware* of and *intended* to facilitate these acts.[31]

The second explicit condition is that the assisting state itself must be bound by the obligation. This criterion loses its relevance in relation to serious breaches of peremptory, or *jus cogens* norms, which are binding on all states.[32] Articles 40 and 41 of the ILC Articles on State Responsibility deal with this type of obligation. Article 40 describes the breach as serious 'if it involves a gross or systematic failure by the responsible State to fulfil the obligation'. Article 41 provides that the states shall cooperate to bring to an end any serious breach, as well as not recognise or render any aid or assistance in maintaining the situation created by this breach. It is not clear from Article 41 whether knowledge or intent is required to hold a state responsible for assisting in the breach of peremptory norm.[33]

The previous draft of the Articles on State Responsibility contained Article 19, which drew a distinction between international crimes and international delicts in the context of the law of state responsibility.[34] Violations of peremptory norms are qualified as crimes. This distinction prompted an extensive debate as to the meaning of state crime and the consequences attached to its commission.[35] However, the contentious nature of this provision prompted the ILC to change its approach and to substitute Article 19 with Articles 40 and 41, which do not mention the word 'crime'.[36]

One of the main controversies surrounding the notion of state crime was the difficulty of punishing a state.[37] The ILC envisaged that the commission of an international crime should vest other states with some remedial rights, without specifying the exact scope of these rights and the mechanisms for their enforcement.[38] Consequently, the debate

[31] ILC Commentary (n 28) 66, 67. See also Nahapetian (n 19); Reinisch (n 28).

[32] The Vienna Convention on the Law of Treaties defines *jus cogens* in Article 53 as 'a peremptory norm of general international law is a norm accepted and recognized by the international community of States as a whole as a norm from which no derogation is permitted and which can be modified only by a subsequent norm of general international law having the same character'. The content of *jus cogens* norms is, however, a subject to academic debate. Verdross provided the following definition: 'they do not exist to satisfy the needs of the individual states but the higher interest of the whole international community'. A Verdross, 'Jus Dispositivum and Jus Cogens in International Law' (1966) 60 *American Journal of International Law* 57, 58.

[33] See Nahapetian (n 19).

[34] Text of Draft Articles Provisionally Adopted by the Commission on First Reading, Report of the ILC to the General Assembly, Forty-Eighth Session, UN GAOR, 51st Session, Suat No 10 UN A/51/10 (1996) 60.

[35] See, eg, A Pellet, 'Can a State Commit a Crime? Definitely, Yes!' (1999) 10 *European Journal of International Law* 425 et seq.

[36] M Shaw, *International Law* (Cambridge, Cambridge University Press, 2008) 807–08; Nollkaemper (n 1) 19.

[37] Jorgensen (n 7) 184.

[38] Article 52 of the Draft Articles adopted in 1996 outlined the specific consequences attached to the commission of a state crime as opposed to a mere delict. They included the

around sanctioning the state turned away from the general preventative side of the concept and focused on the technicalities of defining precise remedies.[39] This, in turn, led to the deletion of Article 19 in favour of Articles 40 and 41 of the ILC Articles on State Responsibility.

An opinion that has received some scholarly support simply leaves aside the label 'criminal' and holds that, for practical purposes, Article 40 'serious breach responsibility' is equivalent to the international criminal responsibility of states.[40] The important aspect is not the labelling, but rather the enactment of a proper enforcement mechanism currently lacking in the law of state responsibility. Zimmermann and Teichmann argued in favour of introducing punitive damages and an obligation to alter one's domestic legal system as new, effective remedies in the context of state crimes.[41]

The final condition of state responsibility for aiding and assisting is not expressly mentioned in Article 16 of the Articles on State Responsibility, but is discussed in the ILC Commentary. The aid and assistance must contribute significantly to the commission of internationally wrongful conduct.[42] The contribution need not, however, be essential to the performance of the act.[43] When the ILC covers the possible ways in which the state may assist human rights violations, it speaks of the 'material aid'.[44]

The ILC Commentary also expressly distinguishes aiding and assisting as recorded in Article 16 of the ILC Articles on State Responsibility from co-perpetratorship (regulated by articles on the attribution of the Articles on State Responsibility) and the substantive rules prohibiting aid or assistance contained in different international instruments.[45]

Aside from the ILC Articles on State Responsibility, 'complicity in genocide' is explicitly outlawed by Article 3(e) of the Convention on the Prevention and Punishment of the Crime of Genocide of 1948 (hereinafter the

removal of limitations on restitution and satisfaction. However, the mechanisms of the implementation of this provision were not explained. Report of the ILC to the General Assembly, Forty-Eighth Session, UN GAOR, 51st Session, Suat No 10 UN A/51/10 (1996) 71–72. See also Jorgensen (n 7) 180.

39 Jorgensen (n 7) 185.

40 Harding (n 1) 82; A Zimmermann and M Teichmann, 'State Responsibility for International Crimes' in Nollkaemper and van der Wilt (n 1) 312–13.

41 Zimmermann and Teichmann (n 40) 312–13.

42 Aust pointed towards the lack of clarity on what constitutes relevant 'aid and assistance' because the ILC is silent on the matter. He concluded: 'Instead, "aid or assistance" is a normative and case-specific concept.' Aust (n 13) 197, 230.

43 ILC Commentary (n 28) 66. Here the parallel can be drawn with the similar requirement for 'aiding and abetting' in international criminal law: many ICTY and ICTR Chambers contended that the contribution of the accused need not be a *conditio sine qua non* for the crime to occur. For more discussion, see Ch 4.I.G and 4.II.B.

44 ILC Commentary (n 28) 67.

45 ibid 66.

Genocide Convention). Article 4(1) of the Convention against Torture and Other Cruel, Inhuman and Degrading Treatment or Punishment of 1984 (hereinafter the Torture Convention) calls on the state parties to criminalise, inter alia, 'an act by any person which constitutes complicity or participation in torture'.

Other international instruments dealing with human rights and humanitarian law such the International Covenant on Civil and Political Rights of 1966 or the Geneva Conventions for the Protection of Victims of War of 1949 do not explicitly mention 'complicity'. There is an emerging view among some scholars[46] that states can nonetheless be complicit in the failure to comply with the positive obligation to respect and ensure rights contained in these instruments.[47] Cerone, for example, argued for a wider understanding of state complicity, which, in his view, can manifest itself in three ways: first, as a state responsibility for the violation of negative obligations on the basis of attributing the conduct of the organs of one state to another state; second, as a derivative state responsibility for the violation of negative obligations within the meaning of Article 16 of the Articles on State Responsibility; and, third, as responsibility for the failure to respect positive obligations contained in primary rules.[48] It remains to be seen whether this approach will be adopted in the future. In the meantime, both cases on state responsibility discussed in this chapter reject this broad view of state complicity.

II. COMPARATIVE ANALYSIS OF COMPLICITY IN INTERNATIONAL CRIMINAL LAW AND THE LAW OF STATE RESPONSIBILITY

A. Complicity in Genocide

i. The Akayesu *Case*

Jean-Paul Akayesu, a father of five, served as a teacher in the Rwandan municipality of Taba. He was a well-respected leader of his local commune and held the position of mayor for some time in 1993 and 1994, overseeing the local economy, the police and law in the village. After the commencement of the Rwandan genocide, he actively urged the population to kill Tutsis. As mayor, he must have known about the atrocities taking part in his municipality, but nevertheless failed to punish the

[46] Clapham (n 1) 62; J Cerone, 'Re-examining International Responsibility: "Complicity" in the Context of Human Rights Violations' (2008) 14 *International Law Students Association Journal of International and Comparative Law* 525; Nahapetian (n 19); *cf* M Jackson, *Complicity in International Law* (Oxford, Oxford University Press, 2015) 190.

[47] Geneva Conventions, art 1; International Covenant on Civil and Political Rights, art 2.

[48] Cerone (n 46).

perpetrators. Moreover, he was present when sexual violence was committed against Tutsi women, encouraging by his presence the further perpetration of crimes.[49]

The *Akayesu* judgment is one of the most significant judgments rendered by the international tribunals as it contains the world's first conviction for the crime of genocide. It is noteworthy that while the prosecution charged Akayesu, inter alia, with both genocide and complicity in genocide,[50] the Trial Chamber disagreed with the prosecutor's decision to charge both modes of participation, stating that an individual cannot be at the same time the principal perpetrator of a particular crime and the accomplice thereto.[51] The Chamber further reasoned that the accomplice can be tried even if the principal perpetrator has not been identified.[52] Consequently, the Trial Chamber analysed whether the actions of Akayesu were merely a manifestation of an accomplice liability or whether they constituted an actual commission.[53] The court drew the distinction between complicity in genocide pursuant to Article 2(3)(e) of the Statute and aiding and abetting genocide in accordance with Article 6(1) of the Statute.[54]

The Trial Chamber established that for the purposes of the substantive provision on complicity in genocide (Article 2(3)(e) of the Statute, which prohibits genocide, conspiracy to commit genocide, incitement to commit genocide, attempt to commit genocide and complicity in genocide),[55] 'complicity' is to be defined as per the Rwandan Penal Code and includes procuring means, aiding and abetting, and instigation. Most importantly, for this crime, an accomplice to genocide need not necessarily possess the *dolus specialis* of genocide, namely the specific intent to destroy, in whole or in part, a national, ethnic, racial or religious group as such; it is sufficient that the accused knew of the genocidal plan and participated in its execution.[56] Aiding and abetting, covered under Article 6(1) of the Statute, is, in the view of the Trial Chamber, similar to the material elements of complicity in genocide. However, by virtue of being linked to the substantive

[49] *Prosecutor v Akayesu*, ICTR Case No 96-4-T, Trial Chamber Judgment, 2 September 1998, paras 12–23.

[50] Articles 2(3)(a) and 2(3)(e) of the ICTR Statute.

[51] *Akayesu* Trial Judgment (n 49) para 468, 532 as discussed by K Kittichaisaree, *International Criminal Law* (Oxford, Oxford University Press, 2002) 237.

[52] *Akayesu* Trial Judgment (n 49) para 531.

[53] For the discussion of 'complicity' in *Akayesu*, see W Schabas, *The UN International Criminal Tribunals: The Former Yugoslavia, Rwanda and Sierra Leone* (Cambridge, Cambridge University Press, 2006) 305–06.

[54] For the views expressed by other ICTY and ICTR Chambers on the distinction between these two provisions, see Ch 4.I.H.

[55] This provision reproduces art 3 of the Genocide Convention.

[56] *Akayesu* Trial Judgment (n 49) 537–44.

crimes listed in Articles 2–4 of the Statute, aiding and abetting genocide requires the person to have acted with specific genocidal intent.[57]

The Trial Chamber held that Akayesu's acts constitute factual elements of the crime of genocide. He incurred individual criminal liability for 'having ordered, committed, or otherwise aided and abetted in the preparation or execution of the killing of and causing serious bodily or mental harm to members of the Tutsi group'.[58] Such an extensive participation in genocidal acts led the Chamber to conclude that Akayesu possessed specific genocidal intent and was thus responsible for genocide and not merely for complicity in genocide.[59] The Trial Chamber sentenced Akayesu to life imprisonment for this offence.[60]

ii. The Genocide Case

In 2007, the ICJ ruled on Bosnia's claim that Serbia had committed genocide during various events that occurred in Bosnia between 1991 and 1995. Bosnia maintained that the pattern of atrocities committed against the non-Serbian population over a long period of time demonstrated that Serbia possessed the specific intent within the meaning of the Genocide Convention. The court rejected this all-encompassing approach by stipulating that specific intent can only be shown by reference to particular circumstances.[61] Consequently, the ICJ established that members of the VRS (the army of the Republika Srpska)[62] committed genocide only in and around Srebrenica starting from about 13 July 1995.[63] In its finding, the ICJ referred extensively to the ICTY jurisprudence on genocide.[64]

[57] ibid, para 546–47. For a slightly different point of view on the interplay between the procedural and substantive provisions on complicity in the ICTR Statute, see C Eboe-Osuju, '"Complicity in Genocide" versus "Aiding and Abetting Genocide"' (2005) 3 *Journal of International Criminal Justice* 56.

[58] *Akayesu* Trial Judgment (n 49) 705–06, as discussed by Cassese (n 3) 217.

[59] *Akayesu* Trial Judgment (n 49) para 734. In addition to convicting Akayesu of genocide, the Trial Chamber found him guilty of ordering the killings of several refugees and civilians, acts of torture committed in his presence, aiding and abetting sexual violence by allowing it to happen close to his office and saying the words of encouragement. See ibid, paras 651–96.

[60] *Prosecutor v Akayesu* ICTR Case No 96-4-T, Sentencing Transcript, 2 October 1998 ('*Akayesu* Sentencing Transcript') 6. In contrast, Radislav Krstić and Dragan Nikolic has been sentenced by the ICTY to 35 years' imprisonment for aiding and abetting the genocide. See *Prosecutor v Krstić*, ICTY Case No IT-98-33-A, Appeal Judgment, 19 April 2004, para 97.

[61] *Genocide* Judgment (n 21) para 373.

[62] Republika Srpska is the Serbian-populated enclave within Bosnia and Herzegovina where the atrocities occurred.

[63] *Genocide* Judgment (n 21) para 297.

[64] For more discussion on this point, see D Turns, 'Application of the Convention on the Prevention and Punishment of the Crime of Genocide: Bosnia and Herzegovina v. Serbia and Montenegro' (2007) 8 *Melbourne Journal of International Law* 398.

The ICJ reviewed the different ways in which Serbia could be held accountable for the atrocities committed by the VRS in Srebrenica. In particular, it examined three issues: first, whether the acts of genocide were committed by persons or organs whose conduct is attributable to Serbia; second, whether the acts enumerated in Article 3 of the Genocide Convention other than genocide itself (for example, complicity in genocide) were committed by persons or organs whose conduct is attributable to Serbia; and, finally, whether Serbia complied with the obligation deriving from Article 1 of the Genocide Convention to prevent and punish genocide.[65]

With regard to the first question, the ICJ held that actions of the VRS cannot be attributed to Serbia on the basis that neither the Republika Srpska nor the VRS were de jure organs of the FRY, nor did they have the status of an organ of that state under its internal law.[66] Similarly, the ICJ rejected Bosnia's argument that the conduct of the VRS was attributable to Serbia based on Article 8 of the ILC Articles on State Responsibility as a conduct directed or controlled by the state.[67] In resolving this issue, the ICJ refused to apply the test of 'overall control' introduced by the ICTY Appeals Chamber in *Tadić* and instead applied a stricter test of 'effective control' developed by the ICJ in the *Nicaragua* case.[68] It explained that while it attached great weight to the ICTY's finding relating to the events that happened during the conflict, it could not use the ICTY's legal test of 'overall control' because it was developed for a purpose unrelated to the attribution of state responsibility for acts committed by paramilitary units.[69]

In relation to the second question, namely responsibility for various acts enumerated in Article 3 of the Genocide Convention, the ICJ rather quickly ruled out all possible forms of committing genocide apart from 'complicity in genocide'.[70] It then made several important pronouncements relating to state complicity in general and complicity in genocide in particular.

First, the ICJ held that 'complicity' needs to be distinguished from the acts of perpetrators acting on the instructions of or under the direction or effective control of Serbia. If such conduct is proved, it is directly attributable to the state without using the concept of complicity.[71] Second, the court clarified that for the purposes of Article 3 of the Geneva Convention, 'complicity' entails 'the provision of means to enable or facilitate

[65] *Genocide* Judgment (n 21) para 379.
[66] ibid, para 386.
[67] ibid, para 412.
[68] *Military and Paramilitary Activities in and against Nicaragua (Nicaragua v United States of America)* ICJ Reports 1986, para 65.
[69] *Genocide* Judgment (n 21) paras 402–04. See also M Shaw, *International Law* (Cambridge, Cambridge University Press, 2008) 791.
[70] *Genocide* Judgment (n 21) paras 416–17.
[71] ibid, para 419.

the commission of the crime'.[72] Third, the ICJ held that although there is no notion of 'complicity' in the terminology of the law of international responsibility, it is similar to the notion of 'aid and assistance' that constitutes the customary rule found in the law of state responsibility and embodied in Article 16 of the ILC Articles on State Responsibility.[73] Consequently, the ICJ found it appropriate to examine Serbia's potential accomplice liability in genocide through the prism of Article 16 of the ILC Articles on State Responsibility.[74] Fourth, the court refused to answer the question of whether the accomplice needs to share the specific intent of the principle perpetrator, but affirmed that it is essential that the person or an organ furnishing 'aid and assistance' to the principal perpetrator needs, at the very least, to be aware of such intent.[75]

This latter point was the sole basis for failing to hold Serbia responsible for complicity in genocide. The ICJ held that it was not satisfied beyond reasonable doubt that Serbia supplied resources to the perpetrators of the genocide with a clear awareness of their genocidal intent—the intent to destroy, in whole or in part, a human group as such. In other words, the court did not find conclusive evidence that the Belgrade authorities were aware that their aid and assistance would be used to commit genocide, especially where the decision to commit genocide had been taken shortly before the act was actually carried out.[76] Judges Keith and Bennouna disagreed with the court on this point, stating in their separate declarations that Serbia must have known about the specific intent of the VRS and provided it with aid and assistance with that knowledge.[77]

Finally, two implicit points emerge from the ICJ's discussion relating to complicity: the state can potentially be an accomplice to the genocide committed by certain entities (and not the other state)[78] and complicity in genocide is possible even when the genocide as a principal wrong has not been attributed to any state.

With regard to the third question relating to Serbia's potential failure to comply with its positive obligation under Article 1 of the Genocide Convention to prevent and punish genocide, the ICJ held that Serbia had indeed violated its obligation in this respect.[79] While a detailed analysis of this finding is beyond the scope of this chapter, it is worth noting that

[72] ibid.
[73] ibid.
[74] ibid, para 420.
[75] ibid, para 421.
[76] Ibid, paras 422–23.
[77] Declaration of Judge Bennouna, *Genocide* Judgment (n 21) 362; Declaration of Judge Keith, *Genocide* Judgment (n 21) 354–58. See also Jackson (n 46) 212.
[78] Jackson (n 46) 215.
[79] *Genocide* Judgment (n 21) para 440.

the ICJ did not award any compensation to Bosnia as a result of finding this breach.[80]

B. Complicity in Torture

i. *The* Furundžija *Case*

Anto Furundžija served as a local commander of the Croatian Defence special unit in one of the municipalities in Bosnia and Herzegovina. At one point during the conflict, the accused subjected a Bosnian Muslim woman to interrogation in the nude in front of 40 soldiers. After this interrogation, the woman was taken to another room where she was raped in the presence of the accused, who did nothing to stop the sexual violence.

The prosecution charged Furundžija with one instance of rape and torture without specifying the mode of liability, thus leaving the question to the Trial Chamber.[81] This lack of clarity regarding the nature of the participation of the accused prompted the Trial Chamber to examine the difference between participating in the joint criminal enterprise and aiding and abetting a crime, using torture and rape as examples for its analysis. Based on a review of the post-Second World War jurisprudence, it concluded that the actus reus for aiding and abetting consists of practical assistance, encouragement or moral support which has a substantial effect on the perpetration of the crime, whereas the mens rea required is the knowledge that these acts assist the commission of the offence.[82] In contrast to aiding and abetting, the notion of common design presupposes the actus reus consisting of participation in a joint criminal enterprise and that the required mens rea is intent to participate.[83]

When applying these principles to the case, the Trial Chamber concluded that to be guilty of torture as a co-perpetrator, the accused must have participated in an integral way in the torture and with the intent of obtaining a confession or punishing and humiliating the victim.[84] In contrast, to be guilty as an aider and abettor, the accused must assist in some way and this assistance must have a substantial effect on the torture. The accused must also have the knowledge that torture is taking place.[85] Following this line of argument, the Chamber noted that aiding and abetting torture may only occur in very limited instances.[86]

[80] Gattini (n 22) 124.
[81] *Prosecutor v Furundžija*, ICTY Case No IT-95-17/1-T, Trial Judgment, 10 December 1998, para 189.
[82] ibid, para 191, as cited by Cassese (n 3) 217.
[83] ibid, para 249, as cited by Schabas (n 53) 307.
[84] ibid, para 249.
[85] ibid, para 245, as cited by Schabas (n 53) 307.
[86] ibid, para 257.

Based on these considerations, the Trial Chamber concluded that the interrogation of a Bosnian woman was an integral part of torture. The accused was therefore guilty of torture as a co-perpetrator.[87] At the same time, the accused was only found guilty of aiding and abetting rape. He himself did not commit the act, but by virtue of being present at the scene of the crime and holding the position of authority, he encouraged the sexual violence.[88]

The Trial Chamber noted that varying degrees of participation may be a matter to consider at sentencing, thereby implying that aiding and abetting may attract a more lenient sentence.[89] Consequently, it sentenced Anto Furundžija to 10 years' imprisonment for torture and eight years' imprisonment for aiding and abetting rape, with both sentences to be served concurrently.[90] It did not explicitly discuss the effect of the mode of participation on sentencing. However, it did make clear that, as he was as responsible for the crime as the person actually inflicting pain, the accused's role in torture as a fellow perpetrator was an aggravating factor.[91] Given that both torture and rape are equally reprehensible crimes, the slightly more lenient sentence for aiding and abetting rape confirms the relative weight the Trial Chamber assigned to the mode of the accused's participation in the crimes.

ii. The Binyam Mohamed *Case*

In 2009, the UK Parliament's Committee issued a report relating to the allegations that UK security services had been complicit in the torture of UK nationals held in Pakistan and elsewhere.[92] The case of Binyam Mohamed was one of the alleged 'torture cases' reviewed by the UK Parliament's Committee.

Binyam Mohamed was a UK resident of Ethiopian nationality arrested in 2002 in Pakistan under the US extraordinary rendition programme on suspicion of alleged links with Al-Qaeda. He was detained and questioned in Pakistan, Morocco, Afghanistan and, finally, Guantanamo, where he was held for more than four years until his release in 2009.[93]

[87] ibid, para 267.

[88] ibid, paras 273–75, as discussed by Cassese (n 3) 218.

[89] ibid, para 257. This is a highly contested topic. For more discussion, see Ch 7.

[90] ibid, para 112.

[91] ibid, paras 281–82.

[92] *Joint Committee on Human Rights—Twenty-Third Report*, http://www.publications.parliament.uk/pa/jt200809/jtselect/jtrights/152/15202.htm.

[93] *See R (Mohamed) v Secretary of State for Foreign and Commonwealth Affairs* [2008] EWCH 2048 (Admin) ('*Binyam Mohamed* Judgment') and *R (Mohamed) v Secretary of State for Foreign and Commonwealth Affairs (Guardian News and Media Ltd and Others Intervening)* [2010] EWCA Civ 65, EWCA Civ 158 ('*Binyam Mohamed* Case').

While detained in Guantanamo, Mohamed brought a claim in a UK court seeking the disclosure of evidence held by the UK government and intelligence services confirming that he was subjected to torture in 2002–04. He needed this information to render his confessions inadmissible in proceedings before the US military commission in relation to charges of terrorist activity. On 21 August 2008, the Divisional Court of the Queen's Bench Division granted his claim and ordered the release of evidence subject to redactions (if any) requested by the Foreign Secretary.[94]

Consequently, at the Foreign Secretary's request, seven paragraphs of the *Binyam Mohamed* judgment, summarising the US reports sent to the UK authorities regarding his mistreatment while he was held in Pakistan, were redacted. Both Mohamed and the media representatives who joined the proceedings questioned whether these redactions were justifiable on appeal. In the meantime, the documents sought by Mohamed were made available to him in the US proceedings, meaning that the only question before the Court of Appeal was whether to restore the seven paragraphs initially redacted from the *Binyam Mohamed* judgment. In February 2010, the Court of Appeal ordered the redacted paragraphs to be restored.[95] It held that where the judgment is concerned with such a 'fundamental and topical issue as the mistreatment of detainees' and the involvement of the UK government in this mistreatment, public interest overrides other considerations.[96]

Neither of the two judgments described above relates directly to the question of UK complicity in torture. The *Binyam Mohamed* judgment does, however, make several points that are important for understanding the scope of the concept in the law of state responsibility.

In *Binyam Mohamed*, the court granted disclosure on the basis of a test developed in the earlier case of *Norwich Pharmacal*.[97] One of the questions that the court had to answer in order to apply the *Norwich Pharmacal* principles was whether there was a wrongdoing and whether the UK government had facilitated such wrongdoing through the security service or its agents being involved in or participating in the alleged wrongdoing.[98]

The court established that in May 2002, the UK security services received reports containing information relating to Mohamed's mistreatment in Pakistan by the US authorities. The court then ruled that the UK government facilitated the interrogation of Mohamed in the knowledge of the reports, which contained information relating to his detention and treatment in the circumstances where his detention incommunicado was

[94] *Binyam Mohamed* Judgment (n 93).
[95] *Mohamed* Appeal Judgment (n 93).
[96] Appeal Judgment, para 184.
[97] *Binyam Mohamed* Judgment, para 61.
[98] ibid, para 71.

unlawful under the law of Pakistan.[99] Consequently, the *Binyam Mohamed* judgment concluded that by seeking to interview Mohamed in such circumstances, 'the relationship of the UK Government to the US authorities in connection with BM was far beyond that of a bystander or witness to the alleged wrongdoing'.[100]

Another important issue discussed in the *Binyam Mohamed* judgment was Mohamed's argument that the UK breached its obligation of disclosure flowing from the particular status of the prohibition on torture in international law as a rule of *jus cogens* binding on states *erga omnes*.[101] Without questioning the *jus cogens* nature of the prohibition of torture, the court rejected Mohamed's argument, stating that at that time there existed no rule of customary international law obliging the UK to make a disclosure to him.[102]

In arriving at this conclusion, the court examined Article 41 of the ILC Articles on State Responsibility, which imposed on all states a twofold obligation resulting from the breach of obligations under the peremptory norms of international law: a positive obligation to cooperate to bring an end to the breach; and a negative duty not to render aid or assistance in maintaining the situation created by a breach of a peremptory norm. With regard to the former obligation, the court referred to Professor Crawford's commentary on Article 41, where he stated that it is an open question whether international law at present prescribes a positive duty of cooperation.[103] The court also noted that currently there is no authority that purports to provide a comprehensive statement of the legal consequences flowing from the *jus cogens* status of the primary rule.[104]

The UK Parliament's Committee elaborated on the notion of state complicity, using the *Binyam Mohamed* case as one of the instances of the UK's alleged complicity in torture. The Committee was confronted with the question whether certain conduct by the UK government, such as asking foreign intelligence known to use torture to detain and question an individual, constitutes complicity in torture. In order to answer this question, the Committee had to define what constitutes 'complicity in torture'. Consequently, the Committee members drew a distinction between 'complicity in torture' for the purposes of individual criminal responsibility and state responsibility. The former required proof of three elements in accordance with *Furundžija*: (1) knowledge that torture is taking place and (2) a direct contribution by way of assistance that (3) has a substantial effect on

[99] *Binyam Mohamed* Judgment, para 147.
[100] ibid, para 88.
[101] ibid, para 162.
[102] ibid, para 183.
[103] Appeal Judgment, para 173.
[104] ibid, para 179.

the perpetration of the crime. The latter, based on the interpretations provided by the UN Committee Against Torture, meant 'simply one State giving assistance to another State in the commission of torture, or acquiescing in such torture, in the knowledge, including constructive knowledge, of the circumstances of the torture which is or has been taking place'.[105]

The UK Parliament's Committee concluded, relying on the opinion of Professor Sands, that a narrower meaning of complicity is likely to be adopted in the context of individual criminal responsibility, whereas determination of state responsibility calls for a wider definition of complicity.[106] The Committee made such a conclusion on the basis of Sand's explanation that 'complicity' within the meaning of Article 4(1) of the Torture Convention has a broader meaning than 'aiding and abetting' within the meaning of Article 7(1) of the ICTY Statute. Despite this difference in the scope of complicity for the purposes of two different legal instruments, Sands advised the UK Parliament's Committee to use the three-prong test developed by the ICTY Trial Chamber in *Furundžija* in order to determine whether the UK incurred liability for complicity in torture.[107] Based on these considerations, the Committee concluded that the government's turning a blind eye, systematically receiving or relying on the information originating from the country known to torture 'might well cross the line into complicity'.[108]

In the *Ahmed and Another v R* case, the Court of Appeal of England and Wales had an opportunity to test this 'wider' understanding of complicity in the law state responsibility.[109] The two appellants were convicted of terrorism offences. One of the appellants, Rangzieb Ahmed, claimed that the prosecution against him should have been stayed on the basis of, inter alia, the UK's alleged complicity in torture.[110] He claimed that he was held in captivity and tortured in Pakistan before being brought to the UK to stand trial. During his time in Pakistan, the UK intelligence officers interviewed him on at least one occasion. His argument was that complicity is demonstrated where State A has any settled practice of information or intelligence sharing with State B, which is known or believed to use torture. Furthermore, according to the argument, wherever such complicity by settled practice is demonstrated and information has been shared in respect of a man prosecuted in England who has been interrogated in

[105] UK Parliament's Report, paras 31, 32, 35.

[106] ibid, para 34.

[107] Supplementary Memorandum Submitted by Professor Philippe Sands QC Following Oral Evidence on 28 April 2009 ('Sand's Memorandum'), http://www.publications.parliament.uk/pa/jt200809/jtselect/jtrights/152/152we23.htm.

[108] UK Parliament's Report, Conclusions and Recommendations, para 3.

[109] *Ahmed and Another v R* [2011] EWCA Crim 184 (25 February 2011).

[110] ibid, para 23.

State B under conditions involving torture, there is a sufficient connection between the complicity and the trial to justify staying the prosecution.[111]

On the face of it, this position appears to be consistent with the broader view of complicity advanced by the UK Parliamentary Committee. However, the court rejected the appellant's claim. It drew the line between the use of materials obtained under torture by the executive and the courts. The court regarded the use of materials obtained under torture by the executive as permissible with a view to the policy objective of protecting citizens. In contrast, the use of such materials by courts should not be allowed.[112] Court proceedings involving a prosecution must only be stayed if there is a connection between the alleged wrongdoing and the trial. In the case at issue, it was not demonstrated that the torture impacted upon the trial.[113] Moreover, the court rejected the extended view of complicity as 'aspirational'.[114] It held:

> On ordinary principles of English law, if A aids or abets (ie assists) B to commit torture, or if he counsels or procures (ie encourages or arranges) torture by B, then A is no doubt guilty, as is B. But simply to receive information from B which is needed for the safety of A's citizens but which is known or suspected to be the product of torture would not, without more, amount in English law to either of these forms of secondary participation.[115]

III. TREATMENT OF COMPLICITY IN TWO AREAS OF LAW: COMMON TRENDS AND DIVERGENCES

There is a connection between the law of state responsibility and international criminal law. As has been discussed above, the two fields complement each other. Article 58 of the ILC Articles on State Responsibility reassures us that 'these articles are without prejudice to any question of the individual responsibility under international law of any person acting on behalf of the State'. Similarly, *Furundžija* confirms that under current international humanitarian law, individual criminal liability may be supplemented by state responsibility.[116]

Complicity is a concept utilised by the law of state responsibility and international criminal law in a very similar manner. Complicity in both areas of law has both broader and narrower meanings. Complicity in

[111] ibid, para 26.

[112] *cf* UN Human Rights Council, 'Report of the Special Rapporteur on the Promotion and Protection of Human Rights and Fundamental Freedoms while Countering Terrorism' (4 February 2009) UN Doc A/HRC10/3, paras 53, 55.

[113] *Ahmed and Another* (n 109) paras 33–40.

[114] ibid, para 44.

[115] ibid, para 42.

[116] *Furundžija* Trial Judgment (n 81) para 142. For further discussion, see Sunga (n 2) 246.

international criminal law can encompass all modes of direct criminal participation apart from commission, while sometimes it is equated solely with aiding and abetting.[117] Similarly, complicity in the law of state responsibility can be understood merely as one state aiding and assisting another state to commit an internationally wrongful act within the meaning of Article 16 of the ILC Articles on State Responsibility, or it can also entail the state's failure to respect positive obligations under the *jus cogens* primary rules of international law. In the latter case, the procedural threshold set by Article 16 for holding the state responsible may arguably be circumvented. However, in *Binyam Mohamed*, the court refused to recognise as binding the positive obligation to disclosure flowing from the prohibition of torture and refused to acknowledge complicity on the part of the UK in torture on this basis.[118]

It is evident from the case law analysis that complicity as a form of participation in both the law of state responsibility and international criminal law is intimately linked to the substantive rules defining the prohibited conduct. The scope of complicity is predefined by the nature of conduct it is attached to. The Trial Chamber in *Furundžija* was able to establish that the accused perpetrated torture, and not merely aided and abetted it, only after having reviewed the elements of torture and the accused's role in relation to these elements. Similarly, Sand's Memorandum discusses complicity in torture from the perspective of the Torture Convention (primary rules) and the ILC Articles on State Responsibility (secondary rules). Both the *Genocide* and the *Akayesu* cases focus on the notion of genocidal intent, or *dolus specialis*, in their reasoning relating to complicity.

Similar principles relating to complicity seem to emerge in both fields of law. First, in the law of state responsibility and international criminal law, it is possible to hold an individual and a state complicit in crime even without a conviction of the principal perpetrator. The *Furundžija*, *Genocide* and *Binyam Mohamed* cases fall under this principle and *Akayesu* explicitly discusses it. Second, both fields of law draw a dividing line between perpetration and complicity. *Furundžija* clearly demonstrates the difference between perpetrating the crime as a part of a joint criminal enterprise and aiding and abetting the crime. Similarly, the ILC Commentary and the *Genocide* judgment explicitly mention the distinction between the two modes of participation.

Finally, the legal requirements of complicity in the law of state responsibility and international criminal law are very similar. The fault requirement

[117] For a discussion of the scope of complicity in international criminal law, see Ch 4.I.B.

[118] Cerone (n 46) also suggested that complicity in the law of state responsibility can fall under the doctrine of attribution, when the conduct of an organ of one state is attributed to another. The *Genocide* case has rejected this wide interpretation of complicity by holding that in such a case, the acts of organs are directly attributable to the state without the doctrine of 'complicity'.

of complicity for the purposes of both state responsibility and individual criminal responsibility seems to be at least knowledge that the acts assist in the commission of the specific crime. However, the mental element is better defined in international criminal law. The ad hoc tribunals require at least 'knowledge',[119] while the ICC has adopted a higher threshold: aiding and abetting must occur 'for the purpose of facilitating the commission of a crime'.[120]

The law of state responsibility offers limited insight on the issue of the fault element. Article 16 of the ILC Articles on State Responsibility incorporates the requirement of 'knowledge' in the definition of aiding and assisting, the ILC Commentary mentions both knowledge and intent, and the *Genocide* judgment, regrettably, falls short of discussing whether intent shared with the principle perpetrator is required to hold a state complicit in genocide. Such a finding would have dealt with the discrepancies in the ILC Commentary, but could have been highly controversial because without the conviction of the primary perpetrator, it seems very difficult, if not impossible, to establish the 'shared intent' of the accomplice. In *Binyam Mohamed*, the UK Parliament's Committee suggested, relying on the international criminal law standards, that knowledge is sufficient to hold a state complicit in torture.

The conduct requirement of complicity is also comparable to some extent in the law of state responsibility and international criminal law. The Trial Chamber held in *Furundžija* that the actus reus of complicity (in a narrow sense) consists of the assistance having a substantial effect on the perpetration of the crime. The ICC is presently in search of the appropriate criterion to assess the effect of assistance on the crime.[121] Both the *Genocide* and the *Binyam Mohamed* cases describe complicity as a certain conduct that 'facilitates' the commission of the wrongdoing. In addition, the ILC Commentaries require that in the context of state complicity, the aid and assistance must contribute significantly to the commission of internationally wrongful conduct. Thus, the impact of assistance has to reach a certain level in order to attract responsibility of both states and individuals.

Despite the close connection between complicity in the law of state responsibility and international criminal law, the present study has revealed a number of important differences between the complicity of states and the complicity of individuals. These distinctions showcase the limits of the cross-disciplinary comparison furnished in this chapter.[122]

[119] For a discussion of this, see Ch 4.I.G.

[120] Rome Statute, art 25(3)(c). For a discussion of this, see Ch 5.I.C.

[121] See Ch 5.II.C.

[122] Aust argued that intra-disciplinary comparisons will not provide for ready-made answers to problems related to the interpretation of art 16 of the Articles on State Responsibility. See Aust (n 13) 194.

One of the main differences between complicity in the law of state responsibility and international criminal law is that the complicity of individuals, as opposed to state complicity, implies more or less clear consequences. The mode of participation is one of the factors that affect sentencing in international criminal law.[123] State complicity, in contrast, has no specific implications attached to it. The question arises whether state complicity entails less severe or simply different countermeasures than those taken against the state primarily responsible for an internationally wrongful act.

One would assume that the general rules regarding the consequences of finding a state responsible for breach of an internationally wrongful act would be applicable to complicit states.[124] However, using these provisions in conjunction with state complicity presents some difficulties. The main source of the problem is that these consequences have been modelled on the bilateral relationship between one wrongdoing state and one injured state.[125] Complicity obscures the matters by introducing an additional legal relationship.[126] Matters are further complicated by the fact that responsibility for aiding and assisting does not require the complicit state to have committed a wrongful act, but that it associates itself with the wrongful conduct of another state.[127]

This distinction between the two fields lies in the fact that international criminal law in general has developed mechanisms for enforcing the individual criminal responsibility as opposed to the law of state responsibility, which still lacks such mechanisms, particularly when dealing with the responsibility of states for grave breaches of peremptory norms. The absence of clear guidelines on enforcing the responsibility of states for failure to respect positive obligations of *jus cogens* nature was one of the reasons for the ILC's rejection of the notion of 'state crimes'. The same reason prompted the court in *Binyam Mohamed* to deny UK responsibility for breaching the Torture Convention. Similarly, the ICJ did not grant Bosnia compensation following the finding that Serbia violated the Genocide Convention by failing to prevent genocide.

Another important distinction between state and individual complicity is that the link between complicity and substantive rules is more evident in the area of individual criminal responsibility. International criminal law usually provides for one comprehensive legal instrument—the relevant

[123] See Ch 7.

[124] Articles on State Responsibility, arts 29–41.

[125] Aust (n 13) 269.

[126] On the impossibility of exercising ICJ jurisdiction in multiparty disputes without the consent of the third party, see *Case of the Monetary Gold Removed from Rome in 1943 (Italy v France, United Kingdom and United States) (Preliminary Question)* ICJ Rep 1954.

[127] Aust (n 13) 272.

statute—that contains both the general rules on attribution of responsibility and the specific provisions relating to crimes. In contrast, the law of state responsibility defines complicity as a mode of participation in the ILC Articles on State Responsibility, while the rules outlining prohibited conduct are found elsewhere in various international treaties.[128] It is true that the Genocide and the Torture Conventions explicitly mention 'complicity'. However, in the context of these instruments, 'complicity' is treated more as a substantive crime itself rather than a mode of participation. This peculiarity prompted the judges in the *Genocide* case to turn to the ILC Articles on State Responsibility for the proper definition of 'complicity'. The UK Parliament's Committee in *Binyam Mohamed* drew inspiration from the definitions provided by international criminal law.

Yet another difference between complicity in the law of state responsibility and international criminal law resides in the definition of legal requirements of complicity. As discussed above, it is well established in the case law of international criminal tribunals that 'knowledge' is sufficient to hold an individual responsible for aiding and abetting the crime if other criteria are met.[129] The ICC has a higher threshold for the fault requirement—acting with a purpose of facilitating the commission of the crime.[130] The situation is much less clear in the law of state responsibility. The ILC Commentaries mention both knowledge and intent as a requirement for aiding and assisting. Similarly, the ICJ has adopted a very careful approach to the fault requirement in the context of state complicity. It did not rule on whether shared intent is necessary for complicity in genocide and it fell short of establishing Serbia's awareness of the genocide about to be committed. This caution can be explained by the general difficulty of ruling on the fault of a collective entity such as state. The legal dilemma lies in the fact that fault is established in relation to state agents who are nonetheless acting in their official capacity. They are implementing state policy in an unlawful manner. The ensuring separation of their individual responsibility as moral agents as a result of their unlawful actions from the responsibility of a state brings about certain level of discomfort.[131]

Consequently, in contrast with the UK Parliament's Committee conclusions, it appears that complicity for the purposes of the law of state responsibility has a narrower scope than complicity for the purposes of

[128] *cf* Jackson (n 46) 149. The author argues that art 16 of the ILC Articles on State Responsibility is a primary rule.

[129] See Ch 4(I)(G).

[130] Rome Statute, art 25(3)(c).

[131] P Allott noted that 'the moral effect of the law is vastly reduced if the human agents involved are able to separate themselves personally both from the duties the law imposes ad from the responsibility which it entails'. P Allott, 'State Responsibility and the Unmaking of International Law' (1998) 29 *Harvard Journal of International Law* 14.

international criminal law. The threshold for holding a state responsible for complicity is higher than the threshold established for complicity in the context of individual criminal responsibility. Of course, this could be partially explained by the lack of relevant cases in the field of the law of state responsibility, but the general principles of complicity developed by both disciplines are nonetheless sufficiently clear to point in the direction of a higher threshold for state complicity.

This finding first seems counterintuitive. A rich jurisprudence relating to individual criminal responsibility clearly dominates the remarkably few cases dealing with state complicity. International criminal law has developed the concept of complicity to a much greater extent than the law of state responsibility. However, the lack of elaboration of the standard of complicity in the law of state responsibility does not cancel out the fact that the requirements for state complicity are more stringent than those applied to individuals. The case of *Ahmed and Another v R* supports this contention. The Court of Appeal of England and Wales, in contrast with the conclusions of the UK Parliament's Committee, rejected the wider notion of state complicity.

One can furnish a number of explanations as to why there exists a higher threshold for state complicity. One reason could be the tension that is still present in the law of state responsibility between the traditional state-centred approach that implies primarily bilateral relations between states and the community-oriented approach that is currently on the rise.[132] In this respect, the prominent international lawyer Roberto Ago already noted in 1939 that it was exactly this bilateral structure of international law which made it impossible to think of state responsibility for complicity.[133]

From a strictly legal point of view, criminal law, from the moment of its conception, was aimed at individuals rather than collective entities.[134] Consequently, applying certain criminal law principles to the state poses challenges. The *Genocide* judgment demonstrated the difficulty of defining the fault requirement for the state.[135] Another challenge is the question of punishment and its enforcement. Domestic criminal law usually provides for a developed criminal justice system encompassing various types of punishment backed up by the state enforcement mechanism. International criminal law is similar to domestic criminal law in that it empowers courts and tribunals to hand down sentences enforced through

[132] Aust (n 13).

[133] ibid 5, citing R Ago, 'Le délit international' (1939-II) 68 *Recueil des Cours* 415, 523.

[134] International criminal law lies at the intersection of domestic criminal law and public international law. It embraces to some extent the collective aspect of international crimes. For more discussion, see Ch 8.

[135] The question of the subjective element of state responsibility for aiding and assisting was already raised during the preparatory work on the provision for the Articles on State Responsibility. Aust (n 13) 231–35.

state cooperation. Therefore, finding an individual to be an accomplice to a crime brings about a very tangible outcome. No equivalent exists at the level of state responsibility.

On a more general level, the reluctance to accept a stricter standard of state criminality, and in particular state complicity, makes it possible to protect states from the stigmatisation that inevitably follows from a finding of criminal responsibility. On a global scale, the consequences of holding an individual complicit in international crimes are less severe than the same finding in relation to a state. This is so because persons incur their punishment individually, while criminally responsible states have to bear the consequences as a collective entity. Thus, state complicity opens the door to severe reputational implications, as well as multiple legal actions, including individual claims for damages originating in foreign countries. These effects could in turn undermine the very essence of statehood—sovereignty—which holds that a state is not subject, within its territorial jurisdiction, to the governmental, executive, legislative or judicial jurisdiction of a foreign state.[136]

In this respect, a parallel can be drawn with corporate complicity, and the caution that the state courts exercise in holding corporations complicit in human rights violations in another state. The recent case law of the US Supreme Court appears to uphold the presumption against extraterritorial application of the US statutes.[137] In *Kiobel*, the US Supreme Court rejected the claim that the Alien Torts Statute covered conduct occurring in a foreign sovereign's territory, even if the corporation is present in the US. The court insisted that for the presumption against extraterritoriality to be set aside, the claims must 'touch and concern the territory of the United States … with sufficient force'.[138] The reasons for this conservative approach to corporate complicity are similar to the concerns related to state complicity—the reluctance to jeopardise another state's sovereignty.

CONCLUSION

International crimes are complex in nature and involve a variety of actors, including states and individuals. It is essential to address the question of responsibility for mass atrocities at each level of perpetration. This is possible because state and individual responsibility are not mutually exclusive and complement each other. In general, individual criminal responsibility

[136] R Bernhardt, *Encyclopaedia of Public International Law* (Oxford, Oxford University Press, 2003) 512.

[137] *Kiobel v Royal Dutch Petroleum* 2013 WL 1628935; *Morrison v National Australia Bank Ltd* 561 US 2010.

[138] *Kiobel v Royal Dutch Petroleum* (n 137).

and state responsibility share similar foundations. Consequently, some theories from one field of law travel to another field of law. Complicity is one example of such a shared notion. However, care needs be applied when comparing the responsibility of a state and the responsibility of an individual. It has been demonstrated in this chapter, using the example of complicity, that there are limits to such a comparison.

It is due to the specific features of the law of state responsibility and international criminal law that the threshold for state complicity is higher than the threshold for individual complicity. Preserving the integrity of 'complicity' as a concept in both areas of law requires maintaining the distinctions. The system of state responsibility at the moment lacks proper enforcement mechanisms when it comes to certain types of violations. It also lacks the proper articulation of some criminal law concepts, such as 'fault'. In contrast, the complicity of individuals in the commission of international crimes enjoys elaborate definitions and the support of the domestic legislator.

Consequently, the direct transposition of the concept of complicity from one area of law to another is not the most desirable approach. It is arguably more efficient to furnish proper analysis and articulation of this principle separately in the context of each discipline, relying on the realities of the particular area. The case law of the international criminal tribunals relating to individual complicity is a useful tool in developing the notion of state complicity, but it can only serve as a reference point and not a substitute.

The *Furundžija* case illustrates this last point. The *Furundžija* Trial Chamber found the accused guilty of perpetrating torture (and not merely aiding and abetting the crime) solely on the basis of the accused being behind the purpose of torture, namely obtaining the information through interrogation. By directly applying the same test to the *Binyam Mohamed* case, one may come to the conclusion that the UK was not merely complicit in torture, but rather perpetrated it because it appears from the facts of the case that the UK's purpose was precisely that of obtaining the information from Mohamed. However, such a conclusion would arguably be too controversial and far-reaching.

7

The Correlation between Complicity and Sentencing

INTRODUCTION

THE QUESTION OF responsibility is closely intertwined with the question of punishment. It is difficult to perceive actions as criminal if they are not subject to punishment.[1] In the dialogue between the offender and the community, punishment is an instrument of communication to the wrongdoer of public reprobation.[2] The pain that the punishment inflicts, or the 'hard treatment elements of punishment', ensures that the offender does not ignore the message that society is trying to deliver to him.[3]

This dialogue between the offender and the community becomes even more intense at an international level: the outrageous nature of international crimes and the amount of suffering sustained by the victims enhance public desire to subject the offender to legal censure. Therefore, sentences handed down by the ICTY, the ICTR, the ICC, the ECCC and the SCSL have a huge impact on the accused, the victims and society.[4] The punishment becomes the measure of responsibility of the convicted person and it is usually widely publicised and discussed. Paradoxically, international criminal law lacks proper guidance on sentencing.[5] There are no appropriate tools to help 'translate' the totality of criminal conduct of the accused into a numerical value. Therefore, it comes as no surprise that some legal

[1] G Fletcher, *The Grammar of Criminal Law* (Oxford, Oxford University Press, 2007) 12.

[2] RA Duff, 'Punishment, Retribution and Communication', in A von Hirsch, A Ashworth and J Roberts (eds), *Principled Sentencing*, 3rd edn (Oxford, Hart Publishing, 2009).

[3] ibid.

[4] MB Harmon and F Gaynor, 'Ordinary Sentences for Extraordinary Crimes' (2007) 5 *Journal of International Criminal Justice*, 707.

[5] N Bernaz, 'Sentencing and Penalties' in W Schabas and N Bernaz (eds), *Routledge Handbook on International Criminal Law* (Abingdon, Routledge, 2009) 289; RD Sloane, 'Sentencing for the "Crime of Crimes": The Evolving "Common Law"' of Sentencing of the International Criminal Tribunal for Rwanda' (2007) 5 *Journal of International Criminal Justice* 714; R Cryer, H Friman, D Robinson and E Wilmeshurst, *An Introduction to International Criminal Law and Procedure*, 2nd edn (Cambridge, Cambridge University Press, 2010) 494.

commentators highlight the difficulty of predicting the length of the sentences to be handed down by the international courts.[6]

Complicity as a mode of liability is an important indicator determining the degree of culpability of the accused during sanctioning in national law. As discussed in some detail in Chapter 2, most domestic legal systems distinguish between primary and secondary perpetrators for sentencing purposes. Mitigation of the sentence is one practical outcome of finding someone complicit in crime, as opposed to rendering him the primary perpetrator. National legal orders are quite explicit in this respect and can be roughly divided into two camps: those that recognise more lenient sentences for accessories and those that treat all crime participants alike.[7]

Common law countries, as well as France, punish principals and accomplices alike. This is stipulated at the legislative level. However, an analysis of jurisprudence and doctrine reveals a more nuanced approach in individual cases. Other national legal systems, such as those in Germany, Spain or Russia, are more explicit in distinguishing between complicity and primary participation, and their statutes ensure that accomplices receive more lenient sentences than primary perpetrators.[8] The justification for a sentencing discount for an accessory is that his act is less wrongful, his state of mind is less culpable or he lacks the requisite hegemony over the act.[9] Yet these explanations raise questions even in the domestic law context. For example, should the accessory still receive a sentencing discount if his motive was worse than that of the primary perpetrator?[10]

As international law targets senior leadership figures often far removed from the scene of the crime, it presents even greater difficulty with respect to punishing accomplices. In many instances, the conduct of these individuals fits the legal definition of complicity. Can one safely assume that their culpability is less simply because they did not directly perpetrate the crime? The ICTY, ICTR, SCSL, ECCC and ICC Statutes do not answer this question or explain the consequences attached to the distinct modes of liability they contain.[11] The matter is further complicated by the introduction in international criminal law of various concepts constituting 'borderline' cases that lie between complicity and the actual commission

[6] G Mettraux, *International Criminal and Ad Hoc Tribunals* (Oxford, Oxford University Press, 2005) 356.

[7] G Fletcher, *Rethinking Criminal Law* (Boston, Little, Brown, 1978) 637; R Haveman and O Olusanya (eds), *Sentencing and Sanctioning in Supranational Criminal Law* (Antwerp, Intersentia, 2006), at 54.

[8] A Cassese, *International Criminal Law*, 2nd edn (Oxford, Oxford University Press, 2008) 188.

[9] Fletcher (n 7) 654–56.

[10] ibid, 651.

[11] Antonio Cassese notes the rudimentary nature of international criminal law when it comes to explaining the consequences attached to different classes of participation. See Cassese (n 8) 188.

of an offence. Joint criminal enterprise and co-perpetration often denote a level of involvement that, while not exactly amounting to direct perpetration, does not belong under the heading of complicity either.

The purpose of this chapter is to explore the correlation between complicity and sentencing in international criminal law. The analysis proceeds in the following order. First, there is an in-depth discussion of the sentencing considerations contained in several judgments that are thought to be representative of the sentencing decision-making process at an international level. This exercise elucidates individual factors affecting the final outcome. Second, the table contained in Appendix II reflects the correlation between the modes of participation and sentencing at the ICTY, the ICTR, the ECCC and the SCSL in a more schematic way. The table lists all persons convicted by the ad hoc tribunals and hybrid courts, the crimes that they were convicted of, their mode of liability and their respective sentences. It demonstrates that the final number of years assigned to the convicted person largely depends on the type of crime charged, the scope of the indictment and the existence (or absence) of the plea agreement. The mode of liability as a factor influencing sentencing is difficult to discern, especially in cases where convictions rely on several forms of participation rather than just one.

This chapter argues three main points. First, the processes of attributing responsibility and the imposition of a sentence are two distinct processes and should continue to be treated as such, especially in the context of international criminal law. This is in line with HLA Hart's separation of conviction and punishment.[12] Second, the mode of liability under which the accused is convicted bears more weight at the attribution of responsibility stage than at the punishment stage. Empirical research of the sentencing practice in international criminal law supports this conclusion and shows that complicity by no means warrants a lesser sentence in international criminal law. Rather, it has *some* impact on the sentence along with other considerations.[13] This is explained by the peculiar nature of international criminal law targeting primarily senior perpetrators who are away from the scene of the crime. Thus, it is the totality of factors that judges take into consideration rather than one particular aspect.[14] Consequently, in contrast with domestic law, the mode of participation does not speak so much to the gravity of the offence.

[12] HLA Hart and J Gardner, *Punishment and Responsibility: Essays on Philosophy of Law* (Oxford, Oxford University Press, 2009) 185.

[13] See Appendix II. For a quantitative study of the ICTY sentencing practice, see also B Hola, A Smeulers and C Bijleveld, 'Is ICTY Sentencing Predictable? An Empirical Analysis of ICTY Sentencing Practice' (2009) 22 *Leiden Journal of International Law* 79.

[14] *Prosecutor v Taylor*, SCSL-03-1-A, Appeal Judgment, 26 September 2013, para 670.

Finally, in the absence of the sentencing regime in international criminal law, judicial discretion in the determination of penalties is essential. The judges' freedom to decide on the appropriate penalty after having taken into consideration the totality of factors—including the mode of liability under which the conviction is entered—is one of the defining features of international criminal law. This is not necessarily a negative sign, but it is important to establish a cap on the exercise of the judicial discretion. The most obvious way to do this is to define and rank the aims of punishment in international criminal law and to elaborate on the scale of crimes according to their gravity.

The first section of this chapter outlines few sentencing principles contained in the Statutes of the ad hoc tribunals and the ICC. The same section explores the effect of the forms of participation, in particular complicity, on sentencing. The conclusions are drawn on the basis of the selected judgments emanating from the ad hoc tribunals, the hybrid courts and the ICC. The second section discusses punishment goals in international criminal law—any discussion on sentencing is incomplete without an elaboration of these goals. This section attempts to link traditional justification for punishment utilised by domestic legal systems with the reality of international criminal law. In addition, the section strives to find a place for the mode of liability within the framework of each sentencing goal. The final third section of the chapter examines judicial discretion at sentencing. It draws a distinction between the two stages of criminal trial—the stage leading to conviction, which places much emphasis on the mode of responsibility of the accused person, and the sentencing stage, which focuses on the totality of factors in determining the punishment.

I. THE CORRELATION BETWEEN COMPLICITY AND SENTENCING

A. Statutory Sentencing Principles

Before turning to the impact of complicity on punishment in the case law, it is important to identify some sentencing principles developed by the international criminal tribunals and the ICC. The Statutes of the ICC, the ICTY, the ICTR and the SCSL, and the ECCC constituent documents provide minimum guidance on this aspect, allowing for wide judicial discretion.[15] One can summarise a few general principles common to all of the abovementioned courts:

1. International criminal tribunals cannot impose the death penalty.
2. There is a limited dialogue with the national criminal justice systems: the ICTY, the ICTR and the SCSL may have a recourse to the general

[15] Cassese (n 8) 51.

practice regarding prison sentences in the courts of the respective state, while the ICC may refer to national sentencing provisions in the complementarity analysis.

3. In imposing the sentences, the Trial Chambers should take into account such factors as the gravity of the offence and the individual circumstances of the convicted person, as well as mitigating and aggravating circumstances.[16]

The first principle limits the Trial Chambers' discretion to imposing custodial sentences only, supplemented by the option of ordering the forfeiture of unlawfully acquired assets. In relation to the ICTY, the ICTR and the SCSL,[17] this excludes other types of punishment such as the death penalty, fines or community service.[18] The Rome Statute provides for an option of a fine in addition to the imprisonment.[19] With regard to the length of imprisonment, neither the ICTY Statute nor the ICTR Statute prohibits life imprisonment,[20] while the Rome Statute sets the maximum term at 30 years, allowing in exceptional cases for life imprisonment if justified by the extreme gravity of crimes and the individual circumstances of the convicted person.[21] The SCSL Statute requires that the imprisonment be for a limited number of years.[22]

The second principle—the recourse to domestic sentencing practice at the ICTY, the ICTR and the SCSL—received some acclaim.[23] However, it is generally not considered to be mandatory.[24] The Appeals Chamber in *Tadić* noted that 'while the law and practice of the former Yugoslavia shall

[16] See ICTY Statute, art 24; ICTR Statute, art 22; Rome Statute, art 78; SCSL Statute, art 19; ECCC Law, arts 38–39; ECCC Agreement, art 10; ICTY, ISTR and SCSL Rules of Procedure and Evidence, r 101; ECCC Internal Rules, r 98(5); and ICC Rules of Evidence and Procedure, r 145, attached in Appendix I.

[17] The ECCC regime differs from that of the SCSL, the ICTY, the ICTR and the ICC in that: 'The ECCC Agreement, the ECCC Law and the Internal Rules are otherwise silent as regards the principles and factors to be considered at sentencing. In particular, they do not indicate whether sentencing before the ECCC is governed by international or Cambodian legal rules, or some combination of each.' See *Prosecutor v KAING Guek Eav alias Duch*, ECCC, Case No 001/18-07-2007/ECCC/TC, Trial Judgment, 20 March 2012 ('*Duch* Judgment'), para 575. The ECCC Supreme Court Chamber established the prevalence of international law over national sentencing provisions by holding that 'in accordance with the principle of *lex specialis*, the ECCC Law shall govern the range of penalty in proceedings before the ECCC'. *Prosecutor v KAING Guek Eav Alias Duch*, ECCC, Case 001/18-07-2007-ECCC/SC, Appeal Judgment, 3 February 2012 ('*Duch* Appeal Judgment'), para 348.

[18] Mettraux (n 6) 343.

[19] Rome Statute, art 77(2)(a).

[20] ICTR Statute, art 23(1) and ICTY Statute, art 24(1).

[21] Rome Statute, art 77(1).

[22] SCSL Statute, art 19(1).

[23] For example, in *Muhimana* the ICTR Trial Chamber examined in detail the sentencing ranges provided by the Rwandan law for murder, genocide and crimes against humanity. See Judgment, *Muhimana* (ICTR 95-1B-T), Trial Chamber, 28 April 2005, para 592.

[24] Cassese (n 8) 51–52.

be taken into account by the Trial Chambers for the purposes of sentencing … a Trial Chamber's discretion in imposing sentence is not bound by any maximum term of imprisonment applied in a national system'.[25] National law plays a greater role when it comes to the enforcement of sentences of the convicted persons.[26] The Rome Statute does not envisage that the ICC should consider the scale of penalties of the relevant states.[27]

Finally, the third principle, namely the factors to be considered at sentencing, received a detailed, albeit somewhat mechanical, explanation in the case law of international tribunals. The first part of the determination, the 'gravity of offence', has been referred to as 'the litmus test for the appropriate sentence'.[28] Despite its apparent importance, this notion is not sufficiently clear in the jurisprudence of the tribunals,[29] especially in the absence of a formal hierarchy of the offences in the statutes of the courts and tribunals.[30] The courts describe 'gravity of offence' in a number of generic terms: the ICTR, for example, stated that in assessing the gravity of offences for which the accused has been found guilty, the Chamber takes into account the particular circumstances of the case as well as the nature and degree of his participation in the crimes.[31]

The ICTY Appeals Chamber in *Krnojelac* adopted a similar understanding of the gravity of the crime, where it held that 'the starting point in any consideration of the appropriate sentence is the gravity of the conduct of the accused in the case in question'. The judges further clarified that the determination of this issue requires analysis 'of the particular circumstances of the case, as well as of the form and degree of the participation of the accused in the crime'.[32] In the RUF sentencing judgment, the SCSL has been more explicit in holding that the following factors need to be taken into account when assessing the seriousness of the offences for sentencing purposes: the scale and brutality of the offences, the role played by

[25] *Prosecutor v Tadić*, Case No IT-94-1-Tbis-R117, Second Sentencing Judgment, 11 November 1999, para 21.

[26] Bernaz (n 5) 289.

[27] Cassese (n 8) 52.

[28] *Prosecutor v Akayesu*, ICTR Case No 96-4-A, Appeal Chamber Judgment, 1 June 2001, para 413.

[29] Sloane (n 5) 722; Harmon and Gaynor (n 4) 696–98; Cryer et al (n 5) 498.

[30] Cryer et al (n 5) 498.

[31] *Prosecutor v Muhimana*, ICTR Case No 95-1B-T, Trial Judgment 28 April 2005, ('*Muhimana* Trial Judgment'), para 591.

[32] *Prosecutor v Krnojelac*, ICTY Case No IT-97-25-T, Trial Judgment, 15 March 2002, para 522, as discussed by K Khan and R Dixon (eds), *Archbold: International Criminal Courts. Practice, Procedure and Evidence* (London, Sweet & Maxwell, 2005) 815. See also *Prosecutor v Delalić et al* ('*Čelebići* Appeal Judgment') ICTY Case No IT-96-21-A, Appeal Judgment, 20 February 2001, para 731; *Prosecutor v Blaskić*, ICTY Case No IT-95-14-A, Appeal Judgment, 29 July 2004, para 683; *Prosecutor v Aleksovski*, ICTY Case IT-95-14/1-A, Appeal Judgment, 24 March 2000, para 182.

accused in their commission, the degree of suffering inflicted on victims and the number of victims.[33]

The ICC, in the *Lubanga* sentencing decision, established that the 'gravity of the crime' is one of the principal factors to be considered in the determination of the sentence. It should be in proportion to the crime and reflect the culpability of the convicted person.[34] The court inferred the requirement of proportionality from Article 81(2)(a) of the Rome Statute providing for the possibility to appeal the sentence if it is disproportionate to the crime. Proportionality also played a major role in the jurisprudence of the other international courts: the ICTR Trial Chamber in *Akayesu* held that the 'sentence must reflect the predominant standard of proportionality between the gravity of the offence and the degree of responsibility of the offender'.[35] The SCSL in the *RUF* sentencing judgment also pointed out that sentences should be individual and proportionate to the severity of conduct of the offender.[36]

In addition to the gravity of the offence, the judges consider mitigating and aggravating circumstances. Instruments of the ICTY, the ICTR and the SCSL do not include the list of such circumstances, deliberately leaving them to the discretion of the judges.[37] Examples of the aggravating factors include the role of the accused in the commission of crimes, his position of leadership, discriminatory intent and the length of time during which the offence continued.[38] The ICC's Rules of Evidence and Procedure contain a non-exhaustive list of mitigating and aggravating factors to be considered at sentencing, including the extent of the damage caused, the degree of participation of the convicted person, the abuse of power and the individual's official capacity.[39]

The SCSL introduced a new aggravating factor in the *Taylor* case, namely the extraterritoriality of the acts of the convicted person. The judges felt compelled to account for the fact that Mr Taylor's support of the crimes in neighbouring Sierra Leone in his capacity as a former President of Liberia resulted in the damage and suffering in the neighbouring country and not simply his own.[40] This freshly discovered aggravating factor reinforces

[33] *Prosecutor v Sesay, Kallon and Gbao*, SCSL-04-15-T, Sentencing Judgment, 8 April 2009 ('*RUF* Sentencing Judgment'), para 18.

[34] *Prosecutor v Thomas Lubanga Dyilo*, ICC-01/04-01/06, Trial Chamber I, Decision on Sentence Pursuant to Article 76 of the Statute, 10 July 2012, para 36.

[35] *Prosecutor v Akayesu* ICTR Case No 96-4-T, Sentencing Transcript, 2 October 1998, at 8.

[36] RUF Sentencing Judgment (n 33) para 18.

[37] ibid, para 25; *Prosecutor v Obrenović*, ICTY Case No IT-02-60/2, Sentencing Judgment, 10 December 2003, para 91; *Blaskić* Appeal Judgment (n 32) para 685.

[38] *Blaskić* Appeal Judgment (n 32) para 686.

[39] ICC Rules of Evidence and Procedure, r 145(1)(c) and (2); see also W Schabas, *The International Criminal Court: A Commentary on the Rome Statute* (Oxford, Oxford University Press, 2010) 902–06.

[40] *Taylor* Sentencing Judgment, para 98.

two key points: first, the sentencing practice at an international level is still evolving; and, second, the individualisation of sentences in international criminal law requires a high degree of judicial discretion to reflect the unique set of facts in each case.[41] In contrast, domestic criminal law, due to the high volume of cases and a different nature of offending at stake, benefits from more regulation in the area of sentencing, for it assists judges with the categorisation of cases based on repetitive scenarios.

The three sentencing principles discussed above provide little guidance on the punishment of convicted persons.[42] While there exist some fundamental sentencing rules, such as the exclusion of the death penalty, the specific length of incarceration is determined by relying on the generic notions, such as the gravity of the offence and the individual circumstances of the accused. The judges thus enjoy broad discretion in crafting the content of these broad terms on a case-by-case basis. The next section demonstrates how judges approach one of the 'ingredients' of sentencing considerations—the form of participation of the convicted person, which is a constituent element of 'gravity of offence'. Its role appears limited.

B. Case Law

In the absence of the rigid statutory guidance, there are a number of factors that international criminal judges take into account at sentencing and it is difficult to single out one aspect as dispositive. Where does complicity fit into the equation? The mode of participation of the convicted person appears to be one of those factors. The SCSL in *RUF* noted that the mode of liability under which the accused is convicted may serve as an indication of his role in the crime and 'aiding and abetting as a mode of liability generally warrants a lesser sentence than that imposed for a more direct form of participation'.[43] Many ICTY and ICTR Chambers made similar pronouncements to that effect.[44] For example, the *Šljivančanin* Appeals

[41] In *Lubanga,* the prosecution appealed the sentence based, inter alia, on the Trial Chamber's failure to expressly consider some evidence deemed relevant for sentencing purposes. The Appeals Chamber refuted this argument and upheld judicial discretion at sentencing. *Prosecutor v Thomas Lubanga Dyilo,* ICC-01/04-01/06 A 4 A 6, Appeals Chamber Judgment on the appeals of the Prosecutor and Mr Thomas Lubanga Dyilo against the 'Decision on Sentence pursuant to Article 76 of the Statute', 1 December 2014 (*'Lubanga* Sentencing Appeal'), para 73.

[42] The lack of statutory guidance as to the specific penalties led some commentators to conclude that the principle of legality of penalties (*nulla poena sine lege*) is not applicable at the international level. See Cassese (n 8) 51; K Ambos, '*Nulla Poena Sine Lege* in International Criminal Law' in R Haveman and O Olusanya (eds), *Sentencing and Sanctioning in Supranational Criminal Law* (Antwerp, Intersentia, 2006) 32.

[43] RUF Sentencing Judgment (n 33) paras 19–21.

[44] See, for example, *Prosecutor v Vasiljević,* ICTY Case No IT-98-32-A, Appeal Judgment, 25 February 2004, para 102; Cassese (n 8) 211.

Chamber acknowledged the practice of treating aiding and abetting as a lower form of responsibility attracting a lesser sentence. However, it held that it is the gravity of the underlying crimes that remains an important consideration in assessing the *totality* of the criminal conduct.[45] The Appeals Chamber in *Taylor* took a different approach. It held that 'there is no hierarchy or distinction for sentencing purposes between forms of criminal participation'.[46]

In practice, the form of participation of the accused bears a relative value.[47] The table on the impact of the liability mode on sentencing at the ICTY, the ICTR, the SCSL, the ICC and the ECCC contained in Appendix II shows that a combination of factors affects the length of a sentence. First, it is clear from the table that the ICTY has on average a more lenient sentencing policy than the ICTR, while the ICTR is in turn more lenient than the SCSL. Second, the types of crime as well as the number of criminal acts underlying the conviction play an important role at sentencing. Genocide usually attracts heavier penalties; the more crimes that the individual is found responsible for, the longer his sentence.[48] Third, plea bargains as a rule significantly reduce the length of imprisonment. Finally, on the basis of the cumulative sentencing principle, internationally convicted persons frequently receive a single sentence for different criminal acts and different modes of participation that attach to these acts. This peculiarity makes it difficult, if not impossible, to distil the exact impact of complicity on the 'final figure'.

The empirical research of the ICTY sentencing dynamics conducted by Hola, Smeulers and Bijleveld pointed to interesting conclusions. It showed that the final average sentence for perpetrators, 17.3 years' imprisonment, is very close in value to the final average sentence for aiders and order givers—16.2 and 16.8 years' imprisonment, respectively. Moreover, the other types of accomplices receive an even more severe punishment than the actual perpetrators—18.5 years is the average sentence for planners and 20.7 for instigators.[49] On the other hand, members of a joint criminal enterprise receive a lenient average sentence of 14.6 years' imprisonment. This is despite the fact that participation in the joint criminal enterprise counts as a primary mode of responsibility.[50]

[45] *Prosecutor v Mrkšić and Šljivančanin*, ICTY Case No T-95-13/1-A, Appeal Judgment, 5 May 2009, para 407.

[46] *Taylor* Appeal Judgment (n 14) para 670.

[47] The aims of punishment in international criminal law are discussed in the subsequent section.

[48] This aspect raises important, charged policy questions. What is the implication of a prosecutorial decision to charge the accused only with a specific type of offence—when evidence on other crimes is abundant—solely for the matters of judicial efficiency?

[49] Hola, Smeulers and Bijleveld (n 13) 91.

[50] *Vasiljević* Appeal Judgment (n 44) para 95; *Prosecutor v Tadić*, ICTY Case No IT-94-1, Appeals Chamber Judgment, 19 July 1999, para 188; *Prosecutor v Krnojelac*, ICTY Case No IT-97-25-A, Appeal Judgment, 17 September 2003, para 29; Mettraux (n 6) 288.

Therefore, one can conclude that it is the combination of factors that predetermines the final sentence, and the mode of responsibility plays only a limited role. In this respect, it is also instructive to look at several cases across the tribunals with the prospect of establishing how complicity, or the mode of participation in general, fits into the pattern of judicial thinking at sentencing. This exercise has the benefit of including the factual component in the discussion on sentencing that is missing from the statistical overview provided in Appendix II.

Tadić, the first international criminal law trial in the modern era, provides a compelling example of the limited significance of complicity and the importance of the other factors at sentencing. Duško Tadić was a member of the Serbian Democratic Party in the town of Kosarić. He was convicted of various acts of violence against the non-Serb population in this district, including aiding and abetting prisoner beatings and killing two Muslim police officers.[51] Tadić's initial sentence of 20 years' imprisonment was largely motivated by the fact that he could not be considered to have played a significant leadership or organisational role in the events that occurred in the Bosnian municipality of Prijedor.[52]

Tadić's sentence has been revisited twice after that: once by the Trial Chamber after the Appeal Judgment came out[53] and again by the Appeals Chamber itself.[54] Upon the first review, the Trial Chamber increased Tadić's sentence to 25 years' imprisonment following the finding that Tadić was responsible for the killing of five men pursuant to the notion of 'common design' of the joint criminal enterprise, as opposed to aiding and abetting these crimes.[55] Tadić appealed against both the initial sentencing judgment and the subsequent one on the basis that the gravity of the offence and his culpability were not sufficiently reflected in the sentence. The Appeals Chamber agreed with him that the sentence of 25 years' imprisonment failed to reflect the relative insignificance of his role in the broader context of the conflict in the former Yugoslavia. The Appeals Chamber reduced his sentence to 20 years, holding that while the conduct of which he stood convicted was heinous, his level in the command structure of the whole ethnic cleaning campaign was relatively low.[56]

[51] *Prosecutor v Tadić*, ICTY Case No IT-94-1-T, First Sentencing Judgment, 14 July 1997, paras 20, 74, 75.

[52] ibid, para 60.

[53] For a discussion of the ICTY Appeal's Chamber decision to convict Tadić of murder as results of his participation in the joint criminal enterprise, see W Schabas, *The UN International Criminal Tribunals: The Former Yugoslavia, Rwanda and Sierra Leone* (Cambridge, Cambridge University Press, 2006) 297.

[54] *Prosecutor v Tadić*, Case No IT-94-1-Tbis-R117, Second Sentencing Judgment, 11 November 1999 ('*Tadić* Second Sentencing Judgment'); *Prosecutor v Tadić*, ICTY Case No IT-94-1-A and IT-94-1-Abis, Third Sentencing Judgment, 26 January 2000 ('*Tadić* Third Sentencing Judgment').

[55] *Tadić* Second Sentencing Judgment (n 54).

[56] ibid.

In contrast with *Tadić*, Zlatko Aleksovski was found guilty of aiding and abetting and not guilty of membership in the joint criminal enterprise. The ICTY held that his presence during the maltreatment of hundreds of non-Croat prisoners in Bosnia in his capacity as commander of the prison represented a tacit encouragement of the crimes.[57] This maltreatment amounted to outrages upon personal dignity as violations of the laws and customs of war.[58] The Trial Chamber sentenced Aleksovski to two and a half years' imprisonment based on the consideration that his direct participation in the commission of the acts of violence was relatively limited.[59] The prosecution appealed, arguing that the sentence of two and a half years' custody failed to achieve the two main purposes of sentencing in international criminal law, it being disproportionate to the magnitude of the offence[60] and lacking a sufficient deterrent effect.[61]

The Appeals Chamber was not especially influenced by the deterrence rationale and used the test developed by previous tribunals in order to assess whether the gravity of the offence was given due consideration. It discussed whether the circumstances of the case as well as the form and degree of participation of the accused in the crime justify such a lenient sentence.[62] It concluded that while the accused may have had a secondary role in the commission of crimes in prison, the Trial Chamber failed to give sufficient weight to the gravity of Aleksovski's conduct because he was a commander and, as such, the person in authority who had the power to prevent crimes in the prison. The Appeals Chamber therefore increased his sentence to seven years' imprisonment.[63]

Aleksovski is one of the infrequent instances when the Appeals Chamber felt compelled to increase the sentence of the accused.[64] It appears that when it initially delivered a lenient sentence of two and a half years, the Trial Chamber was guided by recognition of Aleksovski's peripheral position in the commission of the crimes and the fact that he was not

[57] *Prosecutor v Aleksovski* Trial Judgment, ICTY Case IT-95-14/1-T, 25 June 1999, para 87.

[58] *Aleksovski* Trial Judgment (n 57) 89.

[59] ibid, paras 235 and 244.

[60] For more discussion on proportionality, see K Kittichaisaree, *International Criminal Law* (Oxford, Oxford University Press, 2002) 316.

[61] *Aleksovski* Appeal Judgment (n 32) para 179.

[62] ibid, para 182.

[63] ibid, paras 183, 184 and 191.

[64] *Galić* demonstrates another example of the dramatic increase in the length of the accused's sentence on appeal. The Appeals Chamber in this case struck down the sentence of 20 years' imprisonment imposed by the Trial Chamber for ordering the shelling of Sarajevo and sentenced the accused to life imprisonment. In the view of the Appeals Chamber, the exceptional degree of brutality and cruelty with which the crimes were committed, their prolonged nature and Galić's position of authority rendered the initial sentence of 20 years unreasonable and unjust. See *Prosecutor v Galić*, ICTY Case No IT-98-29-T, Trial Judgment, 5 December 2003, para 769; *Prosecutor v Galić*, ICTY Case No IT-98-29-A, Appeal Judgment, 30 November 2006, para 455.

perpetrating them, but merely aiding and abetting. The mode of liability of the accused was therefore central in the Trial Chamber's reasoning. The Appeals Chamber re-established that *a number* of factors must be evaluated in order to determine the gravity of the crime, not only the degree of the participation of the accused but also his role in the context of the conflict and circumstances of the case.

The *Vasiljevic* case is a rare example of when a sentencing discount was based almost exclusively on the mode of participation of the convicted person. Mitar Vasiljevic was a member of Serbian paramilitary unit operating in eastern Bosnia.[65] The Trial Chamber established that on around 7 June 1992, the accused, together with several other paramilitaries, forcibly transported seven Bosnian Muslim civilians to the eastern bank of the Drina River, where five of the victims were executed while two men managed to escape.[66] Prior to transporting the civilians to the execution site, Vasiljevic held them at gunpoint in a nearby hotel. The Trial Chamber convicted Vasiljevic as a co-perpetrator in the joint criminal enterprise. To incur liability as a member of the joint criminal enterprise, the accused must share a criminal intent with the principal offender.[67] The Trial Chamber in *Vasiljevic* inferred intent from the acts of the accused, holding that 'the only reasonable inference available on the evidence is that the accused, by his actions, intended that the seven Muslim men be killed, whether or not he actually carried out any of those killings himself'.[68] The Trial Chamber convicted Vasiljevic of murder in respect of the five men and inhumane acts in respect of the two survivors.[69] He was sentenced to 20 years' imprisonment.[70]

The Appeals Chamber, on the other hand, held that it has not been established beyond reasonable doubt that the accused shared a criminal intent to kill.[71] However, the Appeals Chamber recognised that Vasiljevic knew that his actions would assist the killings because he guarded the victims prior to the shootings, walked them to the place of the executions, and was present at the time when the killings took place. His actions had a significant effect on the commission of the crime. Based on these considerations, the Appeals Chamber reversed the finding that he was a co-perpetrator in the joint criminal enterprise and found him guilty of aiding and abetting murder and inhumane acts.[72] The new finding in

[65] See the ICTY case information sheet at www.icty.org.

[66] *Prosecutor v Vasiljević*, ICTY Case No IT-98-32-T, Trial Judgment, 29 November 2002, para 97.

[67] See Chapter II.1.iii *supra*.

[68] *Vasiljević* Trial Judgment (n 68) para 113.

[69] ibid, paras 211 and 240.

[70] ibid, para 309.

[71] *Vasiljević* Appeal Judgment (n 44) para 115.

[72] ibid, paras 133–35, as cited by Mettraux (n 6) 284.

relation to his form of liability prompted the Appeals Chamber to adjust his sentence.[73] The Chamber reversed the sentence from 20 to 15 years' imprisonment based on the view that aiding and abetting generally warrants a lesser sentence than is appropriate for responsibility as a co-perpetrator.[74] Such a sentence, in the view of the Appeals Chamber, reflected the inherent gravity of the criminal conduct of the accused, the form and the degree of his participation, and the circumstances of the case.[75]

The ICTR judges also chose between primary and secondary participation on a number of occasions. For example, in the *Akayesu* case, the trial bench analysed whether the actions of the local teacher in the Taba municipality of Rwanda were merely a manifestation of an accomplice liability or whether they constituted an actual commission.[76] The judges held that Jean-Paul Akayesu incurred individual criminal liability for 'having ordered, committed, or otherwise aided and abetted in the preparation or execution of the killing of and causing serious bodily or mental harm to members of the Tutsi group'.[77] Such an extensive participation in genocidal acts led the Chamber to conclude that Akayesu was responsible for genocide and not merely for complicity in genocide.[78]

The Trial Chamber sentenced Akayesu to life imprisonment for genocide and incitement to commit genocide, 15 years' imprisonment for rape and 15 years' imprisonment for murder.[79] In arriving at such a conclusion, the judges assessed his personal role in the crimes committed in Taba. In particular, the tribunal noted Akayesu's position of authority in the local municipality and his duty to protect the population whose confidence he had betrayed.[80] The Trial Chamber pointed out that Akayesu's relatively low ranking in the government of Rwanda could serve as a mitigating factor at sentencing, whereas his deliberate choice to participate in the killings and rapes of members of the Tutsi population through orders and tacit encouragement constituted a powerful aggravating factor, one which clearly outweighed the mitigating factor.

At the sentencing stage, the tribunal placed the magnitude of the crime at the centre of its considerations. Life imprisonment for genocide stands in contrast to the 15 years' imprisonment for all other crimes committed

[73] ibid, para 149.

[74] *Vasiljević* Appeal Judgment (n 44) para 102.

[75] ibid, para 182.

[76] For a discussion of 'complicity', see Schabas (n 53) 305–06.

[77] *Prosecutor v Akayesu*, ICTR Case No 96-4-T, Trial Chamber Judgment, 2 September 1998, paras 705–06.

[78] ibid, para 734. In addition to convicting Akayesu of genocide, the Trial Chamber found him guilty of ordering the killings of several refugees and civilians, acts of torture committed in his presence, and aiding and abetting sexual violence by allowing it to happen close to his office. See *Akayesu* Trial Judgment (n 77) paras 651–96.

[79] *Akayesu* Sentencing Transcript (n 35) 6.

[80] ibid.

by Akayesu, including murder and rape.[81] Despite the fact that the judges went to some lengths in specifying the mode of participation of the accused, this consideration seems to have occupied a rather peripheral role at sentencing, with the gravity of the crime of genocide taking centre stage.

The SCSL sentencing judgment in *Taylor* exemplifies sentencing practice for complicity in war crimes and crimes against humanity. It is not particularly lengthy and builds on the past jurisprudence of the ad hoc tribunals and the SCSL. From the beginning, the Trial Chamber acknowledged that in the case law of the ad hoc tribunals, aiding and abetting attracts a lesser sentence than that to be imposed for primary forms of participation. Despite recognising this, the Chamber highlighted that the unique circumstances of the case are the dominant factor in its sentencing considerations.[82] Charles Taylor's factual contribution to the crimes committed in Sierra Leone appeared to be significant. The Chamber found that the RUF/AFRC heavily and frequently relied on the material aid supplied and facilitated by the convicted person, who also provided other forms of practical assistance that substantially contributed to the commission of the crimes while fully aware of the essential elements of these crimes.[83] The 'label' of secondary participation did not alleviate the gravity of Taylor's acts in the eyes of the Trial Chamber.

Two main aggravating factors appeared to attract the most weight for penalty purposes: Taylor's presidency and the extraterritoriality of his acts. The court placed him 'in a class of his own' when deciding upon the penalty, while stressing that, as President of Liberia and a member of ECOWAS committee, he held a position of public trust with inherent authority that he abused.[84] The fact that he intervened in the affairs of another state by supporting the violence in neighbouring Sierra Leone and not in his own country, thus violating the principle of customary international law, further aggravated his sentence.[85] Consequently, it was his leadership position as the former President of Liberia as well as the extraterritorial nature of his crimes and not the means of his involvement in the crimes that played the key role at sentencing and resulted in him receiving a lengthy sentence of 50 years' imprisonment.[86]

The *Taylor* Appeals judgment upheld Taylor's conviction and 50-year sentence for aiding and abetting and planning murders, rapes and other acts of violence committed during the Sierra Leonean civil war.[87]

[81] The sentences were ordered to be served concurrently.

[82] *Taylor* Sentencing Judgment (n 40) para 21.

[83] *Prosecutor v Taylor*, SCSL-03-1-T, Trial Judgment, 11 May 2012, paras 6920, 6952, 6956.

[84] *Taylor* Sentencing Judgment (n 40) paras 29, 97.

[85] ibid, paras 27, 98.

[86] ibid, para 40.

[87] *Taylor* Appeal Judgment (n 14).

However, the appellate panel disagreed with the Trial Chamber that aiding and abetting generally warrants a lesser sentence than that imposed for primary participation.[88] The judges held that it is unwise to assess the gravity of participation modes in the abstract as it precludes the individualised assessment of cases.[89] Instead, the better approach is to evaluate the totality of factors:

> In light of the foregoing, the Appeals Chamber holds that the totality principle exhaustively describes the criteria for determining an appropriate sentence that is in accordance with the Statute and Rules, and further holds that under the Statute, Rules and customary international law, there is no hierarchy or distinction for sentencing purposes between forms of criminal participation. The Appeals Chamber concludes that the Trial Chamber erred in law by holding that aiding and abetting liability generally warrants a lesser sentence than other forms of criminal participation.[90]

The *RUF* case closely resembles *Taylor* both factually and legally. In this case, the SCSL convicted three high-profile members of the RUF—Issa Hassan Sesay, Morris Kallon and Augustine Gbao—of war crimes and crimes against humanity, stemming from their participation in a single joint criminal enterprise with a broadly defined common criminal purpose to take power and control of Sierra Leone through committing crimes such as terrorism, rape, enslavement, murder, attacks on UN personnel, forced marriages and recruitment of child soldiers.[91] The Chamber held that Sesay and Kallon contributed significantly to the furtherance of the common purpose in the knowledge that their actions were part of the widespread and systematic attack against the civilian population. In contrast, the bench largely inferred Gbao's participation and contribution to the joint criminal enterprise from his 'important role and oversight functions'.[92] This resulted in the conviction of Gbao pursuant to the basic form of joint criminal enterprise for crimes that he did not intend to commit.

Both the Trial and Appeals Chambers held that so long as the accused had agreed to the common criminal purpose, he is responsible for all the natural and foreseeable consequences flowing from the execution of that purpose, however remote they might have been from the defendant's own intentions.[93] This finding represented an unjustified extension of the joint criminal enterprise concept through abandoning the 'intent' requirement

[88] ibid, para 667.
[89] ibid, para 666.
[90] ibid, para 670.
[91] *Prosecutor v Sesay, Kallon and Gbao* ('RUF Case'), SCSL-04-15-T, Trial Judgment, 2 March 2009, paras 1979–85.
[92] RUF Sentencing Judgment (n 33) para 266.
[93] *Prosecutor v Sesay, Kallon and Gbao*, SCSL-04-15-A, Appeal Judgment, 26 October 2009 ('RUF Appeal Judgment'), para 492; RUF Trial Judgment (n 91) para 2109.

for mens rea. Ultimately, Gbao's sentence of 25 years' imprisonment, as opposed to 52 and 40 years for the co-accused, reflects his lower level of participation in the joint criminal enterprise. The Trial Chamber found Gbao's involvement in the overall scheme to be more limited than that of his co-defendants, thus decreasing his degree of culpability for sentencing purposes.[94] In particular, the Chamber noted that Gbao was a functionary of the RUF whose chief contribution to the joint criminal enterprise was ideological inspiration and the enslavement of civilians.[95] If one compares Charles Taylor's role with the role of the accused in the other SCSL cases, such as the RUF case, Taylor's overall contribution to the crimes in Sierra Leone appears more comparable to the contributions of Sesay and Kallon, rather than that of Gbao, whose knowledge and intent were largely inferred.

The ICC is still developing its sentencing policy, so the place it assigns to the modes of liability at sentencing is still unchartered territory. If the idea that the forms of participation in Article 25(3) of the Rome Statute are arranged according to their implicit degree of blameworthiness continues to prevail, the implication in the future might be that the court renders more lenient sentences to accomplices as compared to primary perpetrators.[96] However, this development is rather unlikely because, first, the ICC shows clear signs of disillusionment with the idea of the hierarchy of the modes of liability[97] and, second, the first two available sentencing judgments fail to assign dramatic importance to the form of participation of the convicted person.

The first judgment in *Lubanga* provides some important insights into the issues of sentencing policy. It reinforces the point that it is the totality of factors that shape the punishment of the accused. Thomas Lubanga was convicted as a direct co-perpetrator pursuant to Article 25(3)(a) of the Rome Statute for his role in the implementation of the common plan to build an army for the purpose of establishing and maintaining political and military control over the Ituri region of the Democratic Republic of Congo that resulted in the enlistment, conscription and use of children below the age of 15 to participate actively in hostilities.[98] Following a defence request, the *Lubanga* Trial Chamber held a separate sentencing hearing and delivered a separate sentencing decision, assessing the factors relevant to the sentence of the accused.[99] Thomas Lubanga was sentenced separately for

[94] RUF Sentencing Judgment (n 33) para 271.

[95] ibid, paras 268, 270.

[96] The sentencing decision in *Katanga* expressly rejects this idea. *Prosecutor v Mathieu Ngudjolo Chui*, ICC-01/04-01/07, Trial Chamber II, Decision on Sentence Pursuant to Article 76 of the Statute, 23 May 2014 ('*Katanaga* Sentencing Decision'), para 61.

[97] See Ch 5.II for more discussion on the hierarchy of the modes of liability.

[98] *Prosecutor v Thomas Lubanga Dyilo*, ICC-01/04-01/06, Trial Chamber I, Judgment Pursuant to Article 74 of the Statute, 14 March 2012, paras 1355–57. For a detailed discussion of the *Lubanga* Judgment, see Ch 5.

[99] *Lubanga* Sentencing Decision (n 34) para 20. This sentence was confirmed on appeal. See *Lubanga* Sentencing Appeal (n 41) para 119.

conscripting, enlisting and using children under the age of 15 to participate in the hostilities (13, 12 and 14 years, respectively).[100] His joint sentence amounted to 14 years' imprisonment, which was confirmed on appeal.[101] The Appeals Chamber supported the broad discretion of the Trial Chamber in determining the appropriate sentence in each individual case.[102]

Lubanga's relatively low sentence reflects several considerations by the Trial Chamber. On the one hand, the judges acknowledged that the crimes of conscripting, enlisting and using children are very serious, especially in view of the vulnerability of the victims.[103] In the context of the discussion on the gravity of offences, the panel stressed that the sentence should be proportionate to the crime,[104] reinforcing the retributive rationale at sentencing. The Chamber rejected as disproportionate the approach suggested by the prosecution to set the 'baseline' or starting point for all sentences at approximately 80 per cent from the statutory maximum of 30 years' imprisonment.[105] On the other hand, the Trial Chamber did not find any aggravating factors in the case at issue, while Lubanga's continuous cooperation despite multiple failures of the prosecution was considered a mitigating factor.[106] The prosecution appealed this point, insisting that Lubanga's position of authority and abuse of power must have been considered as an aggravating factor—a claim refuted by the Appeals Chamber, which held that these elements did not require a separate treatment as aggravating factors because they already comprised the assessment of the gravity of the crime.[107]

Moreover, when discussing the degree of participation of the convicted person, the judges attributed particular importance to the fact that the Chamber did not find that Lubanga *meant* to conscript and enlist boys and girls under the age of 15 into the army and use them to participate actively in hostilities, but that instead he was *aware* that, in the ordinary course of events, this would occur.[108] Therefore, he was found to possess indirect intent in the meaning of Article 30 of the Rome Statute.[109] Thus, without discussing the mode of participation as such, the Trial Chamber acknowledged that the fault requirement is an important factor in the determination of sentences.

[100] *Lubanga* Sentencing Decision (n 34), para 98.
[101] ibid, para 99.
[102] *Lubanga* Sentencing Appeal (n 41) para 76.
[103] ibid, paras 37–44.
[104] ibid, para 36.
[105] ibid, paras 92–93.
[106] ibid, paras 91 and 96.
[107] ibid, para 85.
[108] ibid, paras 52–53.
[109] For a discussion of the different forms of intent inherent in art 30 of the Rome Statute, see ME Badar, '*Dolus Eventualis* and the Rome Statute without it?' (2009) 12(3) *New Criminal Law Review* 433 et seq.

The *Katanga* sentencing decision continued to uphold the importance of proportionality by reiterating that the sentence must be proportionate to the offence committed and the degree of culpability of the convicted person.[110] The nature and degree of participation of the convicted person was part of the assessment of the gravity of the offence. Thus, the Chamber took notice of the fact that Katanga was convicted of contribution 'in any other way' to the commission of the crimes by the group of commanders.[111] However, the judges underlined that there is no hierarchy of the modes of liability within Article 25(3) of the Rome Statute; therefore, in the absence of the scale of punishments, the degree of participation of the convicted person and his intent must be evaluated with reference to the specific facts of the case.[112] In line with this reasoning, the Chamber underscored the significance of Katanga's contribution. His logistical support of the Ngiti militia allowed the latter to attack the Bogoro village.[113] The judges also acknowledged his position of authority, but failed to find any aggravating factors, such as the abuse of such authority.[114] The Chamber found the personal situation of Katanga—a father of six children—and his efforts in the demobilisation process in the region to constitute mitigating factors.[115] The final sentence therefore amounted to 12 years' imprisonment.[116]

What follows from *Tadić*, *Aleksovski*, *Akayesu*, *RUF*, *Lubanga*, *Katanga* and *Taylor* is that the mode of liability has limited impact on the sentences of the convicted persons. There are a number of factors affecting the judicial determination of penalties. In *Tadić*, the finding that Dusko Tadić is not a mere aider and abettor but a perpetrator in the joint criminal enterprise led to a slight increase in his sentence. However, the Appeals Chamber felt compelled to reduce this sentence and return to the original length of imprisonment, placing most significance on the fact that Tadić was a low-level perpetrator, and not on his membership in the joint criminal enterprise. In *Akayesu*, the gravity of the crime of genocide occupied a central role at sentencing. The ICC convicted Lubanga as a direct co-perpetrator, yet he received a relatively lenient punishment of 14 years' imprisonment due to his lesser mental state (indirect intent), the absence of aggravating factors and his cooperation with the court as a mitigating factor.

The cases discussed in this section also demonstrate that the relationship between the mode of participation and the severity of punishment

[110] *Prosecutor v Germain Katanga*, ICC-01/04-01/07, Trial Chamber II, Decision on Sentence Pursuant to Article 76 of the Statute, 23 May 2014, para 43.
[111] ibid, para 45.
[112] ibid, para 61.
[113] ibid, para 65.
[114] ibid, para 75.
[115] ibid, paras 88 and 114.
[116] ibid, para 170.

is not straightforward. Complicity does not necessarily warrant a lesser sentence. Taylor received a harsh penalty of 50 years' imprisonment for aiding and abetting war crimes and crimes against humanity. This is a plausible approach: an adequate sentence in international criminal law does not hinge on the abstract label attached to the conduct of the convicted person, but stems from the overall assessment of the various factors on a case-by-case basis—something that can only be performed if enough flexibility is afforded to the judges. However, judicial discretion may have a downside when judges resolve problems associated with the attribution of liability at the stage of sentencing. The latter seems to be the case in *RUF*, where the Trial Chamber struggled to convict the accused Gbao of some the crimes charged under the heading of the joint criminal enterprise—a mode of liability that requires proof of intent. As a result, the Chamber compensated for the tenuous connection between Gbao and some of the crimes in the indictment by imposing a more lenient sentence.

II. SENTENCING OBJECTIVES AT THE CROSSROADS: DOMESTIC AND INTERNATIONAL LAW

A. Sentencing Objectives in International Criminal Law

It follows from the cases discussed in the previous section that complicity, as opposed to primary perpetration, has some impact on the sentence of the accused, yet it is hard to measure this impact due to a number of other factors that affect judicial decision making. Punishment objectives or goals help to systemise these considerations. They may determine the length and the form of punishment imposed upon the offender as well as the weight of the liability form at sentencing. Despite the importance of articulating sentencing rationales, the ICTY, the ICTR and the SCSL Statutes do not specify the aims of sentencing.[117] The Preamble of the Rome Statute of the ICC mentions the objectives of ending impunity and preventing crimes, without any further elaboration.

The first sentencing judgment of the ICC in *Lubanga* embraces the statement in the Preamble, but does not elaborate further on sentencing aims, preferring to focus on the specific sentencing principles instead.[118] The more recent *Katanga* sentencing decision also refers to the Preamble, but is slightly more detailed in that it acknowledges that the sentence has two important functions: reprobation, which is the expression of stigma surrounding the crime and its perpetrator; and deterrence, which aims to

[117] Khan and Dixon (n 32) 808.

[118] *Lubanga* Sentencing Decision (n 34) para 16.

prevent future offending. The sentence must be proportionate to the gravity of a crime. This feature allows for the desire of vengeance.[119]

Examination the case law of the ad hoc international tribunals also appears to point towards retribution and deterrence as the primary aims of punishment.[120] As early as 1996, the *Erdemović* Trial Chamber of the ICTY adopted 'retribution, or "just deserts", as legitimate grounds for pronouncing a sentence for crimes against humanity, the punishment having to be proportional to the gravity of the crime and the moral guilt of the convicted'.[121] The *Erdemović* Chamber also acknowledged the limited value of deterrence at sentencing by reiterating that general prevention is 'intimately related' to the reprobative function of legal punishment.[122] The *Tadić* Appeals Chamber confirmed that deterrence must not be accorded undue prominence in the overall assessment of the sentences to be imposed on the convicted persons.[123] Finally, *Erdemović* mentioned the rehabilitative function of punishment, which in the context of international criminal law should be subordinate to the other two rationales.[124]

Since *Erdemović*, the case law of the ad hoc tribunals has not expounded significantly on sentencing goals.[125] The rehabilitation rationale does not seem to be accepted as relevant at the level of international criminal law, despite occasional passing references.[126] The general discussions relating to the gravity offence reinforce the principle of retribution in international criminal law. The judgments, however, do not provide any further guidance on how retribution as a punishment aim 'works' within the ambit of international criminal law, nor do they explain the consequences of holding retribution and deterrence as the main sentencing goals.

When it comes to deterrence, the courts have been even less explicit. The 2004 appeal judgment in *Kordić and Čerkez* made an attempt to define

[119] *Katanga* Sentencing Decision (n 110) paras 37–38.

[120] *Čelebići* Appeal Judgment (n 32) para 806; *Prosecutor v Kordić and Čerkez*, ICTY Case No IT-95-14/2-A, Appeal Judgment, 17 December 2004, para 1074; *Prosecutor v Popović et al*, ICTY Case No 05-88-T, Trial Judgment, 10 June 2010, para 2128; *Prosecutor v Erdemović*, ICTY Case No, IT-96-22-T, Sentencing Judgment, 29 November 1996 ('*Erdemović* Judgment'), para 64.

[121] *Erdemović* Judgment (n 120) para 64.

[122] ibid, para 65.

[123] *Prosecutor v Tadić*, Case No IT-94-1-A and IT-94-1-Abis, Appeals Chamber, 26 January 2000, para 48. See also *Aleksovski* Appeal Judgment (n 32), para 185; *Čelebići* Appeal Judgment (n 32) para 801.

[124] *Erdemović* Judgment (n 120) para 66.

[125] eg, *Čelebići* Appeal Judgment (n 32) para 806; *Kordić and Čerkez* Appeal Judgment (n 120) para 1074; *Popović* Trial Judgment (n 120) para 2128.

[126] In *Popović*, for example, the Trial Chamber acknowledged that rehabilitation, which is another sentencing objective in addition to retribution and deterrence, does *not* play a predominant role in international criminal law due to the serious nature of the crimes committed under the Tribunal's jurisdiction. *Popović* Trial Judgment (n 120) para 2130. See also *Čelebići* Appeal Judgment (n 32) para 806. *cf Prosecutor v Bralo*, ICTY Case No IT-95-17-S, Sentencing Judgment, 7 December 2005, paras 20, 60, 67, 69.

retribution and deterrence for the purposes of international criminal law.[127] Citing the Supreme Court of Canada, it held that retribution should be seen as:

> [A]n objective, reasoned and measured determination of an appropriate punishment which properly reflects the … culpability of the offender, having regard to the *international* risk-taking of the offender, the consequential harm caused by the offender, and the normative character of the offender's conduct. Furthermore, unlike vengeance, retribution incorporates a principle of restraint; retribution requires the imposition of a just and appropriate punishment. (Emphasis added)[128]

There is a misquotation in the above passage—the original paragraph referred to the 'intentional' and not 'international' risk-taking of the offender. Therefore, there is nothing in the definition originally provided by the Canadian Supreme Court that explains retribution in the *international* context.[129] In fact, the combination 'international risk-taking of the offender' does not entirely 'fit' within the retributive rationale. The inhibition of risk-taking behaviour in potential perpetrators through the fear of punishment is precisely the attribute of the deterrent, not just deserts, philosophy.[130] In the original version, however, the domestic court stressed not the risk-taking per se, but rather the *intentional* risk-taking as an indication of the culpability of the offender. If the word 'intentionally' is omitted or replaced by another word, the description of retribution no longer holds. Moreover, it appears that the quote is taken out of context; in the original paragraph, the court was not concerned with providing a comprehensive definition of the 'retributive' rationale.[131] It is unfortunate that both the *Krajišnik* appeal judgment and *Popović et al* trial judgments copied the above definition verbatim.[132]

The *Kordić and Čerkez* appeals panel also elaborated on the meaning of deterrence. First, the court rightfully pointed out that individual deterrence aims at disheartening the offender from reoffending. It then held that general deterrence refers to the attempt to integrate or to reintegrate those persons who believe themselves to be beyond the reach of international criminal law.[133] This position conflates deterrent and rehabilitative

[127] *Kordić and Čerkez* Appeal Judgment (n 120) paras 1075–78.

[128] ibid, para 1075 (referring to the Supreme Court of Canada judgment *R v. M (CA)* [1996] 1 SCR 500, para 80).

[129] *R v M (CA)* (n 128), para 6.

[130] A von Hirsch, A Ashworth and J Roberts (eds) *Principled Sentencing*, 3rd edn (Oxford, Hart Publishing, 2009) 40.

[131] The original case dealt with a purely domestic issue of the sentencing cap on cumulative sentencing for multiple convictions. The Supreme Court found this cap to be unjustified. *R v M (CA)* (n 128).

[132] *Popović* Trial Judgment (n 120) para 2128; *Prosecutor v Krajišnik*, ICTY Case No IT-00-39-A, Appeal Judgment, 17 March 2009, para 804.

[133] *Kordić and Čerkez* Appeal Judgment (n 120) paras 1077–78.

thinking since the latter prioritises reintegration of the offender over threatening him with sanctions.[134] The subsequent *Krajišnik* and *Popović et al* judgments, despite citing the original *Kordić and Čerkez* judgment, dissolved this confusion by restating that an international penalty 'should be adequate to deter the convicted person from committing any future violation, it must also have the effect of discouraging other potential perpetrators from committing the same or similar crimes'.[135]

The ECCC and the ICC pioneered an important new development in international sentencing—an attempt to incorporate victims' rights, including the rights to reparation and compensation, within the international criminal justice paradigm.[136] This attempt corresponds to the restorative justice philosophy of punishment. The ICC reinforced the restorative rationale in *Lubanga* by setting out the principles on reparation pursuant to Article 75(1) of the Rome Statute and ordered the registry to transmit the individual applications to the Trust Fund for Victims.[137] The court upheld a growing recognition in international criminal law of a need to go 'beyond the notion of punitive justice, towards a solution which is more inclusive, encourages participation and recognizes the need to provide effective remedies for victims'.[138]

The court in *Lubanga* named a few of the functions of reparations: relieving the suffering caused by the offences; affording justice to victims by alleviating the consequences of the wrongful acts; deterring future violations; contributing to the effective reintegration of former child soldiers; and reconciling the offender, the victim and the wider community.[139] The subsequent appeal judgment clarified some of these principles and took a step closer to explaining the process whereby all of these goals could be achieved.[140]

The ICC noted that reparations should not be limited to 'direct' harm or the 'immediate effects' of the crimes of enlisting and conscripting children under the age of 15, and that the standard of 'proximate cause' must be adopted. However, it failed to provide a definition for this standard.[141] The Appeals Chamber acknowledged that the standard of proximate

134 von Hirsch, Ashworth and Roberts (n 130) 2.

135 *Popović* Trial Judgment (n 120) para 2129; *Krajisnik* Appeal Judgment (n 132) para 805.

136 Rome Statute, arts 43, 54, 64, 68, 75, 79; Law on the Establishment of the ECCC, new art 33.

137 *Prosecutor v Thomas Lubanga Dyilo*, ICC-01/04-01/06, Trial Chamber I, Decision establishing the principles and procedures to be applied to reparations, 7 August 2012 ('*Lubanga* Reparation Decision'), para 289.

138 ibid, para 177.

139 ibid, para 179.

140 *Prosecutor v Thomas Lubanga Dyilo*, ICC-01/04-01/06 A A 2 A 3, Appeals Chamber, Judgment on the Appeals against the 'Decision Establishing the Principles and Procedures to Be Applied to Reparations of 7 August 2012', 3 March 2015 ('*Lubanga* Reparations Appeal Judgment').

141 *Lubanga* Reparation Decision (n 137) para 249.

cause is the correct one and that the causal link between the harm suffered and the commission of the crime must be determined in the light of the circumstances of the case.[142] Most importantly, the appellate judges shifted the primary burden of reparations from the Victims Trust Fund to the convicted person according to the principle of accountability.[143] The nature of reparations was defined as compensatory or symbolic.[144]

In contrast with the ICC, the ECCC did not issue a separate decision on reparations, preferring to include the relevant section in the judgment immediately after sentencing.[145] Despite keeping reparations and sentencing separate in the Trial Chamber judgment, the restorative justice discourse affected KAING Guek Eav's final sentence of life imprisonment. The Supreme Court Chamber held that the initial sentence of 35 of years' imprisonment did not appropriately reflect the gravity of his crimes. The underlying rationale for imposing a harsher penalty was the need to address the sufferings of the victims. The Supreme Court Chamber clarified: 'Although the punishment of KAING Guek Eav does not completely cure their suffering, the victims' fair and reasonable expectations for justice deserve to be fulfilled. KAING Guek Eav's crimes were an affront to all of humanity, and in particular, to the Cambodian people, inflicting incurable pain.'[146]

B. Sentencing Objectives in Domestic Law

It follows that most punishment aims cited by international courts and tribunals are borrowed from domestic law, but there is little discussion as to how they could be accommodated in an international criminal law context. Direct transplantation does not appear feasible. As with any other municipal law concept, it should first be reduced to the level of a general principle and then transposed into international law in a way that addresses the reality of the international legal order.[147] This is particularly true when it comes to punishment, if only because sentencing objectives designed for offenders within the domestic penal system may not have the same content or produce the same effect in international criminal law.[148]

142 *Lubanga* Reparations Appeal Judgment (n 140) paras 79–80, 129.

143 ibid, para 69. This shift did not undermine the role of the Victims Trust Fund that was instructed to be seised of the matter and later approved the implementation plan prepared by the Trial Chamber.

144 ibid, para 202.

145 *Duch* Trial Judgment, sections 4.1 et seq; *Prosecutor v Nuon Chea and Khieu Samphan*, ECCC Case No 001/18-07-2007/ECCC/TC, Trial Judgment, 7 August 2014 ('*Chea et al* Trial Judgment'), section 19.

146 *Duch* Appeal Judgment (n 17) paras 381–83.

147 Raimondo (n 17) 52.

148 Bernaz (n 5) 297; Harmon and Gaynor (n 4) 692. For more on this topic, see Ch 8.

However, this does not mean that national sentencing goals are irrelevant for international law. On the contrary, international criminal law requires a profound understanding of the domestic philosophy of punishment in order to formulate sentencing goals at an international level. This, in turn, clarifies to some extent the weight to be attributed to complicity at the sentencing stage.

i. Retribution

Retribution is both a punishment rationale borrowed from domestic criminal law and a broader aim of international criminal law that resonates with the calls for 'bringing to justice those responsible' and 're-establishing the rule of law'. The philosophy of retribution treats punishment as deserved suffering administered in the name of justice.[149] Penalty plays an important role in conveying the censure of the crime both to the offender and to a wider audience.[150]

Limited support for this theory derives from the classical philosophy of Immanuel Kant, which views the principle of punishment as a categorical imperative.[151] Those who commit crimes violate the public order by treating themselves as *exceptions* to the law.[152] They become unworthy citizens and must be penalised for the sake of re-establishing the equilibrium that they broke. Punishment becomes the instrument of justice, and justice is essential for the functioning of society.[153] Kant rejected the imposition of punishment for the sake of attaining any public good, for that, in his view, amounts to treating humans as a means to an end.[154] When it comes to measuring the amount of penalty to be administered, Kant suggested the principle of equality: 'whatever undeserved evil you inflict upon another within the people, that you inflict upon yourself. If you insult him, you insult yourself; if you steal form him, you steal from yourself; if you strike him, you strike yourself; if you kill him, you kill yourself'.[155]

The modern account of the retributive, or 'just deserts', philosophy is less categorical; it no longer requires that the suffering of the offender is *equal* to the harm done. Rather, it calls for the punishments that are individual and *proportionate* to the seriousness of criminal conduct.[156] This

[149] Duff (n 2) 127.
[150] ibid.
[151] I Kant, *The Metaphysics of Morals* (Cambridge, Cambridge University Press, 1991 [1797]).
[152] ibid 140.
[153] ibid 141.
[154] For a contemporary discussion of Kant's view of punishment, see G Fletcher, 'Law and Morality' (1987) 87 *Columbia Law Review* 533.
[155] Kant (n 151) 53.
[156] A von Hirsch, 'Proportionate Sentences: A Desert Perspective' in von Hirsch, Ashworth and Roberts (n 130) 117.

philosophy implies that punishment for crime must be proportionate to its relative seriousness, which is measured by the harm produced by the crime and the culpability of the offender.[157] The idea behind this principle is that individuals should be treated as rational beings capable of making choices, and it is the choice to offend that is chastised, not the individual himself; consequently, punishment must be commensurate to the evil inflicted.[158]

The gradation of sentences depending on the mode of participation best fits within this sentencing objective as it is intrinsically linked to the offender's level of culpability. The understanding that accomplices—as opposed to primary perpetrators—receive a more lenient sentence rests on the assumption that the accomplice's culpability is lower than that of the perpetrator.

ii. Deterrence

In contrast with retribution, which looks back at the past deeds of the offender, the deterrent rationale is forward-looking. It aims at reducing crime through the fear of punishment.[159] Jeremy Bentham and Cesare Beccaria's works account for this philosophy. Beccaria wrote 'the purpose of punishment … is none other than to prevent the criminal from doing fresh harm to fellow citizens and to deter others from doing the same'.[160] Like the retributivists, Beccaria referred to proportionality, emphasising, however, a different meaning of this term. He maintained that proportionality between the crime and punishment is observed if the obstacles that deter men from committing a crime are more formidable than the benefits of offending. The more the crimes are contrary to the public good, the greater are the incentives to commit them.[161]

Beccaria argued against cruel punishments because, in his view, for the punishment to achieve its objective, it is only necessary that the harm that it inflicts outweighs the benefit that derives from the crime and that the punishment is certain.[162] Beccaria also reasoned in favour of punishing accomplices. He drew parallels between those who attempt to commit crimes and accomplices to a crime, not all of whom are its direct perpetrators. His claim was that the action preceding the commission of a crime shows a clear intent to carry it out (be it an attempted crime or an act of

157 ibid 116.

158 A Ashworth, *Principles of Criminal Law*, 2nd edn (Oxford, Clarendon, 1995) 26.

159 J Bentham, 'Punishment and Deterrence' in von Hirsch, Ashworth and Roberts (n 130) 53–57.

160 C Beccaria, *On Crimes and Punishments and Other Writings* (1764), edited by A Thomas (Toronto, University of Toronto Press, 2008) 26.

161 ibid 17.

162 ibid 50.

complicity) and deserves punishment, albeit less severe than what is prescribed for the actual execution of the crime. The punishment is justified by the need to prevent the execution of the crime and the lesser penalty motivates the offender to withdraw from the risk-taking enterprise before its commission.[163]

Jeremy Bentham developed Beccaria's ideas.[164] He argued that in order to prevent the reoccurrence of the offence, it is important to make the offender afraid of offending. This can be achieved by making the pain of punishment outweigh the pleasure of offending. Bentham held that excessive penalties are justified because they deter a particular offender from reoffending (specific deterrence) and instigate fear of offending in all members of the public (general deterrence).[165] With regard to the different ways in which individuals get involved in crimes, Bentham noted that there shall be some general convergence as to the quantity of punishment intended for similar offenders, but individual circumstances need to be taken into account.[166]

iii. Rehabilitation

In addition to deterrence, the reform and rehabilitation of the offender represents another utilitarian sentencing goal in domestic law. As Bentham put it, one of the ways to prevent crime is to take away the desire to offend.[167] The rehabilitative model focuses on reforming the offender's character and motivation to commit crimes by tackling the root causes of offending. The rehabilitative model acknowledges that the majority of offenders come from disadvantaged backgrounds and that it is the state's duty to provide programmes to support them.[168] The mode of participation of the offender could be indicative of his proneness to rehabilitation, but this largely depends on the circumstances of the case.

iv. Restorative Justice

Finally, there is the restorative justice paradigm, which, among other things, emphasises compensation for the harm suffered. The restorative approach as a punishment applies only to the direct or primary victims, while restorative justice in a broader sense also affects secondary victims.[169] In the latter case, punishment may be a side-effect, but the main goal of the restorative

[163] ibid 73.
[164] G Fletcher, *The Grammar of Criminal Law* (Oxford, Oxford University Press, 2007) 15.
[165] Bentham (n 159) 53–56.
[166] ibid 56.
[167] ibid.
[168] ibid 28–32.
[169] Von Hirsch, Ashworth and Roberts (n 130) 164.

approach is restitution and compensation.[170] This rationale is similar to retribution in that it is backward-looking, but it shifts the focus from the offender to the harm caused by the crime and the ways in which this harm can be repaired.[171] The process whereby amends are made is as important as the outcome.[172] Domestic criminal justice systems face a great challenge in combining restoration and retribution in a single punishment. However, the two sentencing aims are not irreconcilable.[173] There are at least three ways of facilitating restoration through retribution: first, through imposing the 'suffering' on the offender by subjecting him to censure; second, by having the offender feel remorse; and, finally, by vesting on the offender an obligation to make reparation to the victim.[174] If one views restorative justice as a punishment goal, it is essential that there is a causal link between the actions of the offender and the harm suffered by the victims.

The mode of participation of the offender arguably, does not play an important role within the restorative paradigm *stricto sensu*. This is because the focus is on the harm done and the relationships broken by the offence, and not merely on the offender. However, this philosophy gives complicity a broader meaning. Kutz, for example, argued that our current practices of accountability (the term he uses to refer to responsibility) are relational and positional rather than individualistic and retributivist. He claimed that accountability should be understood through the relationship between an agent (an individual causing harm) and the respondent (the victim).[175] The individualistic approach to accountability fails to reflect the special nature of associative wrongdoing, in particular the culpability of the agent in the context of his relationship with the respondent. For Kutz, the criminal responsibility of accomplices for their confederates' acts is defensible only if viewed in relation to the actions of the respondent and if the individual differences in culpability are taken into account.[176]

C. The Challenges of Adapting the Sentencing Objectives to International Law

Looking at the sparse account of sentencing aims in international judgments, one gets the impression that punishment rationales are not properly discussed in the context of international criminal law. At times,

170 ibid.

171 Duff (n 2) 187.

172 ibid 182.

173 L Zedner, 'Reparation and Retribution: Are They Reconcilable?' in von Hirsch, Ashworth and Roberts (n 130) 189 et seq.

174 Duff (2) 182.

175 C Kutz, *Complicity: Ethics and Law for a Collective Age* (Cambridge, Cambridge University Press, 2000) 17–19.

176 ibid 8 and 16.

the judges lean towards one specific philosophy without properly justifying it. For example, Taylor's political leadership placed him in a special category for deterrence purposes: the severe penalties in his case highlight the abuse of power and the violation of the duty of care by the former head of state,[177] thereby sending out a powerful message to potential perpetrators. The idea behind such a harsh punishment would be that not even the highest-ranking state official enjoys impunity for international crimes. However, there is no elaborate discussion related to the deterrent rationale in the *Taylor* judgment. Likewise, despite rejecting the importance of the rehabilitative function of punishment, the *Erdemović* Trial Chamber considered the young age of the accused, his family status and cooperation with the Tribunals as 'a series of traits characterising a corrigible personality'.[178] Thus, there is a need in international criminal law to develop a more coherent account of sentencing goals. Below, I discuss some aspects pertaining to retribution, deterrence and restoration in the international context.

When it comes to transplanting retributive philosophy from a domestic to an international level, the major stumbling block is the application of its central element—the principle of proportionality. It is difficult to make international punishment fit mass crimes.[179] Jens Ohlin advanced a theory adapting the conventional principle of proportionality to sentencing in international law.[180] He noted that the sentences handed down by the ICTY suffer from a conflict between two types of proportionality: the offence-gravity proportionality and the defendant relative proportionality. The former refers to the traditional consideration that the punishment is proportionate to the gravity of the offence, while the latter denotes the trend among judges to ensure that less culpable defendants are punished less severely than more culpable ones.[181] While offence-gravity proportionality is normatively superior, the defendant-relative proportionality often overtakes judges' reasoning when they hand down unacceptably lenient sentences to 'reserve space' for those allegedly more responsible.[182]

As a solution, Ohlin suggested reinforcing the offence-gravity rationale by treating punishment in international criminal law as a vindication of the rule of law. He based his theory of international punishment as a vindication of the rule of law in the contemporary formulation of Immanuel Kant's categorical imperative, a principle of moral action

[177] See *Taylor* Sentencing Judgment (n 40) para 97.

[178] *Erdemović* Judgment (n 120) para 111.

[179] Bernaz (n 5) 298.

[180] J Ohlin, 'Proportional Sentences at the ICTY' in B Swaart, A Zahar and G Sluiter (eds), *The Legacy of the International Criminal Tribunal for the Former Yugoslavia* (Oxford, Oxford University Press, 2011) 322 et seq.

[181] ibid 324–26.

[182] ibid 326–31. *cf* Sloane (n 5) 719.

whereby one should not act on a maxim unless one can will that maxim to be a universal law.[183] When someone violates morality, they treat themselves as an exception to universal laws and act against morality. The legal system (or international community), in such circumstances, is allowed to impose harsh treatment on the offender to vindicate the rule of law over criminality.[184] According to Ohlin, international sentences ought to reflect the inherent gravity of the offence in a way that even moderate participation in international crimes would yield a life sentence equal to that received by the highest offenders.[185]

Ohlin's uneasiness with the application of the central consideration of retributive sentencing rationale, the principle of proportionality, to international sentences is well grounded. However, the defendant-relative proportionality does not appear to be the main area of concern. Both the ICTY and the ICTR Appeals Chambers stressed that comparison of one case with another is often of limited assistance, and the differences between two accused convicted of similar crimes in similar circumstances are often more significant than the similarities.[186] Rather, the problem stems from the limitations of international criminal law as such, targeting only a fraction of offenders, namely those most responsible for mass crimes.

It is conceivable to apply the proportionality principle when punishing those few selected for prosecution, but it is impossible at an international level to ensure that the punishment is distributed equally among *all* the offenders for their offences. This is in stark contrast with domestic criminal law, which, at least at the statute level, presupposes its universal application. Fletcher refers to this requirement that the law punish all those guilty as 'positive legality'.[187] Therefore, the essential component of the retributive theory—retribution in the distribution of punishment—is distorted a priori through artificially limiting the pool of potentially accused.

HLA Hart highlighted the difference between retribution as a justifying aim and retribution in the distribution of punishment, the latter having a value independent of the former.[188] Embracing the fact that international criminal law does not, a priori, ensure proportionality in the distribution of punishment could remove some of the concerns related to the dominance of the defendant-relative considerations in the judges' reasoning. It remains equally important to define the gravity of

[183] Fletcher (n 154) 537.

[184] J Ohlin, 'Proportional Sentences at the ICTY' in B Swaart, A Zahar and G Sluiter (eds), *The Legacy of the International Criminal Tribunal for the Former Yugoslavia* (Oxford, Oxford University Press, 2011) 334–35.

[185] ibid 337.

[186] *Čelebići* Appeal Judgment (n 32) para 719; *Prosecutor v Musema*, ICTR Case No 96-13-A, Appeal Judgment, 16 November 2001 ('*Musema* Appeal Judgment'), para 387.

[187] G Fletcher, *Basic Concepts of Criminal Law* (Oxford, Oxford University Press, 1998) 207.

[188] Hart and Gardner (n 12) 9–12.

offence in international criminal law for the purposes of observing the offence-gravity proportionality, as well as to assign weight to other sentencing rationales, such as deterrence, rehabilitation and restorative justice.

As with the retributive perspective, deterrence requires further justification within the context of international criminal law. There are views that more weight should be attributed to deterrence when deciding on the sentences of the accused in international trials.[189] This initiative deserves credit. However, some important considerations must be taken into account. First, there is a need to address the main criticism of the deterrence philosophy, namely the difficulty of measuring the effectiveness of sanctions designed to prevent offending.[190] To date, there is no solid empirical basis supporting the idea that potential perpetrators are intimidated by the international indictments and penalties.[191]

Second, it is important to establish the limits of the applicability of the deterrent rationale in international criminal law and the 'target audience' for the harsh penalties. This is so because deterrence in domestic law targets both the general public (general deterrence) and the particular offender (specific deterrence), whereas international criminal law is particularly concerned with the former, not the latter.[192] When it comes to specific deterrence, many national criminal law provisions reflect the idea that there is a robust connection between the crime and the prior record: offenders with a prior record are more likely to reoffend.[193] Such offenders pose a higher risk to society and thus extra measures should be taken against them. In a purely utilitarian account, persistent offenders shall be sentenced based on the cumulative model with each new offence increasing the severity of the sentence.[194]

However, from an international criminal law perspective, this latter argument loses some of its power because the 'audience' that it targets is different from the 'audience' affected by the escalated sanctions in domestic law. International criminal law deals with a highly specific category of offenders—usually high-level first-time perpetrators responsible for the commission of crimes during war or civil unrest. The deterrent effect of harsh penalties in relation to these offenders is far from clear.[195]

[189] Harmon and Gaynor (n 4) 683 et seq.

[190] Von Hirsch, Ashworth and Roberts (n 130) 43 et seq.

[191] M Mennecke, 'Punishing Genocidaires: A Deterrent Effect or Not?' (2007) 8 *Human Rights Law Review* 323 et seq. See also M Drumbl, *Atrocity, Punishment, and International Law* (Cambridge, Cambridge University Press, 2007) 169 et seq.

[192] Cryer et al (n 5) 497.

[193] J Roberts, *Punishing Persistent Offenders: Community and Offender Perspectives* (Oxford, Oxford University Press, 2008) 31.

[194] A Ashworth, *Sentencing and Criminal Justice*, 5th edn (Oxford, Oxford University Press, 2010) 198.

[195] Drumbl (n 191) 169 et seq.

Nevertheless, one can presume that the sanctions imposed at an international level gain much publicity, at least alerting potential perpetrators of the risks associated with offending.

Finally, a large question mark exists regarding the restorative justice rationale. International criminal law has gradually recognised victims' rights, including the right to reparation.[196] The ICC and the ECCC include restorative elements in their discourse. However, it is crucial to distinguish between restoration as a punishment goal and restoration in a broader sense. The former requires the causal link between the acts of the accused and the harm that he caused to the victims. The broader notion of restorative justice implies reparations to the wider community. Yet, if one accepts that restoration in a broader sense is one of the purposes of international criminal law, it is crucial to define its relationship to the cornerstone legal principles, such as that of individual criminal responsibility. Can the latter be jeopardised in favour of the former?[197]

Restoration as a punishment goal is not entirely inconceivable, nor is it at odds with the traditional retributive approach of international criminal law. However, there are two challenges. The first is emphasising the causation—the offender is responsible for those wrongs that he inflicted upon the victims. By expressing remorse, suffering hard treatment (punishment) and reprobation by international community, he makes amends. The second is that wider harms/grievances need to be addressed outside of the criminal trial, possibly through outreach, fact-finding and truth and reconciliation commissions. This broader restorative justice function of international criminal law, albeit extremely important, cannot fit strictly into the punishment of the accused and needs to be achieved in a different way. The court's only contribution towards this goal should be its adherence to strict legal rules.[198]

Restoration is closely linked with the idea of promoting victims' rights as an independent goal of international criminal justice. One possible implication of prioritising this aim over the other is adopting victim-based reasoning in international criminal law.[199] However, there are dangers in this approach. Robinson pointed out that the tendency to adopt victim-focused teleological interpretations often comes at the expense of the fundamental principles of a liberal criminal justice system. His argument is that teleological methods of interpretation inherent in human rights law

[196] It should be noted that restorative justice and victims' rights are distinct concepts.

[197] For more discussion on this issue, see Ch 8.II.

[198] Unfortunately, the ICC in the reparations decision failed to define the standard of the 'proximate cause' or to distinguish between the broader meaning of reparations and the more narrow restorative justice considerations that affected Lubanga's responsibility in the strict meaning of criminal law.

[199] D Robinson, 'Identity Crisis of International Criminal Law' (2008) 21(4) *Leiden Journal of International Law* 925, 933.

may not be always compatible with the principle of legality and other criminal law principles designed to protect the rights of the accused.[200]

Teleological approach as such does not pose insurmountable obstacles to fairness and due process. It is compatible with the rules of treaty interpretation set out in the Vienna Convention on the Law of Treaties, but places special emphasis on the object and purpose of the treaty.[201] Given the important role that the judges have in ensuring the legitimacy of international criminal law and the great number of legal lacunae and uncertainty that this field still holds, it is reasonable to allow a certain level of flexibility when it comes to interpreting the Rome Statute and other related instruments. It is feasible to provide evolutive interpretation compatible with the fundamental principles of criminal law. One way to do this is to recognise that human rights law and criminal law share the same basic notions—fairness, individual autonomy and legality.

However, the problem arises when the interests of the accused are balanced against the interests of victims.[202] This unqualified balancing act compromises the ideals of the liberal criminal justice system because of the confusion about the aspirations of international criminal law and what it is able to achieve through individual sentences meted out to the accused. In these situations, the limitations of international criminal law are most obvious: punishing only a tiny fraction of perpetrators does not translate automatically into realising justice for victims, for they may wish to see more comprehensive trials, a show of remorse by the convicted person or harsher penalties. The reason for this outcome appears to stem from confusion about the aspirations of international criminal law and what it is able to achieve through the individual sentences meted out to the accused.

III. EMBRACING JUDICIAL SENTENCING DISCRETION IN INTERNATIONAL CRIMINAL LAW

It has been over 15 years since the Appeals Chamber in *Furundžija* refused to accept the existence of an 'emerging sentencing regime' in international criminal law.[203] Arguably, there is remarkably little evidence that any consensus has been reached on this issue since then. As discussed in

[200] ibid.

[201] Vienna Convention on the Law of Treaties, arts 31–32. See also *Golder v UK*, Judgment of 21 February 1975, Series A, No 18.

[202] Jürgen Habermas advised against balancing values, which are relative and subject to change. Instead, he suggested adjudication oriented by principles to decide which claim and which action is right. J Habermas, *Between Facts and Norms: Contributions to a Discourse Theory between Law and Democracy* (Cambridge, Polity Press, 1998) 253–61.

[203] *Prosecutor v Furundzija*, ICTY Case No IT-95-17/1-A, Appeal Judgment, 21 July 2000, para 237.

this chapter, international judges rely solely on the broad provisions of the statutes of international criminal courts and tribunals and formulaic language in the generic case law clarifying these provisions. There are no penalty ranges for the specific crimes or the hierarchy of articulated sentencing rationales.[204] Unfettered judicial discretion leads to a certain level of disparity in sentencing in international criminal law.[205] Disparity occurs when similar cases are dealt with differently and where different cases are treated without reference to those differences.[206] Disparity in sentencing is a form of injustice, yet the choice of techniques to promote consistency is not an easy matter even at the domestic level.[207]

National legal traditions recognise different techniques for ensuring that sentencing complies with the rule of law principles.[208] The most obvious way to reduce disparity is to articulate and prioritise sentencing aims.[209] The other technique of promoting consistency is by establishing sentencing tariffs for particular crimes. In England and Wales, for instance, judges are required to follow guidelines that provide for a penalty range for each particular crime and a set of the mitigating and aggravating factors to move up and down the scale. If judges decide to depart from the guidelines, they have to give reasons for doing so.[210] In fact, most national jurisdictions follow the principle *nulla poena sine lege* by stipulating sentencing tariffs in the statutes or formal sentencing guidelines. The more precise the provisions on penalties, the more the national system leans towards order and regularity at the expense of individualised justice. However, the tension between these two values is always present in domestic jurisdictions.[211]

International criminal law clearly prioritises 'customised' justice. The judges stress the importance of individualised sentences reflecting the totality of the criminal conduct of the particular accused.[212] In the absence of an accurate guidance at the level of statutes and case law, maximum flexibility is granted to international judges at sentencing, ensuring their broad discretion. While the current practice of favouring individualised justice and the totality of factors should not be underestimated, there is

[204] There is no agreement as to the sentencing objectives in international criminal law. During the drafting of the Rome Statute, the issue of objectives in sentencing was rarely considered, except for the discussions on the death penalty. See W Schabas, *The International Criminal Court: A Commentary on the Rome Statute* (Oxford, Oxford University Press, 2010) 899.

[205] See Appendix II.

[206] A Ashworth, 'Techniques for Reducing Sentencing Disparity' in von Hirsch, Ashworth and Roberts (n 130) 253.

[207] ibid.

[208] Ashworth (n 206) 254.

[209] ibid 251.

[210] For example, the sentencing range for non-aggravated robbery is one to three years' imprisonment. See Ashworth (n 206) 245.

[211] Fletcher (n 7) 503.

[212] eg, *Blaskić* Appeal Judgment (n 32) paras 683–85.

room for improvement. Parts of the judgments dealing with sentencing often use formulaic language, leaving the reader with much uncertainty as to how the judges decide on the length of imprisonment. This deficiency can be remedied by adjusting the sentencing goals to an international level and by providing more elaborate reasoning in the sentencing parts of international judgments.[213]

There are two main reasons why judicial discretion at an international level should be defended. First and foremost, there is no established penal regime in international criminal law.[214] In the absence of legal traditions, such as those that aid domestic criminal judges in their sentencing deliberations, international judges face a double task of developing the sentencing regime while simultaneously assessing the facts of the particular case. This duty requires an extra degree of discretion. The final sentence must reflect traditional sentencing goals, such as retribution and deterrence, as adjusted to the international criminal law context. The sentence has to send out a strong message of reprobation addressed to the potential perpetrators and members of the international community without violating the principle of proportionality.

Second, the final punishment needs to embrace the unique considerations characteristic of international criminal law. One limitation of international criminal law bearing heavily on sentencing is the inevitable jurisdictional hurdle *ratione personae*—it restricts prosecutions to the senior leadership figures most responsible for the atrocities. In these circumstances, the pressure to convict and render a harsh penalty is very high. This is so because the punishment is not distributed equally among *all* those responsible, but is focused on a selected few. In these circumstances, the judges are tasked with recognising not only the mode or participation of the accused and the particular crime for which they stand convicted, but also a number of other factors, including the leadership position of the convicted person.

At this point, it is essential to clarify how 'complicity' as a mode of participation fits within the discourse relating to judicial discretion. Frequently, domestic law provisions on sentencing explain the relative weight (if any) to be attributed to the mode of participation of the convicted person.[215] In contrast, complicity in international criminal law bears a relative weight on sentences. In the absence of sentencing scales

213 For more on the adjustment of sentencing goals, see Chs 7.II and 8.

214 Kai Ambos stresses the difficulty of reaching agreement among states as to what concrete penalties should be. For example, during the negotiation process of the ICC Statute, delegations made the case for more precise penalties, yet no agreement was reached. Ambos goes on to state that striving for more precision in the definition of the *nulla poena* principle in international criminal law would enhance the credibility and legitimacy of international criminal justice. See Ambos (n 42) 25–33.

215 Appendix I demonstrates that some countries reserve more lenient punishment for accomplices. See, for example, Estonia and Finland.

or articulated punishment aims in international law, the pronouncement that aiding and abetting generally warrants lesser sentences than those imposed for more direct forms of participation is effectively unenforceable. Judges have no guidance in identifying the starting point from which to mitigate the sentence.[216] This observation, coupled with the need to take into account the totality of factors and not just the mode of participation of the accused, renders complicity less useful as an indicator of the culpability of the accused at the sentencing stage. However, this is not to claim that the mode of participation is irrelevant in international criminal justice or should not influence the sentence of the convicted person. On the contrary, the concept of individual criminal responsibility requires the establishment of the precise way in which the accused became involved in the alleged crimes.

The key distinction to be drawn here is between the two stages of a criminal trial—the stage leading to conviction and the sentencing stage. HLA Hart highlighted the importance of separating these two stages. According to him, responsibility has a value quite independent of retributive or denunciatory theories of punishment.[217] At times, the principle of responsibility may be sacrificed when the social cost of maintaining it is too high, thus violating the principle of proportionality in the distribution of punishment.[218] This, however, cannot affect the principle of proportionality inherent to the punishment *itself*. International criminal law with its limitations *ratione personae* is the best example of how the principle of responsibility may be sacrificed due to the practical impossibility of prosecuting all those responsible at an international level.

There is an implicit recognition of the duality of responsibility and punishment in international criminal law: the parts of international judgments that deal with the factual background, liability modes and the definition of crimes are explicit and lengthy, while the sentencing parts are often curtailed and appear somewhat detached from the findings leading to conviction. At times, questions of guilt and sentencing are dealt with in separate hearings.[219] Therefore, complicity as a mode of participation has two independent functions in each of the two stages: first, it serves as an

[216] *Taylor* Sentencing Judgment (n 40) para 257; *Muhimana* Trial Judgment (n 31) para 593; *Vasiljević* Appeal Judgment (n 44) para 182. The 'baseline' approach was explicitly rejected in *Lubanga* Sentencing Decision (n 34) paras 92–93.

[217] Hart and Gardner (n 12) 185.

[218] ibid.

[219] This was the initial practice of the ICTY until the Rules of Evidence and Procedure were amended to allow for unified trials, which is now the practice in both ad hoc tribunals. The Rome Statute provides for unified trials, but with the possibility of bifurcation if one of the parties so requests. The *Lubanga* Trial Chamber followed the bifurcation path, following the request by the defence. See ICTY and ICTR Rules of Evidence and Procedure, rr 85 and 87; Rome Statute, art 76; ICC Rules of Evidence and Procedure, art 143; *Lubanga* Sentencing Decision (n 34) para 20; Cryer et al (n 5) 502–03.

instrument of attaching liability to the accused, provided the legal requirements for complicity are met; and, second, it becomes one of the indicators of the appropriate sentence.

Although at times it may be very tempting for pragmatic reasons or otherwise, these two functions of complicity should not be conflated. At the stage of attribution of liability, it is vital to adhere to the strict principles of individual criminal responsibility and due process. 'Fair labelling' is important because this is the only way in which the bodies applying international criminal law gain legitimacy.[220] In instances where there is insufficient evidence to meet the legal requirements for the most commonly used modes of liability—joint criminal enterprise or indirect co-perpetration—it is advisable to resort to alternatives, such as various forms of complicity. This approach ensures that the acts of the accused receive the most accurate description in the judgment. Using less stringent criteria for attaching liability undermines the cause of international criminal law by creating the image of 'collective punishment'. This in turn negatively affects its public perception and has a detrimental impact on victims' rights, depriving them of proper recognition.[221]

Modes of liability at sentencing serve a different function—they form part of the picture in assessing the gravity of the conduct of the convicted person. While there is pressure to convict and render a harsh penalty, this should not be done at the cost of circumventing the stringent criteria for the attribution of liability. It is not an adequate solution to grant a convicted person a more lenient sentence due to a lack of evidence as appears to be the case with the accused Gbao in *RUF*. Evidentiary problems need to be addressed at the stage of the attribution of responsibility by, for example, using a mode of liability that best describes the conduct of the accused, and not at sentencing.

The question is whether it is more realistic to employ modes of participation that accurately reflect the contribution of the accused and then determine the appropriate sentence, taking all relevant factors into account. It appears that the Trial Chamber in the *Taylor* and *Lubanga* cases preferred the latter solution. The court in *Taylor* refused to convict Taylor under the joint criminal enterprise doctrine due to insufficient evidence regarding his alleged participation in the common plan.[222] Instead, the judges held the accused accountable as an aider and abetter, or someone

[220] Judge van den Wyngaert stressed the importance of 'fair labelling'. She referred to J Ohlin, 'Joint Intentions to Commit International Crimes' (2011) 11 *Chicago Journal of International Law* 693. See *Prosecutor v Mathieu Ngudjolo Chui*, ICC-01/04-02/12-4, Trial Chamber II, Concurring Opinion of Judge Christine van den Wyngaert to Judgment Pursuant to Article 74 of the Statute, 18 December 2012, para 28.

[221] See Ch 4.II.A.

[222] *Taylor* Trial Judgment (n 83) para 6906.

who knowingly contributed to the commission of crimes.[223] However, despite the fact that Taylor 'merely' aided and abetted and planned crimes in Sierra Leone, his sentence duly recognised other factors such as his overall leadership role and the impact of his actions on the conflict. Likewise, the *Lubanga* Trial Chamber handed down a relatively lenient sentence notwithstanding the finding that Lubanga was a direct co-perpetrator. What mattered to the court was the combination of the mitigating factors, absence of the aggravating factors and a lesser form of intent on part of the convicted person. Therefore, the forms of liability of both accused took a backseat when it came to imposing the penalty. This approach seems reasonable.

CONCLUSION

This chapter has dealt with the role of complicity at sentencing. International judges have declared on a few occasions that aiding and abetting generally warrants a lesser sentence that that rendered for perpetration. However, the case law and the statutory sentencing principles reveal that primary perpetration through the joint criminal enterprise or the concept of 'co-perpetration' does not automatically warrant a more severe sentence than that rendered for aiding and abetting (or any other forms of complicity), nor does it imply a higher degree of culpability. Rather, the mode of participation forms part of the discussion of the appropriate punishment, along with a number of other factors.

In contrast with many domestic legal systems that already include a sentencing discount for aiding and abetting at the statutory level, complicity in international criminal law is fully compatible with lengthy sentences at the level of primary perpetration for two main reasons. First, international criminal law still lacks a coherent sentencing regime; therefore, judicial discretion is guided solely by a small number of generic formulas found in the case law. The scarce statutory provisions on penalties establish some broad principles such as prohibition of the death penalty, but are hardly sufficient to assign weight to the modes of participation or set the scales of punishment for each particular crime. At a theoretical level, international criminal law does not rank or properly define the goals of punishment—a step that could potentially indicate the role of the mode of liability for sentencing purposes. Therefore, international judges are left with the freedom to decide on the appropriate punishment in each case, taking into consideration a combination of factors, including the form of participation.

[223] ibid, paras 6907 et seq.

The second reason why complicity is compatible with longer sentences in international criminal law is its unique nature, which focuses on the senior leadership figures, therefore reducing the number of direct perpetrators in the dock and prioritising those who masterminded the offences. The latter category most frequently meets the fault and conduct requirements of complicity. In this situation, only individualised assessment of the circumstances and the particular facts of the case makes it possible to determine whether the culpability of the accomplice is less or more than that of the actual perpetrator.

Finally, it is essential to recognise the duality of criminal proceedings. The mode of participation serves different purposes at trial and sentencing. At trial, complicity or any other form of participation is used for 'labelling' the conduct of the accused. The goal is to provide the precise description of the person's role in the commission of the crime. This is in line with the principle of individual criminal responsibility. At the sentencing stage, the form of participation is one of several indicators for measuring the level of culpability of the accused. Depending on the factual circumstances of the case, complicity may or may not indicate the lesser involvement of the convicted person. As the case law has shown, the mode of participation usually plays a peripheral role in sanctioning due to the presence of other factors that account for harsher penalties, such as the individual's leadership role or the grave nature of crimes.

8

Conclusion: The Place of Complicity in International Criminal Law

INTRODUCTION

PREVIOUS CHAPTERS ANALYSED complicity from different angles. Chapter 1 introduced the problem. Chapter 2 explored complicity in domestic law. The study of the liability modes covered 31 domestic jurisdictions. It showed that complicity in its various forms is rooted in all of the legal systems under consideration. Even countries adhering to the unitary model of participation—ie, not distinguishing between different forms of participation at the legislative level—recognise in both doctrine and case law the different roles of those involved in offending. The boundary between primary perpetration and secondary liability shifts from country to country, and within a single system, depending on the factual circumstances. However, the functional core of complicity does not depend on this shifting border; complicity is a legal construction that serves to determine the circumstances in which liability is attributed to those who do not physically perpetrate the crime. Because of the wide recognition that complicity enjoys in national law, it is fair to assume that it has the status of a general principle of international law recognised by 'civilised nations' and is therefore embedded in a source of law.

Chapter 3 showed that historically one of the main challenges of international criminal law was attributing individual criminal responsibility for collective wrongdoings. There were different mechanisms employed to solve the problem—from ignoring the distinctions between crime participants in favour of a fact-based approach to holding the accused responsible under the broad umbrella of conspiracy. Under the influence of continental lawyers, in particular those coming from France, complicity also made its way into modern international criminal law as one of several means for attaching liability to those removed from the scene of the crime.

Chapters 4 and 5 focused on contemporary international criminal law and the jurisprudence emanating from the ICC, the ICTY, the ICTR, the SCSL and the ECCC. The analysis in these chapters showed that forms of participation occupy a distinct place in the statutes and case law of international courts and tribunals, all of which recognise different forms of complicity. However, there are several problematic areas pertaining to the law on complicity that require attention. Among these issues is the frequent 'mismatch' between the facts of the case and the legal labels attached to them, the failure to distinguish between the elements of the substantive offence and the legal requirements of liability modes, the introduction of competing models for dealing with collective criminality that are not firmly grounded in international law, the shifting standard of causation and finally 'downgrading' complicity by unduly associating it with a lower degree of blameworthiness.

Chapter 6 compared complicity in the law of state responsibility and international criminal law. It established certain limits of cross-fertilisation between the two fields of law, which differ in terms of their objectives and methods. This difference places a limit on the transferability of legal notions from one domain to another. However, despite this divergence, both disciplines share a number of problems with the application of the concept of complicity, such as linking the form of liability to the substantive crime or defining the fault requirement.

Finally, Chapter 7 explored the consequences of complicity. It assessed critically the statement made by several Chambers that aiding and abetting generally warrants a lesser sentence than primary perpetration. This statement was dismissed as mechanical on the basis of the analysis of individual cases, supplemented by the table on the correlation between the modes of participation and sentencing in Appendix II. The study in this chapter revealed that it is the totality of factors that influence the sentence rather than the liability mode alone. Moreover, the chapter distinguished the two stages of the criminal process—the stage of attribution of responsibility and the sentencing stage. It was argued that the principle of fair labelling requires describing the conduct of the accused in precise terms; hence, complicity occupies a prominent role during the first stage. At the same time, forms of participation are not dispositive at the second stage, that of sentencing, which is characterised by a high degree of judicial discretion.

The analysis in the previous chapters outlined various aspects of complicity in international criminal law—its historical origins, its roots in domestic law, its philosophical underpinnings and the problems with its application in an international context. However, the predominant question of how to deal with collective criminality remains. Is complicity an adequate construction to describe the conduct of international offenders? Does the context of mass atrocities affect the way in which legal concepts are interpreted and applied by international courts and tribunals?[1] Do we even need to 'fine-tune' the forms of liability in international criminal

[1] Mark Osiel noted that the law 'has been largely content to rely on fictions remote from the empirical reality of mass atrocity discerned by historians and social scientists'. This observation served as an impetus for the full-fledged study of the 'empirical reality of mass

law?[2] Osiel posed an important question in this respect: 'Does a preoccupation with individual culpability prevent proper recognition of the collective origins and nature of mass atrocity?'[3]

The answer to these questions lies in the sphere of the objectives of international criminal justice. This concluding chapter argues that the main and overarching purpose of international criminal law is its symbolic significance as the flagship of values shared by humanity. Symbolism manifests itself procedurally—international criminal law strives to be an exemplary justice mechanism and substantively—through setting the threshold of behaviour that is no longer accepted by the international community. This overarching goal creates space to accommodate the limitations of international criminal law—its aspirational character, its lack of supranational enforcement powers, the dissonance between targeting individual perpetrators and the collective nature of offending, and, finally, the distinct and complex criminological reality of mass atrocities.

If we accept that international trials aspire to set an example of how justice must be administered, then the principles of fairness and individual criminal responsibility require us to define the precise way in which the accused is connected to the crime. International criminal law targets those most responsible—leaders and 'masterminds'. These individuals are frequently removed from the scene of the crime, yet they are responsible for planning or substantially assisting mass criminality. This particular focus of international criminal justice makes secondary forms of liability indispensable.

Section I of this chapter briefly defines the limitations of international criminal law. This exercise lays the ground for section II of the chapter, which discusses symbolism as an overarching objective of international criminal justice. It is argued that conceptualising international criminal law as symbolic serves a dual purpose: first, attaining a high standard of procedural justice and defining the type of conduct that humanity rejects is an objective in its own right; and, second, it allows us to embrace the limitations in respect of the plethora of other goals pursued by international criminal law. Finally, section III builds on the rest of the book to schematically outline a number of areas in the law on complicity requiring attention.

atrocity' by Mikaela Heikkilä. See M Osiel, 'The Banality of Good: Aligning Incentives against Mass Atrocities' (2005) 105 *Columbia Law Review*, 1751, 1752; M Heikkilä, *Coping with International Atrocities through Criminal Law: A Study into the Typical Features of International Criminality and the Reflection of these Traits in International Criminal Law* (Turku, Åbo Akademi University Press, 2013) 356.

[2] James Stewart argues in favour of abandoning the modes of liability all together. J Stewart, 'The End of "Modes of Liability" for International Crimes' (2012) 25 *Leiden Journal of International Law* 165.

[3] Osiel (n 1) 1753.

I. THE LIMITATIONS OF INTERNATIONAL CRIMINAL LAW

As the name suggests, international criminal law combines the features of two disciplines: public international law and domestic criminal law. These form the core of international criminal law.[4] This is not to suggest that other disciplines do not have any influence—international humanitarian law and international human rights law inform the content of international criminal law. However, the fundamental principles upon which international criminal law operates come from the two founding disciplines. For example, the principles of individual criminal responsibility, legality and equality of arms, which are fundamental for international criminal justice, all derive from domestic criminal law.[5] Yet, reliance on national concepts has its limits. At times, the principles emerging at an international level conflict with the fundamental principles of domestic criminal law, as in the case of selective prosecutions, for instance. There is a strong political and international element embedded in international criminal law that cannot be ignored. International criminal law tends to fall back on its public international law origins in difficult situations. The limitations of international criminal law can thus be revealed through the tensions between the two different fields of law.

A. Conservative versus Progressive

Domestic criminal law is a highly conservative institution aiming to preserve the social order and enforce social norms through criminal sanctions.[6] It exemplifies the conflict between individual autonomy and collective interests.[7] In Mill's philosophy, self-protection is the sole end for which humankind is allowed to interfere with the individual liberty of any of their number. Consequently, the only purpose for which power can be exercised is to prevent harm to others.[8] The definition of harm depends on the values embedded in society. Usually the ruling classes define these values over time, and the threat of penal sanctions protects the equilibrium attained in a particular society.[9]

[4] eg, R Cryer, H Friman, D Robinson and E Wilmeshurst, *An Introduction to International Criminal Law and Procedure*, 2nd edn (Cambridge, Cambridge University Press, 2010) 16.

[5] The first international trials at Nuremberg and Tokyo represented a compromise between different domestic legal systems.

[6] A Ashworth, *Principles of Criminal Law*, 2nd edn (Oxford, Clarendon, 1995) 15.

[7] ibid 29.

[8] JS Mill, 'On Liberty' in L May and J Brown (eds), *Philosophy of Law: Classic and Contemporary Readings* (Chichester, Wiley-Blackwell, 2011) 369.

[9] Ashworth (n 6) 16.

Durkheim explained the traditionalist nature of penal law by the fact that it denotes the feelings collectively shared by society.[10] The authority of the penal rule is thus a societal custom formed over time.[11] Domestic criminal law has an indispensable regulatory function because by guarding the dominant values shared by its citizens, it may be said to preserve the identity of the state. Punishment in domestic law is administered in a systematic fashion because all members of the society are presumed to share the values and agree to submit the offender to censure.[12] Society can be said to 'outsource' the imposition of penalty to an organised body, which administers this process in a consistent way.

In contrast, international criminal law is a relatively new field of law that dates back just a few decades to the establishment of the International Military Tribunal in Nuremberg.[13] International criminal law does not limit itself to the values shared by the citizens of a particular state, but claims universality and adherence to the project of protection of the fundamental legal values of humanity as a whole.[14] It is highly aspirational—many customs are not yet embedded in the international community and are still in the process of being formed. Despite its great importance for the development of humanity, international criminal law, unlike its domestic counterpart, has arguably not yet achieved the status of being an indispensable regulatory instrument in international affairs as it lacks consistency in the imposition of punishment that domestic criminal law offers. International trials are just 'samples' of justice in the situations where political reality and the international climate allow for prosecution and conviction.

B. Deviance versus Conformity

Domestic and international offending differ from a behavioural point of view. Criminology offers a number of theories explaining why people commit traditional crimes. These explanations vary significantly. Some criminologists believe that people offend due to being exposed to an unfavourable environment; others claim that economic inequality prompts criminality, while the third group believes that humans act as rational beings and seize any suitable opportunity to offend.[15] What unites these approaches is that criminality is regarded as a form of deviance from the norm.

[10] E Durkheim, *The Division of Labour in Society* (New York, Free Press, 1984) 37.

[11] ibid 35.

[12] ibid 45.

[13] London Agreement, 8 August 1945, 82 UNTC 280.

[14] K Ambos, *Treatise on International Criminal Law, Volume 1: Foundations and General Part* (Oxford, Oxford University Press, 2013) 65.

[15] GB Vold, TJ Bernard and JB Snipes, *Theoretical Criminology*, 4th edn (Oxford, Oxford University Press, 1998) 4.

The responses of the domestic criminal justice system are consequently geared towards ensuring conformity and preventing deviance.[16]

International criminal law deals with a different type of criminality. It often stems from obedience rather than from deviance.[17] Political violence usually changes the context in which humans operate and authority is exercised to induce offending rather than desistance. Its responses have therefore to be attuned to breaking the patterns of compliance rather than ensuring conformity. Mass violence requires structure and organisation because its continuation depends on human cooperation within the system. The only way to induce individuals to be part of the enterprise that commits crimes is to instil in their minds that they are simply small cogs with no responsibility.[18] It is almost as if individuals submit their individual autonomy, their freedom of choice, to a higher authority, and in return they expect to feel absolved of responsibility.

Hannah Arendt explored this phenomenon by asking how was it possible for the individual and collective conscience to disappear, with some notable exceptions, in Nazi Germany?[19] She looked at the example of Adolf Eichmann, a Nazi bureaucrat whose trial she observed. He did not enter the criminal system for sadistic motives, but to pursue a career, and his conscience functioned in the expected way for about four weeks until it began to function abnormally.[20] The reason behind this shift was the effect of a substitution of values promoted by the Nazi Party. Instead of perceiving themselves as murderers, the functionaries felt that they were involved in something historic, grandiose and unique.[21] The duty to obey orders overshadowed any possible conscientious objections.[22]

Stanley Milgram conducted a number of experiments designed to test the capacity of individuals to defy authority when put under pressure to perform acts that went against their conscience. The participants were instructed by an authoritative figure to gradually administer electric shocks to another individual (actor) in cases when the latter gave the wrong answers to the predetermined questions. The declared goal of the experiment was to test the effects of punishment on learning, but the real aim was to see how far individuals could go in inflicting pain

[16] In the words of Hart, the criminal law sets up in its rules standards of behaviour to encourage certain types of conduct and discourage others. See HLA Hart and J Gardner, *Punishment and Responsibility: Essays in the Philosophy of Law* (Oxford, Oxford University Press, 2009) 6.

[17] For a sociological perspective, see S Milgram, *Obedience to Authority: An Experimental View* (Tavistock, Pinter & Martin, 1974).

[18] H Arendt, *Eichmann in Jerusalem: A Report on the Banality of Evil* (New York, Viking Press, 1965) 57.

[19] ibid 91.

[20] ibid 95. This narrative is now being contested as the evidence of Eichmann's sadistic inclinations has emerged. See D Lipstadt, *The Eichmann Trial* (New York, Nextbook Press, 2011).

[21] ibid 105.

[22] ibid 91.

on another human being. The results were shocking: while people were experiencing severe strain and discomfort following the orders from the person in charge, very few participants found the strength to resist authority and stop the experiment. This is despite the fact that they perceived their acts as immoral. This outcome led Milgram to conclude that values are not the only forces that drive a person in an ongoing situation—context is equally important. He argued that the level of obedience can be altered and defiance can be stimulated when multiple authority figures are not in agreement with each other (diffusion of authority) or when an individual is exposed to group pressure (someone else refuses to obey).[23]

C. Legitimacy through Enforcement versus Legitimacy through Fairness

Domestic criminal law and international criminal law gain their legitimacy in a different way. National criminal law is the product of the separation of powers: the legislators enact positive law in the form of statutes; the courts apply the law as a principle and determine whether a technical violation of law constitutes a wrongdoing; while the executive branch frames public discussion about the criminalisation or decriminalisation of certain conduct. What is extremely important is that domestic law does not need to legitimise itself. The state system provides for a basic rule of recognition that allows us to determine *before* a rule is actually made that it will be valid *if* it conforms to the requirements of the rule of recognition.[24] If a criminal law provision fulfils these requirements, it is automatically valid and citizens are obliged to obey. The state machinery ensures compliance through its enforcement powers.

International criminal law functions in an entirely different way. It is a branch of public international law that benefits neither from a basic rule providing general criteria of validity for its norms nor from an enforcement apparatus akin to that of the state. International law is not entirely without 'teeth' as it envisages coercion, just not in the form of criminal sanctions.[25] Its persuasive force is of a political nature. For meaningful executive powers, international criminal justice must rely on states.[26] The dialogue with national governments is thus essential to maintain the functioning of the discipline as a failure to perform enforcement functions may lead to the denial of justice, as, for instance, with the pending ICC arrest warrant against the President of Sudan, Omar Al Bashir.

23 Milgram (n 17) 118.
24 Hart and Gardner (n 16) 235.
25 M Shaw, *International Law* (Cambridge, Cambridge University Press, 2008) 7.
26 eg, art 27 of the ICTY Statute and art 26 of the ICTR Statute (enforcement of sentence).

How do international courts achieve the full cooperation of domestic institutions? The key is to be perceived as legitimate.[27] This can be accomplished through enhancing the quality of international criminal justice. International trials should be a matter of quality, not quantity. The legitimising effect of exemplary justice cannot be understated.

International courts and tribunals are thus essential mechanisms for bringing to life international legal norms through interpreting its sources—treaty, custom and the general principles of law.[28] HLA Hart maintained that it is perfectly conceivable in a less advanced legal culture (such as international law) to have binding rules supported by appropriate forms of social pressure that do not refer to the ultimate rule of the system.[29] The social pressure required to keep the system operational rests on the global acceptance of the moral foundation of international criminal law.

A constant need for legitimation underscores the importance of the rigorous approach of international courts and tribunals in dealing with the sources of international law. Shklar drew attention to the propensity of the analytical legal mind for thinking of the law as 'there' or 'not there' at all times and in all places when it is rather a question of degrees of legalism in politics of complex social orders.[30] The truth is that international criminal law began in a legal vacuum—the International Military Tribunal in Nuremberg was created when there was no law, no government and no political order.[31] The principle of legality had to be circumvented to some extent as the law was gradually developed.[32] Consequently, the quality of work of the international courts predetermines the perceived legitimacy of the outcome.

D. Individual versus Collective Aspect

Liberal domestic criminal law theories are built upon the principle of individual autonomy, which respects an individual's freedom to act as a rational being.[33] Pursuant to this principle, an individual can only be held

[27] Here I use legitimacy in a sociological sense as a belief by actors that certain rules are legally or morally binding. See CA Thomas, 'The Uses and Abuses of Legitimacy in International Law' (2014) 34(4) *Oxford Journal of Legal Studies* 729, 754.

[28] Hart (n 16) 235–36.

[29] ibid 234–36.

[30] J Shklar, *Legalism: An Essay on Law, Morals and Politics* (Cambridge, Mass, Harvard University Press, 1964) 148.

[31] ibid 153.

[32] However, there is an argument that international criminal law has its distinct process of criminalisation; affecting the way in which the principle of legality must be understood within the discipline. See B van Schaack, '*Crimen Sine Lege*: Judicial Lawmaking at the Intersection of Law and Morals' (2008) 97 *Georgetown Law Journal* 119.

[33] Ashworth (n 6) 26; D Robinson, 'Identity Crisis of International Criminal Law' (2008) 21(4) *Leiden Journal of International Law* 926.

liable for voluntary conduct.[34] International criminal law recognises this central rule. The challenge lies in reconciling the individual nature of criminal responsibility and the group aspect of crimes: how does one attribute responsibility for mass atrocities? International criminal law has struggled with this problem since its inception. The difficulty arises from the enormity of crimes in question, the collective nature of offending that involves many individuals at the different levels within the state hierarchy and the strong organisational element inherent in international criminality.

In his opening address to the tribunal, Robert Jackson, the chief prosecutor for the US at Nuremberg, summarised the challenges of opening the first trial in history for crimes against peace: 'Never before in legal history has an effort been made to bring within the scope of a single litigation the developments of a decade, covering a whole continent, and involving a score of nations, countless individuals, and innumerable events.'[35]

II. SYMBOLISM AS AN OVERARCHING AIM

The UN Secretary-General claimed in his 2004 report to the Security Council that the objectives pursued by the special criminal tribunals include bringing to justice those responsible for serious violations of human rights and humanitarian law, putting an end to such violations and preventing their recurrence, securing justice and dignity for victims, establishing a record of past events, promoting national reconciliation, re-establishing the rule of law and contributing to the restoration of peace.[36] These goals, which were never formalised or ranked, have different timeframes, but are all equally ambitious: some look backwards, others dwell on the present-day reality, while a third type of objectives are focused on the future.[37]

The desire to fulfil all of the stated goals without clearly defining them—the desire for an ultimate success in achieving each stated objective—also became the weakness of international criminal justice. A unifying principle that limits our expectations and curtails the multiple ambitious

[34] Hart (n 16) 174.

[35] The Trial of German Major War Criminals by the International Military Tribunal Sitting at Nuremberg, Germany, 21 November 1945 (1946), http://avalon.law.yale.edu/imt/11-21-45.asp.

[36] The Secretary-General, Report of the Secretary-General on the Rule of Law and Transitional Justice in Conflict and Post-Conflict Societies, UN Doc. S/2004/616 (2004), 38.

[37] It is essential to point out that not all of the objectives can be achieved through criminal punishment. While 'bringing to justice those responsible' corresponds to the retributive punishment rationale, preventing the reoccurrence of the violations of human rights and humanitarian law corresponds to the logic of deterrence, and to some extent securing justice and dignity for victims to restoration. There are broader goals that cannot be achieved through punishment *stricto sensu* such as reconciliation, setting the historical record and re-establishing the rule of law.

objectives can make international criminal law more coherent. Without such a principle or an overarching aim, the system is prone to provoking disappointment, disapproval or even abuse. The criticism ranges from the ineffectiveness of international courts and tribunals to their over-politicisation and the selectivity of prosecutions.

It seems that one of the most important, tangible achievements of international criminal law is changing the way in which the world community perceives political violence.[38] This is significant progress for a field of law that was created relatively recently. International crimes are no longer tolerated as the 'necessary evil'. Rape, for instance, is no longer perceived as one of the 'spoils of war', but as a crime against humanity deserving of condemnation along with other hideous acts.

Symbolism therefore emerges as the leading objective of international criminal justice. The term 'symbolism' is meant to refer to the mission of international criminal law in creating a space for the shared, immutable values of the international community through the administration of exemplary justice. Symbolism seems to be the best fit because it denotes the strengths of international criminal justice to transcend state borders and to serve as a reminder that mass atrocities do not go unpunished. At the same time, this objective also stresses the unique features of international criminal law discussed in the previous section.

Perceiving international criminal justice as symbolic helps to manage expectations bestowed on the international criminal justice system while maintaining a sense of coherence. For example, because of the collective nature of mass atrocities as well as a frequent lack of enforcement powers, international criminal law is capable of addressing only a limited number of situations and reaching only a handful of perpetrators. This is in stark contrast with domestic criminal law, which, at least at the statutory level, presupposes universal application.[39] Viewed through the lens of retribution or deterrence (typical domestic sentencing rationales) requiring the law to punish all the guilty and not just a selected few, there is a problem with this discrepancy in international criminal law.[40]

However, if one accepts that the role of international criminal law is symbolic, this caveat no longer appears problematic. The very few instances when the responsible individuals stand trial in the context of international criminal law become representative of a broader consensus amongst international community rejecting political violence as a threat to

[38] D Luban, 'After Honey Moon: Reflections on the Current State of International Criminal Justice' (2013) 11 *Journal of International Criminal Justice* 505.

[39] Fletcher refers to this requirement that the law must punish all those guilty as 'positive legality'. G Fletcher, *Basic Concepts of Criminal Law* (Oxford, Oxford University Press, 1998) 207. For a discussion of this limitation, see Ch 7.II.C.

[40] For a detailed analysis, see Ch 7.II.C.

international peace and security. They serve as a symbol of condemnation and the mature status of international society. In the criminological reality of mass atrocities, in the midst of which individuals tend to abandon their will and follow a manipulative higher authority when put under pressure, international criminal law has no other choice but to focus primarily on breaking the patterns of obedience when violence is about to happen. It must also address circumstances inducing violence in the first place. One way to achieve this is to conceptualise international criminal law as an alternative source of authority or an instrument of group pressure—a loudspeaker for transmitting universal values with the view of preventing criminal obedience.[41] This is precisely the symbolic function of international criminal law.

The rhetoric of symbolism emphasises the limited scope of legal inquiry for the purposes of creating a comprehensive historical account. Acknowledging that international criminal law is symbolic in that it allows for prosecuting only a handful of perpetrators relieves the courts of some of the pressure to uncover all the truth about the conflict.

The symbolic function also tackles the limitations of the deterrence rationale in international criminal law—namely, the lack of a solid empirical basis supporting the idea that potential perpetrators are intimidated by the international indictments and penalties. Symbolism allows us to think about international criminal law as a showcase for the emerging values of international community. Those few judgments that are issued at an international level gain a lot of publicity and at the very least alert potential perpetrators to the general risks associated with offending. In addition, international criminal law triggers predeterrence,[42] which implies creating conditions whereby individuals do not even contemplate taking part in political violence because of certain assumptions about lines not to be crossed, or the moral minima, instilled in their minds. The symbolic role of international criminal law is thus antecedent to its deterrent power.

When it comes to the considerations of restorative justice that receive increased recognition in international criminal law, the main problem seems to be that the rights of the accused are often balanced against the rights of the victims.[43] For example, Judge Odio Benito in her separate and dissenting opinion to the *Lubanga* judgment argued that it is incumbent on the ICC to regard the interests of victims and, as a result, to provide comprehensive legal definitions that go beyond the circumstances of

[41] I Tallgren, 'The Sensibility and Sense of International Criminal Law' (2002) 13 *European Journal of International Law* 3, 592.

[42] M Damaška, 'What is the Point of International Criminal Justice?' (2008) 83 *Chicago-Kent Law Review* 329, 347.

[43] See Ch 7.II.

each individual case.[44] This view seems to extend the powers of the Trial Chamber beyond those envisaged in Article 64(2) of the Rome Statute.[45] Furthermore, over-expansive legal definitions are at odds with the rights of the accused, in particular the right to be informed about the charges, to have adequate time for preparation and to be tried without delay.[46] The approach that seeks to counterpoise the rights of the accused and the victims' rights entirely transforms the focus of a criminal trial. The question remains whether such a shift faithfully serves the end goal of offering justice to the victims.

A more coherent approach would be to strive for the quality of individual judgments by strict adherence to the principles of liberal criminal justice. The aim should be to ensure that the rights of the accused are respected to the fullest extent possible.[47] In this way, the perceived legitimacy of the tribunals would increase and, with it, hopefully victim satisfaction and the potential for reconciliation. If international justice is viewed as legitimate, it is easier to use it as a tool to empower local communities to pursue accountability at the national level through, for example, the principle of complementarity promoted by the ICC.[48] Increased accountability at the local level then leads to a 'change from within'—the sign of true reconciliation.

'Symbolism' is the term used in this book, but there are other names for this goal—there is a growing trend in legal scholarship recognising it as 'didactic' or 'expressivist'.[49] Mirjan Damaška draws attention to the problem posed by a number of unranked goals in international criminal law and addresses it by proposing a leading objective, which he calls 'didactic' or 'socio-pedagogic'. He maintains that international criminal courts should place more emphasis on persuasion and strengthen a

[44] *Prosecutor v Thomas Lubanga Dyilo*, ICC-01/04-01/06, Separate and Dissenting Opinion of Judge Odio Benito to the Trial Chamber I, Judgment Pursuant to Article 74 of the Statute, 14 March 2012 ('Separate and Dissenting Opinion of Judge Odio Benito'), para 7.

[45] Article 64(2) reads as follows: 'The Trial Chamber shall ensure that a trial is fair and expeditious and is conducted with full respect for the rights of the accused and due regard for the protection of victims and witnesses.'

[46] Rome Statute, art 67(1)(a)–(c).

[47] *Prosecutor v Germain Katanga*, ICC-01/04-01/07, Trial Chamber II, Minority Opinion of Judge van den Wyngaert to Judgment Pursuant to Article 74 of the Statute, 7 March 2014, para 311.

[48] Rome Statute, art 1.

[49] M Drumbl, *Atrocity, Punishment, and International Law* (Cambridge, Cambridge University Press, 2007) 173; Damaška (n 42) 345; H van der Wilt 'Why International Criminal Lawyers Should Read Mirjan Damaška' in C Stahn and L van den Herik (eds), *Future Perspectives on International Criminal Justice* (The Hague, TMC Asser Institute, 2010) 99; S Mohamed, 'Deviance, Aspiration, and the Stories We Tell: Reconciling Mass Atrocity and the Criminal Law (2015) 124 *Yale Law Journal* 1628.

sense of accountability for international crime by exposing these extreme forms of inhumanity.[50] The purpose is to establish moral minima that are universal.[51]

Mark Drumbl calls the same goal 'expressivism' and maintains that an expressivist punishes to strengthen faith in the rule of law among the general public, as opposed to punishing simply because the perpetrator deserves it or because potential perpetrators will be deterred by it.[52] This reasoning is close to retribution, which is about treating the wrongdoer as a moral agent.[53] The communicative function of punishment conveying blame through deprivation is a valid attribute of the retributive rationale.[54] This is somewhat different from the broader symbolic function of international criminal law as a flagship of shared values.[55] The distinctive objective of symbolism is delivering a certain message to the community as a whole rather than to a certain offender. Harmen Van der Wilt's view is possibly the closest to the one advocated in this book. He contends that the role of the expressive theory is to imbue the general public with core values and with faith in the rule of law.[56]

Symbolism receives limited coverage in the case law of the ad hoc tribunals, hybrid courts or the ICC primarily because there is a thin line between proclaiming the symbolic value of international justice and sliding towards rhetorical restatements devoid of legal content. The judgments acknowledge to some degree that there is something different about international crimes and the need to punish them, but this is done more on an intuitive level than by explicitly integrating the emblematic value of international criminal law in the reasoning.[57] The tendency of international judges is to concentrate on the punishment rationales as they appear in the domestic context—retribution and deterrence, with some attention given to victims' rights and reconciliation.[58] The following passage from

[50] Damaška (n 42) 345.

[51] ibid 347.

[52] Drumbl (n 49) 173. For a general account of this goal of punishment in domestic law, see J Feinberg, *Doing and Deserving: Essays in the Theory of Responsibility* (Princeton, Princeton University Press, 1974).

[53] A von Hirsch, 'Proportionate Sentences: a Desert Perspective' in A von Hirsch, A Ashworth and J Roberts (eds), *Principled Sentencing*, 3rd edn (Oxford, Hart Publishing, 2009) 117. See Ch 7.II.

[54] RA Duff, 'Punishment, Retribution and Communication', in von Hirsch, Ashworth and Roberts (n 53) 127–35.

[55] For a detailed account of retribution, see Ch 7(II)(B).

[56] H van der Wilt, 'Joint Criminal Enterprise: Possibilities and Limitations' (2007) 5(1) *Journal of International Criminal Justice* 99.

[57] Heikkilä noted: 'From the point of view of the phenomenology of international criminality, it is noteworthy that many other typical features of international criminality are not considered at attribution.' Heikkilä (n 1) 366.

[58] See Ch 7.II.

Aleksovski is sometimes cited in support of a limited recognition of the symbolic function of international criminal law:[59]

> [A] sentence of the International Tribunal should make plain the condemnation of the international community of the behaviour in question and show that the international community was not ready to tolerate serious violations of international humanitarian law and human rights.[60]

This rhetoric is indeed very powerful. However, there is no separation of retribution and symbolism in this judgment that speaks in the preceding phrase about the fact that *retribution* is not fulfilling the desire for revenge, but is an expression of the outrage of international community.[61] Reference is made to the function of retribution as a medium for voicing public disapproval of the deeds of the offender. This is slightly different from symbolism because the channel of communication is with the particular offender and not the general public.

The *Krstić* appeal judgment recognised to some extent the symbolic function of international criminal law by singling out one particular offence, genocide, as deserving of 'special condemnation and opprobrium'.[62] The reasoning is that genocide 'is a crime against all of humankind, its harm being felt not only by the group targeted for destruction, but by all of humanity'.[63] Similarly, the only sentencing judgment of the ICC in the *Lubanga* case made no direct reference to the function of international criminal law in propagating values shared by humanity, but incidentally pointed towards the unacceptable nature of crimes against children.[64] The considerations in *Krstić* and *Lubanga* are crime-specific, but they show how international judgments become the point of reference for the behaviour that is not tolerated by humankind.

The *Taylor* appeal judgment came closest to an express recognition of the symbolic function of international criminal law. The Appeals Chamber upheld Charles Taylor's conviction and a 50-year sentence for aiding and abetting and planning murders, rapes and other acts of violence committed during the Sierra Leonean civil war.[65] As the former President of Liberia, Taylor was involved in organising and funding attacks on the civilian population in the neighbouring country. The appellate judges held that the sentences imposed by the court reflected 'the revulsion of mankind, represented by the international community, to the crime

[59] Van der Wilt (n 56) fn 39; Damaška (n 42).

[60] *Prosecutor v Aleksovski*, ICTY Case IT-95-14/1-A, Appeal Judgment, 24 March 2000, para 185.

[61] ibid.

[62] *Prosecutor v Krstić*, ICTY Case No IT-98-33-A, Appeal Judgment, 19 April 2004, para 36.

[63] ibid.

[64] *Prosecutor v Thomas Lubanga Dyilo*, ICC-01/04-01/06, Trial Chamber I, Decision on Sentence Pursuant to Article 76 of the Statute, 10 July 2012, paras 37–44.

[65] *Prosecutor v Taylor*, SCSL-03-1-A, Appeal Judgment, 26 September 2013.

and the convicted person's participation in the crime'.[66] Thereby, they recognised that culpable involvement of the heads of state in political violence in another state is no longer accepted. Justice in this case serves as a yardstick of the shared global values.

It follows that accepting the symbolic role of international criminal law helps in containing expectations and bringing some coherence to the plethora of proclaimed objectives of international criminal law. The question is how does one integrate this overarching aim into judicial reasoning? One way to do this is to see the symbolic function of international criminal law as a substantive and procedural consideration. From a substantive point of view, international criminal law plays a crucial role in defining the forms of political violence that are not accepted by the international community. It shapes our perception of the shared values that must be upheld universally.[67] For example, the Rome Statute represents an up-to-date codification of international crimes. Arguably, the role of the ICC is not only to provide the jurisdictional framework for international prosecutions but also to spread the values embedded in the Statute through enhancing national legislation. Pursuant to the complementarity principle, the ICC promotes the implementation of the Rome Statute into the domestic legislation of the countries that are parties to the Statute.[68]

The symbolic function of international criminal law can also be seen as a procedural tool for interpreting the administration of justice. It appears that international criminal justice attains legitimacy not only through delivering the final outcome—the conviction or acquittal—but also through the way in which it reaches this outcome. Justice becomes a matter of outcome *and* process. If we conceive international trials as symbols of exemplary justice, then the principles of fairness and due process must inform every step of the way.

The role and place of complicity in international criminal law becomes evident if one looks at it through the lens of symbolism. The principle of fairness demands that offenders are labelled and punished in proportion to their wrongdoing.[69] Andrew Ashworth suggested that fair labelling requires us to maintain the distinctions 'to ensure a proportionate response to law-breaking, thereby assisting the law's educative and declaratory

[66] ibid, para 663.

[67] The Committee of French jurists participating in setting up the ICTY suggested that the proposed tribunal 'must be universal, because the crimes it is to punish are an affront to the conscience of all humanity'. See *Report of the Committee of French Jurists to study the establishment of International Criminal Tribunal to judge the crimes committed in the Former Yugoslavia* appended to the letter dated 10 February 1993 from the Permanent Representative of France to the United Nations addressed to the Secretary General, UN DOC S/25266, para 23(b).

[68] There are initiatives facilitating the implementation.

[69] Ashworth (n 6) 87.

function in sustaining and reinforcing social values'.[70] This is precisely the symbolic function of law discussed above. Ashworth referred to the definitions of the substantive offences, but the same consideration applies to the modes of responsibility—the notion of fairness insists that we describe the conduct and the mental state of the accused in the most precise terms.

Ohlin argued in favour of the distinction between principals and accessories in international criminal law because collapsing this distinction sends the wrong message to the world—it inflates the culpability of accessories and deflates the culpability of principals.[71] Perhaps the main problem with attaching the same label to all crime participants is not necessarily 'evening out' their level of culpability, since this primarily depends on the factual circumstances rather than the mode of participation, but the violation of the principle of legality. Labels are important for reinforcing this principle—an individual must be fairly warned prior to any demands on his liberty and have a crystal-clear idea as to why and how he incurs individual criminal responsibility. Another argument for maintaining the distinction is that an accurate description of the conduct and mental state of the accused contributes to the perceived legitimacy of international courts and tribunals. For example, in respect of setting the lower limits of superior responsibility, Damaška claimed that: 'Ordinary people do not lump together intentional perpetrators of heinous crimes and those who failed to bring them to justice.'[72]

Labelling certain acts 'complicity' as opposed to 'perpetration' does not undermine the symbolic, or expressive, function of international criminal law by signalling a lesser degree of culpability of the accomplice. The idea of the hierarchy of participation forms—principal perpetration being considered the most blameworthy—must therefore be rejected. Judge van den Wyngaert relied on the principle of fair labelling when she criticised the emerging hierarchy at the ICC.[73] This highly questionable position reinforces the tendency to make the conduct of political and military leaders 'fit the mould of principal liability' by using implied theories such as that of 'control of the crime'.[74] Judge van den Wyngaert accurately observed that the drafters of the Rome Statute have not elaborated forms of criminal responsibility for this specific category of offenders, and characterising them as principals is problematic from the legal and conceptual

[70] ibid 86.

[71] J Ohlin, 'LJIL Symposium: Names, Labels, and Roses', *Opinio Juris* blog, 23 March 2012, http://opiniojuris.org/2012/03/23/ljil-names-labels-and-roses.

[72] Damaška (n 42) 350.

[73] For more on the hierarchy of participation modes at the ICC, see Ch 5.

[74] *Prosecutor v Mathieu Ngudjolo Chui*, ICC-01/04-02/12-4, Trial Chamber II, Concurring Opinion of Judge Christine van den Wyngaert to Judgment Pursuant to Article 74 of the Statute, 18 December 2012, para 29.

point of view.[75] The legal difficulty is precisely the violation of the principle of fair labelling—the juridical description of the conduct has to match the facts of the case rather than be based on an artificially constructed notion. If the leader is removed from the scene of crime, then he may just as easily be held complicit in the crimes occurring in the field rather than 'perpetrating' them.

III. IMPROVING THE CURRENT PRACTICES OF ATTACHING LIABILITY FOR COMPLICITY

The previous section justified the idea of distinguishing between different forms of participation in international criminal law. The reason for this is to uphold the principle of legality and to create a precedent of a fair trial for the world community. Different forms of complicity—explicitly provided in the statutes of international courts and deeply rooted in domestic legal systems—are often the most appropriate mechanisms for attaching the liability to the offenders removed from the scene of the crime.

There are a number of concluding observations resulting from the discussion throughout this book that may contribute to improving current practices on accomplice liability in international criminal law:

1. Legal requirements of complicity—conduct and fault requirements—need to be sufficiently clear and linked to the facts of the particular case. It is essential to treat these two elements not as two autonomous units, but as parts of the same whole.
2. Because of its evolving nature, international criminal law is characterised by a high degree of judicial discretion not only at the sentencing stage, but also at the stage of the attribution of responsibility. However, there must be limits to judicial creativity. It is advisable to adopt a more rigorous methodology when it comes to processing the sources of international criminal law. Decisions to create new forms of liability beyond those expressly provided for in the statutes or to introduce new elements to the existing forms call for further justification.
3. Complicity is an intricate balancing exercise. It may seem that it casts its net too wide by not requiring that the act of the accomplice caused the principal to act. The lack of causation loosens the conduct requirement. The equilibrium is restored by an enhanced fault requirement: the knowledge of the crime and the intent to assist or encourage the commission of the principal's crime.[76] The Rome Statute demands that

[75] ibid, para 15.
[76] Ashworth (n 6) 409.

the aider and abettor acts with a *purpose* of facilitating the commission of the crime.[77]

4. The practical implication of the balancing exercise is that the further the accomplice is removed from the scene of the crime, the more emphasis must be placed on his mental state. From the evidentiary point of view, this may imply avoiding a fully inferential analysis when it comes to assessing an accomplice's culpability. Knowledge that the crime is being committed is an essential element of complicity.[78] If the accomplice is found to be close to the scene of the crime, his fault may be implied, while his contribution has to be spelled out—mental state alone is not sufficient to bring about criminal responsibility. In contrast, in cases of removed assistance or encouragement, knowledge about the crimes and the intent to be involved in their commission become dispositive for attaching responsibility to the accomplice. This consideration is particularly relevant in the context of mass atrocities—the gap between the accomplice and the crime is often very wide, and the only way to compensate for this distance is to focus on individual culpability.
5. The requirement that the aid of the accused is specifically directed towards the crime is arguably part of the fault—rather than conduct—requirement of complicity.[79] The necessary extent of an accessory's knowledge of the principal offence is a complex consideration that depends largely on the circumstances of the case.[80] The test in English law would be whether the offence committed was within the contemplated range of offences and, if not, whether it was of the same *type* as any of those offences contemplated.[81] International criminal law has to devise its own approach to the required level of specificity of the accused's knowledge. For example, it may be said that the threshold of specificity is met if the accomplice supplies material aid to the rebel groups with the knowledge that the rebels are involved in large-scale mass violence and the furnished aid will almost inevitably be put to criminal use.
6. From a criminological point of view, it seems that the context of political violence has a bearing on the culpability of the accused—offending often stems from obedience rather than defiance. This aspect has to be accounted for when assessing the accomplice's culpability. Which factors shaped the accomplice's wrongful decisions? What were the courses of action available to the accused?

[77] Rome Statute, art 25(3)(c).

[78] W Schabas, 'Enforcing International Humanitarian Law: Catching the Accomplices' (2001) 83 *International Review of the Red Cross* 842, 450.

[79] *cf Prosecutor v Perišić*, ICTY Case No 04-81-A, Appeal Judgment, 28 February 2013, para 73.

[80] KJM Smith, *A Modern Treatise on the Law of Criminal Complicity* (Oxford, Clarendon, 1991) 161 et seq.

[81] ibid 167.

7. The collective nature of international criminality is also an important consideration for the purposes of establishing accomplice liability. Factual scenarios of mass atrocities are diverse, but are all equally complex. They presuppose the cooperation of individuals at different levels of the military and political apparatus. It is essential to establish the links between different actors. Culpability in criminal law is individual, but should be assessed in relation to the acts of the other perpetrators.
8. The hierarchy of the modes of participation implicit in the reasoning of some ICC, ICTY and ICTR Trial Chambers should be abandoned. The degree of blameworthiness should not hinge on the legal label attached to the conduct of the accused, but should rather be a reflection of the factual circumstances. In the context of political violence, the acts of accomplices are often more reprehensible than those of the primary perpetrators. Accomplices issuing orders from the safety of their desks frequently have more freedom to act in accordance with their conscience than the participants in the crime pulling the trigger of the gun. Accomplices also frequently enjoy the benefit of time—an opportunity to reflect on the consequences of their conduct—an option that is not available to the principals. This too must be brought to bear on the assessment of the individual criminal responsibility of accomplices.

Appendix I

National Legislation on Complicity

*The translation of the terms used in this table may vary due to linguistic peculiarities.

Country	Participants in crime	Term 'complicity' mentioned	Sentencing discount for any mode of participation	Conspiracy	Comments	Reference to legislation
Albania	1. *Organisers* organise and manage the activity to commit the criminal act. 2. *Executors* carry out direct actions to realise the criminal act. 3. *Instigators* instigate the other collaborators to commit a criminal act. 4. *Helpers*, through advice, instructions, concrete means, abolition of obstacles, promise to hide collaborators' tracks or things relevant to the criminal act, help to carry it out.	No	No	Creation and participation in a criminal organisation, terrorist organisation, armed gang or structured criminal group constitutes a crime and is punished according to the provisions of the special part of the Penal Code or other special criminal provisions.		Articles 25–28 Albanian Penal Code.

Country	Participants in crime	Term 'complicity' mentioned	Sentencing discount for any mode of participation	Conspiracy	Comments	Reference to legislation
Argentina	1. *Executors.* 2. *Accomplices* without whose help the crime would not have been executed. 3. *Other accomplices* involved in the execution of the crime.	Yes	Yes Mandatory discount for other accomplices (category 3).		Accomplices are punished only for what they intended.	Articles 45–48 Argentinian Penal Code.
Austria	*Persons involved in the execution of the crime.*	No	Yes Discretionary sentencing discount for those participating in an ancillary manner.		Every participant is punished according to his guilt.	Sections 12–13, 34(1) Austrian Penal Code.

Country	Participants in crime	Term 'complicity' mentioned	Sentencing discount for any mode of participation	Conspiracy	Comments	Reference to legislation
Bangladesh	1. *Executors.* 2. *Abettors.* a. Instigators. b. Members of a conspiracy provided it results in an illegal act or omission c. Aiders.	No	No		Abettors are punished for the result. Abettors are punished even in cases where the crime is not executed. Abettors are always removed from the scene of the crime. If they are present, they are deemed to have committed the offence.	Chapter 5 Penal Code of Bangladesh.
Bolivia	1. *Author*: any party without whose contribution the crime would not have been executed 2. *Instigator*. 3. *Accomplice*: contributes intentionally to the crime, which would have would have been executed even without such help	Yes	Yes Mandatory discount for other accomplices (category 3).			Articles 20–24 and 39 Bolivian Penal Code.

Country	Participants in crime	Term 'complicity' mentioned	Sentencing discount for any mode of participation	Conspiracy	Comments	Reference to legislation
Bosnia and Herzegovina	1. *Perpetrator.* 2. *Accomplices* (joint perpetrators). 3. *Inciter.* 4. *Accessory* (helps in the commission of the crime).	Yes	Yes Discretionary mitigation for accessories (category 4).		The accomplice shall be considered criminally responsible within the limits set by his own intent or negligence, and the inciter and the accessory within the limits of their own intent.	Articles 29–32 Penal Code of Bosnia and Herzegovina.
Bulgaria	Accomplices in crime: 1. *Actual perpetrator.* 2. *Abettor*: the one who has deliberately persuaded somebody else to commit the crime. 3. *Accessory*: the one who has deliberately facilitated the commitment of the crime through advice, explanations, promise to provide assistance after the act, removal of obstacles, providing resources or in any other way.	Yes	Yes Discretionary discount for aiding when the degree of participation is small.		The abettor and the accessory shall be responsible only for deliberate aid.	Articles 21, 22, 55, 58 Bulgarian Penal Code.

Country	Participants in crime	Term 'complicity' mentioned	Sentencing discount for any mode of participation	Conspiracy	Comments	Reference to legislation
Canada	1. *Actual perpetrator*. 2. *The one who does or omits to do anything for the purpose of aiding* any person to commit the crime. 3. *Abettor*. 4. Persons carrying out the common purpose. 5. *Counsellor* (procures, solicits and incites).	No	No			Articles 20–24 Canadian Penal Code.
China	1. *Principal offender*: one who organises and leads a criminal group in conducting criminal activities or plays a principal role in a joint crime. 2. *Accomplice*: one who plays a secondary or supplementary role in a joint crime. 3. *One who is coerced* into committing a crime. 4. *Instigator*.	Yes	Yes Mandatory discount for accomplices and those coerced into committing a crime. Discretionary discount for instigators.	A criminal gang is a more or less permanent criminal organisation composed of three or more persons for the purpose of jointly committing crimes. The head, who organises or leads a criminal gang, shall bear criminal responsibility for all the crimes committed by the gang.		Articles 25–28 Criminal Law of the People's Republic of China.

Country	Participants in crime	Term 'complicity' mentioned	Sentencing discount for any mode of participation	Conspiracy	Comments	Reference to legislation
Cuba	1. *Authors* (including those who execute, organise or use an innocent agent to commit crime). 2. *Accomplices* (including those who encourage others to commit a crime, facilitate its commission through advice or help its commission in other ways).	Yes	Yes Mandatory discount for accomplices.			Articles 18.1–19.1 Cuban Penal Code.
England	1. *Principals.* 2. *Whoever aids, abets, counsels or procures a principal.*	Not mentioned in the legislation, but in the doctrine.	No	Conspiracy occurs in both English and American law as a distinct offence, consummated upon entering into the agreement to commit criminal acts. Conspiracy also generates a standard for holding each conspirator complicitous in the crimes of fellow conspirators.	The general part of criminal law relies heavily on case law.	1861 Aiders and Abettors Act, case law.

Country	Participants in crime	Term 'complicity' mentioned	Sentencing discount for any mode of participation	Conspiracy	Comments	Reference to legislation
Estonia	1. Principal offender—unaided principal offender, the one committing crimes through an innocent agent and jointly with other offenders pursuant to an agreement embracing the elements of the offence. 2. *Accomplice*: a. *Abettor*: intentionally induces another person to commit an intentional unlawful act. b. *Aider*: intentionally provides physical, material or moral assistance to an intentional unlawful act of another person.	Yes	Yes Discretionary discount for aiders (category 2(b)). Mandatory discount for the accomplices who lack the specific personal characteristics, which pursuant to law constitute prerequisites for the liability of the principal offender.			Articles 20–24 Estonian Penal Code.

Country	Participants in crime	Term 'complicity' mentioned	Sentencing discount for any mode of participation	Conspiracy	Comments	Reference to legislation
Finland	1. *Accomplices*: two or more persons have committed an intentional offence together. 2. *Instigator*: intentionally persuades another person to commit an intentional offence. 3. *Abettor*: before or during the commission of an offence, intentionally furthers the commission by another of an intentional act or of its punishable attempt, through advice, action or otherwise.	Yes	Yes Mandatory discount if the perpetrator is convicted as an abettor, or his complicity in the offence is otherwise clearly less than that of other accomplices.			Chapter 5 (515/2003) Finnish Penal Code.
France	1. *Perpetrator*: commits the criminally prohibited act. 2. Accomplice: a. knowingly, by aiding and assisting, facilitates its preparation or commission; or b. by means of a gift, promise, threat, order, or an abuse of authority or powers incites the commission of an offence or gives instructions to commit it.	Yes	No	Conspiracy is a distinct offence defined as a criminal association established with a view to the preparation of the crime, marked by one or more material actions in furtherance of that crime.	Accomplice is punishable as a perpetrator.	Articles 121-4–121-7 French Penal Code.

Country	Participants in crime	Term 'complicity' mentioned	Sentencing discount for any mode of participation	Conspiracy	Comments	Reference to legislation
Georgia	1. *Performer (and co-performer)*. 2. *Organiser*: a person who organised the commission of a given crime or who guided its execution, as well as a person who created an organised criminal group. 3. *Abettor*: a person who inclined another person to the commission of a given crime by way of persuasion, subornation, threat, or by any other method. 4. *Accomplice*: a person who cooperated in the commission of a crime by advice, instructions, granting of information, instruments or means for the commission, or by elimination of the impediments for the commission of a crime etc.	Yes	No	The creator and/or organiser of a criminal group is liable in cases specified in the special part of the Penal Code.	Criminal liability of a participant in the crime shall be determined by the character and degree of participation of each participant in the commission of a given crime. The commission by a person of a crime which was not covered with the intent of other co-participants shall be recognised as an excess of a co-participant. Other participants in a given crime shall not be subject to criminal liability for an excess.	Articles 27–31 Georgian Penal Code.

Country	Participants in crime	Term 'complicity' mentioned	Sentencing discount for any mode of participation	Conspiracy	Comments	Reference to legislation
Germany	1. *Perpetrator*: commits the crime himself or through another. 2. *Co-perpetrator*: commits a crime jointly with one or more other people. 3. *Instigator*: intentionally induces another to commit an unlawful act. 4. *Accessory*: intentionally renders aid to another in that person's intentional commission of an unlawful act.	No	Yes Mandatory discount for accessories (category 4).	A person who declares his willingness or who accepts the offer of another or who agrees with another to commit or abet the commission of a felony shall be liable under the same terms.		Sections 25–30, 49 German Penal Code.
India	1. *Executors* 2. *Abettors*: a. instigators; b. Members of a conspiracy provided it results in an illegal act or omission c. aiders.	No	No	When two or more persons agree to do or cause to be done an illegal act, or an act which is not illegal by illegal means, such an agreement is designated a criminal conspiracy.	Abettors are punished for the result. Abettors are punished even in cases where the crime is not executed. Abettors are always removed from the scene of the crime. If they are present, they are deemed to have committed the offence.	Articles 107–20 Indian Penal Code.

Country	Participants in crime	Term 'complicity' mentioned	Sentencing discount for any mode of participation	Conspiracy	Comments	Reference to legislation
Indonesia	1. *Principals*: a. those who perpetrate, cause others to perpetrate or take a direct part in the execution of the act; b. those who provoke the execution of the act by gifts, promises, abuse of power etc. 2. *Accomplices*: a. those who deliberately aid in the commission of the crime; b. those who provide the opportunity, means and information for the commission of the crime.	Yes	Yes Mandatory discount for accomplices.		Complicity to commit a misdemeanour shall not be punished.	Articles 55–62 Indonesian Penal Code.

Country	Participants in crime	Term 'complicity' mentioned	Sentencing discount for any mode of participation	Conspiracy	Comments	Reference to legislation
Iraq	1. *Principal*: a. commits an offence by himself or with others; b. participates in the commission of an offence that consists of a number of acts and wilfully carries out one of those acts during the commission of that offence; c. incites another in any way to commit an act contributing to an offence if that person is not in any way criminally liable for the offence. 2. *Accessory*: a. incites another to commit an offence and that offence is committed on the basis of such incitement; b. conspires with others to commit an offence and that offence is committed on the basis of such conspiracy;	No	No	A criminal conspiracy is considered to be an agreement between two or more people to commit a felony or misdemeanour such as theft, fraud or forgery, whether or not it is a specified offence or arises out of acts that are aided and abetted, even though that agreement is in the initial planning stages or has been in existence only for a short time.	Any person who participates in the commission of an offence as a principal or an accessory is punishable by the penalty prescribed for that offence unless otherwise stipulated by law. An accessory is considered to be a principal to an offence if he is present during the commission of that offence or any act contributing to that offence.	§§ 47–59 Iraqi Penal Code.

Country	Participants in crime	Term 'complicity' mentioned	Sentencing discount for any mode of participation	Conspiracy	Comments	Reference to legislation
	c. knowingly supplies the principal to an offence with a weapon, instrument or anything else to commit an offence or deliberately assists him in any other way to carry out those acts for which he has received assistance.					
Israel	1. *Perpetrator*: a. perpetrator; b. joint perpetrator (performing all acts jointly or having some acts performed by another person); c. perpetrator using another person as an instrument. 2. *Instigator*: causes another to commit an offence by means of persuasion, encouragement, demand or cajolery. 3. *Accessory*: if a person does anything, before an offence is committed or during its commission, to make its commission possible, to support or protect it, or to prevent the perpetrator from being taken or the offence or its proceeds from being discovered, or if he contributes in any other way to the creation of conditions for the commission of the offence.	No	Yes Mandatory discount for accessories (category 3).			Articles 29–34 Israeli Penal Code.

Country	Participants in crime	Term 'complicity' mentioned	Sentencing discount for any mode of participation	Conspiracy	Comments	Reference to legislation
Italy	*Persons cooperating in crime.*	No	No Penalty is increased for those who led others to cooperate.	Agreement to commit a crime is not punished if the crime is not carried out. Conspiracies to commit specific offences form an exception to the general rule.	Each of the co-operators is subject to penalties prescribed for the crime itself. Penalty can be increased or decreased (within the sentencing range) using the provision on aggravating and mitigating circumstances.	Articles 110–18 Italian Penal Code.
Japan	1. *Principals.* 2. *Accomplices*: a. co-principals; b. inducers; c. aiders.	Yes	Yes Mandatory sentencing discount for aiders (category 2(c)).	A person who did not actually take part in committing a crime, but masterminded it and conspired with others, is usually punished as a principal because, as held by the Supreme Court, he uses the acts of the others as an instrument to commit a crime (judgment of the Supreme Court, 28 May 1958, *Keishu* 12-8-1718).		Articles 60–65 Japanese Penal Code.

Country	Participants in crime	Term 'complicity' mentioned	Sentencing discount for any mode of participation	Conspiracy	Comments	Reference to legislation
Kenya	1. *Actual perpetrator.* 2. *A person who does or omits to do any act for the purpose of enabling or aiding* another person to commit the offence. 3. *A person who aids or abets* another person in committing the offence; 4. *A person who counsels or procures* any other person to commit the offence.	No	No		Each of the participants in the crime is deemed to have committed the offence and is guilty of that offence.	Articles 20–23 Kenyan Penal Code.
Norway	Modes of participation are not listed in the general part of the code; rather, they form a part of the description of specific offences in the special part of the code.	No	No Depending on the particular offence in question, the same penalty is fixed for all participants in the crime.	Conspiracy to commit certain crimes is punishable—for example, conspiracy to commit a homicide.		

Country	Participants in crime	Term 'complicity' mentioned	Sentencing discount for any mode of participation	Conspiracy	Comments	Reference to legislation
Philippines	1. *Principals*: a. those who take a direct part in the execution of the act; b. those who directly force or induce others to commit it; c. those who cooperate in the commission of the offence by another act without which it would not have been accomplished. 2. *Accomplices*: persons who, not being principals, cooperate in the execution of the offence by previous or simultaneous acts. 3. *Accessories*: persons who knowingly take part in the crime subsequent to its commission by various forms of assistance.	Yes	Yes Sentencing discount by one degree for accomplices (category 2) and two degrees for accessories (category 3).	Conspiracy exists when two or more persons come to an agreement concerning the commission of a felony and decide to commit it. Conspiracy is only punishable when the law specifically provides for this.	Accessories are only punished for grave felonies.	Articles 8, 16–20, 52–59 Philippines Penal Code.

Country	Participants in crime	Term 'complicity' mentioned	Sentencing discount for any mode of participation	Conspiracy	Comments	Reference to legislation
Poland	1. *Perpetrators*: a. actual perpetrator; b. joint perpetrator; c. the one who ordered the commission of the act; d. the one who directed the commission of the act. 2. *Instigators*. 3. *Aiders and abettors*: a. the one who, with intent that another person should commit a prohibited act, facilitates by his behaviour the commission of the act, particularly by providing the instrument, means of transport, or giving counsel or information; b. the one who, acting against a particular legal duty of preventing the prohibited act, facilitates its commission by another person through his omission.	No	Yes Discretionary mitigation for aiders and abetters (category 3).		Each person cooperating in the perpetration of a prohibited act shall be liable within the limits of his intent or a lack of it, irrespective of the liability of others cooperating in the perpetration.	Articles 18–24 Polish Penal Code.

Country	Participants in crime	Term 'complicity' mentioned	Sentencing discount for any mode of participation	Conspiracy	Comments	Reference to legislation
Russia	1. *Perpetrator* (including joint perpetrator and perpetrator using an innocent agent). 2. *Organiser*: one who has organised the commission of a crime or has directed its commission—also a person who has created an organised group. 3. *Instigator*: one who has abetted another person in committing a crime by persuasion, bribery, threat or by any other method. 4. *Aider*: one who has assisted in the commission of a crime by advice, instructions on committing the crime, the removal of obstacles to it etc.	Yes (as an umbrella term for all the participants in the crime).	No	The creator and/or organiser of a criminal group is liable in cases specified in the special part of the Penal Code.	The responsibility of accomplices in a crime shall be determined by the character and the degree of the actual participation of each in the commission of the crime. The commission of a crime that is not covered by the intent of other accomplices shall be deemed to be an excess of the perpetrator. Other accomplices to the crime shall not be subject to criminal responsibility for the excess of the perpetrator.	Articles 32–36, 67 Russian Penal Code.

Country	Participants in crime	Term 'complicity' mentioned	Sentencing discount for any mode of participation	Conspiracy	Comments	Reference to legislation
Switzerland	1. *Perpetrator*. 2. *Those who intentionally participate in crime*	No	Yes Mandatory discount for those who intentionally provided assistance to the perpetrator.			Articles 24–27 Swiss Penal Code.
United Arab Emirates	1. *Principal*. 2. *Accomplice*: a. direct accomplice: i. joint perpetrator, ii. perpetrator of an act that constitutes part of the crime, iii. perpetrator through an innocent agent; b. accomplice to crime by causation: i. abettor, ii. conspirator, iii. aider (by providing weapons, tools and facilitating the commission of the crime by other means).	Yes	No		Accomplices are punished for the result, even if the other crime was intended. Whoever takes part in a crime in his capacity as a direct or causative accomplice shall receive the penalty for said crime unless the law provides otherwise.	Articles 44–52 UAE Penal Code.

Country	Participants in crime	Term 'complicity' mentioned	Sentencing discount for any mode of participation	Conspiracy	Comments	Reference to legislation
US	1. *Direct perpetrator*: one who personally engages in the proscribed conduct. 2. *Indirect perpetrator*: one who causes an innocent or irresponsible person to engage in the proscribed conduct. 3. *Accomplice*: one who, with the purpose of promoting or facilitating the commission of the offence: a. solicits such other person to commit it; b. aids or agrees or attempts to aid such other person in planning or committing it.	Yes	No Each person's criminal liability should reflect his individual culpability.	Conspiracy exists in both English and American law as a distinct offence, consummated upon entering into the agreement to commit criminal acts. Conspiracy also generates a standard for holding each conspirator complicitous in the crimes of fellow conspirators.	American law is highly fragmented due to the existence of both federal and state legal systems and because not all states have adopted the Model Penal Code.	Section 2.06 Model Penal Code.
Venezuela	1. *Perpetrator*. 2. *Immediate cooperator*. 3. *Instigator*. 4. *Accessories* (facilitating the commission of the crime, providing means and assistance before or after the act).	No	Yes Mandatory discount for accessories (category 4) provided their aid was not indispensable for the commission of the crime.			Articles 83–84 Venezuelan Penal Code.

Appendix II

The Correlation between the Forms of Liability and Sentencing

Name of the accused	Level	Date	Crimes	Mode of participation	Sentence length/number of years
			ICTY		
Aleksovski Zlatko	Appeal	24 March 2000	Outrages upon personal dignity	Aiding and abetting, superior responsibility	7
Babić, Milan	Appeal	18 July 2005	Persecutions on political, racial and religious grounds	Joint criminal enterprise	13
Bala, Haradin	Appeal	27 September 2007	Torture, cruel treatment, murder	Direct perpetration (murder and cruel treatment), aiding and abetting torture	17
Banović, Predrag (guilty plea)	Trial	28 October 2003	Persecutions on political, racial or religious grounds	Joint criminal enterprise	8
Beara, Ljubiša	Appeal	30 January 2015	Genocide, conspiracy to commit genocide, extermination, murder, persecutions	Joint criminal enterprise	Life
Blagojević, Vidoje	Appeal	9 May 2007	Murder, persecutions on political, racial and religious grounds and inhumane acts, forcible transfer	Aiding and abetting	15

Name of the accused	Level	Date	Crimes	Mode of participation	Sentence length/number of years
Blaškić, Tihomir	Appeal	29 July 2004	Inhumane treatment	Perpetration, ordering, planning, aiding and abetting	
Borovčanin, Ljubomir (guilty plea)	Trial	10 June 2010	Extermination, persecutions, forcible transfer and murder	Aiding and abetting	17
Brahimaj, Lahi	Appeal	21 July 2010	Cruel treatment and torture	Perpetration	6
Bralo, Miroslav (guilty plea)	Appeal	2 April 2007	Murder, persecutions on political, racial and religious grounds, rape, torture, inhumane treatment	Perpetration	20
Brđanin, Radoslav	Appeal	3 April 2007	Persecutions, torture, deportation, inhumane acts (forcible transfer), wanton destruction of cities, towns or villages or devastation not justified by military necessity, destruction or wilful damage done to institutions dedicated to religion, wilful killing, torture	Aiding and abetting, instigating	30
Čerkez, Mario	Appeal	17 December 2004	Persecutions on political, racial, or religious grounds, imprisonment, unlawful confinement of civilians	Co-perpetration, superior responsibility	6
Češić, Ranko (guilty plea)	Trial	11 March 2004	Murder, humiliating and degrading treatment	Perpetration	18

Name of the accused	Level	Date	Crimes	Mode of participation	Sentence length/number of years
Ćorić, Valentin	Trial	29 May 2013	Persecutions, cruel treatment, unlawful labour, inhumane treatment, wilful killing, unlawful deportation	Joint criminal enterprise	16
Delić, Hazim	Appeal	8 April 2003	Wilful killings, torture, wilfully causing great suffering or serious injury, inhuman treatment	Perpetration	18
Delić, Rasim	Trial	15 September 2008	Cruel treatment	Superior responsibility	3
Deronjić, Miroslav (guilty plea)	Appeal	25 July 2005	Persecutions on political, racial and religious grounds	Joint criminal enterprise	10
Đorđević, Vlastimir	Appeal	23 February 2011	Deportation, other inhumane acts (forcible transfer), murder, persecutions on political, racial and religious grounds, murder	Joint criminal enterprise, aiding and abetting	27
Došen, Damir (guilty plea)	Trial	13 November 2001	Persecutions on political, racial or religious grounds	Superior responsibility	5
Erdemović, Dražen (guilty plea)	Trial	5 March 1998	Murder	Perpetration	5
Furundžija, Anto	Appeal	21 July 2000	Torture, outrages upon personal dignity, including rape	Co-perpetration, aiding and abetting	10

Name of the accused	Level	Date	Crimes	Mode of participation	Sentence length/number of years
Galić, Stanislav	Appeal	30 November 2006	Acts of violence the primary purpose of which is to spread terror among the civilian population, as set forth in Article 51 of Additional Protocol I to the Geneva Conventions of 1949, murder and other inhumane acts	Ordering	Life
Gvero, Milan	Trial	10 June 2010	Persecutions and forcible transfer	Joint criminal enterprise	5
Hadžihasanović, Enver	Appeal	22 April 2008	Cruel treatment	Superior responsibility	3,5
Jelisić, Goran	Appeal	5 July 2001	Murder, cruel treatment, plunder, inhumane acts	Perpetration (not specified)	40
Jokić, Dragan	Appeal	9 May 2007	Extermination, persecutions on political, racial and religious grounds and murder	Aiding and abetting	9
Josipović, Drago	Appeal	23 October 2001	Persecutions on political, racial or religious grounds, murder, inhumane acts	Perpetration, co-perpetration	12
Kolundžija, Dragan (guilty plea)	Trial	13 November 2001	Persecutions on political, racial or religious grounds	Superior responsibility	3

Name of the accused	Level	Date	Crimes	Mode of participation	Sentence length/number of years
Kordić, Dario	Appeal	17 December 2004	Unlawful attack on civilians, unlawful attack on civilian objects, wanton destruction not justified by military necessity, plunder of public or private property, destruction or wilful damage to institutions dedicated to religion or education	Planning, instigating, ordering	25
Kos, Milojica	Trial	2 November 2001	Persecutions on political, racial or religious grounds, murder, inhumane acts, murder, torture	Joint criminal enterprise	6
Kovač, Radomir	Appeal	12 June 2002	Rape, enslavement	Perpetration, aiding and abetting	20
Krajišnik, Momčilo	Appeal	17 March 2009	Persecution on political, racial or religious grounds, deportation, inhumane acts (forced transfer)	Joint criminal enterprise	20
Krnojelac, Milorad	Appeal	17 September 2003	Torture, murder, persecutions and cruel treatment	Joint criminal enterprise, superior responsibility	15
Krstić, Radislav	Appeal	19 April 2004	Genocide, murders, extermination and persecutions	Aiding and abetting	35
Kubura, Amir	Appeal	22 April 2008	Plunder of public or private property	Superior responsibility	2

Name of the accused	Level	Date	Crimes	Mode of participation	Sentence length/number of years
Kunarac, Dragoljub	Appeal	12 June 2002	Torture, rape, enslavement	Perpetration, aiding and abetting	28
Kvočka, Miroslav	Appeal	28 February 2005	Persecutions on political, racial or religious grounds, murder, torture	Joint criminal enterprise	7
Landžo, Esad	Appeal	8 April 2003	Wilful killing, torture, wilfully causing great suffering or serious injury	Perpetration	9
Lazarević, Vladimir	Appeal	23 January 2014	Deportation, other inhumane acts (forcible transfer)	Aiding and abetting	14
Lukić, Milan	Appeal	4 December 2012	Persecutions on political, racial and religious grounds, murder, inhumane acts, and extermination, murder and cruel treatment	Perpetration	Life
Lukić, Sredoje	Appeal	4 December 2012	Inhumane acts, aiding and abetting persecutions on political, racial and religious grounds, murder, cruel treatment	Perpetration, aiding and abetting	27
Lukić, Sreten	Appeal	23 January 2014	Deportation, other inhumane acts (forcible transfer), murder, persecutions on political, racial or religious grounds, murder	Joint criminal enterprise	20

Name of the accused	Level	Date	Crimes	Mode of participation	Sentence length/number of years
Martić, Milan	Appeal	8 October 2008	Persecutions on political, racial and religious grounds, murder, imprisonment, torture, inhumane acts, deportation, inhumane acts (forcible transfers), wanton destruction of villages or devastation not justified by military necessity, destruction or wilful damage done to institutions dedicated to education or religion, plunder of public or private property, attacks on civilians	Joint criminal enterprise	35
Martinović, Vinko	Appeal	3 May 2006	Inhumane treatment, wilfully causing great suffering or serious injury to body or health, wilful killing, unlawful transfer of a civilian, unlawful labour, plunder of public or private property, persecutions on political, racial and religious grounds, inhumane acts, murder	Perpetration, ordering, aiding and abetting, instigation, superior responsibility	18
Miletić, Radivoje	Appeal	30 January 2015	Murder, persecutions, forcible transfer	Joint criminal enterprise	18

Name of the accused	Level	Date	Crimes	Mode of participation	Sentence length/number of years
Milošević, Dragomir	Appeal	12 November 2009	Terror, murder and inhumane acts	Ordering, superior responsibility	29
Mrđa, Darko (guilty plea)	Trial	31 March 2004	Murder, inhumane acts	Perpetration	17
Mrkšić, Mile	Appeal	5 May 2009	Murder, torture, cruel treatment	Aiding and abetting	20
Mucić, Zdravko	Appeal	8 April 2003	Wilfully causing great suffering or serious injury, unlawful confinement of civilians, wilful killings, torture, inhuman treatment	Superior responsibility	15
Naletilić, Mladen	Appeal	3 May 2006	Torture, wilfully causing great suffering or serious injury to body or health, unlawful transfer of a civilian, unlawful labour, wanton destruction not justified by military necessity, plunder of public or private property, persecutions on political, racial and religious grounds	Perpetration, ordering, aiding and abetting, instigation, superior responsibility	20
Nikolić, Dragan (guilty plea)	Appeal	4 February 2005	Persecutions on political, racial and religious grounds, murder, sexual violence, torture	Perpetration	20

Name of the accused	Level	Date	Crimes	Mode of participation	Sentence length/number of years
Nikolić, Drago	Appeal	30 January 2015	Genocide, extermination, murder, persecutions	Aiding and abetting genocide, joint criminal enterprise (persecutions)	35
Nikolić, Momir (guilty plea)	Appeal	8 March 2006	Persecutions on political, racial and religious grounds	Perpetration	20
Obrenović, Dragan (guilty plea)	Trial	10 December 2003	Persecutions on political, racial and religious grounds	Superior responsibility	17
Ojdanić, Dragoljub	Trial	26 February 2009	Deportation, other inhumane acts (forcible transfer)	Aiding and abetting	15
Pandurević, Vinko	Appeal	30 January 2015	Murder, persecutions, extermination, forcible transfer	Aiding and abetting, superior responsibility	13
Pavković, Nebojša	Appeal	23 January 2014	Deportation, other inhumane acts (forcible transfer), murder, persecutions on political, racial or religious grounds	Joint criminal enterprise	22
Petković, Milivoj	Trial	29 May 2013	Persecutions, cruel treatment, unlawful labour, inhumane treatment, wilful killing, unlawful deportation	Joint criminal enterprise	20
Plavšić, Biljana (guilty plea)	Trial	27 February 2003	Persecutions on political, racial and religious grounds	Individual criminal responsibility	11

Name of the accused	Level	Date	Crimes	Mode of participation	Sentence length/number of years
Popović, Vujadin	Appeal	30 January 2015	Genocide, conspiracy to commit genocide, extermination, murder, persecutions	Joint criminal enterprise	Life
Praljak, Slobodan	Trial	29 May 2013	Persecutions, cruel treatment, unlawful labour, inhumane treatment, wilful killing, unlawful deportation	Joint criminal enterprise	20
Prcać, Dragoljub	Appeal	28 February 2005	Persecutions on political, racial or religious grounds, murder, torture	Joint criminal enterprise	5
Prlić, Jadranko	Trial	29 May 2013	Persecutions, cruel treatment, unlawful labour, inhumane treatment, wilful killing, unlawful deportation	Joint criminal enterprise	25
Pušić, Berislav	Trial	29 May 2013	Persecutions, cruel treatment, unlawful labour, inhumane treatment, wilful killing, unlawful deportation	Joint criminal enterprise	10
Radić, Mlađo	Appeal	28 February 2005	Persecutions on political, racial or religious grounds, murder, inhumane acts, torture	Joint criminal enterprise	20

Name of the accused	Level	Date	Crimes	Mode of participation	Sentence length/number of years
Rajić, Ivica (guilty plea)	Trial	8 May 2006	Wilful killing, inhumane treatment (including sexual assault), appropriation of property, extensive destruction not justified by military necessity and carried out unlawfully and wantonly	Planning and ordering	12
Šainović, Nikola	Appeal	23 January 2014	Deportation, other inhumane acts (forcible transfer), murder, persecutions on political, racial or religious grounds, murder	Joint criminal enterprise	18
Šantić, Vladimir	Appeal	23 October 2001	Persecutions on political, racial or religious grounds, murder, inhumane acts	Perpetration, co-perpetration	18
Sikirica, Duško (guilty plea)	Trial	13 November 2001	Persecutions on political, racial or religious grounds	Superior responsibility, perpetration	15
Simić, Blagoje	Appeal	28 November 2006	Persecutions, cruel and inhumane treatment including beatings, torture, forced labour, and confinement under inhumane conditions, and deportation and forcible transfer	Aiding and abetting	15
Simić, Milan (guilty plea)	Trial	17 October 2002	Torture	Perpetration	5

Name of the accused	Level	Date	Crimes	Mode of participation	Sentence length/number of years
Šljivančanin, Veselin	Appeal	8 December 2010	Torture	Aiding and abetting	10
Stakić, Milomir	Appeal	22 March 2006	Extermination, murder and persecutions	Joint criminal enterprise	40
Stanišić, Mićo	Trial	27 March 2013	Persecutions on political, racial or religious grounds, murder and torture	Joint criminal enterprise	22
Stojić, Bruno	Trial	29 May 2013	Persecutions, cruel treatment, unlawful labour, inhumane treatment, wilful killing, unlawful deportation	Joint criminal enterprise	20
Strugar, Pavle	Appeal	17 July 2008	Attacks on civilians, destruction or wilful damage done to institutions dedicated to religion, charity and education, the arts and sciences, historic monuments and works of art and science, devastation not justified by military necessity, unlawful attacks on civilian objects.	Superior responsibility	7,5
Tadić, Duško	Appeal	26 January 2000	Wilful killing, torture or inhuman treatment and murder	Joint criminal enterprise	20

Name of the accused	**Level**	**Date**	**Crimes**	**Mode of participation**	**Sentence length/number of years**
Tadić, Miroslav (guilty plea)	Trial	17 October 2003	Persecutions based upon deportation and forcible transfer	Aiding and abetting	8
Tarčulovski, Johan	Appeal	19 My 2010	Murder, wanton destruction, cruel treatment	Ordering, planning and instigating	12
Todorović, Stevan (guilty plea)	Trial	31 July 2001	Persecutions on political, racial and religious grounds	Ordering, perpetration, superior responsibility	10
Tolimir, Zdravko	Appeal	8 April 2015	Genocide, conspiracy to commit genocide, extermination, murder, persecutions and forcible transfer	Joint criminal enterprise	Life
Vasiljević, Mitar	Appeal	25 February 2004	Persecutions on political, racial or religious grounds and murder	Aiding and abetting	15
Vuković, Zoran	Appeal	12 June 2002	Torture and rape	Perpetration	12
Zarić, Simo	Trial	17 October 2003	Persecutions based upon cruel and inhumane treatment including beatings, torture, and confinement under inhumane conditions	Aiding and abetting	6
Zelenović, Dragan (guilty plea)	Appeal	31 October 2007	Torture and rape	Co-perpetration	15
Žigić, Zoran	Appeal	28 February 2005	Persecutions on political, racial or religious grounds, torture, cruel treatment	Joint criminal enterprise	25

Name of the accused	Level	Date	Crimes	Mode of participation	Sentence length/number of years
Župljanin, Stojan	Trial	27 March 2013	Persecutions on political, racial or religious grounds, extermination, murder and torture	Joint criminal enterprise	22
ICTR					
AKAYESU, Jean Paul	Appeal	1 June 2001	Genocide, incitement to commit genocide, rape, murder, cruel treatment	Perpetration, instigation, ordering and aiding and abetting	Life
BAGARAGAZA, Michel (guilty plea)	Trial	17 November 2009	Complicity in genocide	Individual criminal responsibility (substantial assistance)	8
BAGOSORA, Théoneste	Appeal	14 December 2011	Genocide, murder, extermination, rape, persecutions, serious violations of Article 3	Ordering, superior responsibility	35
BARAYAGWIZ, Jean Bosco	Appeal	28 November 2007	Genocide, extermination, persecution	Instigation, ordering	32
BIKINDI, Simon	Appeal	18 March 2010	Direct and public incitement to commit genocide	Perpetration	15
BISENGIMANA, Paul (guilty plea)	Trial	13 April 2006	Extermination	Aiding and abetting	15
BIZIMUNGU, Augustin	Appeal	30 June 2014	Genocide, murder, extermination, rape	Superior responsibility	30

Name of the accused	Level	Date	Crimes	Mode of participation	Sentence length/number of years
'GAA' (guilty plea)	Trial	4 December 2007	Giving false testimony	Perpetration	9 months
GACUMBITSI, Sylvestre	Appeal	7 July 2006	Genocide, extermination, murder and rape	Committing, ordering, instigating, aiding and abetting	Life
GATETE, Jean Baptiste	Appeal	9 October 2012	Genocide, extermination, conspiracy to commit genocide	Joint criminal enterprise	40
HATEGEKIMANA, Idelphonse	Appeal	8 March 2012	Genocide, rape, murder	Joint criminal enterprise	Life
IMANISHIMWE, Samuel	Appeal	7 July 2006	Torture, murder, cruel treatment, imprisonment	Ordering, aiding and abetting	12
KAJELIJELI, Juvénal	Appeal	23 May 2005	Genocide, direct and public incitement to commit genocide, extermination	Ordering, instigating, and aiding and abetting	45
KALIMANZIRA Callixte	Appeal	20 October 2010	Genocide	Aiding and abetting	25
KAMBANDA, Jean (guilty plea)	Trial	19 October 2000	Genocide	Instigation, aiding and abetting	Life
KAMUHANDA, Jean de Dieu	Appeal	19 September 2005	Genocide, extermination	Ordering	Life
KANYARUKIGA, Gaspard	Appeal	8 May 2012	Genocide, extermination	Planning	30

Name of the accused	Level	Date	Crimes	Mode of participation	Sentence length/number of years
KANYABASHI, Joseph	Appeal	14 December 2015	Direct and public incitement to commit genocide	Committing	20
KAREMERA, Edouard	Appeal	29 September 2014	Direct and public incitement to commit genocide, genocide, rape, extermination, and killing and causing violence to health and well-being	Committing, ordering, instigating	Life
KARERA, François	Appeal	2 February 2009	Genocide, extermination, murder	Instigating, committing, ordering, aiding and abetting	Life
KAYISHEMA, Clément	Appeal	1 June 2001	Genocide	Committing, instigating, ordering, aiding and abetting	Life
MUHIMANA, Mikaeli	Appeal	21 May 2007	Genocide, rape, murder	Instigating, committing, abetting	Life
MUNYAKAZI, Yussuf	Appeal	28 September 2011	Genocide, extermination	Commission	25
MUSEMA, Alfred	Appeal	16 November 2001	Genocide, extermination	Ordering, committing	Life
MUVUNYI, Tharcisse	Appeal	1 April 2011	Direct and public incitement to commit genocide	Committing	15

Name of the accused	Level	Date	Crimes	Mode of participation	Sentence length/number of years
NAHIMANA, Ferdinand	Appeal	28 November 2007	Direct and public incitement to commit genocide, persecution	Superior responsibility	30
NCHAMIHIGO, Simeon	Appeal	18 March 2010	Genocide, murder, inhumane acts	Ordering, instigating	40
NDAHIMANA, Gregoire	Appeal	16 December 2013	Genocide, extermination	Committing through joint criminal enterprise, superior responsibility	25
NDAYAMBAJE, Elie	Appeal	14 December 2015	Genocide, direct and public incitement to commit genocide, extermination, persecution	Instigating, aiding and abetting	47
NDINDABAHIZI, Emmanuel	Appeal	16 January 2007	Genocide, extermination	Committing, instigating, aiding and abetting	Life
NGEZE, Hassan	Appeal	28 November 2007	Genocide, incitement to commit genocide, extermination	Aiding and abetting	35
NGIRUMPATSE, Mathieu	Appeal	29 September 2014	Direct and public incitement to commit genocide, genocide, rape, extermination, and killing and causing violence to health and well-being	Committing, instigating, aiding and abetting	Life
NIYITEGEKA, Eliezer	Appeal	9 July 2004	Genocide, conspiracy to commit genocide, direct and public incitement to commit genocide, murder, extermination, other inhumane acts	Ordering	Life

Name of the accused	Level	Date	Crimes	Mode of participation	Sentence length/number of years
NIZEYIMANA, Idelphonse	Appeal	29 September 2014	Genocide and murder	Joint criminal enterprise, ordering	35
NSABIMANA, Sylvain	Appeal	14 December 2015	Genocide, extermination, violence to life, health and physical or mental well-being of persons	Aiding and abetting	18
NSENGIYUMVA, Anatole	Appeal	14 December 2011	Genocide, murder, extermination, persecutions, serious violations of Article 3	Ordering, aiding and abetting	15
NSHOGOZA, Léonidas	Appeal	15 May 2010	Contempt of the court	Committing	10 months
NTABAKUZE, Aloys	Appeal	14 December 2011	Genocide, murder, extermination, persecutions, serious violations of Article 3	Superior responsibility	Life
NTAHOBALI, Arsène Shalom	Appeal	14 December 2015	Rape, persecution, outrages upon personal dignity	Committing, ordering, and aiding and abetting, superior responsibility	47
NTAKIRUTIMANA, Elizaphan	Appeal	13 December 2004	Genocide, extermination	Aiding and abetting	10
NTAKIRUTIMANA, Gérard	Appeal	13 December 2004	Genocide, murder, extermination	Committing, aiding and abetting	25
NTAWUKULILYAYO, Dominique	Appeal	14 December 2013	Genocide	Aiding and abetting	20

Name of the accused	Level	Date	Crimes	Mode of participation	Sentence length/number of years
NTEZIRYAYO, Alphonse	Appeal	14 December 2015	Direct and public incitement to commit genocide	Not specified	25
NYIRAMASUHUKO, Pauline	Appeal	14 December 2015	Genocide, conspiracy to commit genocide, rape, outrages upon personal dignity	Ordering, superior responsibility	47
NZABIRINDA, Joseph (guilty plea)	Trial	23 February 2007	Murder	Not specified	7
NZABONIMANA, Callixte	Appeal	29 September 2014	Genocide, conspiracy to commit genocide, direct and public incitement to commit genocide, extermination	Committing, instigating	Life
RENZAHO, Tharcisse	Appeal	1 April 2011	Genocide, murder	Ordering, aiding abetting, superior responsibility	Life
RUGAMBARARA, Juvénal (guilty plea)	Trial	16 November 2007	Extermination	Superior responsibility	11
RUGGIU, Georges (guilty plea)	Trial	1 June 2000	Direct and public incitement to commit genocide, persecution	Committing	12
RUKUNDO, Emmanuel	Appeal	20 October 2010	Genocide, murder, extermination	Aiding and abetting	23
RUTAGANDA, George	Trial	6 December 1999	Genocide, extermination, murder	Committing, aiding and abetting	Life
RUTAGANIRA, Vincent (guilty plea)	Trial	14 May 2005	Extermination	Aiding and abetting (by omission)	6

Name of the accused	Level	Date	Crimes	Mode of participation	Sentence length/number of years
RUZINDANA, Obed	Appeal	1 June 2001		Committing, instigating, ordering, aiding and abetting	25
SAGAHUTU, Innocent	Appeal	11 February 2014	Murder	Committing, ordering, aiding and abetting	15
SEMANZA, Laurent	Appeal	10 May 2005	Genocide, complicity in genocide, extermination, rape, torture	Committing, aiding and abetting, ordering	35
SEROMBA, Athanase	Appeal	12 March 2008	Genocide, extermination	Committing, aiding and abetting	Life
SERUGENDO, Joseph (guilty plea)	Trial	12 June 2006	Genocide and persecution	Committing	6
SERUSHAGO, Omar (guilty plea)	Trial	5 February 1999	Genocide, murder, extermination, torture	Not specified	15
SETAKO, Ephrem	Appeal	28 September 2011	Genocide, extermination, murder	Committing, ordering	25
SIMBA, Aloys	Appeal	27 September 2007	Genocide, extermination	Joint criminal enterprise	25
SCSL					
Brima, Alex Tamba	Appeal	22 February 2008	Extermination, murders, act of terrorism, outrages upon personal dignity, sexual slavery and rape	Committing, ordering, planning, superior responsibility	50

Name of the accused	Level	Date	Crimes	Mode of participation	Sentence length/number of years
Fofana, Moinina	Appeal	28 May 2008	Murder, violence to life, health and physical or mental well-being of persons, other inhumane acts, pillage	Aiding and abetting, superior responsibility	15
Gbao, Augustine	Appeal	26 October 2009	Extermination, murder, rape, sexual slavery, other inhumane acts, violence to life, health and physical or mental well-being of persons, intentionally directing attacks against peacekeepers	Joint criminal enterprise	20
Kallon, Morris	Appeal	26 October 2009	Extermination, murder, rape, sexual slavery, other inhumane acts, violence to life, health and physical or mental well-being of persons, intentionally directing attacks against peacekeepers, conscripting or enlisting children under the age of 15 into armed forces or groups	Joint criminal enterprise	40
Kamara, Brima Bazzy	Appeal	22 February 2008	Extermination, murders, act of terrorism, outrages upon personal dignity, sexual slavery and rape	Ordering, planning, aiding and abetting	45

Name of the accused	Level	Date	Crimes	Mode of participation	Sentence length/number of years
Kanu, Santigie Borbor	Appeal	22 February 2008	Extermination, murders, act of terrorism, outrages upon personal dignity, sexual slavery and rape	Planning, superior responsibility	50
Kondewa, Allieu	Appeal	28 May 2008	Murder, violence to life, health and physical or mental well-being of persons, other inhumane acts, pillage, cruel treatment	Aiding and abetting, superior responsibility	20
Sesay, Issa Hassan	Appeal	26 October 2009	Extermination, murder, rape, sexual slavery, other inhumane acts, violence to life, health and physical or mental well-being of persons, intentionally directing attacks against peacekeepers, conscripting or enlisting children under the age of 15 into armed forces or groups	Joint criminal enterprise	42
Taylor, Charles	Appeal	26 September 2013	Murder, rape, enslavement, terrorism, outrages upon personal dignity, violence to life, health and physical or mental well-being of persons (in particular, cruel treatment), pillage	Planning, aiding and abetting	50

Name of the accused	Level	Date	Crimes	Mode of participation	Sentence length/number of years
			ICC		
German Katanga	Trial	23 May 2014	Murder, attacking a civilian population, destruction of property and pillaging.	Contribution to the crime committed by a group	12
Lubanga Dyilo, Thomas	Appeal	1 December 2014	Enlistment, conscription and use of children below the age of 15 to participate actively in hostilities	Direct co-perpetration	14
			ECCC		
KAING, Guek Eav alias 'DUCH'	Appeal	3 February 2012	Persecution, extermination (encompassing murder), enslavement, imprisonment, torture, and other inhumane acts.	Joint criminal enterprise, planning, instigating, ordering, aiding and abetting	Life
Nuon Chea and Khieu Samphan ('Case 002/01')	Trial	7 August 2014	Crimes against humanity	Joint criminal enterprise, planning, ordering, instigating, superior responsibility	Life

Bibliography

R Ago, 'Le délit international' (1939-II) *Recueil des Cours* 68

M Akehurst, 'Custom as a Source of International Law' (1976) 47 *British Yearbook of International Law* 1

M Aksenova, 'The Specific Requirement for Aiding and Abetting: A Call for Revisiting Comparative Criminal Law' (2015) 4(1) *Cambridge Journal of International and Comparative Law* 88

M Aksenova, 'The Modes of Liability at the ICC: The Labels That Don't Always Stick' (2015) 15 *International Criminal Law Review* 629

P Allott, 'State Responsibility and the Unmaking of International Law' (1998) 29 *Harvard Journal of International Law* 1

D Anzilotti, *Cours de Droit international* (Hudson, 1920–42)

A di Amato, *Criminal Law in Italy* (Alpen aan den Rijn, Wolters Kluwer, 2011)

K Ambos, 'The First Judgment of the International Criminal Court (Prosecutor v. *Lubanga*): A Comprehensive Analysis of the Legal Issues' (2012) 12 *International Criminal Law Review 2, 115*

K Ambos, 'Individual Criminal Responsibility' in GK McDonald and O Swaak-Goldman (eds), *Substantive and Procedural Aspects of International Criminal Law* (The Hague, Martinus Nijhoff 2000)

——. 'Commentary to Article 25 of the Rome Statute' in O Triffterer (ed) *Commentary on the Rome Statute of the International Criminal Court: Observers' Notes, Article by Article* (Baden-Baden: Nomos, 1999, Second Edition, 2003)

——. '*Nulla Poena Sine Lege* in International Criminal Law' in R Haveman and O Olusanya (eds), *Sentencing and Sanctioning in Supranational Criminal Law* (Antwerp, Intersentia, 2006)

——. *Treatise on International Criminal Law, Volume 1: Foundations and General Part* (Oxford, Oxford University Press, 2013)

H Arendt, *Eichmann in Jerusalem: A Report on the Banality of Evil* (New York, Viking Press, 1965)

A Ashworth, *Principles of Criminal Law*, 2nd edn (Oxford, Clarendon, 1995)

——. 'Techniques for Reducing Sentencing Disparity' in A von Hirsch, A Ashworth and J Roberts (eds), *Principled Sentencing*, 3rd edn (Oxford, Hart Publishing, 2009)

——. *Sentencing and Criminal Justice*, 5th edn (Oxford, Oxford University Press, 2010)

——. 'UK Criminal Law' in M Dubber and K Heller (eds), *The Handbook of Comparative Criminal Law* (Stanford, Stanford University Press, 2011)

A Aust, *Modern Treaty Law and Practice* (Cambridge, Cambridge University Press, 2000)

H Aust, *Complicity and Law of State Responsibility* (Cambridge, Cambridge University Press, 2013)

ME Badar, '*Dolus Eventualis* and the Rome Statute without it?' (2009) 12 *New Criminal Law Review* 3

M Bagaric, 'Double Punishment and Punishing Character: The Unfairness of Prior Convictions', in *Punishment and Sentencing: A Rational Approach* (London, Cavendish Publishing, 2001)

J Bell, S Boyron and S Whittaker (eds), *Principles of French Law* (Oxford, Oxford University Press, 2008)

C Beccaria, *On Crimes and Punishments and Other Writings* (1764), edited by A Thomas (University of Toronto Press, 2008)

J Bentham, Punishment and Deterrence, in A von Hirsch, A Ashworth and J Roberts (eds), *Principled Sentencing*, 3rd edn (Oxford, Hart Publishing, 2009)

M Bergsmo, M Harlem and N Hayashi (eds), *Importing Core International Crimes into National Law*, 2nd edn (Berlin, Torkel Opsahl Academic EPublisher, 2010)

GA Bermann and Etienne Picard, *Introduction to French Law* (Dordrecht, Kluwer Law International, 2008)

N Bernaz, 'Sentencing and Penalties' in W Schabas and N Bernaz (eds), *Routledge Handbook on International Criminal Law* (Abingdon, Routledge, 2009)

R Bernhardt, *Encyclopaedia of Public International Law* (Oxford, Oxford University Press, 2003)

N Birkett, 'The Law of the Nuremberg Trial' in G Mettraux (ed), *Perspectives on the Nuremberg Trial* (Oxford, Oxford University Press, 2008)

Black's Law Dictionary, 6th edn (St Paul, West Publishing, 1990)

G Boas, JL Bischoff, NL Reid, *International Criminal Law Practitioner Library International Criminal Procedure* (2 vols) (Cambridge, Cambridge University Press, 2007)

N Boister, *The Tokyo International Military Tribunal: A Reappraisal* (Oxford, Oxford University Press, 2008)

——. 'The Application of Collective and Comprehensive Criminal Responsibility for Aggression at the Tokyo International Military Tribunal' (2010) 8 *Journal of International Criminal Justice* 425

M Bohlander, *The German Criminal Code: A Modern English Translation* (Oxford, Hart Publishing, 2009)

A de Brouwer, 'Gacumbitsi Judgement' in Goran Sluiter and Andre Klip (eds), *Annotated Leading Cases of International Criminal Tribunals: The International Criminal Tribunal for Rwanda* (Antwerp, Intersentia, 2005–06)

I Brownlie, *Principles of Public International Law*, 7th edn (Oxford, Oxford University Press, 2008)

A Cassese, *International Criminal Law*, 2nd edn (Oxford, Oxford University Press, 2008)

——. (ed), *The Oxford Companion to International Criminal Justice* (Oxford, Oxford University Press, 2009)

A Cassese, P Gaeta and JRWD Jones (eds), *The Rome Statute of the International Criminal Court: A Commentary* (Oxford, Oxford University Press, 2002)

J Cerone, 'Re-examining International Responsibility: Complicity in the Context of Human Rights Violations' (2008) 14 *ILSA Journal of International and Comparative Law*

J Chen, *Chinese Law: Towards an Understanding of Chinese Law, its Nature and Development* (Dordrecht, Kluwer Law International, 1999)

B Cheng, *General Principles of Law as Applied by International Courts and Tribunals* (Cambridge, Cambridge University Press, 1987)

W. Chenguang and Z. Xianchu, *Introduction to Chinese Law* (Petaling Jaya, Sweet & Maxwell Asia, 1997)

A Clapham, 'Issues of Complexity, Complicity and Complementarity: from Nuremberg Trials to the Dawn of the Next International Criminal Court' in P Sands (ed), *From Nuremberg to the Hague: The Future of International Criminal Justice* (Cambridge, Cambridge University Press, 2003)

D Cohen, M Hyde and P van Tuyl, 'A Well-Reasoned Opinion? Critical Analysis of the First Case against the Alleged Senior Leaders of the Khmer Rouge (Case 002/01)', WSD HANDA CENTER for Human Rights and International Justice, Stanford University (EastWestCentre.org 2015)

P de Cruz, *Comparative Law in a Changing World*, 3rd edn (Abingdon, Routledge-Cavendish, 2007)

R Cryer, H Friman, D Robinson and E Wilmeshurst, *An Introduction to International Criminal Law and Procedure*, 2nd edn (Cambridge, Cambridge University Press, 2010)

M Damaška, 'What is the Point of International Criminal Justice?' (2008) 83 *Chicago-Kent Law Review* 329

AM Danner and JS Martinez, 'Guilty Associations: Joint Criminal Enterprise, Command Responsibility and the Development of International Criminal Law' (2005) 93 *California Law Review* 75

R David and JEC Brierley, *Major Legal Systems in the World Today: An Introduction to the Comparative Study of Law* (London, Stevens, 1985)

H Donnedieu de Vabres, 'Le process de Nuremberg devant les principes modernes du Droit Penal International [The Nuremberg Trial and the Modern Principles of International Criminal Law]' (1947-1) 70 *Recueil des Cours de l'Academie de droit international de la Haye* 477

M Drumbl, *Atrocity, Punishment, and International Law* (Cambridge, Cambridge University Press, 2007)

M D Dubber, 'Criminalizing Complicity: A Comparative Analysis' (2007) 5 *Journal of International Criminal Justice* 4

M Dubber and K Heller, 'Introduction' in M Dubber and K Heller (eds), *The Handbook of Comparative Criminal Law* (Stanford, Stanford University Press, 2011)

RA Duff, 'Punishment, Retribution and Communication' in A von Hirsch, A Ashworth and J Roberts (eds), *Principled Sentencing*, 3rd edn (Oxford, Hart Publishing, 2009)

E Durkheim, *The Division of Labour in Society* (New York, Free Press, 1984)

R Dworkin, *Taking Rights Seriously* (Cambridge, Mass, Harvard University Press, 1977)

C Eboe-Osuju, '"Complicity in Genocide" versus "Aiding and Abetting Genocide"' (2005) 3 *Journal of International Criminal Justice* 56

A Eser, 'The Importance of Comparative Legal Research for the Development of Criminal Sciences' in R Blancpain (ed), *Law in Motion: Recent Developments in Civil Procedure, Constitutional, Contract, Criminal, Environmental, Family & Succession, Intellectual Property, Labour, Medical, Social Security, Transport Law* (The Hague, Kluwer, 1997)

——. 'Individual Criminal Responsibility (Article 25)' in A Cassese et al (eds), *The Rome Statute of the International Criminal Court: A Commentary* (Oxford, Oxford University Press, 2002)
J Feinberg, *Doing and Deserving: Essays in the Theory of Responsibility* (Princeton, Princeton University Press, 1974)
G Fletcher, *Rethinking Criminal Law* (Boston, Little, Brown, 1978)
——. 'Law and Morality' (1987) 87 *Columbia Law Review* 533
——. *Basic Concepts of Criminal Law* (Oxford, Oxford University Press, 1998)
——. *The Grammar of Criminal Law* (Oxford, Oxford University Press, 2007)
J Gardner, 'Complicity and Causality' in *Offences and Defences: Selected Essays in the Philosophy of Criminal Law* (Oxford, Oxford Scholarship Online, 2007)
A Gattini, 'A Historical Perspective: From Collective to Individual Responsibility and Back' in A Nollkaemper and H van der Wilt (eds), *System Criminality in International Law* (Cambridge, Cambridge University Press, 2009)
M Giles, 'Complicity: The Problems of Joint Enterprise' [1990] *Criminal Law Review* 383
LC Green, 'Comparative Law as a Source of International Law' (1967) 42 *Tulane Law Review*, 52
K Gustafson, 'Case Note' in A Cassese (ed), *The Oxford Companion to International Criminal Justice* (Oxford, Oxford University Press, 2009)
V Haan, 'The Development of the Concept of Joint Criminal Enterprise at the ICTY' (2005) 5 *International Criminal Law Review* 167
J Habermas, *Between Facts and Norms: Contributions to a Discourse Theory between Law and Democracy* (Cambridge, MA, MIT Press, 1996)
K Hamdorf, 'The Concept of a JCE and Domestic Modes of Liability for Parties to a Crime' (2007) 5 *Journal of International Criminal Justice* 208
C Harding, 'Human Action or State Action? Locating the Site of Supranational Criminality' in R Haveman and O Olunsanya (eds), *Sentencing and Sanctioning in Supranational Criminal Law* (Antwerp, Intersentia, 2006)
MB Harmon and F Gaynor, 'Ordinary Sentences for Extraordinary Crimes' (2007) 5 *Journal of International Criminal Justice* 683
HLA Hart and J Gardner, *Punishment and Responsibility: Essays on Philosophy of Law* (Oxford, Oxford University Press, 2009)
HLA Hart and T Honoré, *Causation in the Law* (Oxford, Oxford University Press, 1985)
M Heikkilä, *Coping with International Atrocities through Criminal Law: A Study into the Typical Features of International Criminality and the Reflection of these Traits in International Criminal Law* (Turku, Åbo Akademi University Press, 2013)
K Heller, *The Nuremberg Military Tribunals and the Origins of International Criminal Law* (Oxford, Oxford University Press, 2011)
S Horwitz, 'The Tokyo Trial' (1950) *International Conciliation* 465
G Ireland 'Uncommon Law in Martial Tokyo' (1950) 4 *Year Book of World Affairs* 54
M Jackson, *Complicity in International Law* (Oxford, Oxford University Press, 2015)
R Jackson, 'Nuremberg in Retrospect: Legal Answer to International Lawlessness' (1949) XXXC *American Bar Association Journal* 813 and 881, reproduced in G Mettraux (ed), *Perspectives on the Nuremberg Trial* (Oxford, Oxford University Press, 2008)
RY Jennings, 'The Identification of International Law' in Bin Cheng (ed), *International Law, Teaching and Practice* (Stevens, London, 1982)

JRWD Jones and S Powles, *International Criminal Practice*, 3rd edn (Oxford, Oxford University Press, 2003)

W Jordash and J Coughlan, 'The Right to Be Informed of the Nature and Cause of the Charges: A Potentially Formidable Jurisprudential Legacy' in S Darcy and J Powderly (eds), *Judicial Creativity at the International Criminal Tribunals* (Oxford, Oxford University Press, 2010)

NHB Jorgensen, *The Responsibility of States for International Crimes* (Oxford, Oxford University Press, 2000)

SH Kadish, 'Complicity, Cause and Blame: A Study in the Interpretation of Doctrine' (1985) 73 *California Law Review* 2

I Kant, *The Metaphysics of Morals* (Cambridge, Cambridge University Press, 1991 [1797])

K Khan and R Dixon (eds), *Archbold: International Criminal Courts. Practice, Procedure and Evidence* (London, Sweet & Maxwell, 2005)

H Kelsen, *The Law of the United Nations: A Critical Analysis of its Fundamental Problems* (London, Stevens, 1950)

K Kittichaisaree, *International Criminal Law* (Oxford, Oxford University Press, 2002)

G Knoops, *Theory and Practice of International and Internationalized Criminal Proceedings* (Dordrecht, Kluwer Law International, 2007)

C Kutz, *Complicity: Ethics and Law for a Collective Age* (Cambridge, Cambridge University Press, 2000)

——. 'The Philosophical Foundations of Complicity Law' in J Deigh and D Dolinko (eds), *The Handbook of Philosophy of Criminal Law* (Oxford, Oxford University Press, 2011)

H Lauterpacht, *The Development of International Law by the International Court* (Cambridge, Cambridge University Press, 1958)

D Lipstadt, *The Eichmann Trial* (New York, Nextbook Press, 2011)

D Luban, 'After Honey Moon: Reflections on the Current State of International Criminal Justice' (2013) 11 *Journal of International Criminal Justice* 505

S Manacorda and C Meloni, 'Indirect Perpetration versus Joint Criminal Enterprise: Concurring Approaches in the Practice of International Criminal Law' (2011) 9 *Journal of International Criminal Justice* 1

S Manacorda in A Cassese (ed), *The Oxford Companion to International Criminal Justice* (Oxford, Oxford University Press, 2009)

M Mennecke, 'Punishing Genocidaires: A Deterrent Effect or Not?' (2007) 8 *Human Rights Law Review* 319

G Mettraux, *International Criminal and Ad Hoc Tribunals* (Oxford, Oxford University Press, 2005)

——. *The Law of Command Responsibility* (Oxford, Oxford University Press, 2009).

——. (ed), *Perspectives on the Nuremberg Trial* (Oxford, Oxford University Press, 2008)

S Milgram, *Obedience to Authority: An Experimental View* (Tavistock, Pinter & Martin, 1974)

J S Mill, 'On Liberty' in L May and J Brown (eds), *Philosophy of Law: Classic and Contemporary Readings* (Chichester, Wiley-Blackwell, 2011)

S Mohamed, 'Deviance, Aspiration, and the Stories We Tell: Reconciling Mass Atrocity and the Criminal Law (2015) 124 *Yale Law Journal* 1628

M Moore, 'Causation in the Criminal Law' J Deigh and D Dolinko (eds), *The Handbook of Philosophy of Criminal Law* (Oxford, Oxford University Press, 2011)

K Nahapetian, 'Confronting State Complicity in International Law' (2002) 7 *UCLA Journal of International Law and Foreign Affairs* 99

A Nollkaemper, 'Introductions' in A Nollkaemper and H.V.D Wilt (eds), *System Criminality in International Law* (Cambridge, Cambridge University Press, 2009)

A Nollkaemper and H van der Wilt, 'Conclusions and Outlook' in A Nollkaemper and H van der Wilt (eds), *System Criminality in International Law* (Cambridge, Cambridge University Press, 2009)

J Ohlin, 'Joint Intentions to Commit International Crimes' (2011) 11 *Chicago Journal of International Law* 693

——. 'Proportional Sentences at the ICTY' in B Swaart, A Zahar and G Sluiter (eds), *The Legacy of the International Criminal Tribunal for the Former Yugoslavia* (Oxford, Oxford University Press, 2011)

H Olasolo, 'Complementarity Analysis of National Sentencing' in R Haveman and O Olunsanya (eds), *Sentencing and Sanctioning in Supranational Criminal Law* (Antwerp, Intersentia, 2006)

——. *The Criminal Responsibility of Senior Political and Military Leaders as Principals to International Crimes* (Oxford, Hart Publishing, 2009)

——. 'Complementarity Analysis of National Sentencing' in *Essays on International Criminal Justice* (Oxford, Hart Publishing, 2012)

——. *Essays on International Criminal Justice* (Oxford, Hart Publishing, 2012)

R Overy, 'The Nuremberg Trials: International Law in the Making' in P Sands (ed), *From Nuremberg to the Hague: The Future of International Criminal Justice* (Cambridge, Cambridge University Press, 2003)

M Osiel, 'The Banality of Good: Aligning Incentives against Mass Atrocities' (2005) 105 *Columbia Law Review* 1751

——. *Making Sense of Mass Atrocity* (Cambridge, Cambridge University Press, 2009)

A Pellet, 'Can a State Commit a Crime? Definitely, Yes!' (1999) 10 *European Journal of International Law* 425

S Powles, 'Joint Criminal Enterprise: Criminal Liability by Prosecutorial Ingenuity and Judicial Creativity?' (2004) 2 *Journal of International Criminal Justice* 606

FO Raimondo, *General Principles of Law in the Decisions of International Criminal Courts and Tribunals* (The Hague, Martinus Nijhoff, 2008)

——. 'General Principles of Law, Judicial Creativity, and the Development of International Criminal Law' in S Darcy and J Powderly (eds), *Judicial Creativity at the International Criminal Tribunals* (Oxford, Oxford University Press, 2010)

A Reinisch, 'Aid or Assistance and Direction and Control between States and International Organizations in the Commission of Internationally Wrongful Acts' (2010) 7 *International Organizations Law Review* 63

J Roberts, *Punishing Persistent Offenders: Community and Offender Perspectives* (Oxford, Oxford University Press, 2008)

P Roberts, 'Comparative Law for International Criminal Justice' in E Orucu and D Nelken (eds), *Comparative Law: A Handbook* (Oxford, Hart Publishing, 2007)

D Robinson, 'Identity Crisis of International Criminal Law' (2008) 21 *Leiden Journal of International Law* 4

P H Robinson, 'Comparative Summary of American Criminal Law' in M Dubber and K Heller (eds), *The Handbook of Comparative Criminal Law* (Stanford, Stanford University Press, 2011)

C Romano, A Nollkaemper and J Kleffner, *Internationalized Criminal Courts* (Oxford, Oxford University Press, 2004)

——. 'Crimes as Part of Organized Power Structures' (1963) *Goltdammer's Archiv für Strafrecht* 193

C Roxin, *Täterschaft und Tatherrschaft*, 6th edn (Berlin, de Gruyter, 1994)

L Sadat and J Jolly, 'Seven Canons of ICC Treaty Interpretation: Making Sense of Article 25's Rorschach Blot' (2014) 27 *Leiden Journal of International Law* 755

P Saland, 'International Criminal Law Principles' in Roy Lee (ed), *The International Criminal Court-The Making of the Rome Statute: Issues, Negotiations, Results* (Dordrecht, Kluwer Law International, 1999)

W. Schabas, 'Enforcing International Humanitarian Law: Catching the Accomplices' (2001) 83 *International Review of the Red Cross* 842

——. *The UN International Criminal Tribunals: The Former Yugoslavia, Rwanda and Sierra Leone* (Cambridge, Cambridge University Press, 2006)

——. *An Introduction to the International Criminal Court*, 3rd edn (Cambridge, Cambridge University Press, 2007)

——. *The International Criminal Court: A Commentary on the Rome Statute* (Oxford, Oxford University Press, 2010)

M Shaw, *International Law*, 6th edn (Cambridge, Cambridge University Press, 2008)

J Shklar, *Legalism: An Essay on Law, Morals and Politics* (Cambridge, Mass, Harvard University Press, 1964)

U Sieber, 'Participation in Crime: Criminal Liability of Leaders of Criminal Groups and Networks, A Comparative Analysis' in *Expert Opinion by the Max Planck Institute for Foreign and International Criminal Law as Commissioned by the ICTY* (Freiburg, Max Planck Institute Report, 2006)

B Simma and P Alston, 'The Sources of Human Rights Law: Custom, *Jus Cogens*, and General Principles' (1988–89) 12 *Australian Yearbook of International Law* 82

I Sinclair, *The Vienna Convention on the Law of Treaties* (Manchester, Manchester University Press, 1984)

R Skilbeck, 'Case Note' in A Cassese (ed), *The Oxford Companion to International Criminal Justice* (Oxford, Oxford University Press, 2009)

E van Sliedregt, *The Criminal Responsibility of Individuals for Violations of International Humanitarian Law* (The Hague, TMC Asser Press, 2003)

——. 'System Criminality at the ICTY' in A Nollkaemper and H van der Wilt (ed), *System Criminality in International Law* (Cambridge, Cambridge University Press, 2009)

——. *Individual Criminal Responsibility in International Law* (Oxford, Oxford University Press, 2012)

RD Sloane, 'Sentencing for the "Crime of Crimes": The Evolving "Common Law" of Sentencing of the International Criminal Tribunal for Rwanda' (2007) 5 *Journal of International Criminal Justice*

JC Smith and B Hogan, *Criminal Law*, 10th edn (London, Butterworths, 2002)

KJM Smith, *A Modern Treatise on the Law of Criminal Complicity* (Oxford, Clarendon, 1991)

R Steinke, *The Politics of International Criminal Justice: German Perspectives from Nuremberg to the Hague* (Oxford, Hart Publishing, 2012)

J Stewart, 'The End of "Modes of Liability" for International Crimes' (2012) 25 *Leiden Journal of International Law* 165

LS Sunga, *The Emerging System of International Criminal Law* (The Hague, Martinus Nijhoff, 1997)

I Tallgren, 'The Sensibility and Sense of International Criminal Law' (2002) 13 *European Journal of International Law* 3

V Thalmann, 'Case Note' in A Cassese (ed), *The Oxford Companion to International Criminal Justice* (Oxford, Oxford University Press, 2009)

CA Thomas, 'The Uses and Abuses of Legitimacy in International Law' (2014) 34(4) *Oxford Journal of Legal Studies* 729

D Turns, 'Application of the Convention on the Prevention and Punishment of the Crime of Genocide. Bosnia and Herzegovina v. Serbia and Montenegro' (2007) 8 *Melbourne Journal of International Law* 398

A Verdross, 'Jus Dispositivum and Jus Cogens in International Law' (1966) 60 *American Journal of International Law* 57

G Vetter, 'Command Responisibility of Non-military Superiors in the International Criminal Court' (2000) 25 *Yale Journal of International Law* 89

GB Vold, TJ Bernard and JB Snipes, *Theoretical Criminology*, 4th edn (Oxford, Oxford University Press, 1998)

T Weigend, 'Perpetration through an Organization: The Unexpected Career of a German Legal Concept' (2011) 9 *Journal of International Criminal Justice* 91

R Weisberg, 'The Model Penal Code Revisited: Reappraising Complicity' (2000) 4 *Buffalo Criminal Law Review* 217

G Werle, 'Individual Criminal Responsibility in Article 25 Rome Statute' (2007) 5 *Journal of International Criminal Justice* 4

G Werle, B Burghardt, F Jessberger, *Principles of International Criminal Law* (The Hague, TMC Asser Press, 2009)

G Werle and B Burghardt, 'Indirect Perpetration: a Perfect Fit for International Prosecution of Armchair Killers? Foreword' (2011) 9 *Journal of International Criminal Justice* 85

——. 'Establishing Degrees of Responsibility: Modes of Participation in Article 25 of the ICC' in E van Sliedergt and S Vailiev (eds), *Pluralism in International Criminal Law* (Oxford, Oxford University Press, 2014)

L van den Herik, 'Using Custom to Reconceptualise Crimes against Humanity' in S Darcy and J Powderly (eds), *Judicial Creativity at the International Criminal Tribunals* (Oxford, Oxford University Press, 2010)

H van der Wilt, 'Joint Criminal Enterprise: Possibilities and Limitations' (2007) 5 *Journal of International Criminal Justice* 5

——. 'Why International Criminal Lawyers Should Read Mirjan Damaška' in C Stahn and L van der Herik (eds), *Future Perspectives on International Criminal Justice* (The Hauge, TMC Asser Institute, 2010)

A von Hirsch, 'Proportionality in the Philosophy of Punishment' (1992) 16 *Crime and Justice*

——. 'Proportionate Sentences: A Desert Perspective' in A von Hirsch, A Ashworth and J Roberts (eds), *Principled Sentencing*, 3rd edn (Oxford, Hart Publishing, 2009)

A von Hirsch, A E Bottoms, E Butney, P-O Wikstrom, *Criminal Deterrence and Sentence Severity* (Oxford, Hart Publishing, 1999)

B Hola, A Smeulers and C Bijleveld, 'Is ICTY Sentencing Predictable? An Empirical Analysis of ICTY Sentencing Practice' (2009) 22 *Leiden Journal of International Law* 79

G van Hoof, *Rethinking the Sources of International Law* (Boston, Kluwer, 1983)

B van Schaack, '*Crimen Sine Lege*: Judicial Lawmaking at the Intersection of Law and Morals' (2008) 97 *Georgetown Law Journal* 119

Q Wright, 'The Law of the Nuremberg Trial' (1947) 41 *American Journal of International Law* 38

S Yeo, 'Comparative Summary of Indian Criminal Law' in M Dubber and K Heller (eds), *The Handbook of Comparative Criminal Law* (Stanford, Stanford University Press, 2011)

A Zahar and G Sluiter, *International Criminal Law: A Critical Introduction* (Oxford, Oxford University Press, 2008)

L Zedner, 'Reparation and Retribution: Are They Reconcilable?' in A von Hirsch, A Ashworth and J Roberts (eds), *Principled Sentencing*, 3rd edn (Oxford, Hart Publishing, 2009)

A Zimmermann and M Teichmann, 'State Responsibility for International Crimes' in A Nollkaemper and H van der Wilt (eds), *System Criminality in International Law* (Cambridge, Cambridge University Press, 2009)

K Zweigert and H Koetz, *An Introduction to Comparative Law*, 3rd edn (Oxford, Clarendon, 1998)

Index